War and Nationalism in South Asia

I0127766

This book presents and analyses the oldest sub-national war of post-colonial South Asia, between the Indian state and the Nagas of Northeast India. It offers a serious and thorough political history on the Naga region over three periods: pre-colonial, colonial and post-colonial.

Drawing on a wealth of primary sources and comparative and theoretical literature, Marcus Franke demonstrates that agency and identity formation are an ongoing process that neither started nor ended with colonialism. Although the interaction of the local population with colonialism produced a Naga national elite, it was the emergence of the Indian political class, with access to superior means of nation and state-building, that was able to undertake the modern Indo-Naga war. This war firmly made the Nagas into a 'nation' and that set them onto the road to independence.

War and Nationalism in South Asia fundamentally revises our understanding of the existing 'histories' of the Nagas by exposing them to be influenced by colonial or post-colonial narratives of domination. Furthermore, by placing the region into the *longue durée* of state formation with its involved technique of imperial rule, the book presents a new approach to the study of nationalism and war in South Asia in general.

This book will be of interest to students and scholars of politics, history, anthropology and South Asian studies.

Marcus Franke is Visiting Lecturer at the South Asia Institute, Heidelberg, Germany. His current research focuses on the cosmology of political elites.

Routledge Advances in South Asian Studies
Edited by Subrata K. Mitra
South Asia Institute, University of Heidelberg, Germany

South Asia, with its burgeoning, ethnically diverse population, soaring economies and nuclear weapons, is an increasingly important region in the global context. The series, which builds on this complex, dynamic and volatile area, features innovative and original research on the region as a whole or on the countries. Its scope extends to scholarly works drawing on history, politics, development studies, sociology and economics of individual countries from the region as well as those that take an interdisciplinary and comparative approach to the area as a whole or to a comparison of two or more countries from this region. In terms of theory and method, rather than basing itself on any one orthodoxy, the series draws broadly on the insights germane to area studies, as well as the tool kit of the social sciences in general, emphasizing comparison, the analysis of the structure and processes, and the application of qualitative and quantitative methods. The series welcomes submissions from established authors in the field as well as from young authors who have recently completed their doctoral dissertations.

War and Nationalism in South Asia

The Indian state and the Nagas

Marcus Franke

R Routledge
Taylor & Francis Group

LONDON AND NEW YORK

First published 2009
by Routledge
2 Park Square, Milton Park, Abingdon, Oxon OX14 4RN

Simultaneously published in the USA and Canada
by Routledge
711 Third Avenue, New York, NY 10017

Routledge is an imprint of the Taylor & Francis Group, an informa business

First issued in paperback 2011

© 2009 Marcus Franke

Typeset by Swales & Willis Ltd, Exeter, Devon

British Library Cataloguing in Publication Data
A catalogue record for this book is available
from the British Library

Library of Congress Cataloging in Publication Data
A catalog record for this book has been requested

ISBN13: 978-0-415-50216-0 (pbk)
ISBN13: 978–0–415–43741–7 (hbk)
ISBN13: 978–0–203–88487–4 (ebk)

To the Naga people

Contents

Preface and acknowledgements

The work on this topic had already started for me in 1997 when I chose to write on the genesis of war in the Naga hills in my *Magister*-thesis at the Social Anthropology Department of the South Asia Institute of the University of Heidelberg, Germany. Before that, I had done extensive reading on historical anthropology and Southeast Asian history, politics and anthropology and felt I was in a familiar area when studying the Nagas. Initially, I turned to anthropological literature on war to come to terms with the topic and in order to adhere to disciplinary purity, but realised that most of it was ethology, not anthropology, that separates the reasons for wars among ahistorical tribals etc. from the reasons for wars among us historical beings, a distinction I found unjustifiable. Hence, I decided to do away with any disciplinary purity and draw on several disciplines – history, historical anthropology and politics – that I found contributed to my understanding.

In 1998 I signed up with the *International Committee of the Red Cross* as an English-Urdu translator for Jammu and Kashmir for a little over a year. I believe that my experiences in this theatre of war considerably helped my further engagement with the Naga case, but also assisted my understanding of the dynamics and complexities of comparable armed conflicts in general. The most astounding thing I found was that I had to revise or abandon most of what I had believed before I arrived there. It took me approximately nine months in the field with access to all sides, readings and discussions with knowledgeable colleagues, before I was able to understand the different lines of conflict and common interests. This taught me a lesson about the complexities of such wars and how much effort is required to understand them. When on leave during that year, I gathered material on the Naga case in the newspapers, magazines, bookshops and libraries of Srinagar, Jammu, Delhi and Calcutta, and had tentative conversations with Nagas I ran into.

Returning to Heidelberg in spring 1999 I wrote my *Magister*-thesis. In this I established a narrative of modern Naga political history with the help of secondary sources, available at or via the University of Heidelberg, while also clarifying some points in interviews with Nagas. The thesis questioned concepts of state, nation and nationalism, ethnicity and ethnic group and war and their inherent relationships.

In summer 2000 Subrata Mitra invited me to continue the work on the Nagas at the University of Hull, and I registered for the Ph.D. training course there under Gurharpal Singh, who remained my supervisor following his departure to

Birmingham. In spring the following year, I was invited to Bangkok to meet and interview representatives of the National Socialist Council of Nagalim (Isaak-Muivah) NSCN (I-M) for about three weeks, where I had extensive talks with its General Secretary Th. Muivah.

From June 2001 to June 2002 I researched Naga history in the archives of the British Library in London, in addition to holding an ongoing series of interviews with Nagas there. Because I was already acquainted with most of what had been published relating to the Nagas, I decided I would leave that aside and take as little for granted as possible in order to arrive at my findings afresh, with the help of new sources and a critical reading of them. Consequently, for the whole year, I combed through every relevant volume and folder and gathered the material which I then wrote up, analysed, contextualized and finally wrapped up into a Ph.D. thesis by the end of 2004, after having returned to Heidelberg.

It was then in 2006, after Subrata Mitra had already invited me to be a regular member of his methodology colloquium and to teach as a visiting lecturer at his politics department at the University of Heidelberg, he asked me to revise my thesis into a book for his Routledge Advances in South Asian Studies which I readily accepted and set out to do. And now, since this task seems to be accomplished, I realize that it was my companion for quite a while.

Most of the debts I have incurred in the course of the research and writing process for this book will have to go unnamed, simply because the list would become too long. But a good start are the two academics that accompanied the work in different ways: I am grateful to Subrata Mitra, on whose recommendation I got the opportunity to pursue doctoral research at the Department of Political and International Studies at the University of Hull and for the possibility to publish this book in his series; and I want to express my gratitude to Gurharpal Singh, my supervisor, who, with his rare mixture of protestant work ethic, faculty and good humour, provided invaluable support in the course of this research.

I am also grateful to the Ferens Educational Trust of the University of Hull for funding and thus enabling my research during the first three years, and especially to Rachel Blakey for her invaluable work solving the practical problems involved.

I acknowledge my thanks to the staff of the Graduate Research Institute of the University of Hull and of the Brynmor Jones Library, Hull; the staff of the library of Delhi University; the National Library Calcutta; the British Library; the SOAS library, London; the library of the Red Cross delegation in Delhi; the library of the South Asian Institute, the University Library, and the library of the Max Planck Institute for Comparative Public Law and International Law – all at Heidelberg.

I also have to thank many Nagas, of whom I want to name only two: Luithui Luingam and sadly the late Mr. Yong Kong; the conversations and friendship with both were not only of great personal worth but also of invaluable importance for the conduct of this research. Friends who happen to be Nagas are not named here intentionally, in order not to associate them unnecessarily with contentious political views.

Thanks also go to Jens Franz and Jeffrey Kile for both being friends in London and beyond, and for correcting early versions of some of my chapters, and Jens for helping in the final stages of the thesis that builds the basis for this book. And I cannot thank enough Paul Bilic and Chris Masters – my former colleagues at Collingham College, London – for their straightforward and positive responses when I asked them to correct the English. And thanks go also to Sonja Lenk in Heidelberg, for proofreading the new chapters that were added.

Finally, thanks, gratitude and love go to my family and friends who not only kept me company but also kept me going and who had to bear the brunt of the ups and, I fear, maybe even more of the many downs that come along with such a project: Angela Spencer and Baz Strickland, as well as Jeffrey Kile and Katrina John, in London; my parents Helga and Heinrich Franke in Wittighausen; my sister Ulrike Steegmüller, her husband Walter and their (grown-up) kids Sarah and Ruben in Heidenheim; my brother Stephan and his partner Carolin in Freiburg; my son Rainer and his mother Erika in Gerlachsheim; my friend Gereon Wetzel and his partner Anna Ginesti in München; Ulrike Umstätter, Sonja Lenk, Ralph Stütz, Ralf Rehberger and his partner Marion Jourdan, all friends in Heidelberg.

Although I surely have forgotten many, I feel I have to express my special gratitude to Ralf Rehberger who definitely had to listen to most of my doubts and who has been an invaluable friend for all these years.

Of course, no one but me is responsible for the content of this book.

Marcus Franke
Heidelberg, May 2008

Abbreviations

AFSPA	Armed Forces Special Powers Act
CC	chief commissioner
DC	district commissioner
GOI	government of India
INA	Indian National Army
ISF	Indian Security Forces
MOD	Ministry of Defence
MP	Member of Parliament
NEFA	Northeast Frontier Area
NFG	Naga federal government
NHD	Naga hills district
NLSG	Nagaland state government
NNC	Naga National Council
NPC	Naga People's Convention
NSCN	National Socialist Council of Nagalim
NSCN (IM)	National Socialist Council of Nagalim (Isaak – Muivah)
NSCN (K)	National Socialist Council of Nagalim (Khaplang)
NWS	Naga Women's Society
NYM	Naga Youth Movement
PIL	People's Independence League
SDO	sub-divisional officer
TFD	Tuensang frontier division
UDF	United Democratic Front
ULFA	United Liberation Front of Assam

Introduction

The ceasefire in the Naga hills is a product of the war there, that is the consequence of the continuation of conquest and subjugation of segmentary societies at the hands of centralised states. It is imperialism in the service of state formation which today, with the means and the objectives of the modern nation-state, more often than not leads to violent repression and the threat of it. In these times of the accepted principles of democracy, the rule of law and universal human rights, this should be intolerable.

However, the overwhelming majority of the literature about the Nagas does not say that at all. To the contrary, one encounters mostly three interdependent arguments appearing in different compositions: First, in good imperialist manner, the Nagas themselves are blamed for their own subjugation, by claiming at least implicitly that they should be ruled by others for their own good, even if against their will. This is connected to the second, that the violence that necessarily must be employed to bring them to order, or into one's own state, is the necessary price to pay for the larger good of good governance that comes once successfully incorporated. For the second argument to be tolerable, requires the third, that is the trivialization of the war, the denial that there is anything like a war or excessive violence going on there at all.[1]

The first two arguments are easily countered: we no longer accept the wholesale incapacitation of whole populations.[2] And we do not accept sacrificing people as a means to a higher end,[3] because this always leads to misery, bloodshed and terror, phenomena we value negatively.[4] This shows that it is the third argument we have to invalidate to prove the proposition made initially. We have to show that the Nagas did not and still do not want to be ruled by others and that this showed itself in their war against their conquerors. That is, we will demonstrate that the conquest triggered unified resistance, that the people unified against the intruders and warred to preserve their self-determination. In its general features it is an omnipresent product of state formation, but in its specific features is clearly identifiable in the post-colonial, neo-imperial world where South Asia poses no exception to the rule.

Theory and methodology

Political science, as it is practised in this book, rests on the understanding that our theorizing is based on our belief of what it is to be human,[5] that is to say there is no brute data to be measured neutrally.[6] Our understanding as it is guided by theory and fed by political philosophy is thus inherently historical and geographical.[7] We make sense out of the subject matter for us in a narrative way. Moreover we are doing this with the help of concepts and categories that are first of all our own,[8] that is to say we use a familiar terminology that we, as we proceed, have to fill with local and historical sense. In this way, our narrative ideally should make sense also for those described by it that is, we have used a familiar structure and have filled it with new content. This builds a conceptual bridge that allows us to explain what happened. Furthermore, if we have been able to explain what happened then we have penetrated some inherent logic that in turn may make it possible to make predictions about what will happen in the future.[9] In order to gain this local and historical sense we have to come from the detail, the mass of data,[10] and embed this in the wider regional and global context to reduce the danger of misinterpretation.[11] As we proceed in our analytical narrative,[12] we have to allow our protagonists the ability to learn, and for the respective outcomes that they may be different from the ones intended and that the irreversible was not necessarily the inevitable, and finally we have to abstain from any teleological temptation.[13] Yet, this would contradict what I have claimed above and so we have to grant some internal, local, historical logic, some pan-human, which, if it were not empirically attested to, would have to be a normative one. So I shall claim that, from the actions witnessed over the last 180 years or so in the Naga hills, the outcome, which for most of the time was war and suffering, can be explained and maybe even understood. This is so, since the general pattern of actions met a general pattern of outlooks and convictions that are attestable for in the Naga hills, which, not only there but in all comparative cases, would result in the same answers.

In this inter-subjectivity it becomes as objective as it gets in the social sciences.

From this followed the methodology of this study. First, a historical narrative was established as far as possible with primary sources, in chronological order and not yet analysed. The second step was the identification of the relevant social agents that then were generalized for the sake of describability into 'types of action', though individuals had been given more space in the narrative due to the exceptional reach of their actions or their exemplary quality to illustrate a point. Third, the pertinent concepts were pinpointed as factors that were and are decisive for the either peaceful or violent course of action. The task was to discern the understanding that the collective agents had of them at respective times. These were the conceptions of what is a social and political unit, of rulership and sovereignty, of freedom and dignity, of fighting, war and capitulation. Fourth, it was necessary to draw parallels to comparable contexts and cases, and to take into consideration the wider historical framework in order to come to grips with the happenings, events, changes, transformations etc. on the ground. Basically, what was to be understood again and again were the reasons for actions, their effects and the transformations they triggered on our established concepts out of the peculiarities of our collective agents under consideration.

So we had the local politics as it reacted to the challenges of the colonial and post-colonial state. These reactions were based on the Nagas' understanding of the situation that was mostly based on some experience or historical knowledge, or knowledge that had been gained about the contemporary situation. Then we have the actions conducted by the agents of the colonial and post-colonial state, directed by elites themselves acting on their understanding, yet in a wider field and being more powerful, they more or less determined what was staged in the local field of action. The conquest of the Naga hills followed from the wider geopolitical and regional logic and triggered the war in the Naga hills; that in turn was the dominant factor unifying the Nagas: hence, we have geopolitics and regional tradition and history determining state politics, triggering local resistance (read war) that created local political unity. Of course, the local reaction was an action based on its own history and tradition itself, but in its scope of action limited by far more powerful adversaries.

Organisation of the book

The chapters in the book are arranged with the more powerful actors (British and Indians) preceding the less powerful (Nagas):[14]

Chapter one deals with the initial phase of contact between the British and the Nagas, and the diverse manifestations of the former's desire to subjugate the latter, until this was abandoned due to high costs. This runs against established historiography that claims British imperial indifference towards the Naga hills at this stage and holds the Nagas responsible for British retribution and conquest. Moreover, by embedding British actions into the general context of British imperialism, I show that British movement into the Naga hills at this time was perfectly in accord with the overall imperial project.

Chapter two attempts to render Naga behaviour understandable in the face of British encroachments. I do this via a careful reading of colonial sources, then by placing them into the wider history of that region and by looking at comparative cases. Here in relation to one Naga group I am able to stress several things distorted or neglected in the established historiography: first, that these hill societies can only be understood when placed into the wider context, which is especially true for the practice of headhunting; second, that the Naga hills were not a murderous zone of headhunting machines; third, that the Nagas were politically conscious of themselves in contradistinction to their plains' neighbours; fourth, that they were also aware about the superior power of their centralised neighbours and thus as a rule refrained from provocative acts; fifth, that when they surrendered they did it out of the belief the victors would not want to stay and would finally return to the plains; and sixth, and more implicitly, they also surrendered because they were aware of the general practice of imperialism (i.e. of rule over others) and thus more willing to accept it.

Chapter three then returns to the British agents, explaining their return to and partial conquest of the Naga hills, the way they ruled them and the reasons for retreat. I am able to show here that the British, when the Transfer of Power was nearing, never wanted the Nagas to be independent, as it is widely believed, but were only interested in some safeguards for them, and then only in the beginning. Further, this chapter describes in detail the specific colonial administration and thus presents us with the basis for rendering the consequences of this rule meaningful in regard to Naga social identity formation.

This process of ethno- or nation-genesis under colonial rule is addressed in chapter four. At this juncture I first demonstrate that colonial rule did not have the salutary effects it is professed to have had in colonial historiography. Further, that the impact of colonial administration was only enough to produce an elite Naga nation, but inconsequential in this respect for the mass of the Nagas who only were sensitised to their elite's concerns by the cataclysm of the Second World War, staging one of its decisive battles in the Naga hills.

Chapter five outlines the policy of the post-colonial political Indo-Assamese elite towards the Nagas that was characterised by paying lip service to granting free choice to the Nagas and sympathy with them, but on the other side, by a determination to keep them within the Indian Union, which found its equivalents in the Indian constitution and in the actions of the Indo-Assamese agents on the ground who treated the Nagas as politically immature savages. It is shown that the Indian state, in the logic of the nation-building process of post-colonial states, employed massive armed force, qualifying as state terror and genocide, to make the Nagas accept the occupation of their country.

Chapter six expounds how the Nagas, initially voting for immediate return to their independence, then acquiesced to an interim solution before they, because of what they perceived as insincere Indian policy, again returned to their initial demand. Further, it examines how the Nagas, in emulation of the Indian Congress, fought with non-violent non-cooperation until the violence, employed by the Indo-Assamese administration, became intolerable in their eyes resulting in them taking recourse to armed resistance. The ensuing war not only served as a real catalyst for Christianity among the Nagas but also for the Naga nation.

Chapter seven tries to grasp post-Nehruvian policy towards the Northeast in general and the Nagas in particular. It shows how the benevolent discourse more and more is belied by an uninspired approach that continues the old imperial divide-and-rule device that combines ruthless repression with the creation of a comprador class. The necessary and most probably calculated result is the spread of violence to an ever wider field that allowed the ruling elite to retain unchallenged, undivided control of the territory and its resources.

Chapter eight describes how the Nagas, in the course of protracted warfare, split into warring factions; but since the 1980s Naga civil society had already started to unify and exert pressure on their armed groups to do the same and search for a peaceful solution of the political problem.

This was due to its vibrant civil society – that may be rooted in their traditions – that propagated a strong ethos of freedom and independence and may point the way out of the reactive politics of violence and counter-violence that afflicts an ever wider territory of the Indian periphery today.

1   British imperial expansion and historical agency, 1820s–1850s

Introduction

That the British never intended to conquer the Naga hills and that this was forced on them by the Nagas themselves is a myth in the modern sense. The aim to defeat the Burmese, to expel them from Assam and to reinstall the native governments in between as a buffer zone, made the hill people surrounding Assam initially into potential allies, to be drawn into the violent conflict and made instrumental in the war efforts. At this stage they are by no means portrayed as negative and are treated as equals in the colonial documents. The prospect for economic profit, and the discovery of the strategic value of the mountains surrounding Assam, then led to the decision to keep Assam and to reinstall only some of the native governments, and then only as dependent ones. The hill people now were turned from sensible and potential allies into irrational, irresponsible, barbarous savages, from whom the Assamese had to be protected. The reason for keeping Assam under British rule was to safeguard it from these 'viles'. In the case of the Nagas, the dependent government of Manipur was encouraged to subjugate them. When that stratagem failed and led to retaliation, carried out by the Nagas, the British in turn changed tactics and tried to make them comply with what they called 'punitive expeditions'. These punitive expeditions involved foraging into the Nagas' territory, destroying their villages and defences together with their grain stores, leaving them resourceless and defenceless, at the mercy of often hostile neighbours, and trying to overawe them into subjugation. Yet when this also failed to achieve the desired effect, the British added to their strategy the component of the economic break-up and incorporation of the Naga hills into their market sphere, combined with the threat of military force. Simultaneously they were closing in on the Naga hills by settling other cultivator populations around them, as well as allowing the extensions of the tea estates up to the foothills. But this was all to no avail. The Nagas were under no central rule that could have made them comply. The terrain and the weather were so difficult for the British that the Nagas, when changing to guerrilla tactics, could not be controlled easily by them. Hence a rational calculation brought the British to disengage from the Naga hills. More than a decade later the British reversed that policy; for reasons lying beyond the Naga hills, they attempted to progressively conquer them, but never brought them entirely under their control (see chapter three).

The Tengimas were part of the later Angami Nagas, and at the time of British arrival were organised in a ranked clan system that can be taken as a segmentary political system (see chapter two). The clans rivalled each other for hegemony that expressed itself in tribute and enforced following in case of external threat, thus constituting a parallel, penetrated, territorial polity based on conflict and consensus. Historically Southeast Asian, the Tengimas inhabited a refuge area whose inhabitants had developed their identity by stressing individual autonomy and collective consensus in conscious opposition to the hierarchically constituted lowland societies. Since they were aware of the numerical, material and technological superiority of their centrally organised plains neighbours, they carefully tuned their policy towards them, appeased at one time and deterred the other. Being at the same time conscious of the fact that it was the very inaccessible nature of their territory that allowed for their independent way of life, they put up staunch resistance when threatened with large-scale invasions, but gave in when resistance seemed futile. Plains kingdoms in Southeast Asia had thus far not seen any incentive to direct control or to subjugate hill regions.

Radcliffe-Brown was at pains to justify such processes in African societies as politics.[1] Politics was the business of states, and real states were nation-states, and nation-states, in turn, were European or of European descent, since only rational Europeans could devise, erect and man them. Non-Europeans, devoid of self-consciousness, were excluded from progress and history, and thus unable to develop a national consciousness, form a nation or build a nation-state. These non-nations, had to be ruled by the enlightened nations, in this way conveying legitimacy to the imperial project.[2] So when we speak about nation or non-nation we have to be aware of this legacy, on the normative content of this statement, and the empowering or disempowering consequences that may come with it. The term nation, I would argue, always was more normative than it was descriptive – which is not to deny its relative reality, but to doubt its real reach and extent.

I will argue that the Tengimas were conscious of themselves as politically different, and determined to retain that difference, as is proven by their sustained resistance. This consciousness of being different qualifies to be called national, in the sense of a self-conscious political community. To measure and evaluate Tengima nationalism against an idealised modern European nation is not only part of the above-mentioned legacy, but in its teleology obstructs our view and inhibits us from understanding both phenomena.

The evidence is overwhelming that the British had no preconceptions of the region where they were to encounter the hill tribes, who at that time were already called 'Nagas' by the inhabitants of the plains. The meeting of the British and the Nagas was the result of the war of the former with the Burmese in 1824–26. The Burmese had invaded Assam and threatened territory of the East India Company until the British declared war and decided to expel the Burmese from the Northeast. At first the British did not want to stay in Assam, but rather intended to create a buffer zone between British India and the court of Ava. As long as the Burmese threat continued to exist, the British planned to enlist the hill tribes for purposes of gathering intelligence, maintaining logistics and fighting the Burmese

as British troops. The British had used hill tribes in this way before. At this historical juncture, the British perceived and portrayed the Nagas with moral indifference.
This, however, quickly changed when the British discovered that the Arakan
mountain range potentially formed a natural (geopolitical) boundary thus rendering
Assam important from a strategic point of view. Immediately following this reve-
lation, strategic and economic reasons for keeping Assam within the empire were
brought forward. With an ever-increasing accumulation of intelligence, the British
fortified their strategic and economic rationale for occupying Assam, as well as the
necessity for British civilisation[3] and administration, until they both merged into
one. Such rationales were superseded and at the same time justified by a new British
awareness of their duty to protect Assam from the 'barbarians', the name then given
to the hill tribes. In other words, perception and description of land as well as
people varied in accordance with the changing imperial interests.

Interpreting the actions of Cortés during the conquest of Mexico, Tzetevan
Todorov suggests that '. . . in the world of a Machiavelli and a Cortés the
discourse is neither determined by the object, which it describes, nor by congruence
with a tradition, but follows in its construction only the aim, which it is pursuing'.[4]
Todorov explicates this argument with a theoretical analysis of language,
beginning with the publication of the first grammar of a modern European language
in 1492. This characterised an attitude shift from one of obedience to analysis
and the concomitant consciousness that one may as well utilise language for
practical purposes.[5] This may be likened to what Max Weber has termed the
'disenchantment of the world': the knowledge or belief of being able to understand
everything about the conditions of life by way of calculation, in order to dominate
them.[6]

For the Spaniards the spread of Christendom provided ideological legitimacy for
conquest, expansion and the hunt for gold. They gave Christianity and took the
gold, with material subjugation thus a prerequisite for the spread of Christianity and
the taking of the gold. As such, means and ends merged into one. In cases of resistance, the Other had to be seen as inferior, thereby providing justification for conquest.[7] The Other had to be denied equality, and was not to be taken as a subject, but
as an object. Or, as Todorov phrases it: 'The other human is discovered and
refused/rejected at the same time'.[8] In this respect, the British may be seen to have
followed the pattern of their Spanish forerunners.

The first Anglo-Burman war, February 1824 – March 1825

The British 'military-fiscal state', itself a product of permanent warfare on a global
scale with its rival France,[9] acquired actual control over the East India Company's
holdings in South Asia by the end of the eighteenth century.[10] The British possessions in India developed into state-like structures that were equally militarised, its
personnel poised for conquest and thus were adequately described as 'garrison
states'.[11] Military force, or force as such, seemed to be the natural tools of British
policy. War was not the continuation of politics with other means, the policy was
war.[12] The British state and its ruling class was a martial one.[13] Perpetual warfare

made fighting into something very normal and necessary, lest there was the danger of becoming too soft.[14]

Subjugation and colonisation, the business of empire building was, for Europeans in general, rooted in European tradition, praxis and experience.[15] Ever since Aristotle's theory of natural slavery, the Greek conception of themselves and the *barbaroi*, and the Romans seeing themselves as the only power, the legitimacy for empire (that is to say, rule over others by asserting it is for their own good) was provided for in European ideology.[16] Thus we may locate the reasons for British expansion into Naga territory in the general ideology of the empire and in the constant search for new revenues to finance the military-fiscal state.

From August 12th 1765, the EIC was the de facto ruler of the lower Gangetic valley. By 1766, the provinces of Bengal, Bihar and Orissa had been added, including '. . . the present district of Goalpara in the State of Assam [being] . . . a border area, separating the Ahom kingdom in Assam from the Company's dominions'.[17] Although Koch Bihar was made a tributary by 1773, there was no British move to interfere in Assam in any political way. Banerjee sees the reason for that in the purely commercial nature of British interest.[18] Peers, on the contrary, sees the contemporary concept of 'natural frontier' as responsible for the lack of British interest into what is nowadays Northeast India. While the Indus river or the Hindu Kush mountains to the north-west and the Himalayas to the north clearly could be taken as such a 'natural frontier', the terrain north and east of Chittagong, on the other hand, with all its hills and jungles, presented itself to the British rather as a zone than a frontier.[19] Furthermore, the territory was considered as anything but salubrious, the Burmese market as too unpromising, and the Burmese empire as such not perceived as a threat. However, reasons for war with the Burmese had been given from the time of Hastings.[20] Nonetheless, the British did interfere in the Assam disturbances, raging from the 1780s,[21] the first time from 1792 – 1794.[22]

The Burmese, on the other side of the theatre, were asked by the Moamarias, the Singphos and by the Ahom monarch to intervene on their behalf in Assam. Following their annexation of Arakan between 1784 and 1785, the Burmese increased their activity in Chittagong but had no intention of intervening on either side in Assam.[23] Yet in 1819 the Burmese invaded Assam for the second time (the first having been in 1817) and installed themselves in Gauhati (today Guwahati).[24] By 1822 the Burmese had complete control over Assam, subsequently seen as a province of the Burmese empire.[25] The historical basis of British and Nagas coming into contact includes this Burmese conquest of Assam and Manipur, the Burmese threat of annexing Cachar and Synthia (the latter then considered a dependency of East Bengal), and of invading British territory itself. This was the situation, or how it was described, at least, in contemporary British correspondence. From the same documents we may infer that the British would have preferred to avoid confrontation, by respecting one another's respective zones of influence, which were guaranteed by a buffer zone between the two powers.[26] By February 1824, the British no longer believed in the possibility of a peaceful settlement with Ava.[27] In a private letter, Scott (the then agent to the governor general on the Northeast Frontier) to Swinton (the then secretary to the governor general in Fort William) praised the strategic value of the Assam valley, south of the Brahmaputra,[28] offering evidence for reasons to extend British territory into Assam. In a declaration to the council on February 24th 1824, Governor General Amherst justified this position with an account of Burmese aggression against the British, going on to declare war on the Burmese with the aim of dislodging them from Assam, where they threatened the eastern frontier of Bengal.[29] The British used the border disputes and skirmishes with the Burmese as a pretext to start a full war, despite Amherst starting with an explicit order to abstain from any offensive action.[30] For Peers it was Anglo-Indian militarism again that led him to believe the Burmese threat was one that was capable of inciting the whole of India, and/or suspected that the Russians might be behind it. In addition in 1824 six years of peace had already prevailed, putting at risk the vigilance of the troops. Consequently, a show of force was deemed necessary and Amherst was pressured into it by those he was supposed to govern.[31]

Revenue stagnation and decline in the 1820s might have been a further incentive to look for prospective territory.[32] Bengal's agency houses may also have played an important role. Established during the 1780s by merchants pooling their resources to cope with the new opportunities and demands of the China trade, they became the locus for investment for company employees, having been barred from conducting private trade by Cornwallis' reform of 1793. These agency houses on the one hand used this capital for commercial expansion into Southeast Asia, and on the other hand '. . . also became major creditors to the company administration in India, financing warfare, and the general costs of territorial expansion'.[33] They entered into a symbiotic and influential relationship with military-fiscal British-India, and were allowed a great deal of say on company's policy in Southeast Asia and its eventual expansion.[34] The Burmese kingdom and British India were two expanding empires. While the British gave refuge to rebels operating from their territory against the Burmese, the latter tested the former by violating their territory. Both had already known each other intimately for decades before the British finally decided to wage war. Thus we may say that although the Burmese were expansionist towards the smaller kingdoms in their neighbourhood, they did not seek a full-scale war with the British, and were thus completely taken aback by their response and assault even on mainland Burma. This is to say that the evidence seems to agree with Peers, and that it was Anglo-Indian militarism that provoked and exaggerated the Burmese threat to give a pretext for further conquest.[35]

On 5th March 1824, the official proclamation of war against the Burmese by the Governor General followed. The initial aim proclaimed in the proceedings was to reinstall the smaller kingdoms as a buffer zone between the two bigger powers,[36] although the ultimate aim was already to strike at Rangoon.[37]

Pushing the frontiers, February 1831 – October 1839

The decision to keep Assam and to annex Cachar, and the installation of dependent governments in Upper Assam and Manipur brought the British to the foot of the hills separating Assam from Burma. The British intention to develop the plains adjoining the hills to their gain, to exploit them economically by way of searching for natural resources, as well as by settling farmers there who could be taxed and encouraged to grow cash crops, added an additional incentive to have a closer look at the hills themselves. First, they surveyed them to find out whether there were profitable resources in the hills, and second, they secured the plains by bringing the hills under control and opened up and secured communications from Manipur to Assam through these very hills. Therefore, the British saw it as beneficial to subjugate the Nagas between Assam and Manipur, and, because it presented itself as the cheaper option, asked the state of Manipur to do the job for them. With the Nagas there, the Angamis resisted and retaliated against British held territory itself. The British then decided to take the matter into their own hands and planned to make the Angamis pay with one punitive expedition. Yet, since there rarely was a real battle to be won, or a head of state or regime to be defeated, war had to be waged on the people.[38]

Attempted economic integration, December 1839 – March 1843

The end of the 1830s saw the first military action of the British against the Angamis. It involved a policy in which the British burned the villages and destroyed the food stores of those Nagas who did not welcome them. This policy was supplemented by the order to the Nagas to refrain from any active fighting, to surrender their own means of defence and attack to the British. The Angamis' reply was to shake their spears at Grange (Sub-assistant of Nowgong) on his second expedition, shouting that '. . . their spears were their Rajas'.[39] The British promised the Nagas to refrain from any interference into their local affairs, but that the Nagas should give some symbolic tribute as a sign of acceptance of British supremacy. Furthermore, the Angamis were ordered to surrender those of their chiefs whom the British held responsible for attacks on what the British had decided was their territory; otherwise close relatives would be taken hostage. Subsequently, to avoid creating a power vacuum, the population was to choose and install new chiefs. These new chiefs, in turn, would be held responsible by the British for the conduct of the tribes, that is to say the British would rule through them. The chiefs would be told of economic rewards via trade and it was this opening up of the hills by which the British hoped on the one hand to civilise, domesticate and dominate the Nagas,[40] and on the other, to profit from this trade themselves by incorporating the Naga hills into their market system and possibly extract resources. This in the end meant subjugation via economic penetration for which it was necessary to open up the lines of communication, if possible without high-cost military intervention. To ensure that all this would prove successful, the British intended to establish a military post, that is to say a bridgehead, in the Angami hills, at the same time assuring them that this did not allude to any encroachment on their sovereignty.

Grange, who commanded a Shan militia, was ordered for his second expedition into Angami country to go via Mohong Dijua, close to Dimapur, in order to clear the road as far as the Dhansiri river, and to establish there a '. . . godown for Storing provisions, as also huts for the Sepoys have been ordered to be built at the different stages'.[41] Captain Brodie was instructed to join Grange at the Dhansiri river. Identified as the main perpetrators of the raids were the '. . . tribes, under the chiefs Ikari and Inpoji inhabiting the villages of Mangoan and Sukungo . . .'[42] The aim was to pacify without occupying, to pursue the chiefs '. . . to agree to exert themselves, to restrain the predatory habits of their tribes . . .' to put themselves under British protection. There was not to be any reduction of their power and authority. As a sign of their acknowledgement of British protection they should send an annual present of elephant tusks. Nevertheless, Grange was to take hostages if he had reason to suspect that their consent was only given due to the presence of British troops. Ikari and Inpoji should either be surrendered, or their close relatives should be taken hostage to ensure their good conduct. In the event of any resistance they should be attacked, apprehended and then treated as prisoners of war. Grange was to find out which chiefs the tribes wanted and should ensure their installation, so that no power-vacuum would lead to instability and chaos. The chiefs were to be made to understand that the British government did not want to deprive them of their power, and that they would only be held responsible for the peaceful conduct of their tribes and that they would profit from a '. . . free intercourse with traders and others . . .' but would be attacked in any case of misconduct.[43]

Lieutenant Bigge informed Grange that a permanent military post was to be established and he, Grange, should suggest a location for this. The Shan were to man this post and to be asked to settle there. The native officers were not to exercise any control over the native chiefs and should avoid any offence towards them and were to act in a conciliatory manner towards the people.[44] The government approved of these instructions.[45]

Grange was ambushed during this expedition. He took the village of Khonoma by force and destroyed it together with its hidden store of grain.[46] When retreating he realised that the Nagas had *panjied*[47] every path. On his way back he encamped in two further villages, one of which he also destroyed, together with all of its grain stores.[48] Captain Frances Jenkins (agent to the governor general on the Northeast Frontier) reported to the Government about his hope that Grange's expedition had had the desired effect on the Angami Naga tribes:

> The repetition of our incursion & the punishment inflicted on two of the largest Villages of the Angami confederacy Haplongmie and Juppama the former for attacking him on returning from his search after the Munipoorees and the latter for killing one of the Asamese Coolies during his absence cannot but convince the Nagas that we have power of punishing them for any offences upon our subjects, & it is gratifying to know that the murderous attacks of these Nagas upon the Cacharee Villages have been entirely suspended during the past year; & that our Ryats have been enabled to advance their cultivation along the Dheensiri to the South much beyond its former limits.[49]

Grange had taken prisoners from these 'hostile and powerful tribes' who were to be used as messengers to exert influence on them.[50] The projected pacification was obviously necessary to allow further settlement and cultivation bordering the hills, indispensable for the extraction of revenue. Jenkins summarised and commented upon the communication between his assistant Bigge and Gordon in a dispatch to Fort William. Therein Jenkins informed the government that Gordon was in favour of establishing a *thana* in the Angami country, in order to dominate it and completely subjugate the Nagas. This would ensure an easy communication between Assam and Manipur via a road between these two parts through Angami territory. Bigge, on the other hand, was of the opinion that there was nothing to trade there to justify the expense of building such a road. He instead would have preferred to go on a leisurely tour through Naga country to bring them in line and Jenkins supported this idea of a four-month tour with only a small detachment. Furthermore, Jenkins was of the opinion that a military post at Dimapur on the Dhansiri, on the northern frontier of North Cachar, and at Semkhur, at the south-eastern frontier of the district, would not only discourage attacks but also encourage settlers to extend their settlement towards the hills and if necessary Gordon's plan of a road from Manipur to Assam via Angami land could be implemented.[51] The government approved of Bigge's plan to carry out a public relations tour through the Naga villages.[52]

A few months later in April 1841 Jenkins reported the success of these measures to the government, that the raids of the Angamis had already stopped after Grange's first expedition and that during each of these raids approximately 40–50 people had been killed or abducted. Thus Jenkins suggested to go one step further and to incorporate the Naga hills economically and to send the *ryats* of the company there.[53] The governor general expressed his satisfaction with the development, encouraged frequent mutual intercourse and, if possible, the avoidance of force and the use of peaceful means to encourage the Nagas to abstain from hostilities between themselves and their neighbours.[54] The government wanted to acquire an acknowledgement as soon as possible from the Angamis of their submission to British authority, and in general desired to open up and gradually civilise the Naga hills through roads, trade, traders etc.[55] However, raids were resumed in December 1841. The government ordered action to be taken especially regarding the fixing of boundaries (e.g., between Manipur and Angami Naga territory) and the protection of the frontier by the set-up of a '. . . permanent chain of Military posts in the hills for checking the aggression of the Angami and other neighbouring tribes'.[56] In March 1842 the government decided against the establishment of a post among the Angamis in favour of frequent visits for '. . . the conciliation and civilization of the [Angami] tribes'.[57] Meanwhile, inroads by Angamis to villages in Manipur and Cachar were continuously reported.[58] However, a turning point seemed to be reached when Jenkins euphorically informed the government of India (GOI) in March 1843 that he believed, that the Nagas in this area (Angamis and Rengmas) had now accepted British supremacy. The advantages he saw, or which he at least wanted the government to believe, were the expected revenue through house-tax, the addition of the Nagas to the market as consumers and producers, the full development and cultivation of the ostensible fertile country bordering on Naga territory, since it was now pacified and safe, and the cultivation of some high quality tea in the Naga hills themselves. He evoked a new flourishing area, which he would have liked to be supported and connected by a school in Dimapur, helping to facilitate trade relations between the hills and the plains – at this stage the British, on economic grounds, wanted to enhance the relationship between these two areas.[59] Only later, when they realised that the enforced fusion between hills and plains brought about conflicts that often precipitated unrest and rebellion, as for example already experienced by the British in Bengal,[60] and that then, as a rule, order had to be reinstalled with expansive counter-insurgency operations, was a policy of separation followed. This policy afterwards could be presented as philanthropic, devised to safeguard the interests and the way of life of the hill people. Much later, in the 1920s when the Nagas resistance had been crushed, and when they had stopped posing even a remote danger or challenge, some of the British officers, serving long terms among them, would come to admire the Nagas and the way of life they had developed. Yet, there was nothing of that in the nineteenth century; the Nagas, together with the difficult terrain they lived in, were simply enemies of the British. Consequently, the British had developed certain strategies to deal with those, and one of them was to try to incorporate them into the market system. The trade goods and opportunities were meant to be the carrot; the striking power of the *sepoys*, the stick.

After the policy to delegate the task to subjugate the Angamis to Manipur had failed and had instead resulted in them fighting back, the British changed their strategy. They had wanted to incorporate the Nagas into their market sphere with a mixture of intimidation, by appointing and holding chiefs accountable to the British, and opening up lines of communication and securing them through the establishment of a military post, by encouraging settler colonisation into and around the Naga hills and in placing the Kukis in Cachar to check possible forays. The so-called punitive expeditions were also used to gather intelligence on a wide range of topics: there was the military necessity to collect and document the data about the geo- and topography of the area, as well as the distribution of populations, their cultural identification and social and political order.[61] Then there was the hunt for, and documentation of, possible natural resources or the likelihood for growing cash-crops, as well as the discovery of trade opportunities.

Direct intervention and retreat, November 1844 – February 1851

Encouraging trade and contact between the plains and the hills was hitherto the strategy of the British to incorporate the Naga hills into their economic sphere. This was to be the first step and should have had the effect of pacifying the Nagas, to civilise them in British or European terms, to make them dependent on trade, and hence incorporate them into their empire. But it was not the opening up of the Naga hills towards modernity; it was to take away their independence, or we could say to dispossess them of their means of defence and production, and therewith their self-determination.[62]

In the process of doing so, the British drew the circle closer and clashed with the dominant Angami groups, to whom they represented rivals. The Angami power field was characterised by a constant struggle between leading clans, correlating to the territorial unit of the *khel*. It was common practice to temporarily seek allies among the powers surrounding the hills to finish off a local rival. We will have a

closer look at who the Angamis were in the next chapter. The British, seeing themselves as the paramount power of order, were drawn into the local power struggle,
not realising that the Nagas saw them as just another contestant, and did not want
them to stay, nor did they believe that they could wish to do so.[63] Local British officers, far away from any direct control, also had their role in this drama, and some
decided not to inform the government about the real situation on the ground. The
government, once it had found out, and predominantly motivated by commercial
interests, did give the order for retreat and non-interference, once face-keeping
retaliation strikes had been carried out. Subsequently, for more than a decade,
affairs other than the Nagas were more important for the British. Only after further
parts of Lower Burma had been conquered and incorporated into the *raj*, did the
Naga hills come back onto the British political agenda.

By November 1844 the Shan militia, stationed at the village of Lamkaje, a small
outpost of Hosung Hajo, was attacked by Angamis.[64] British investigations established that Khonoma was behind this attack on the Shan Militia. The involved
Angamis had announced that they would make war on the 'sepoys', seeing themselves as the strongest village, and therefore convinced that the others had to do
what they said.[65] The local officers Eld and Wood were ordered to arrest with cau-
tion the most powerful Khonoma chief.[66] Both officers led the two columns of the
military operation, which burned down three villages in the process, including
Khonoma, for not surrendering its men.[67] However, this time the government did
not approve of the practice of burning down villages:

> The burning of these villages was not justifiable and the Officers engaged with
> these half civilized tribes on the Frontier of our possessions would in the opin-
> ion of the Governor General in Council gain more influence with them and be
> better able to carry out measures for the protection and benefit of our own
> Frontier and Subjects by acting in all circumstances with Strict Justice and
> moderation, than by having recourse to these harsh measures of General and
> indiscriminate Vengeance.[68]

The British had entered into a local power struggle and were seen by the Angamis
both as rivals and as potential allies. Therefore, the local officers saw the only solution in the establishment of a permanent military post among the Angamis.[69]
Additionally, the most important chiefs should be taken hostage to ensure the submission of the rest of the tribe.[70] After renewed forages by Angamis in 1846,[71] the
government sanctioned all measures, especially the opening up of communications
(roads), to enable the establishment of a temporary military post at Samaguting,
with the aim of suppressing future Angami raids. The government was then still
hoping to find natural resources in the Naga hills, for example coffee etc.[72] For his
next expedition into Angami territory, Butler was especially called on to collect
botanical and geological information.[73] The government was eager to find something to pay the expenses.

The post at Samaguting was for a long time a success, the place itself flourishing
with settlers pouring into North Cachar to start cultivation,[74] until the British

decided to move their militia headquarters into the centre of Angami country.[75] This intrusion and interference resulted in a surprise attack on their militia with thirteen personnel killed.[76] The militia was attacked because it got itself involved in a local feud.[77] Thereupon, the government sanctioned immediate and strong measures; the dispatch of military forces into the Angami hills were permitted, as a last resort, to burn the villages and destroy the crops.[78] Military operations inside Angami country were carried on for months and, for the first time, the British stayed on in the hills during the rains.[79] When in May 1850 the government grew impatient and requested the agent to the Northeast to submit more information about the situation in the Angami hills,[80] Jenkins reported on the impending success of the operation, that the Nagas were coming in one by one and were offering submission. Further, that the commanding officer in the hills, Lieutenant Vincent, asked to stay on in the hills during the rains. Jenkins, on this occasion, conveyed his opinion that the mere destruction of the offending villages was not enough and suggested as a further measure the destruction of the crops to prevent the Nagas from cultivation, a strategy of scorched earth, but that this would necessitate the permanent stationing of an European officer. This, so he continued, would finally bring them to submission, but involved '. . . the necessity of proceeding to the harsh but unavoidable infliction of destroying villages and crops'.[81] Jenkins warned not to call off the operation at this stage, since this would send the wrong signals. There was, so Jenkins thought, every justification to make an end to their '. . . useless striving for their rude independence and the right to plunder and murder their neighbours . . .'[82] The government gave its approval, since it '. . . may be productive . . .'[83] Jenkins continued to portray the course of events in the Naga hills as very positive, that the British had very good relations with the Nagas, yet, at the same time he requested artillery support to dislodge a stockade above Khonoma.[84] The government, now alarmed by the sudden request for artillery, ordered that no offensive step should be undertaken before Jenkins had submitted the details.[85] Nevertheless, the government sanctioned the building of roads, necessary to take action against the Angamis, including one to be built from Golaghat and Nowgong via Dimapur to Samaguting,[86] and from there the extension up to Mozema and the transformation of Dimapur into a permanent military post.[87] They also finally agreed on Jenkins' request for two mountain howitzers from the Assam Local Mountain Artillery.[88]

Information from around the time painted a dramatic picture of the situation for the British in the Angami hills. The Nagas were not at all willing to go into submission and only a force of 500 men with mountain guns were seen as sufficient to effect that. The whole of the hills was either hidden or open against the British.[89] Grey, the then officiating under-secretary to the GOI, had undertaken the task of analysing all the previous communications dealing with the events that led to the then present situation in the Naga hills, and came to the conclusion that most of the killings had occurred since they, the British, had started their intervention:

> The present state of affairs in the Naga Hills bordering upon Nowgong to the eastward and lying North of Muneepore would seem to have arisen entirely out

of the endeavours made by the British authorities in Assam to restrain the violent and deadly feuds existing among different tribes and villages of Nagas.[90]

Of course, Grey had to portray here the British endeavour to subjugate the Nagas as an altruistic, humanitarian intervention. Nevertheless, he had come to the conclusion that the raids had become more lethal, that is to say, the number of killings during single raids had become higher. Every intervention, so he continued, was a failure, the adopted measures led to new failures and the result was that the whole race was up in arms and prepared to offer the most determined opposition to the British troops.[91]

This brought the matter to the higher levels of the British hierarchy, so the governor general of India, Lord Dalhousie, expressed his complete displeasure with the conduct of Jenkins and his subordinates, and also stated that the government now had to act with military power to support him and restore the '. . . influence of our power . . .' About the future policy he wrote as follows:

> It would be premature perhaps to state now my views as to what ought to be our subsequent course, as farther information has been called for by His Honour in Council – But I can have no hesitation in declaring my opinion, that our past proceedings of late years with the Nagas have not been for our advantage – I deprecate the continuance of any such relations with barbarous tribes as tend directly to the mischievous occurrence of 'little Wars': and I hold that on this as on all other frontiers where wild and plundering clans are seated, our true policy is to stand strictly on the defensive; to protect as fully as we can our own border, and its inhabitants, but not to interfere beyond it from any motive however laudable. In short we ought to mind our own business and not to meddle with other peoples.[92]

Dalhousie ordered a strictly defensive stand, and discouraged any attempt to impose authority over the Nagas: 'I . . . deprecate entirely any seizure of useless and embarrassing territory . . .'[93] The orders were to defend strictly only the British borders, to protect only their own subjects and to abstain from any interference '. . . all further relations with the hill chiefs or attempted authoritative influence should be avoided'.[94] In a further protocol Dalhousie underlined his stand vis-à-vis Angami country:

> I dissent entirely from the policy which is recommended of what is called obtaining a control, that is to say of taking possession of these hills and of establishing our sovereignty over their savage inhabitants. Our possession could bring no profit to us; and would be unproductive.[95]

Again his order was strict non-interference, and regarding the defence of the frontier, which Jenkins had said was impossible, Dalhousie wrote that it should be possible with spirit, that the withdrawal after a military victory signalled British power and the will to enforce, and '. . . our desire to show that we have no wish for territorial aggrandisement, and no designs on the independence of the Naga tribes'.[96] As long as the Angamis were peaceful, trade should be carried out with them, once they offend British territory or subjects, the trade should be interrupted '. . . to allay their natural fears of our aggression upon them . . .'[97] On the next day the order to withdraw was immediately relayed to Jenkins.[98]

The stationing of a military post inside Angami territory had first drawn the British into local Naga politics and then made them a target for the Angamis who were then rallying around the flag to expel the intruder and finally managed to do so. The local officers, guided by the problems on the ground were called back by their superiors, once they had realised that the cost-benefit calculation would come up with a deficit. Hence, the first phase of interaction between British and Nagas ended in 1851 with a decision in favour of non-interference, a conviction that it would not pay to colonise the Nagas and that the troubles with them were instigated by the interference into their affairs.

Conclusion

Strategic rationale and the promise of profit brought the British to the foot of the hills separating Burma from Assam. Strategic and economic considerations made them want to gain ascendancy over the hill tribes, especially since they first thought it could be done by Manipur, and then, after that had failed, that one powerful strike would scare the natives into compliance.

The empire, cautiously, hesitatingly, yet steadily, expanded its search for natural and tradable resources, for markets, and above all for taxable populations. This expansion was furnished with legitimacy by inventing the mission to deliver its rule and administration and save the people from oriental despotism or unspeakable savage cruelties. One people after the other had to be redeemed when commercial interests conflated with the ideological, covering up the mere predatory enterprise. The British agents, we may assume, lived in their ideology, only sometimes questioning their right to be there, to conquer. Typically enough, these reflections were always made by the senior officials in Calcutta or London, when expecting an unprofitable enterprise.

Military force, or force as such, seemed to be the natural tool of British policy. War was not the continuation of politics with other means, the policy was war.[99] The British state and its ruling class were a martial one, '. . . dressed to kill'.[100] Perpetual warfare made fighting into something very normal and necessary, lest there were the danger of degenerating.[101] Or as Edmund Burke, staunch critic of the empire noted in 1784:

> The main drift of their policy was to keep the natives totally out of sight. We might hear enough about what great and illustrious exploits were daily performing on that great conspicuous theatre [India] by Britons. But . . . we were never to hear of any of the natives being actors.[102]

We will now try to remedy this, despite the scarcity of sources, and will try our best to understand who these Nagas were who resisted, if only for a time, the onslaught of the garrison state.

2 The Nagas, the Angami case – polity and war, 1820s–1880

Introduction

This chapter aims to demonstrate that the British, when they tried to subjugate the Naga hills lying between Assam and Manipur, bordering Northern Cachar, encountered a number of clusters of polities of which one group, calling themselves 'Tengima', took centre stage in the resistance. Why is this important? I will argue at a later stage that the societies of these polities shared a similar culture that allowed them to identify themselves in a political way and of which the former Tengimas only formed a part. Further, the hardening of the surrounding cultural and societal boundaries defined the extent of the conglomeration of polities. That is to say it was to a lesser extent the colonial vis-à-vis his boundaries and administration, but to a far greater one the policy of the post-colonial successor that merged these polities into one, forming the Naga nation. This is an ongoing process, and will become clearer in the course of the following chapters.

Our data stems from the pens of the British conquerors. When trying to make sense of their writings, we have to interrogate them carefully and to keep in mind what we learned in the previous chapter on the garrison state, its personnel, their culture and interests. They basically give us some ethnographic accounts, but data is most comprehensive where some form of violence was involved. Our main problem will thus be to decipher their polities via an interpretation of contemporary Naga practice, as it had been handed down to us. This will necessitate an additional and framing discussion of Southeast Asian history, concepts of rule, and understanding of war. In addition, wherever it seems helpful, I will also fall back on literature dealing with cases in other regions and times that show similarities to our case and were termed by Gellner 'peripheral areas'.[1]

The outer circle

What nowadays is named Northeast India represented a long-standing crossroads between China and Southeast Asia on one side and the subcontinent and Afghanistan on the other. Chinese and Greek sources from the second century BC onwards tell us about routes leading from southern China via northern Burma through the Brahmaputra valley: one through the Patkoi range and Upper Burma, another through Burma alongside the Chindwin valley, and yet another through the Arakan along the Irrawaddy valley.[2] China aside, Southeast Asia was connected to South Asia by sea and land routes, the latter via the difficult terrain of the mountain chain between Assam and Burma.[3] Archaeological findings and observations suggest that the hill regions definitely, and also very likely the Assam valley, were influenced rather by Southeast Asia, than by South Asia.[4] While immigration from the subcontinent by the twelfth century nearly consolidated the Sanskritisation of the Brahmaputra valley, the hills did not respond to the new religion.[5] Alastair Lamb delineated Northeast India and mainland Southeast Asia as one region into which the migration from areas corresponding to modern southern China had taken place. It was only the British annexation, having its administration centre in South Asia, that removed the hills of these regions from Southeast Asia.[6]

Southeast Asia was characterised by low population density as a result mostly of incessant warfare. War, however – and we will come back later to this point – was fought to acquire manpower not to waste it.[7] Adding to that precariousness was what Anthony Reid, following Victor Lieberman, names 'law of imperma- nence', cultural tendencies operating in favour of the overthrowing of dynasties and change of the location of their capitals.[8] This fluid state of affairs is best described with Stanley Tambiah's coinage of Southeast Asian polities as 'galactic', that is to say, they were oriented towards a centre, that assembled around itself in concentric circles. This follows the geometric example of the *mandala*, identical to itself but diminishing in power, polities, that were in effect autonomous, but over which it would overlord ritual authority. Competing with this centre were others that attracted or lost these minor polities to rival centres depending on the respective power constellation.[9] This pulsating picture replicating in increasing or decreasing scope in a varying but identical pattern was, in essence, built on the societal principle of leader-follower, delivering the building blocks of the tradi- tional polity in Southeast Asia.[10] In between these polities were stretches of terri- tory which were difficult to access, either because they were mountainous or heavily forested or both, providing a refuge for a life outside these kingdoms, and creating

> a fundamental dualism of hill and valley, upstream and downstream, interior and coast. (. . .) No state incorporated such dependents fully; they remained a stateless penumbra of the state, often indispensable providers of forest or sea products, messengers, warriors and slaves – tributary but distinct, and perceived as uncivilized but also as free.[11]

Although Lieberman sees a continuity of centralisation and state-building for mainland Southeast Asia, that was to a large degree comparable to what hap- pened in Europe, and for him thus resembling a common Eurasian pattern, he nevertheless admits that until the arrival of the European colonial powers, mainland Southeast Asian polities retained their galactic quality as ascribed by Tambiah, and that the hill areas had by then not been affected by the state-building measures.[12]

To war or not to war

The Angamis had been spared the depredations of the wars including and preceding the first Anglo-Burman war. Yet the *raja* of Manipur, after his re-enthronement had been effected by his British protectors, lost no time in his zeal to make tributary the hill people surrounding his kingdom, including the Angamis.[13] In addition, we have evidence that during the winter months of 1831/32 and 1832/33 respectively, strong expedition forces, each consisting of around 1,500 personnel, including 800 troops, crossed the Angami hills and were ferociously opposed at every step of their progress. The Angamis acted in unison and in some cases even went so far as to burn their own villages and crops, leaving a torched earth for the intruder.[14] The British had ordered Manipur to subjugate the Angamis[15] and equipped its troops for this purpose with guns and ammunition.[16] The Angamis, possibly in retaliation, raided North Cachar and Manipur, however, without us being given any specifics.[17]

The first details on an Angami intrusion into North Cachar originate from February 1835, stating that the Angamis demanded tribute from Naga villagers living there, and in case the latter refused, burnt their houses and took by force what had not been given freely. That the British called this an intrusion is due to the fact that they only recently considered North Cachar as their territory. It is, however, very likely that the Angamis were not yet conscious of this, and thus from their side it constituted no intrusion at all.[18] The next incident on which we happen to possess concrete information was reported two years later, in May 1837, when Angamis killed five people and abducted thirty;[19] and another raid more than a year later in October 1838, with again five homicides and twenty abductions.[20] The affected area was that around Haflong. Who and what exactly was behind these raids is difficult to establish. There is the above-mentioned possibility that they were retaliation for prior Manipuri and Cacharie attacks, or that a dispute over salt wells was involved. The documents also say that these were a mixture of headhunting and slave-capturing raids, for the latter could either be sold to Bengali slave traders or ransomed to their respective villages.[21] Thus these raids, carried out on Naga villages, could also have been part of their feuding system. But whatever the real reasons for them or who the actual perpetrators were, and whether the accounts themselves were part of the violent conflicts between rival groups to direct the wrath of the British against ones' enemy, we probably never will be able to say with certainty. What becomes evident though, is that the extent and the number of incidents seems to have been greatly exaggerated by the British officers, the portrayal of an escalation solely the produce of the reports' ever faster circulation. British officers on the ground, on the one hand dramatised the situation to render intervention necessary; on the other hand, they exaggerated the economic potential of the area and the willingness of the inhabitants to be taken under British protection. In this way they created the pretext for pushing the frontier further.

Thus, from the late 1830s the British decided to take affairs into their own hands,[22] resulting a decade later in an escalation during which, for the first time, British troops, almost without interruption, stayed on in the Angami hills, moving about destroying villages and crops, but for most of the time were besieged in their

own stockades. The Angamis, in retaliation, attacked villages under British jurisdiction that in turn, were armed with guns by the British. More and more Angami
clans and villages united and finally forced the British to withdraw from the hills
and contributed to their decision to disconnect themselves from Angami affairs.
From all the evidence we have, it seems that the presence and conduct of the British
troops triggered a temporary rallying-around-the-flag in these hills. The British had
to call on artillery and regular troops and still were only able to take a formidable
fortress above Khonoma because it was vacated by the Angamis. The massive out-
lay on the fortress alone shows the extent of collective endeavour, though it might
have been brought about in an egalitarian way. The Angamis did not have to hold
on to villages or fortresses, since the British could not at all control their movements, and were soon not able anymore to distinguish between population and foe.
British presence also triggered challenges of neighbouring mighty villages, located
further to the east, and not under the political influence of the Tengima group of
villages. Those Nagas were obviously unaware of the firepower of British arms and
stubbornly engaged them in open combat, resulting in hundreds of casualties.[23]

The endemic violence prevailing on the edges of and within the Angami hills was
an invention of the officers on the ground, designed to convey legitimacy to their
desire for conquest. It was British intervention that then created the havoc that it
was allegedly in the first place intended to stop. Grey, the then officiating under-
secretary to the GOI, came to pretty much the same conclusion when analysing the
communications of the officers on the frontier:

> The present state of affairs in the Naga Hills bordering upon Nowgong to the
> eastward and lying North of Muneepore would seem to have arisen entirely out
> of the endeavours made by the British authorities in Assam to restrain the vio-
> lent and deadly feuds existing among different tribes and villages of Nagas.[24]

It was only the missing evidence of the reality of the 'deadly feuds' within the hills
that eluded Grey, but he had established the fact that the raids had become more
lethal, in other words the number of killings during single raids had increased.
Every intervention, so he continued, was a failure, and the adopted measures had
led to new failures, and on the situation of the British troops, that had then been in
the Angami hills '. . . with the exception of Jabulee's immediate followers [the one
allied clan from Mozema], the whole race is up in arms and prepared to offer the
most determined opposition to the British Troops.'[25] Approximately thirty years
later, when the British were in the process of establishing themselves in the middle
of the Angami hills, with preceding events similar to the one we have described
here, an attack of the Merhema clan of Khonoma on a British detachment again
unleashed a general uprising. In the process of this the British were besieged in their
stockade by thousands of Angami warriors, busy driving trenches up to the British
fortification. One of the besieged later narrated the following incident:

> On the night of 24th, a Nága who spoke Hindustani harangued us from behind
> one of the barricades. He said we had come here and occupied land, we had cut

their trees, bamboos, and grass, we wanted revenue from them and made them furnish coolies. His speech ended with a query. – 'What will happen now?'[26]

The British finally were relieved, and the Angamis, after a protracted war, defeated. We will now try to find out why the Nagas took up general resistance and why they finally surrendered.

Refuge-area warrior society

The title of this sub-chapter is taken from Boehm's study on feuding,[27] and nicely depicts that we are only to understand these hill societies by placing them into the wider political context.[28] We will now do just this by subsequently turning to the phenomena of headhunting, raiding, feuding and war, in order to try to make our deductions on the constitution of contemporary Angami society.

Headhunting has to be differentiated from pure trophy taking in wars and raids, existing at all times in all places, and may be defined as '. . . an organized, coherent form of violence in which the severed head is given a specific ritual meaning and the act of headtaking is consecrated and commemorated in some form.'[29] There is no one symbolic meaning or reasoning, hence social and political factors have to be taken into consideration when trying to make sense out of headhunting acts.[30] For the Angamis, we have very little evidence of such pure headhunting cases. One of these was the killing of four women: 'These murders were committed . . . as propitiatory offerings for a good harvest, the limbs of the persons killed as well as the skulls being carried off to be stuck up in the rice fields.'[31] The explanation given here points to some fertility concept involved, a reasoning widely accepted among Nagas today (personal communications) and in the literature on them. The headhunter was glorified as life-giver, and thus was his status enhanced.[32] However, we have to keep in mind that the evidence about actual headhunting cases is scant, and that the existence of the practice was welcomed by the British as conveying further legitimacy to their conquest, as was the case elsewhere in Southeast Asia: 'The battle over tribal sovereignty was largely waged over the suppression of headhunting.'[33] Headhunting was always the outcome of considerations at a specific time and place and did not follow from an automatic application of rules.[34] Moreover, headhunting acts could as well be understood as statements on power relations,[35] and related to that, as acts that symbolised one's political autonomy.[36]

Raids, as Boehm has demonstrated with the help of his Montenegrin case study, were especially conducted when subsistence failed and/or to prove oneself as a man, in which case heads were also taken to give evidence of one's deeds.[37] Thus raiding for Montenegrins could be a *rite de passage*, as was headhunting for Ilongots.[38] Raiding depended as much on historical circumstances and contemporaneous considerations as did headhunting, that is to say it was undertaken only after weighing the pros and cons, and not if severe retribution was to be expected in return.[39] Also, the composition of raiding parties could reflect real or projected political alliances, and thus could be an instrument of home politics.[40] Raiding among the Angamis will have been motivated and regulated in the same way. Yet in addition to the material and status enhancing incentives, raiding in Southeast Asia could also be driven by the desire for captives that could be ransomed or sold as slaves, or to adopt them into one's own society and in this way acquire manpower, a general objective of Southeast Asian warfare, as we have learned above.

Raiding, on the other hand, has to be differentiated from feuding, and Boehm follows here Radcliffe-Brown, Evans-Pritchard and Gluckman[41] in stating that feuding happened only inside the tribe between its component clans and had a regulatory function.[42] The basis of feuding was the moral system in which everyone was the Other's equal and had the obligation that he was taught from childhood on, to defend one's honour and revenge one's blood.[43] Yet to escape the crude and ahistorical functionalism of the British school of social anthropology, Boehm states that the institution of feuding was a conscious historical solution to the problem of the possibility of homicidal violence in a society without central authority and therefore contributing to social stability.[44] Boehm stresses that the extent of feuding was always exaggerated by visiting foreigners and that the percentage of people actually involved in feuding at any time, constituted only a tiny fraction of the total population, so that casualties were low and the majority of the people could conduct their daily affairs in peace.[45] Moreover, feuding did not evolve in an automatic and inevitable fashion, every stage rather presented a turning point at which several considerations had to be made, and where arbitration to prevent escalation could either be offered or enforced by the community. Honour had to be bent and truces announced for the sake of social stability or in case of an outside threat or simply during harvest. Feuding was thus rather characterised by invention and modification rather than by following tradition,[46] as must have been the feuding units, the clans: '... the bertan [Ilongot for clan] and the feud, far from being a timeless bedrock of synchronic social structure, are historically conditioned and socially constructed.'[47]

The Montenegrins, according to Boehm, constituted a segmentary political system, in which households made up clans, and clans made up tribes. Clans were military and feuding units and tribes made up the one for territorial defence. The constitution of the tribes was, as the one of the clans, situational. While clans were competing with each other, inter-tribal feuding, which, if it happened, could develop into warfare, was rare. Rather they were conscious of the larger and more powerful plains neighbour (in this case, the Turks) and united in case of threats coming from this side '... to defend their territory and autonomy.'[48] The term 'segmentary political systems' was coined by Meyer Fortes and Evans-Pritchard to come to terms with African societies that lacked any discernible central authority that could be co-opted or coerced into the imperial enterprise.[49] The evidence for the Angamis, in our case and period of scrutiny, represented rather a polity that was constituted out of ranked clans that vied with each other for dominance. In other words, they were organised in an egalitarian way internally, and their composition must have been changing, reflecting ideology, not sociology,[50] but these clans were ranked among themselves, and thus egalitarianism extended only as far as clan boundaries. The reach of the clans' ritual dominance, that should not be confused with effective rule, depended on their respective power, in accord with Tambiah's galactic polity. Also it seems from our evidence (and this would differentiate it from Tambiah's concept) that several clans could radiate their dominance at a time inside the same space (though it seemed that newly acquired firearms worked towards a centralisation of power), and Reid gives us examples of indigenous Southeast Asian state formations based on balancing clans making up a federal structure:

> Though tension between these rival authorities was the rule, in the ideal Southeast Asian polity they could be overcome by a process of discussion and consensus. At their best, these institutions of pluralism provided a modest basis for contractualism within state structures. Most often, however, they also inhibited progress towards the bureaucratic institutionalization of state authority.[51]

For African societies – which shall serve to give us a rough idea, despite all their fission and fractions – unity as whole was produced and perceived by the people themselves through numerous cross-cutting kinship ties, material interests and common ritual values. Political units, that may be defined narrowly in relation to military actions and legal sanctions, could under no circumstances be understood in isolation. They were based on interlocking social systems transgressing their highly unstable political boundaries, and made the drawing of the latter to a certain degree into a wanton matter.[52] The mobility of African people made rights over people important, not over things; borders had less importance which in turn was assigned to key points and centres rather than to bounded space,[53] and again is congruent to Tambiah's findings that we discussed above, that, as we have just learned, have to be qualified by our own evidence and Reid's that several clans could rule a territory in a pluralist way.

In chapter four we shall hear more on the political constitution of the populations inhabiting the Naga hills with the help of later dating evidence and literature. Here it shall suffice to liken contemporary Angami polity to segmentary political systems described elsewhere at other times. Without further research in oral history[54] (and maybe not even with that) we will not be able to pin down how exactly the Angamis then were politically constituted.

Yet from what has been hitherto discussed, it should have become clear that there existed no such social and ritual ties or relations with the newly arrived British conquerors. The British were clearly located outside the social systems, perceived as radically different and as predatory. This may account for the general resistance that was rallied to oppose British intrusion. Like Boehm's Montenegrins the Angamis united to fight this obvious Other. Although they fought in a decentralised way, they not only concerted their actions to a certain degree but also hit at their enemy's bases and allies. The totality of armed interactions and confrontations can safely be called war, according to modern definitions.[55] That the Angamis in general avoided high numbers of casualties was in accord with the warfare then practised in Southeast Asia that for one avoided the wasting of precious manpower,[56] but also becomes understandable from the fact that it was fought along real or fictional kinship ties that, as was explained above, did not allow for the idea of dying for a higher good. That the Angamis surrendered relatively easily in 1880 can be ascribed to the fact that it was beyond their imagination that the British would want to stay.[57] They surely must have thought that this campaign, as all the ones before, was a temporary affair, and that the British, once they had received their tribute and were assured of allegiance, would return back to whence they had come. In other words, the surrender in the 1880s meant something else for the Angamis than for the British. The actual surrender of the Angamis was not a punctual affair but a slow process of disbelief and realisation, a successive accommodation to the presence of the foreign occupants. The rather light administration that the British kept up, once the Angami hills were pacified, certainly helped the people acquiesce to it.

In order to investigate further into the reasons for resistance, I want to make another leap, right into this century. In summer 2001 I conducted interviews with several Nagas in London. One of my main interviewees was Mr. Yong Kong, an elderly Ao Naga gentleman who came to London in the early 1960s to support Zaphu Angami Phizo, the pivotal figure of Naga nationalism, of whom we will hear more later, in his struggle to make the Naga case publicly known. My main interest was to find out why the Nagas had taken up arms against the Indian state and were still fighting after nearly 50 years. After three days, we continued to come back to the reason why the Nagas had given in to the British and why suddenly they demanded independence from the Indians. I argued in a very hair-splitting way and managed to greatly annoy him, but suddenly, leaving all the proximate reasons aside, he very angrily said:

> No, you see, what the outside world, or even people like you, do not understand is the Nagas are not fighting for independence, they are defending their territory, their territory, if your country is invaded.[58]

As Walker Connor writes: '... grasping the obvious has always been a problem for academics and policy-makers.'[59] There is a difference between 'fighting for independence' and 'defending one's territory', or homeland as Connor would term it.[60] I would say that the Angamis from the 1830s to 1880 were defending their territory, the occupation was not yet effected, everyone could see the actual act of violent penetration of the foreign conquerors, and that they were in the wrong place. Yet, since the British were very thinly present in the Naga hills, the subsequently subjugated groups could somehow arrange themselves under their ineffective rule. Though they had lost their political freedom, for most of the time they retained their individual freedom. The case was different with the sudden influx of Indian personnel in the aftermath of the Transfer of Power. Now their land was really taken away. Of course there were other factors too, but here I must stress that what happened in 1947, and before in 1849 and 1879, were invasions, but that by 1947 the Nagas already knew that the Indians came to stay. We will come back to this in chapter six. Here I simply want to suggest that the reason for the Angamis fighting the British in 1849/50 as in 1879/80 was that they were defending their territory. As Connor has demonstrated not only intra- but also inter-state wars were and are fought by individuals on grounds that he calls homeland psychology and which in turn eludes cold academic analysis: 'Psychological perceptions of homelands and the emotions to which they give rise are the stuff that dreams – *and nightmares* – are made of.'[61]

In pre-colonial Southeast Asia wars were not fought for land, but over populations and they generally moved away in case of an attack.[62] How then can I claim that the Angamis and later the Nagas fought to defend their territory? One factor might have been that the villages of the Nagas, other than those of their plains neighbours, were in general heavily built and resembled fortresses with a high labour input; the same was (and still is) true for the terraced rice fields of the Angamis. Yet the solution to our impasse may lie rather more in the fact that the lowland peasants simply moved from one polity and ruler to another, in case of a threat, or a too oppressive regime, or they were forcibly moved. That is to say for lowland inhabitants it was (and still is) the normal state of affairs to live under one or the other regime. Hill people, on the other hand, lived in these 'peripheral areas' in conscious opposition to and rejection of lowland tutelage as Gibson has stated for three Southeast Asian peoples.[63] In Schiller's *Wilhelm Tell* Walter asks his father Tell whether there existed countries where there were no mountains, and Tell confirming this describes the plains to him in the lushest detail. Walter then with incomprehension queries why they then should toil and fear in the mountains instead of quickly descending into the paradisiacal lowland. Tell explains to him that the fields, forests, lakes and rivers of the plains belong not to the people themselves but to the king and church, and that the people in turn receive protection instead of bravely protecting themselves. Thus sobered Walter replies that he would feel rather confined in the wide plains and so would prefer to live under threat of avalanches and glaciers.[64] The Angamis, like the Swiss and Montenegrins, inhabited a refuge-area, had a distinct sense of their individual and collective autonomy and were conscious about the fact that their freedom depended on the inaccessibility of their territory that they, in turn, were willing to defend. The defence was conducted by every man, voluntarily, since everyone was one's own master, fighting for one's own independence. And to bring in the female perspective, the band of brothers would have been encouraged by their mothers, sisters, wives and wives to be, as Gertrud in Schiller's Tell sweeps away her husband's hesitation to fight, with her affirmation that they (the Swiss), too, are men (and maybe that he should not make her question that), that they also know how to handle a battle-axe, and that God helps the brave.[65] Gertrud's husband was left with neither choice nor excuse. While in the lowlands legitimacy trickled down to the people from the god-king, in the hills it was constituted out of the consensus of the collective will and at all times open to negotiation, a fact bringing us to our last point in this chapter.

Nationalism, nothing new in the West

Assamese historiography, in trying to trace the prehistoric racial and genetic core of the Nagas in order to demonstrate their mixed origin,[66] serviced the project of a greater Assam. The same is true for their opposite number. Naga scholars too feel the need to legitimise present-day demands for recognition as a separate nation with the demonstration of Naga foreign relations going back to the third century AD.[67] Both claims follow the logic of nationalism that demands a nation in order to legitimately set up a state, i.e., a nation-state. A nation, in turn, must be presented as something like an endogamous kinship group that has already existed from time immemorial.

Following the same logic are efforts to find historical sources purportedly relating to the Nagas in Vedic or ancient Greek or Chinese sources that,[68] though interesting per se, and demonstrating the long history of settlement in those hills, will yet not have been the decisive element in the formation of Naga polities in the eighteenth and nineteenth century. Thus neither can be made accountable for the resistance to the British, nor, for that matter, for the formation of modern Naga nationalism and resistance to Indian occupation in the twentieth century.

This school of thought implicitly carries the notion that there are discrete, bio-logically self-reproducing groups that share and possess a distinct language and culture, a congruence of race, language and culture, whose bearers should make up one society, its nation, and in turn be granted with its territory, its nation-state.[69] Cultures and their bearers travelled through time in an unadulterated way '. . . they could not mix, they had hard edges like billiard balls.'[70] Yet since there is no scientific way to determine who belongs to what people, ethnic group or nation, such undertakings in the end boil down to a blatant racist point of view and always are the product of politics.[71]

Frank Proschan takes the widespread existence of orally transmitted myths of origin in highland Southeast Asia as evidence for the existence of autochthonous, i.e., pre-colonial, conceptualisations of ethnicities that he considers as primary, and the colonial influence as secondary, in opposition to Benedict Anderson. The myths decidedly conceptualise and represent a world of common humanity, that is pluralistic, multiethnic, multilinear and inegalitarian in which different groups may be differentiated according to phenotype, cultural markers, social status, economic opportunity, technological knowledge, and, and this is important for us, political authority.[72] Butler (the principal assistant of Nowgong) related the kind of myth prevalent among the Angamis in the first half of the eighteenth century, and this alone could suffice to support us in our statement that the Angamis had a conception of themselves as different and that this under any circumstances also included a political notion of them. Proschan draws support from Ronald R. Atkinson who, with the help of oral history, re-constructed the pre-colonial:

> . . . ideological underpinnings and sociohistorical processes that contributed to the development . . .(. . .)[of a] common social order and political culture . . . over almost all of what is now the Acholi District of Uganda – processes that laid fundamental foundations and set crucial parameters for the further evolution of Acholi societal formation and ethnic consciousness over the nineteenth and twentieth centuries.[73]

Atkinson's central point is that we have to go back to pre-colonial times to understand the effect (and maybe the approach also) of colonial workings. Acholi by the mid- to late-seventeenth century was characterised by kinship-based groups inhabiting single-village political communities, with occasional multi-village groupings. At that time it constituted a '. . . multicultural frontier region . . .' in which the inhabitants shared common features but did not form a single society. This changed with immigration in the course of the eighteenth century when new populations brought with them the new ideas and institutions of chiefship that brought about increased centralisation, which in turn resulted in the processes described in the previous quote.[74]

Prasenjit Duara argues that to conceptualise political identity as only modern is wrong, and criticises the notion

> . . . that nationalism is a radically novel mode of consciousness. . . . because this position ignores the complexity of the nature of historical memory and causality and because it remains tied to the idea of self-consciousness as a uniquely modern phenomenon. In neither modern nor premodern society is it possible to sustain the notion of a unified consciousness presumed by the concept of nationalism.[75]

He continues:

> Whether in India or China, people historically identified with different representations of communities, and when these identifications became politicized, they came to resemble what is called modern 'national identities'.[76]

And:

> I will argue that there were totalizing representations and narratives of community with which people identified historically and with which they may continue to identify into the modern nation. Of course, premodern political identifications do not necessarily or teleologically develop into the national identifications of modern times and there are significant ruptures with the past. A new vocabulary and a new political system – the world system of nation-states – selects, adapts, reorganizes and even recreates these older representations. But the historical memory of archaic totalizations does not always disappear, and as this memory is periodically re-enacted, it often provides potent material along which to mobilize the new community.[77]

The Tengima group of the later Angamis and Nagas, as becomes evident from our data, constituted such a politicised community that, according to Duara, qualifies as nation. Since Walker Connor sees passive resistance to an authority that is perceived as foreign as sufficient evidence for the existence of popular national consciousness, and hence the existence of a nation,[78] the prolonged and sustained violent resistance to the British invasion demonstrated here by the Tengimas might then surely suffice to prove my point. The Naga hills were home to a whole range of political identities whose bearers were as conscious of themselves as of that fact. How and that these identities transformed into a larger one was not due to some genes but to history, and it will be this history that will form the subject of the remaining chapters of this book.

Conclusion

Hill people, as has become evident here, were conscious of the fact that their lowland neighbours were superior in numbers, arms and organisation to them, and that it was the inaccessibility and undesirability of their territory that protected them from permanent subjugation, if not from occasional devastating invasions. Hence they were cautious not to unnecessarily provoke the wrath of their mighty neighbours. So far we have seen that the extent and number of raids carried out by the Angamis was greatly exaggerated by the men on the ground, the murderous zone a product of their reports. We have evidence of two, sometimes one, but also of no violent assaults per year – attacks that have been mixtures of raids for property and testing one's manliness, and those exclusively to attain heads and limbs of victims to ensure fertility for the fields. Also, we have clearly political operations aiming at British forces and their bases, or as sanctions against subordinate villages for not opposing the British intruder. Finally, we witnessed a power struggle between two of the more powerful clans, a fight that must have been greatly exacerbated by the additional firepower gained with either directly winning British support or the acquisition of guns, when we remember the fortress-like villages. However, the two years of peace from 1847 to 1849 show that the Angamis for one had decided to give in to the British, if only for the moment, and that this must have been understood by all Angami clans, or they were made to understand by the stronger clans. This period of intensified communication between British held territory and Angamis, in a way a blind spot, since peace makes bad (in the sense of little) news, must have greatly enlarged the Angamis' knowledge of their white adversaries, and thus influenced their decisions in their dealings with them. On the other hand the pattern of the interaction will in general have followed the one the Angamis had with the central organised predecessors of the British. The point here is to reiterate that neither feuding nor headhunting were automatic reflexes of Angami culture but subject to political considerations and decision-making.[79] Further, the Angami hills were, at the time we are concerned with here, a polity organised in a segmentary way, in which clans may have split and rivalled each other for domination, in which clans also may have called in outside allies for support in this internal power struggle, but on the understanding that these outsiders never wanted to stay on permanently. In this the Angamis simply mirrored the alliance politics of their lowland neighbours. Finally, the Angamis were conscious about themselves as being different and separate in a political way, and thus determined to govern themselves, as may be surely deducted from the concerted and determined resistance to the British invasion. This resistance easily renders the whole sum of events from 1849 to 1851 liable to be qualified as war, respectively of conquest or resistance, depending on one's point of view, but confirming the notion of two opposed polities.

3   Imperial conquest and withdrawal, 1860s–1947

Introduction

The concerted resistance of the Tengima group of the Angami Nagas and the limited interest of the British in the Naga hills brought about a change in British policy by 1851. Pivotal in this decision to call back the imperial personnel from the Naga hills was the then Governor General Dalhousie, who was inclined to entertain an aggressive forward policy, as can be seen, for instance, in his handling of the neighbouring Burma case unfolding at the same time.[1] This chapter explains the Naga hills' place in the British empire during the time of 'high imperialism', documents and delineates the partial conquest of the Naga hills and the type of regime the British set up there, and their eventual retreat.

Imperialism unbound

Chapter one located the reasons for British expansion into Naga territory in the general ideology of the empire and in the search for ever new revenues to finance a military-fiscal state that had resulted out of the incessant warfare among competing European states at the global level. In this respect the picture didn't change much from the middle of the nineteenth century onwards. Quite to the contrary, once acquired, the facticity of empire created an understanding of the British of themselves as an imperial race, and the more the real empire was falling to pieces the more British greatness and empire-being was enacted, evoked and asserted.[2]

To be more precise, global competition between European states provided the main incentive for attacks on extra-European countries leading to massive territorial occupations between 1760–1830.[3] Geopolitics, though a little more relaxed in the post-1815 period, continued to shape British foreign policy and often provided the impulse for territorial expansion. This drive was heightened again by renewed imperial rivalries after 1870.[4] Adhering to the same logic, British cabinet members' war aims in the First World War were the dismantling of rival empires and the enlargement of their own, an attitude that Edwin S. Montagu, secretary of state for India, found quite agonising:

> . . . equally acquisitive [as his cabinet colleagues] was the rounded Lord
> Curzon who for historical reasons of which he alone is master and geographical

considerations of which he has peculiarly studied, finds reluctantly, very much against his will, that it would be dangerous if any country in the world is left to itself, or in control of any other country but ourselves, and we must go there, as I have heard him say, 'for diplomatic, economic, strategic and telegraphic reasons'.[5]

Even after the Second World War neither US-Americans nor Europeans wanted to de-colonise Asia and Africa but faced with the cold war planned to exchange formal for informal control.[6]

Certainly for this later period also, generally described as high imperialism, reasons for empire are not only seen to be rooted in geopolitics: one approach fuses metropolitan geopolitics and peripheral interests, seeing the first as the driving force and the second as shaping the peculiar form of the actual outcome;[7] another one argues in favour of the decisive role the personnel of the proconsuls played in the overseas possessions;[8] then there is still the reasoning for British finance being the driving and determining force behind British imperialism and its disengagement.[9] Furthermore, we come across the factor of imperial politics serving home and party political interests in an age of increased suffrage;[10] and we encounter an ideological hardening, the belief in the racial superiority of the British race having the duty to rule others for their own good, resulting from the facticity of an extensive existing empire and the necessity to justify that.[11] The latter two rationales are new, compared to those we encountered in chapter one. Hence, even more so in what Bayly has called the first age of global imperialism, the reasons for empire during the age of 'high imperialism' were equally profound as they were diverse, or as Uday Singh Mehta puts it:

> The empire was a complex phenomenon informed by the multiple purposes of power, commerce, cultural and religious influence, and the imperatives of progress, along with the myriad subsidiary motives of pride, jealousy, compassion, curiosity, adventure, and resistance.[12]

Hence it would be absurd, in David Cannadine's words, to reduce a phenomenon as complex as the British empire to single causes that are supposed to be applicable across the imperial period and for all affected places, as well as for all involved processes and events. Rather, it was the study of factors in isolation leading to a neglect of scrutiny of '. . . essential connections between overseas expansion, foreign policy, international relations and great-power rivalries . . .'.[13] An integral approach bringing the strands together concludes that, in principle, mid-Victorian British imperial expansionism knew no limits, but was constrained by the practical considerations a widely overstretched power had to make that at best '. . . enjoyed an extra-European 'semi-hegemony' – a series of discontinuous regional hegemonies.'[14] It was therefore limitations in power that tamed an otherwise unbound and all-out British drive for expansionism.

Though it is an important lesson to learn that there existed a (near) pan-British acceptance of, a dedication to, and a desire for British imperialism, and that this ambition was only curbed by a lack of means, and it might help to explain why which territories were annexed or not, subjected to informal control or not, it does not absolve us from looking into the intricacies of every single case, since the mixture of motivations and factors for the followed up policies varied and determined the actual outcome and performance of, for example, a respective imperial occupation. To phrase it differently, if we want to understand a certain territory and its people under imperialism and after, as is the case for this work, we do best to look into the details of the given case, and then embed it into the wider field. This sounds trivial, but I think we might be able to make statements about British imperialism by comparing superficially several cases of British imperial holdings; but we will only be able to do the same on the respective holdings when we have examined their precolonial time, as well as having looked precisely into their specific cases of colonial subjugation and occupation, if we want to understand their post-colonial predicament. That is to say we understand the particular only against the General, but it is also necessary to conduct detailed case studies in order to fathom the General, or as Bayly puts it: 'The effects of imperialism are as much part of its character as its causes.'[15]

The conquest of India was the result of the war with France. Once it had been conquered its paramount significance and considerations of how to protect it and how to ensure the communication with it determined the conquest of new territories that served either as buffer or support bases for either military or trade.[16] Taking this into account, the importance of the *Raj* for the empire in its material and psychological effect might explain the general reluctance to let go of it.[17] India was only surrendered since it was becoming ungovernable, the Indian army seen as unreliable and authoritarian rule thus not possible,[18] since this then would have involved massive military action and cost,[19] and would furthermore not have been condoned by the United States upon which the British then depended.[20] In this particular case it was the shifting balance in power to the advantage of the Indian independence movements that forced the British to yield, otherwise it held true what Burke, according to Mehta, had already been conscious of: 'Another people's independence . . . is always the limiting point of our vision – the darkness that reason does not illuminate.'[21]

Return to the Naga hills

The renewed British forward policy leading to the partial annexation and occupation of the Naga hills is explained in retrospect by the failure of the policy of non-interference. The retreat into the plains and protection of the frontier had proved itself unfeasible. More than 150 people, whom the British considered as their subjects, were reported to have either been killed or abducted in 1851 alone. In 1854 Manipur invaded the Angami hills and the Angamis in turn asked the British for protection, which was declined. The British shortened their line of defence, but were still unable to defend North Cachar, which remained subject to incursions by the Angamis. The proposal was made to give up North Cachar and the district commissioner (DC) of Assam approved it. Yet, this was rejected by the then lieutenant governor of Bengal Sir C. Beadon,[22] who did not like the idea of giving in to 'wild tribes'.[23] The reality of the raids and the direction they came from should not be taken at face value, since these reports were certainly bent to suit the personnel of the garrison state and condoned by the presence of interests, transcending the field of Assam, for instance the competition with the colonial rival France in neighbouring Southeast Asia, the surge for trade routes in Assam, and possibly also the search for oil in Upper Burma.[24] Over the next two decades a forward policy was pursued that accelerated at the end of the 1870s.

This change of policy, in turn, marked the end of a series of weak viceroys that entertained a spectrum of foreign policy that had moved from passive non-interference to one of active alliance-building. With the return of the Conservatives to power in Britain, and Disraeli as prime minister and Salisbury as secretary of state for India, this changed, and '. . . was the beginning of the new Conservative imperialism, motivated by a determination to make Britain a great power in Asia.'[25] Lytton, who became viceroy in 1876, was briefed to entertain a forward policy expressed in regard to Afghanistan, but his desire for conquest was also directed to Upper Burma and together with the general inclination to expansion might well have influenced the policy towards the Naga hills. The move into the Naga hills in winter 1877–78 was heavily resisted by the Angamis,[26] followed by the cessation of hostilities in February 1978. However, the Angamis did stop fighting for the moment, and the British on their part also halted their attacks, in their words, to avoid further destruction, suffering and antagonising.[27]

By March 1878 it was decided to shift the headquarters to the site of Kohima into the middle of the Angami Naga hills.[28] Six months later, in November, the assistant secretary to the chief commissioner (CC) of Assam notified the foreign secretary in Lahore by telegram that Kohima had been occupied without opposition on November 14th.[29] Shortly after, by 5th December 1878, the secretary of state agreed to the gradual extension of British power over the Nagas.[30] By April 1879 the CC of Assam notified that the headquarters of the Naga hills district (NHD) had been transferred from Samaguting to Kohima on 24th March 1879.[31] In August 1879 Ridsdale reported to the government that, after having established themselves at Kohima, the Nagas still could hardly believe that the British would want to stay.[32] In October of the same year the political officer Damant and some of his men were killed by men from Khonoma.[33] This marked the starting point to the collective uprising of the Angamis, answered by the British with massive military operations[34] that lasted until the end of March 1880, and ended with the submission of the Angamis.[35] By August 1880 London gave its permission for the extension of the NHD so as to include the Lhota and Angami Nagas.[36]

Penetration and consolidation

In early 1881 the British contemplated the measures to be taken to install their rule in the Naga hills.[37] First, the boundaries of the district and its sub-divisions were to be fixed, to delineate the geographic extent of the measures to be taken.[38] The next step was the assessment of revenue to finance or at least levy a contribution to the financing of the administration. Revenue was fixed at two rupees per house per year, and was to be paid in two instalments. In March 1881 more than a hundred Naga villages had already paid house-tax.[39] The British still had to rely on the village elders for information about the number of houses in each village, but projected to change this and check these themselves.[40] This was to turn into one of the major tasks for the district officials during their incessant touring through the district. Related to this was the creation and keeping of revenue registers.[41] The revenue register seemed to have been the mother of all files, this documentation having immediately followed the geological, topographical and meteorological data that had been necessary for the conquest.[42] The measure that followed was directly connected with the collection of revenue: the creation of a new authority – the elected or appointed headmen – who were to be responsible for the collection of revenue and who were to receive a commission for that service. This is more interesting since the British here aimed to transform the society of the Angamis from a radical democratic into a hierarchical one. The CC of Assam, Elliot, suggested:

> ... the appointment of elected headmen, who might ... become the nucleus of some sort of village organization, and gradually grow to be possessors of power and authority over the young men of the village. Such a change, from the democratic and independent habits which the people now practice into one of subordination to a council of elders under a village headman, must necessarily be slow, but, if it can be effected, it will be a great help to good government.[43]

'Good government' obviously was the result that was the cheapest to the British and structures of hierarchy allowed them the form of indirect rule involving the minimum of their own resources. Further, Elliott suggested the registration of all adult males, who were each to work for the British for 15 days a year.[44] In addition to that he proposed the establishment of a small staff of permanent 'coolies' to be flexible in regard to transport.[45] After revenue, power-structure, labour supply and transport were addressed, Elliott went on to argue for the disarmament of the Nagas:

> In order to change the Nágas from a warlike and marauding to a peaceful race, it is essential that the habit of carrying arms around should be stopped, and that everything should be discouraged which has a martial tendency, or leads the people to believe that they can successfully resist our arms. (...) Thus in a few years the habit of handling arms, and the proficiency in their use acquired by warlike exercises, will have passed away.[46]

The colonialists thus engaged in the conscious demartialisation of the Nagas, although the British were and still are blamed by post-1947 Indian media, and also political and anthropological writings, for being responsible for what they see as the Nagas having become a martial race. However, this is to be discussed at a later stage. The biggest obstacle to achieving this demartialisation was seen by Elliott to be the formidable defences of the villages:

This practice must be altogether put to a stop. (. . .) . . . the villages should be
made as open and accessible to attack as the natural difficulties of their sites
permit. (. . .) . . . it is no longer necessary that they should take upon themselves
the burden of private defence.[47]

To relieve the Nagas of the burden of private defence was clearly not asked for in a
perfectly altruistic state of mind, but to remove, together with the village defences,
the will of the Nagas to defend themselves, above all against their new masters. The
fall of the material fences was to be followed by the fall of the defences in their
minds.[48] Moreover, the use of the dispensary in Kohima would be encouraged to
convince the Nagas via the healing of their ulcers, prevalent among them, of the
good intentions of the British. The same was to be done regarding vaccinations, and
here especially against the, by then rampant, smallpox: '. . . it has often been found
that wild and savage races recognise these benefits, and are led, by the receipt of
medical treatment, to acknowledge with gratitude the benevolence of our
motives.'[49]

After Elliot had stressed the importance of medical work, he emphasised the
'civilising and pacifying influence' of schools. He lamented the ignorance of Naga
languages among the British officers and urged teaching the Nagas Assamese and
Bengali.[50] The local officers were also to be encouraged to learn the local Naga languages and rewarded for achieving proficiency in them, as well as for the preparation of Naga grammar and vocabulary books. In addition, the younger officers were
to conduct an ethnography of the Nagas; not only was this interesting in itself, but
also important from a conservative point of view, and showed the rulers' interest in
matters of the ruled.[51] Another point of interest was the preservation of forest, and
related to that the restriction of slash and burn cultivation, or *jhuming*, and the
encouragement of permanent, that is to say, terraced and irrigated cultivation.[52]
Finally, the CC of Assam highlighted the paramount importance of direct and personal intercourse between ruler and ruled that had to be achieved through the incessant touring of the district officers and their assistants.[53] Elliott's scheme for the
administration of the Naga hills received approval from the government.[54] The
boundaries of the NHD now included: '. . . the Angamis, the Lhotas in the neighbourhood of Wokha, and a small portion of the Semas dwelling to the west of the
Doyong, with the Rengma Nága lying between them and the Angami country . . . .'[55]

This excluded the people then known by the British as Ao Nagas, then still called
Hatigorias, the Eastern Angamis and the greater part of the Semas. The eastern
boundary was roughly constituted by the Doyang river, the northern by the Inner
Line of the Sibsagar, the western by the Nowgong district, and the southern boundary by the North Cachar district.[56]

In August 1884, three and a half years after Elliott's memorandum, the officiating secretary to the CC of Assam, Stack, complained about the high wages in the
NHD, that they were hindering progress, and about the intention of the administration to gradually reduce them, however, without knowing how this was to be
achieved.[57] House-tax was paid by 164 villages of the five tribes of the Angami,
Kacha, Sema, Lhota and Rengma Nagas, totalling 17,933 houses. Yet the revenue

did not even cover a quarter of the expenses of the administration.[58] Excise was mainly on opium, *ganja*, country-spirits and imported wines. Large bodies of 'coolies', working in transport or in roadwork, contributed heavily to the consumption of country-spirits. Further sources of revenue were the selling of stamps, licences to capture elephants and fishery rights.[59] A mission school had been opened at Kohima, teaching Assamese and English, in order to train copyists or clerks for the administration.[60] For regular police work the British had enlisted a small body of detectives from among the Angamis, Semas and Kukis, since the normal police force was, despite promised rewards, not competent in any Naga languages.[61]

Together with the administration the British also had started to build-up the infrastructure; the houses for the officers in Kohima, a fort, *cutchery*, treasury and jail were in the progress of being built. The water supply had been established and the filter-bed was projected. Several rivers had been bridged, roads, bridle and foot-paths were either in the progress of being built or planned. Immigration from Assam and Nepal was encouraged, since local labour was hard to come by and forced labour difficult to find, but still used as a means of transport. A postal line was established between Dimapur, Kohima and Wokha. Medical help was increasingly being accepted by the Nagas; an Assamese doctor in Kohima and a young Naga had been trained as vaccinators. Importance was still laid on the acquirement and textualisation of Naga languages.[62]

Policy towards trans-frontier tribes

The newly established NHD, still in the process of being realised, was a frontier district of the British empire. Although the British had tentatively laid down boundaries, in reality they were frontiers, unmarked, zones rather than lines. Local people used to cross them without being aware of them. The problem the British faced there was how to deal with the Nagas living beyond the line the British themselves had marked on their maps as boundaries. In June 1884 the DC of the NHD requested advice and guidance from the CC of Assam on the policy to be pursued vis-à-vis these trans-frontier Nagas. Up to that point the DC had punished those raids conducted among those Nagas residing inside the British district, then those carried out by those living under British jurisdiction on those living outside and, finally, raids by trans-frontier groups on villages under British jurisdiction, leaving aside only those among the trans-frontier people themselves. The DC also tried to serve as mediator in the area adjacent to its district. This territory contiguous with the district boundaries was described by the British as being under 'political control', yet ill-defined in territorial extension and depth as well as in what kind of influence and authority should be exercised there. The DC thus advocated the slow but decisive extension of British control over the whole of the Nagas, since he was of the opinion that nothing else would work with the Nagas other than direct subjugation.[63] The report of the DC suggested an increase in violent raids. So it was that the secretary to the CC of Assam wrote about a considerable increase in incidents when referring this question to the government.[64] This notwithstanding that the government this time did not agree to any change of policy since it feared it would result in an extension of the administrated area. The territory concerned was the hill area bordering on the districts of Lakhimpur, Sibsagar and Naga hills. The extent of the area under political control was to be decided by the CC Assam but there was not to be a change in policy:

> ... interference with inter-tribal quarrels should, as a rule, be limited to those cases where they involve-
>
> 1 Outrages on British subjects.
> 2 Violation of the Inner Line.
> 3 Danger to the interests of people inside the British borders by reason of the proximity of disturbances outside, such disturbances, for instance, as would be likely to intimidate coolies employed upon tea-estates or cultivators.[65]

Over the next three and a half decades the British slowly and only partially extended their control over the Naga hills and by the early 1920s the NHD included Angamis, Kacha Nagas, Kukis, Kacharies, Rengmas, Lhotas, Semas, Southern Sangtams, Aos, some Konyaks and some Kalyo-Kengyus.[66] Not all Naga-inhabited territory had been incorporated. The area outside of the district, by the British called the 'Naga Tribal Area', remained until the end of British colonial rule only under political control.[67] The term 'Tribal Area' described territory, which belonged neither to British India nor to any other state, and legally was regarded by the British as being under the direct executive power of the governor general. This status was only reversed after the Transfer of Power.[68] Later, with the proclamation of the state Nagaland, this territory was turned into the Tuensang district. The NHD initially constituted administratively a part of Assam, but was excluded from the criminal code of India through the application of the *Assam Frontier Tracts Regulation* (1880) on April 22nd 1884.[69] The Morley-Minto constitutional reform in 1909 was not even concerned with the hill areas surrounding Assam.[70] In the next phase – the Montagu-Chelmsford reform in 1919, brought about by the major contribution India had made to the British war efforts[71] – the hill districts of the province of Assam were entirely excluded and put under the administration of the governor, based on paternal principles.[72] The committee did so on the advice of the CC of Assam, whom they met in Calcutta. The committee did not visit the province itself.[73]

Self-rule, Simon Commission and exclusion of backward tracts

In the middle of December 1928 the sub-divisional officer (SDO) NHD C. R. Pawsey, based in Mokokchung, brought forward a proposal for the formation of a tribal authority among the Nagas, firstly for the Lhotas only, as a test-run for self-government. The DC, Hutton, was positively inclined to the proposal but the Assam government called them back. It did not wish the scheme to be carried out at this particular time, when the statutory commission was on its way to India. It wanted the NHD separated from Assam and therewith removed from the reach of the legislative council and hoped to win over the statutory commission for this exclusion of the hill districts. More self-government in the hills would only have endangered this.[74]

The statutory commission, composed of English members of parliament, was also called the Simon Commission, after their chairman Sir John Simon. The commission was appointed in 1927 and sent to India in 1928 to inquire into a new reform scheme that resulted in the *Government of India Act* of 1935.[75] Hutton, the then DC of the NHD, called in a meeting with the Naga leaders, to be briefed about how they envisioned the time after the British departure. The Nagas, although isolated from the Indian independence movement, had realised that the British would not remain on the subcontinent for ever and so had started their own national movement for the regaining of their sovereignty.[76] It seems certain to most of the authors that the Nagas had conveyed to Hutton their desire for independence. Hutton passed his report on, which resulted in the visit, to Kohima, in January 1929, of the Simon Commission, led by John Simon, Clement Attlee and E. Cadogan.

When the commission arrived in Kohima on January 10th 1929, members of the Naga Club handed over a memorandum in which they described themselves as the representatives of their people, empowered to articulate its wishes. The memorandum furthermore said that the Nagas had already heard about reforms, but since they were still administered by the British, they did not see a reason to complain. Now they realised, to their regret, that they were included in future reforms without their knowledge, and that they would fall under any provincial government; they demanded to be administered in the future directly by the British government: 'We never asked for any reforms and we do not wish for any reforms.'[77] The *Naga Memorandum to the Simon Commission* continued that they always had been at war with the Indians and Assamese before the advent of the British and that they had never been conquered, that they were not unified among themselves, and that the only thing unifying them was the British administration. Education was still only rudimentary among them, and they had as yet no one who could represent all the tribes to the outside world, let alone in a provincial council. Their population was small, compared to those in the plains and a however designed representation on their side would have no weight at all. Their languages were completely different from those of the plains and they had not the slightest social affinities with either Hindus or Muslims who looked down on them, the former because the Nagas ate beef, the latter due to their diet of pork; both despised them on grounds of their lack of education which was not the Nagas' fault. These statements were followed by fear of becoming dominated socially, culturally, politically and economically by the Assamese and Indians, if the Nagas were included under the reforms. Thus they asked to remain either under British protection and administration or to be left alone:

> If the British government, however, want to throw us away, we pray that we should not be thrust to the mercy of the people who could never have conquered us themselves, and to whom we were never subjected, but to leave us alone to determine for ourselves as in ancient times.[78]

The memorandum was signed by 20 members of the Naga Club – mainly inter-preters by profession – representing the different tribes. It was not so much the desire for independence speaking out of the memorandum, but the realisation – filled with consternation – that their future could lie with the plainsmen who were superior to them in every way, especially in numbers. The fear they might be cul-turally and economically overpowered by those who despised them, and the reali-sation that they themselves were not yet advanced enough to represent their political interests to the outside world, led them to ask for a postponement.

The government of Assam suggested in their memorandum to the commission the exclusion of the backward tracts – including the Naga hills – following the advice of the then DC NHD Hutton. The backward tracts were to be continued to be administered by British officers,[79] under the '. . . Governor-in-Council, as agent for the Governor-General in council, and at the cost of central revenues.'[80] Therewith the Naga hills were to be put under central rule. Hutton, who had been working on this proposal together with other officers stationed in the hills, mainly argued that the union between the plains and the hills was artificial, only brought about by British conquest and that their inclusion into any legislative scheme would be a farce, since the hill people neither had the education nor were they politically united in any organised form as to make sense for them to be part of a representa-tion scheme.[81] The Simon Commission then consequently followed their advice in their recommendation for constitutional reform, without working out a specific scheme:

> Nowhere in India is the contrast between the life and outlook of these wild hill-men and the totally distinct civilisation of the plains more manifest. The main areas classed as backward tracts are the Lushai Hills, the Naga Hills, the Garo Hills, the North Cachar Hills, and the British portion of the Khasi and Jaintia Hills. To these must be added the Lakhimpur frontier tract, the Balipara fron-tier tract, and the Sadiya frontier tract – the last running up to the Abor country and the borders of Tibet. (. . .)
>
> These races must be among the most picturesque in the world, and until their energies are sapped by contact with civilisation they remain among the most light-hearted and virile. To the economic self-sufficiency of the indigenous hill races – the Nagas, Kukis, Mishmis, and the rest – the tea-planter and the immigrant Bengali alike constitute a real danger. To the loss of self-respect, of confidence in their warlike prowess, of belief in their tribal gods, and of unfet-tered enjoyment in their patriarchal (or rather, in some tribes, matriarchal) cus-toms – changes which tend to exterminate so many primitive races – there has now been added the curtailment of freedom to burn down the forest and sow seeds in its ashes. The process has already begun and the best judges doubt how far the recent quiescence of the hill tribes – for the last expedition against them was in 1918 – is due to contentment. If progress is to benefit, and not to destroy, these people, it must come about gradually, and the adjustment of their needs with the interests of the immigrant will provide a problem of great complexity and importance for many generations to come.

The great majority of the hill tribes are far from forgetting their warlike past, with its long record of raids upon the plains. Many of them probably regard the *pax Britannica* as a passing inconvenience.[82]

The Assam government's stand was motivated on the one hand by a concern for the survival of the hill people: '. . . the lesson of the history throughout the world appears on the best authority that primitive tribes, robbed of their own culture and faced with the competition of another on unequal terms, speedily decay and die out.'[83] This lesson, it reads, caused them to question their own moral responsibility: '. . . it is a matter for the most serious consideration whether the British Government, which found the hill tribes independent, can leave them dependent.'[84] This consideration would later be drowned in the empire's post-war struggle to muddle itself out of the *raj*. A rather weightier motivation would have been the fear of rebellion, if the hill tracts were included into the constitutional reforms, with the following change of rule and administration: '. . . it would be difficult, and might be dangerous, to entrust to the Legislative Council the final administrative control of the hill districts and frontier tracts.'[85] Its fears of the consequences would prove prophetic:

> The Ministers of the future would find the demand that the hill districts should be brought into line with the regulation districts in the plains irresistible, both on political and financial grounds. Any uncontrolled invasion of foreign officials into the Naga Hills, the frontier tracts or the Lushai Hills, would inevitably cause serious trouble.[86]

The government resolved that the hill areas should be excluded, and be put under the control of the governor of Assam, as agent for the central government.[87] Furthermore, that officials, missionaries, ethnologists and leading natives should in cooperation develop a policy to guide the hill people to self-organisation and eventually to self-rule, aiming at the political unification of the hills: 'What is needed for the future is a policy of development and unification on lines suited to the genius of the hill peoples . . .'.[88] In the Naga hills that meant to continue with the establishment of tribal committees and tribal self-rule. The Lhotas were, as mentioned before, the first instance, and in 1934 it was a success and supported by every Lhota village.[89] Alemchimba writes that the Lhota council was already founded in 1923, and that it continued from then on. The Aos had theirs running only from 1939, and the other tribes from the middle of the 1940s, yet he does not specify anything further.[90]

In May 1935 the report of the Simon Commission was fiercely debated in the British parliament and the members of the commission said the Nagas did not ask for self-determination, but for protection.[91] On the basis of the recommendation of the commission, the NHD was declared an excluded area of the Assam province on April 1st 1937.[92] This meant the exclusion of the NHD from all reforms carried out in the rest of India, and that the legislation was not applicable there. The NHD was to be administered on the orders of the governor of Assam who again functioned as deputy for the governor general of India. This arrangement remained active until the Transfer of Power.[93]

The Transfer of Power

The Second World War took the initiative from the British colonialists. Though they hadn't lost the war they had lost what they had possessed in hegemony to their ally the United States. In India that meant they had to organise their departure. Although basically of least importance, this was true for the Northeast in general and the Nagas in particular; the British felt they had a moral obligation towards the 'backward tribes' and their future protection. While it seems that there had been plans back in 1928 to exclude the tribal areas of Burma and Assam and bring them together under a separate but united provincial administration, by 1944 it was recognised that such a scheme would be unworkable, since it would incur the ferocious opposition of the Indian National Congress.[94] And while in August 1944 Amery still envisioned a crown colony scheme, with the accession of that territory to the Indian Union after a generation or so,[95] he dropped this scheme a month later as being impracticable for a number of reasons, among them again the objection of the Indian National Congress, but also the lack of any strategic or economic benefit that could arise out of such an arrangement for Britain. Hence, a tentative scheme was agreed to put the 'backward tribes' under the central government in order to protect them from provincial politics and legislature, and, for this reason to appoint an adviser on the backward tribes to the central government.[96] To work out the details of a future constellation, the governor of Assam Clow supported the set-up of a special commission to investigate on the ground.[97] The representatives of Congress and League for Assam, respectively Bardoloi and Sa'adullah, on their part were also only marginally interested in the tribes' fate, but both took their inclusion into a provincial scheme for granted, albeit for different and conflicting reasons.[98] By May/June 1946 it had been decided that the constitution-making body, the union constituent assembly, was to set up an advisory committee that had to deal and make recommendations for the proper representation of India's minorities in independent India. Due to the fundamentally different situations of, for example, the tribals in the Northwest and those in the Northeast, the advisory committee was to set up special subcommittees that should deal with these respectively. Stress was laid on the expertise and independence of its personnel and the weight that its suggestions should carry forward vis-à-vis the constituent assembly.[99] Yet by the end of the year the Congress-dominated preliminary constituent assembly had decided that the advisory committee's proposals could be overruled by the constituent assembly, making sure to grant just as many safeguards as were necessary not to endanger Congress dominance.[100] The constitutional safeguards reached by this procedure for the Northeast were later called 'sixth schedule'. When by February-March 1947 the Naga National Council (NNC) sent a memorandum to the British prime minister, with copies to Simon and Churchill, asking for the setting-up of a ten-year interim government, during which they could develop themselves politically and decide afterwards whether they would prefer complete independence or some arrangement with the Indian Union, the secretary of state for India Pethick-Lawrence was assured by Sir Henry Knight, former short-time acting governor of Assam, that the NNC represented no one but itself and hence might be safely ignored.[101] When shortly after the governor of Assam Clow confirmed to the contrary, this did not matter much, and Mountbatten, on pragmatic grounds, agreed to the inclusion of the Naga hills into Assam, with some safeguards.[102] In July, Hydari informed Mountbatten of his reaching an agreement with the Nagas[103] and with the *Independence Act* the Nagas were ceded to the Indian Union.[104]

More suspense can be found in the developments on the ground in the Northeast. The British officers there thought they actually had the task of arranging matters for the hills in relation to the new state of independent India; they were searching frantically for a solution. At first they also didn't take the Nagas seriously as actors on the political scene,[105] seeing themselves as their advocates who would represent and negotiate their case vis-à-vis the Indians. Yet, the NNC fast emerged as the political mouthpiece of the Nagas, so that the British officers found themselves in the role of mere interlocutors, or advisors to the Nagas. The problem here for Pawsey was that the NNC consisted mainly of government servants. So if he advised them, as they expected from him, this would have been unacceptable to both Congress and League, and Pawsey would have risked his own transfer.[106] By February 1947, the superintendent of Lushai hills, in a document that was supposed to serve as one of the models, and addressed to the secretary to the governor of Assam, with respect to the Lushai hills and other previously excluded areas, suggested autonomous self-rule, except in areas of foreign policy and defence.[107] The governor of Assam Sir Akhbar Hydari, in a personal answer to these suggestions, disagreed with him, and demanded on the contrary a single administrative unit, since the autonomy Macdonald was proposing was associated with 'independent sovereignty'. Furthermore, he maintained that the hill people had been isolated too long, and would greatly profit from intense intercourse with the plains. Finally, he asserted that the plains would pay for many of the facilities in the hills, consequently the hill people would have to give back something in return – the governor here was thinking in terms of cooperation and participation in the running of the province.[108]

Special consideration was given to the tribal areas. Walker, the political officer of the Tirap frontier tract, had beforehand uttered his concerns to Mills and had asked him for advice. This Walker did, although he had been informed by Sir B. N. Rau, constitutional adviser to the constituent assembly, that no constitution could be forced upon the Naga hills tribal area. Mills, in his position as adviser to the governor of Assam for tribal areas and states further cautioned Walker by quoting Nehru who, in Mills' opinion, had gone even further in saying during a speech held on 13th April 1947: 'We do not want to compel any Province or portion of the country to join Pakistan or Hindustan.' It is clear that both these statements assured Mills that the tribal areas were to be dealt with in, what he considered, a decent way, and so he told Walker to advise the Nagas in Tirap that they should ask for the present system to be continued. Furthermore, that they should be aware of being part of India which might put up military posts in their area, and would also give them assistance in other respects. All in all Mills was satisfied with developments at this stage and had faith in the continuation of an administration that he deemed appropriate.[109] This is also shown by the fact that he sent a copy of this document to Pawsey, commenting that he did not see any reasons why the Nagas in the tribal area might not accept any constitutional arrangement that might be made for the NHD.[110] The British officers in the Northeast therefore contacted the Nagas and informed them about what would happen and how they could take part in shaping the changes.

The drama had fully unfolded by the end of April 1947, when Mills, now visibly alarmed, informed the British officers that the advisory subcommittee indeed came with a pre-fabricated plan and was determined to push that through.[111] Consequently, he urged the officers to advise the hill people to be unanimous in their negotiations with the subcommittee, and in case of any surprise questions, to ask for time to think it over, although this had been taken as differences of opinion in the case of the Lushais. Secondly, he stressed that excluded and tribal areas should, under any circumstances, be dealt with separately, since the latter were '... completely independent and at liberty to negotiate its own terms ...'.[112] Mills had attached to this memorandum a draft he had written on the legal status of the tribal area, where he came to the conclusion that the '... Naga Tribal Areas of the Naga Hills District and Tirap Frontier Tract are both technically and for practical purposes outside British India, for there is a statutory boundary between them and the adjoining districts of the Province.'[113] Of course, Mills considered them independent as Indian states under the suzerainty of the British crown, not as having the right to stay outside the new Indian Union, although for the most part they might not have been aware of either. The reason why Mills wanted to ascribe to the tribal areas the status of Indian states was because he was convinced that the tribals were not able to speak for themselves and that the Indians could not do that either, since the latter were in no way acquainted with the former. Mills felt that British officers should therefore be made representatives of the tribal areas, although he was aware of the fact that this was unacceptable to the subcommittee.[114]

Mills reported that the subcommittee gave considerable weight to the written word, such as recorded treaties; likewise his own draft on the legal status of the tribal people was based on recorded treaties. Pawsey, however, wrote to Mills saying that any divided administration for the Naga hills (i.e., separate solutions for the tribal area and the excluded area or NHD) was unworkable, and he suggested a unitary solution under the central government. This would also have the advantage of being compatible with the NNC's demand for a ten-year interim period, in order to establish their own standing. The only problems Pawsey saw were that Hydari was utterly opposed to it, and the question as to what the subcommittee was up to.[115]

Archer, SDO Mokokchung, agreed with Mills that the required solution was the creation of a state under the central government, which would allow for the gradual development of relations with the province of Assam, but was aware that his Prime Minister Attlee had said in the House of Commons that the hills of the Northeast would be grouped with Assam. Attlee, as quoted by Archer, said: 'In regard to the hills in the Northeast frontier, they come into the Province of Assam and they will be dealt with by the Constitutional Assembly of which Assam forms a part.'[116] Mills then informed Archer that the ministry had declared him a *persona non grata* and that he would have to leave by the 1st August. Mills by then was convinced that everything he suggested was refused, simply because it was him who had said it.[117]

Eight days later we encounter a much more liberated Mills who, in very personal language, informed Archer that the Transfer of Power was now definitely fixed for the 16th August that year, and that due to the drain of Indian civil service officers out of Assam, Archer, if he so wished, might be able to stay on without any problem, as Pawsey was to do until January 1948.[118] In a last and desperate stand, just before his departure, Mills informed the governor that, according to the *Indian Independence Bill*, the tribal areas had to be considered as independent and free to decide whether they would wish to join India or not.[119] Mills was not suggesting that the people in the tribal areas should be independent, but that a legal exposition on their constitutional status should be drawn up and that they in turn were to be informed about it.[120]

Pawsey, in a pre-Transfer of Power communication to Archer, laid open his antipathy to the demands of some Nagas (a minority in his opinion) for complete independence, and gave his assurance that the British needn't have any reason to feel guilty. At the same time he regretted that they did not have more time to set everything right:

> I don't know what the eventual fate of the Nagas will be – there's nothing we can do to help them that we haven't already done. But it seems a pity that we couldn't have had a few more years to get things straight.[121]

This letter exemplifies the mental position of the British officers on the ground in the Northeast. They were, in a paternal way, genuinely concerned about the future fate of the Nagas. They were surely averse to the Indian takeover, but they were enough children of their time, enough propagandists of nineteenth-century state theory, to be utterly opposed to the idea that the Nagas could be independent again. Their antagonism towards the Nagas' demand for independence and later to their struggle for freedom followed from that. As agents in the field of action we may safely assume that as long as they were on the ground they did work for an integration into the Indian Union, even though they would have preferred a more protective scheme. This is demonstrated by the fact that they sided with the group of the Nagas that was opposed to complete independence.[122] And although the British officers of the NHD were advising the Nagas and trying to exert their influence on them,[123] we now know that the British officials wanted to have a protected arrangement for the Nagas, but under no circumstances did they want them to become independent, nor did they believe that the majority of them wanted that in the first place.[124] The more the NNC demanded independence the more hostile the British became towards them, and even advised their successors to just ignore them. The then president of the NNC, Aliba Imti, was singled out as hate figure – the caricature of the westernised savage.[125]

Conclusion

The partial conquest of the Naga hills and the light administration that was imposed on them followed from the interplay between, on the one side, the metropolitan and global imperial orientation that, as we have learned, was only restrained by its limitations in means and power, and, on the other side, from the *raj's* personnel's inclination to ever further annexations. The retreat from the subcontinent and the handover of the Naga hills to the successor creation of the *raj*, the Indian Union, was forced on the British by their dramatic loss in standing and power in the course and wake of the Second World War. We have seen that there had never been serious contemplation on the side of the British decision-makers to give back the Nagas their independence. This was never a matter of concern to them.

The colonial conquest was followed by the delineation of the area to be permanently occupied and the efforts to acquire the geographical knowledge about it, including its inhabiting populations. The next step was the enforcement of the monopoly of violence, the disarmament of the population and the removal of the village defences, followed by the levying of house-tax and the installation of headmen responsible for its collection. Then, a labour force was registered, permanent cultivation was encouraged and *jhuming* discouraged. The forests were taken into British possession, as were rivers, lakes and wild animals. Medical services and schools were established and efforts made to acquire knowledge on Naga languages and society. Immigration was encouraged to supply the labour market. The hardware, the infrastructure – public buildings, roads, bridges, paths – were built or extended and the Nagas asked or encouraged to move around, to travel, to go on trade excursions, to appreciate their newly won general freedom, even when it was forced upon them. However, the administrative penetration was incomplete and rudimentary. As we shall see in the following chapter, all this had profound but far from determining consequences on the Nagas' socio-political identity formation.

4 The transformation of Naga societies under colonialism

Introduction

In the previous chapter we learned why the Naga hills were partially conquered and how they were administered. In this chapter the aim will be to delineate the consequences British colonial rule had for the populations of the Naga hills in respect of their socio-political identity formation. It is often argued that the post-independence Indo-Naga war is a child of British colonialism, the result of their devious divide-and-rule policy. The line of argument runs roughly like this: before the British arrival, the Nagas originally did not exist as a distinct people and entertained cordial relations with the plains population. Through British categorisation and the drawing of administrative boundaries the people of the hills became the Nagas, now separated from the people of the plains. In short, the British and missionaries then made the Nagas into Christian nationalists and implanted in them their hatred for the Indians.[1] It is striking that European agency and its rudimentary rule is ascribed the power to have created radical new political identities.

At the end of colonial rule the Nagas had an elite that was conscious of its own nation-being, and could consequently form themselves into a national organisation. We may say that five factors – categorisation, administration, Christianity, the First and the Second World Wars – in their interplay with local agency, were decisive in this. For, since most of the factors were driven or at least imported by foreign agency, it will in the end have been the local people who decided how to act on them, and thus shaped the outcome. The organisation of this chapter will be as follows: first a brief theoretical discussion of the above-mentioned process, followed by a discussion on the possible pre-colonial socio-political organisation of the Nagas, and finally an assessment of Naga identity formation.

Colonialism, categorisation, administration and war

Colonial empires were conquered by violence, with often devastating consequences for the conquered.[2] Where the colonial powers did not encounter central organised polities, their personnel set out to bring what lay before them into a meaningful order.[3] They assumed that these stateless societies were organised in tribes, and tribes were socially, politically, culturally, and even biologically bounded units. Administrators, who turned into anthropologists, were there to identify and understand these tribal units as a basis for indirect rule.[4] To what extent new categories concurred with old ones will have to be different in every case, but we can assume, that as a rule, colonial categorisations had to be congruent, at least partially, with existing identifications, to be effective.[5] Further, that assumptions of '... discrete, bounded groups, whose distribution could be captured on an ethnic map',[6] were then as they are today: not corresponding with a more complex and interconnected reality. Neither was the unit monolithic – other units of identification remained intact – nor completely bounded to the outside: the so-called tribes were overlapping socially, politically, culturally and biologically with other formations.[7] How these networks worked in detail would have to be the topic of intense further research, but how we may have to imagine, at least approximately, the dynamic of more inclusive identity formation and delimitation might become clearer with the following observation of Prasenjit Duara:

> Sociologically, communities may be thought of not as well-bounded entities but as possessing various different and mobile boundaries that demarcate different dimensions of life. These boundaries may be either soft or hard. One or more of the cultural practices of a group, such as rituals, language, dialect, music, kinship rules or culinary habits, may be considered soft boundaries if they identify a group but do not prevent the group from sharing and even adopting, self-consciously or not, the practices of another. Groups with soft boundaries between each other are sometimes so unselfconscious about their differences that they do not view mutual boundary breach as a threat and could eventually even amalgamate into one community.
>
> An incipient nationality is formed when the perception of the boundaries of community are transformed, namely, when soft boundaries are transformed into hard ones. This happens when a group succeeds in imposing a historical narrative of descent and/or dissent on both heterogeneous and related cultural practices.[8]

Seen like this, in the case of Southeast Asia, including the Indo-Burma region, there are only soft boundaries among the hill people, and Leach considered them as essentially one people. Thus from a hill people perspective, the potential for hard boundaries runs between hills and plains.[9]

However, the relative impact of colonial categorisation and of the other factors associated with colonialism on the life and consciousness of the local populations depended on the respective penetration of the lived reality through the colonial actors, their assistants and institutions. Communications, density and effectiveness of administration, proximity to economic and administrative centres, and the change of the mode of production – from subsistence economy to employment, from barter to money economy – all played a role.[10] Dependent on the relative confrontation with the Other and its categorisation, will have been the impact on self-identification.[11]

An important factor for the reformulation, extension and strengthening of social identities in the colonial encounter were the standardisation and textualisation of languages and the introduction of school systems.[12] This was mostly done by missionaries, who functioned as an informal extension of the colonial state in the area of cultural politics,[13] and who in turn trained locals who, as a rule, were more successful in the execution of the proselytising project. Their task necessitated the establishment of educational and religious centres that provided a network in which members of previously often different and more localised societies now conversed in a common medium. But in stressing local agency, we have to see education and Christianity, made accessible by missionary translations, as welcome new means to counter white dominance, which the converts could turn to their own advantage, and which had an empowering and liberating effect. So did, for instance, the impact of the existence of indigenous missionaries convey the message of equality.[14]

Further, social identity by its very nature depends on the context: group borders that tend to change with the political context. One of the most important factors of the political context are, in Horowitz's view, territorial borders, which tend to give rise to persistent groups, because they are structuring the context for group interaction.[15] During colonial time, territorial horizons were widened in Africa and Asia and led to a corresponding subgroup-amalgamation. The colonial masters created territories out of loosely connected villages and regions, which led to the formation of many new groups.[16] Important herein was not the drawing of arbitrary borders, but the creation of territories that by far surpassed in size preceding political units.[17] This could have led to the adaptation of prior existing social institutions, which were not posing a danger to colonial rule, meaning that prior existing kinship-based groups became more inclusive.[18] Colonial units of administration turned into the dominant frames of reference for their inhabitants.[19] The more the colonial administration effectively penetrated the respective territory, the more this was the case for its population. The local elite was probably the first to be affected by the drawing of the colonial boundaries; their journeys and activities inside the administrative unit helped them to develop a growing sense of community.[20]

Yet, as already noted, we should not see these factors as starting out on a blank page, but as adapting to the existing situation:

> The state and its agencies certainly penetrated and modified society itself, but they entered it as tree-roots grow into rock – along its extant fractures and potential flaws. Dissatisfied claimants and feuding subalterns often sought such intervention against their enemies. Social groups usually knew and sometimes had to account for their members, and enumeration was used and understood.[21]

Further, as discussed in chapter two, political communities and societies existed prior to the advent of European colonialism:

> Community structures of feeling and communication survived into the colonial era, and used the colonial public sphere to assert their claims. Some fissures closed and others opened. . . . These communities had always been political; they now responded to the dialectic of colonialism and the

opportunities of a new politics without being thereby transformed into crea-
tures of the colonial or post-colonial imagination.[22] . . . the social processes of
identity formation continued independent of the official classifications.[23]

That is to say we have to do more research into local agency, and that always has to
be placed into the interplay with the wider framework. We have to take both seriously, and we have to take into account the limitations of a foreign power stretched
thin on the ground, or we may adopt its self-image of an omnipotent culture-hero
(or villain). To try to ridicule people's assertions of their own differences as
colonial, post-colonial, modern etc. constructs an assertion that often is formulated

> . . . precisely in opposition to a foreign-imperial presence. (. . .) [and] . . . entails
> the people's attempt to control the technical and political means that up to now
> have been used to victimize them. . . . an attack on the cultural integrity and
> historical agency of the peripheral peoples, . . .[and is to] do in theory what
> imperialism attempts in practice.[24]

Having made space for this authoritative voice, it is time to explore briefly the
pre-colonial socio-political organisation of the Naga hills.

The pre-colonial socio-political organisation

To understand the consequences of colonialism we have to try to fathom the pre-
colonial starting point. In chapter two we tried to embed the Nagas in their pre-
British colonial, political landscape and showed, with the help of the example of the
Tengima group of the later Angamis, that there were groups around the Naga hills
which had a consciousness that was political and not much different from nationalism. We will now set out to sketch a little more closely the socio-political design of
several groups that later would be called tribes and today make up parts of the Naga
nation.

However, since our data is unfortunately itself the product of colonial investigation we will consider our findings as preliminary.[25] The easiest way to describe the
social organisation of the Nagas is that it consisted of crosscutting ties among different groups. To be more precise, the individual and the household were integrated
into society via being part of different units such as lineages, clans, age groups,
classes, *morungs*[26] and villages. These attachments were sometimes complemen-
tary and at other times in conflict with each other, for instance ,when a *morung* had
members from two or more clans, this opened the possibility for conflicting loyal-
ties to either *morung* or clan. The Konyaks considered loyalty towards the clan to
be of paramount importance, while the Aos, on the other hand, rated loyalty
towards the *morung* as higher. But in general, no one was allowed to kill someone
from one's own clan.[27] A child, as a rule, belonged to the clan of the social father,
and clans often stretched over several villages. These clans, sharing and extending
through a number of villages, came closest to something like a tribe-type community. A clan, per definition, is a kinship group with an assumed common ancestor.

Clan relationships among the Nagas, however, could be manipulated to establish the desired constellation between lineages. The clan defined how one was to address others, what one was allowed to eat, who one could marry and whom one's most likely foes were.[28]

A village consisted of different groups. The respective importance of these lineages, clans, age groups, *morungs* and classes depended on the emphasis that the different communities put on them, and varied from one to the other. Among the Semas and Thendu Konyaks, the structuring principles were the rules of residence; among the Aos and Thenkohs this role was taken on by the age groups, and among the Angamis by kinship relations. The respective dominant units among these groups, therefore, were the village, the *morung* and the village council, and the clan.[29] This very brief sketch of the social and political organisation of different Naga societies is an idealised and standardised description for which always only a part served as model for what was claimed to be covered. From the data hitherto available, I would say that Aos and Lothas had a different and more elaborate system than the others, and that theirs was not simply the democratic end of the scale (that in my view was wrongly ascribed to the Angamis, who tended to be more dominated by pure clan politics), but an elaborate system that seemed to incorporate more segments of society and to have in-built checks and balances that may have made it possible for large populations to live together in a democratic way. However, before we proceed, we have to state the obvious, namely that these sketches, though presented and received as extra-temporal truths, were taken at a particular time (that is in the main during the first quarter of the twentieth century) and only conditionally transferable to, for instance, earlier periods. There is some evidence that the Angamis might have had real chiefs at an earlier stage,[30] like their neighbours the Semas still had.[31] Among the Konyaks, the population of a village unsatisfied with the rulership, killed the chief and his family, and installed his son as chief, but with lesser powers.[32] Other villages of the Konyaks had given up their democratic practice only shortly before the contact with the British, and invited *angs* from hierarchically organised villages to settle among them.[33] The democratic villages of the Konyak were those bordering their democratic neighbours the Aos and were the same that had been annexed by the British in 1910, both facts that might have contributed to the decision in favour of a more democratic constitution. Moreover, in the year of the annexation, the SDO Naga hills still says that 'There are Chiefs in every village who command a lot of authority.'[34] The Lhotas, on their part, once had powerful chiefs and then also developed a more egalitarian system of ruling councils of elders.[35]

At the beginning of the 1870s the British still knew only a little about the populations living in the Naga hills, except that they had to be Nagas. Butler, who was DC in the Naga hills in 1873, left us the following description of the area of settlement of the Nagas:

> Roughly speaking, they may be said to extend from the Kopili River on the west to the Bori Dihing on the east. Towards the north they occupy the whole hill country bordering upon the plain districts of Nowgong, Seebsaugor, and

Luckhimpore. In a southerly direction we now know positively that they not only extend up to, but actually cross over, the great main watershed between the Irrawaddy and Brahmaputra, how far, however, they really go down and extend into the valley of the Kaindwen or Ninghti[36] has never yet been clearly ascertained.[37]

He went on:

> . . . our knowledge of a great portion of the Naga country really rests almost entirely upon 'pure conjecture', and that beyond the fact of its mountainous character we know nothing at all about it up to the present date . . .[and called the Naga Hills a] . . . very terra incognita . . . .[38]

Butler tried to isolate the tribes as units, having observed their relatedness.[39] In the beginning, the British perceived smaller units of villages as tribes, whose boundaries were small streams and rivers, and easy recognisable. Later on, however, the tendency was towards the identification of larger units,[40] and despite the cursory knowledge and the well-perceived differences, there was no doubt for Butler about the unity of the 'race'.[41] Yet other opinions existed as well, for the *Assam Census Report* of 1881[42] and the *The Pioneer* from March 24th 1870[43] the term 'Naga' was seen as a generic term for a whole group of unconnected tribes who inhabited a certain geographical region and who only unite to fight off enemies from outside, like the Manipuris or British, but with the external threat the internal coherence would also disappear.[44]

Woodthorpe, on the contrary, in 1881 divided those then known as Nagas into 'Angami' and 'non–Angami', who, for him, represented two different people.[45] And Hutton later, after a long service first as SDO, then as DC among the Nagas with extensive studies among and of them, concluded that it was impossible to differentiate between those groups called Nagas and other groups living in Assam and Burma.[46] At the same time the Nagas themselves fell into a variety of linguistic sub-groups and a multitude of cultural features,[47] manifesting themselves even in physical appearance and cementing their image as being a mongrel race.[48]

The question 'Who are the Nagas?' was overshadowed for the British by the question of what kind of political organisation their adversary had. Between the rivers Dikhu and Doyang the British had, on earlier expeditions, encountered villages that seemed to have proper chiefs, yet west of the Dikhu, in an area better known to the British, the villages seemed to be ruled in a democratic way. Hence Butler wrote in his report:

> . . . that a Naga nowhere really accepts a chief in our sense of the term. Chiefs they do have, but they are merely the nominal heads of each clan, men who by dint of their personal qualities have become leaders of public opinion but without the least particle of power beyond that given them by the vox populi and that only pro tem, upon the particular question that may happen to be exciting

attention at the time being. The Government of every Naga tribe with whom I have had intercourse is a purely democratical one, and whenever anything of public importance has to be undertaken, all the Chiefs (both old and young) meet together in solemn conclave, and then discuss and decide upon the action to be taken, and even then it often happens that the minority will not be bound by either wish or act of the majority; and as to any one single Chief exercising absolute control over his people, the thing is unheard of.[49]

Woodthorpe reported about the Angamis in 1881: '. . . virtually every man does that which is right in his own eyes, and is a law unto himself.'[50] Both Butler and Woodthorpe were influenced by their contact with the democratically organised groups of the Nagas.

The British, in Jacobs' view, were confronted with what presented itself to them as an ethnographic chaos: '. . . hundreds, if not thousands, of small villages seemed to be somewhat similar to each other but also very different, by no means sharing always the same customs, political system, art or even language.'[51] Moreover, the Nagas seemed to live in a constant state of inter-tribal warfare,[52] in which even parts of the same village seemed to fight against each other, while neutral groups in between went ahead with their daily routines unhindered.[53] Though the classification of the different groups as 'Nagas' was not without difficulties, the British had to agree with the fact that had been established before their arrival: that the hill dwellers had been ascribed the generic term 'Nagas' by the Ahom. Subsequently they had to begin with the identification of effective administrative units, the tribes. Today the tribe is an important unit of identification and no Naga contemporary has any doubts about her tribal belonging, as there are no doubts about being a Naga. Moreover, tribes played, and still play, an important political role in the history of resistance, and as a product of a well-aimed, divide-and-rule policy carried out by the Indian state, tribalism today provides one excuse for the Indian administration not to tackle the Naga question in earnest.

In the course of the gradual extension of their control over the Naga hills, the British first preferred natural borders, then a mixture of the former and perceived tribal borders, in order to draw, if possible, tribal borders and not to split tribes by this.[54] Then the British government asked its officers on the ground to write studies about the subjugated societies, which would serve as handbooks for future administrators, something to base their policy on.[55] The British government made an effort to understand the hill communities since its aim was a cheap administration. Misunderstandings, resulting out of ignorance, led to problems, insurgencies, and those had to be countered with costly punitive expeditions, that were to be avoided if possible. As a result, several voluminous monographs were written about some of the groups that had been identified and delimited as tribes. British knowledge in the beginning was based on old Ahom maps that divided the Naga hills into districts that supposedly referred to different tribes. The names of the districts were at the same time names of the different tribes, derived from the names of the paths into the plains, which were used by different groups. The Nagas themselves did not know anything about these names.[56] It was then up to the British to understand the bases for these categorisations. Ahom practice had resulted in the division into smaller units, i.e., small congregations of villages represented tribes, as it was for the British in the beginning. Therefore, in the reports of the nineteenth century one often comes across tribal names that later on do not turn up again, or tribal names get an adjectival direction attached or simply village names. In the course of time, however, with more knowledge, the tendency was to be more inclusive.

However, as the British acquired more and more knowledge about the Nagas, the writing of monographs about separate tribes did not become any easier. The culture of the Semas, for example, was for Hutton just a conglomeration of different elements, which they adopted on their migrations from other groups.[57] Mills and Hutton had lived and worked long enough among the Nagas to be aware of the complexities of life on the ground, but as children of their time they subscribed to one people, one race, one origin, one language etc., and therefore tried to identify the pure forms and when and where the mixing happened, which they encountered every day:

> No Naga tribe is of pure blood, but the area which they inhabit has been the scene of a series of immigrations from north-east, north-west and south, and the different stocks introduced in this way have entered into their composition.[58]

Hence tribal entities could only be represented as either ideal-typical or as relative.[59] Still the same sense of duty that made them reveal the incongruities also encouraged the British to at least try to relate to existing structures in their process of categorising. So we learn from Mills that the Lhotas were only known to the British government by this name, and they called themselves 'Kyon', meaning 'human' in their own language. Further, they had also a generic term for western and eastern Kyon, respectively called 'Ndrung' and 'Liye'.[60] In addition oral traditions testified a common origin of Lhotas and Southern Sangtams, Rengmas and Semas,[61] and relate to us that parts of the Aos were driven out[62] or assimilated,[63] that refugees of the Semas were ancestors of Lhota–clans,[64] and that both – Lhotas and Rengmas – formed one common tribe in the past.[65] The same was the case with all the groups other than the Lhotas. The Aos called themselves 'Aor', possessed a tribal consciousness and fenced themselves off vis-à-vis other groups.[66] Hutton wrote on the Semas that they, without having the respective organisations, nevertheless possessed a clan and tribal consciousness,[67] and the Konyaks called themselves 'Yamenu Ha', composed out of two clans, called 'Then Ko' and 'Then Du'.[68] Were these historical facts or invented traditions? We have to keep in mind that both Mills and Hutton wrote in the 1920s, several decades after the subjugation of most of the groups concerned here.

All tribes were divided into phratries (compositions of several clans) and clans that more or less influenced types of rule, marriage rules, war and headhunting. Yet, those phratries and clans did not stop at the limits of the respective tribes, but had their equivalents in all other neighbouring groups, serving for instance as marriage partners and in this way had population exchanges as a consequence. Thus a network of relationships between the tribes developed,[69] which made the borders fluid and therefore also the therewith delineated units, called tribes or not. The same was true for the periphery of the tribes designed as Nagas, where they lived in interaction with other groups that today are not Nagas.

So it seems that units were there that could be called tribes, but they were not the sole ordering principle, not a unified whole, so they could split and rearrange, and consequently were not hermetically sealed and self-reproducing.[70] Rather to the contrary, they were embedded in a network of, at least, social relations, with possibly the religious and the political ones following from that. The Naga tribes had soft boundaries, which could have allowed for a process of fusion with relative ease. The lack of communications and possibly also of hard boundaries, however, made this process of wider nation-building neither possible nor necessary. If we take this as the pre-colonial starting point, then we now may try to find out what consequences the British colonial period had for the social identity and nation-formation of the groups that would develop into the Nagas.

Colonial conquest, rule and impact on Naga identity

British colonial rule in the Naga hills was always portrayed as a success story: it stopped headhunting and perpetual warfare, and brought peace and prosperity. Even the Nagas themselves today look upon the time under the British as having been greatly beneficial. This, however, is nostalgia, resulting from a contrast of the past with the bleak present of the ongoing military occupation. Contemporary reports in the wake of conquest from the Naga hills painted a dark picture on the dramatic deterioration of the living conditions. Fields and grain stores were destroyed, epidemics of smallpox and cholera were rampant, the British demanded house-tax, supplies in rice, and pressed the Angamis into the forced labour of 'coolie' work. So, the political agent major T. B. Michell reported that the house-tax of 2 *rupees* was the maximum that the Angamis were able to pay and consequently he recommended dropping the extraction of rice from them.[71] Michell and the brigadier general, J. S. Nation, were arguing for the establishment of permanent transport arrangements that would mean the hiring of 'coolies' and ponies from somewhere else, since the Nagas were so averse to what the reports then called 'excessive seizure' for coolie labour. To keep the peace other means of transport had to be used.[72] And yet in 1884 the DC NHD noted:

> Hillmen generally have a strong dislike to any restrictions on their liberty . . . [t]hey are too well off to necessitate recourse to seeking employment. They can earn an easier livelihood by cultivating their fields or by trading than would be offered under the most liberal terms Government could give.[73]

The Nagas not only had an aversion towards dependent labour, but also could make a better living without it. Either they had to be dispossessed of their means of production, or they had to be made to want to enter into dependent work.

The NHD under British rule was part of the province of Assam. The district was divided into the two sub-districts of Kohima and Mokokchung. The head-quarters for the whole district was in Kohima. There the DC was posted, who was responsible for the whole and also functioned as SDO for the sub-district of Kohima, both connected by a bridle path. Mokokchung was the base of the SDO. Among the most important tasks the DC and SDO had to perform was the estimation and collection of taxes, as well as the settlement of disputes.[74] The DC had almost unlimited powers and only in extreme cases was he required to get the permission of the CC of Assam. He also had to write an annual report for the British-Indian government.[75] The administration was supposed to be based on the principle of personal rule, not only on an apparatus or an institution.[76] Present were a veterinary surgeon, a surgeon, an assistant of the DC, recruited among the Anglo-Indians,[77] and four British officers, who commanded the paramilitary police-battalion of the Assam Rifles, manned mainly by Gurkhas or members of other hill tribes. The British also had created a regular police force, whose jurisdiction was limited to the city of Kohima and the road leading to Manipur.[78]

In villages without chiefs the British asked the village population to elect or decide on one chief who was then supposed to function as the representative of the village vis-à-vis the British government, and had to be confirmed in office by either the DC or the SDO.[79] These chiefs, called *gaonburas,* turned into the representa-tives of the British administration. Granted official authority, they were empow-ered to collect taxes or functioned as village police officers, entitled to settle minor disputes, and could impose fines up to 50 *rupees.*[80] As a sign of their authority they either received a scarlet jacket or blanket.[81] The British employed interpreters, called *dobashis,* among whose tasks it was to translate from the different languages into Nagamese, a regional lingua franca, and to advise the DC or SDO in matters of culture and tradition of the respective groups. They were, by virtue of their office, the guardians, i.e., the interpreters, of traditions.[82] The *dobashis* received, like the *gaonburas,* scarlet jackets and blankets as signs of their office.[83] The British tried to decide disputes on the basis of tradition, '. . . except where it is repugnant to our sense of justice. . .',[84] for which they needed the *dobashis,* about whom Mills wrote:

> They are very carefully picked men and the posts are much sought after, for though the pay is not high, the prestige is great. Care is taken that no tribal interests are overlooked. For instance, at Mokokchung there are interpreters from every tribe of the Subdivision. Among the Ao interpreters the interests of Ancients and Christians, of Chongli, Mongsen and Changki and of each phratry are represented.[85]

Minor disputes, however, were decided by the *gaonburas* and the councils of elders, in order not to subvert their sense of responsibility. Despite being not valid in the NHD, justice was dispensed by the DC and SDO in the spirit of the *Indian Penal Code* and the *Codes of Criminal and Civil Procedures.*[86]

The taxes per annum and per household for the Angamis were three *rupees*, for the other groups two, and for foreigners five.[87] The *gaonburas*, old and sick people and those having served with the Naga Labour Corps in France, were exempted from taxes, as were government servants, whose salary was below 30 *rupees* a month. As noted in the previous chapter, a register for every village was established, listing all houses, those taxed and those exempted. The number of houses was periodically checked by the DC, SDO and their assistants, also revising and/or granting tax exemptions.[88] The actual collection of taxes was done by the *gaonburas*, who received for that a commission of 12.5 per cent of the revenue. In addition, a kind of indirect tax for the population was their duty to look after the bridle paths, carry loads for government expeditions, and, if necessary, to supply them with provisions. Besides this, they had to provide construction material for inspection bungalows and other government buildings, which were spread all over the country. For all other possible public works the Nagas were paid.[89]

This burden was heavy at times. The former governor of Assam, Sir Robert Reid, reported complaints among the Angami in the years 1886–87, due to the extensive recruitment for forced labour for the army, in addition to the 16,500 Nagas, who were enlisted as porters.[90] In 1891–92 the British again enlisted 20,500 Nagas for forced labour.[91] This is in line with the situation described at beginning of this section.[92] In return the Nagas received security. The battalion of Assam Rifles guaranteed a complete end to raids inside the district. Further, all homicides committed inside the distance of a two-day journey outside the district borders, i.e., in the Tuensang area, were punished. In addition, the Nagas had access to free education,[93] free treatment, medicine and food in the dispensaries, and a team of veterinary surgeons looked after the working animals, free of charge. Further, rivers were bridged that previously were impossible to cross for six months a year, and thus trade flourished, due to the improved communications and the abolition of headhunting.[94]

However, the increased interaction and communication inside the Naga hills, and again between them and the plains, resulted in a devastating spread of diseases.[95] And so it happens that the overall impact of the civilising mission on the Naga hills was in Mills' eyes a negative one, and we find him writing about the good old headhunting times.[96] The conversion of the administrative centres into little towns, the above-mentioned improvement of communications, and the payment for services, food and other goods, had the monetization of trade as a consequence and the emergence of a small community of shop-keepers and petty entrepreneurs in the hills.[97] Chaube further sees the erosion of the clan, and for the first time the introduction of a territorial authority in this area, as a product of the British administration:

> . . . at the beginning of British rule . . . the people's primary loyalty was to the clan. Inter-clan disputes used to be solved either in conferences or through clashes. The 'village authority' under the new procedure was a territorial chief and the disputing clans were to accept his verdict.[98]

The delegation of disputes to the DC or SDO widened the perspective of the village population up to the borders of the district and weakened the orientation towards kinship in favour of a territorial one.[99]

The *dobashis* were the bridge between the British and the *gaonburas* and were, according to Chaube, the first privileged class in the Naga hills. They were educated and came mostly from wealthy families, and in the beginning there was no other job opportunity for them. Only much later were administrative positions made accessible to Nagas, which were then, in most cases, filled with *dobashis*.[100] These young Nagas, who either were able to acquire higher education in Assam or Bengal, due to the financial power of their families, or on grounds of the help of church institutions, turned into a new elite and they began '. . . to look upon Europeans as models and tended to become pro-western in taste and attitude.'[101] They received their education in English, which gave them access to western literature and ideas. Traditional claims to their land were now fed with the concepts of self-determination, democratic principals and nationalism, and later on, would also be termed as such. The English language enabled Nagas from all areas to communicate for the first time with each other and represented '. . . eventually a common unifying bond among themselves as well as with the outside world.'[102] This new elite claimed leadership in the political as well as religious sphere.[103]

Colonial administration was reduced to a minimum. With reference to Jenkins and Young we are in a position to assume that the relative confrontation of the Nagas with colonial categorisation was nearly non-existent. The category 'Naga' remained irrelevant for the majority of the Nagas. The emerging monetization and the extension of methods of communication also remained modest until the Second World War. Among the collective identities tribes became more relevant, though the clan and other foci of identity retained their importance. The impact of the administrative borders was also of much less relevance than the determining role that is ascribed to them by Anderson and Horowitz, simply due to the persistence of social, cultural, economic and political ties which could not be superseded or substituted by the weak structures of the colonial administrative unit. Even though the categorisation of the Nagas by the British remained for the average village people negligible in its impact, it nevertheless was not lost on the elite of the Nagas. They began to think in the category of the 'Nagas', thus seeing themselves as a nation that was entitled to self-determination, but were also aware of the fact that the nation in its consciousness about itself was yet to be realised.

Furthermore, the data on Christianity suggests that it was always other events that served as catalysts for Christianity and not the other way round. An Andersonian approach might be true for the elite but not for the mass of the Nagas, and it is the overwhelming majority that is decisive when we want to make statements on whether an agglomeration of individuals, or groups, is a nation, proven by a collective expression of will, like, for instance, a protracted guerrilla war. Lastly, the idea of independence in this language and terminology surely came with Western education spread by Christian institutions, but was only a translation of an indigenous concept that had even more radically and decidedly insisted on personal freedom, compared with the independence of the whole people, which the Nagas now had to adopt to survive in the new state system. As we have seen, both the First and Second World Wars served as catalysts for the spread of Christianity, and thus were instrumental in making large parts of the Naga populations approachable for their small westernised, educated and often young elite, and we will come to this shortly. Proof of this is that the Indo-Naga war, though started only in the 1950s, turned out to have been the decisive catalyst for Christianity (and the Naga nation), and not the other way round – as was claimed by the Indian Government's agents and press alike.[104] And it is the continuation of that war and/or that military occupation by India that gave the dominant role it has today.

The two World Wars

In the course of the First World War the British asked every village in the Naga hills to provide a certain number of men for deployment for work on the battlefields in France and the Middle East. Consequently approximately 4,000 Nagas joined the Naga Labour Corps and were deployed to the respective theatres of war. Apart from those serving in the Labour Corps, there were also Nagas who, being part of regular units in Manipur and Assam, saw active service.[105] In his 'Foreword' to Hutton's monograph on the Semas, Henry Balfour wrote that he came across several Nagas in France and wondered what consequences these experiences might have on the Nagas, and how they would look at the British afterwards:

> In September, 1917, in Eastern France, I came across a gang of Nagas, . . . engaged in road-repairing in the war-zone, within sound of the guns. They appeared to be quite at home and unperturbed. Earlier in that year I just missed seeing them in Bizerta, but the French authorities there described to me their self-possession and absence of fear when they were landed after experiencing shipwreck in the Mediterranean – a truly novel experience for these primitive inland hill-dwellers!
> One wonders what impressions remain with them from their sudden contact with higher civilisation at war. Possibly, they are reflecting that, after what they have seen, the White Man's condemnation of the relatively innocuous headhunting of the Nagas savours of hypocrisy. Or does their *sang-froid* save them from being critical and endeavouring to analyse the seemingly inconsequent habits of the leading people of culturedom? Now that they are back in the hills, will they settle down to the indigenous simple life and revert to the primitive conditions which were temporarily disturbed?[106]

According to Naga authors (who as a rule do not give their sources) it was indeed the case that the Nagas perceived what they saw on the European battlefields as contradictory to the statements of condemnation about their barbarous headhunting practices. The same 'civilised' people engaged in the conduct of a massive carnage, stretching over years, forbade the Nagas a comparatively harmless, yet for their culture essential, practice.[107] The Nagas, according to Horam, saw therein a heightened hypocrisy, and this contributed to the general discontent and resentment against the British that had always been there. Even after sections of the Nagas had converted to Christianity and entertained a friendly intercourse with missionaries and administrators, they were, as Horam expresses it, '. . . never crazy about the British.'[108] Initially the Nagas called the British 'half-cooked' and perceived them as portentous, yet accommodated themselves with their presence, and tried to make the best of it, believing anyhow that it would only be a temporary affair.[109] Further, Nagas returning from the front lines brought home with them stories about how their imperial rulers took severe beatings at the hands of the Germans. If the deteriorating image of and growing resentment against the British was one outcome of this war, so, as Horam argues, did the contact and interaction in France and the Middle East between Nagas of all different groups, including those from the unadministered areas, give rise to a sense of belonging among them.[110] The majority of the recruits of the Labour Corps had been recruited from the '. . . independent transfrontier Nagas . . .', as they were called then, and this resulted in a closer relationship between the British and those Nagas.[111] Alemchimba goes even further and says that it was now that the Nagas saw the necessity for their political unification to be able to represent their interests in a world that would never be the same.[112] Yonuo writes that the Nagas in France had passed a verbal resolution to resolve all their differences and disputes on their return and to work from then on for the political unification of the Nagas, and this, for Yonuo, constituted '. . . the spirit which spearheaded an upsurge of the Naga nationalist movement.'[113] On their return some of those Nagas founded the Naga Club in Kohima and Mokokchung in 1918, which for Panmei marked a turning point in the history of the Nagas, since it was the first organisation representing all tribes.[114] Among the founding members were important *gaonburas*, *dobashis*, government servants, priests and other educated Nagas.[115] The club was unofficially supported by the local administration.[116] In the beginning the club's objectives were more social than political; the members ran a cooperative shop, founded a football team and were supposed to support the district-administration, yet it developed into a political force, and, according to Yonuo, '. . . raised its will against the British imperialism . . .',[117] although in a peaceful and loyal manner.[118] Panmei, in the same vein, sees the Naga Club as an instrument against British imperialism,[119] and Horam assumes that the members of the club already anticipated the dawning of India's independence:

> They were preparing themselves politically in the event of India gaining her Independence from the British – a happening they then visualized as being imminent. Thus their chief concern was the political future of their homeland after the exit of the British. The Naga Club was still in its infancy then, but the pattern of the future had already been installed in their minds.[120]

None of the authors writing about the Naga club identifies his source of information. There are few details subsequent to its foundation, solely that it grew into the centre of social and political gatherings, and represented a '. . . sustained pressure group . . .'.[121] When we recall the contents of the *Memorandum to the Simon Commission* (see previous chapter), we may agree that here Nagas had come together who, discussing their predicament, were aware of their plains neighbours' superiority; there was a danger that their future could be with them; were cognisant of their own disunity, and lack of consciousness on the part of the majority as Nagas; and that despite these negations, formed themselves as Naga populations. However, they failed to realise that there was no way back to an existence outside of the state system, and thus, rather than starting to work on a unification of the Nagas, they accepted the disunity as given. That being so, we may speak of an incipient national elite, whose characteristic trait was passivity, possibly rooted in the understanding of their people's indifference towards potentially national affairs.

This was to change with the Second World War, which led to the most dramatic disruption and radical change of people's lives in the Naga hills. Before 1942 there were no lines of communication capable of supporting large numbers of troops east and south of the Brahmaputra. While the Northwest had always been expected to be the most likely route for a potential invader, the Arakan chain was simply seen as too difficult and unhealthy terrain. The Japanese assault on Burma, however, proved this view wrong and the threat to India's Northeast Frontier set off a massive allied war effort to connect Assam with the rest of India by rail, road, river and air. With that the Naga hills became firstly part of a potential and then virtual barrier against a Japanese invasion, and finally the central part of the front. Dimapur was turned into a base depot, initially to handle 1,000 tons of supplies per day.[122] As a consequence thousands of Nagas and other workers, recruited from all over India, were used by the British as forced labour to build this infrastructure. In Mountbatten's own words:

> In Assam, as in Arakan, we were faced with considerable difficulties. At Dimapur (Manipur Road), which was the advanced base for the Central front, work on a completely new base had had to be undertaken in a highly malarial area. In addition to the operational troops, there was a labour force of about 60,000 employed on the construction of roads, airfields and other works.[123]

The central office of information gives different numbers. Here, from March 1942 onwards 28,000 tea estate labourers were working on the Dimapur–Kohima–Imphal road, provided by the India tea association. Later that number was to increase to 82,000 as a regular labour force. However, the total number of the labour force employed on the central front was three times as high, in other words approximately 250,000 labourers, consisting of imported but also local (Naga) labour.[124]

In 1942 streams of Indian refugees coming from Burma flooded through the Naga hills.[125] Almost 190,000 of them reached Imphal alone, while others used more northern routes, following the retreating Indian, British, and Chinese forces.[126] The Indian auxiliary troops escaping from Burma, chased by the advancing Japanese, in the course of their escape route to the plains, fell upon the villages of the Nagas, drove their populations out, looted them,[127] and finally burned them down.[128] In addition to that east-to-west invasion of the hills, a large number of

Indian auxiliary troops had been already stationed in the Naga hills.[129] Imphal plain was made into the allied advance base for the defence of India and the re-conquest of Burma. The material was transported via air and the Dimapur–Kohima–Imphal road, which had been turned into a two-lane, all-weather route.[130] In 1943 alone the tonnage per month transported along this road increased from 17,000 to 40,000, and again in 1944 to 2,500 a day.[131] By January 1944 the lines of communication of Assam maintained 450,000 men, and by April 620,000.[132]

By the end of March 1944 three Japanese divisions (approximately 100,000 men) had fought their way westward into the Naga hills and encircled 155,000 British and Indian troops in the Imphal area, and in early April they reached Kohima and besieged the garrison there.[133] The battles of Imphal and Kohima were among the toughest in the war in this part of the world and were fought with enormous deployment of planes, tanks, artillery and men,[134] thus leading to comprehensive destruction.[135] To supply the Imphal area by air alone it needed 300 sorties or supply flights per day, adding up to 8,000 in total.[136] To prevent the Japanese from outflanking them, allied troops also were dispatched further north and east into the Naga hills, to Jotsoma, Phekekrima, Mokokchung, Sakhalu, Zubza, and Wokha, and Japanese troops advanced to these positions,[137] extending the area directly affected by the war over the majority of the hills, which brought them temporarily under Japanese administration:

> When the Japanese offensive was fully extended, only 25,000 tribesmen remained under our administration; but by the end of June, when the Naga Hills and other territories had been recovered, their number rose to 186,000.[138]

The Japanese remained for roughly four months in the Naga hills, set up their administration and tried to win over the Nagas to cooperate with them. Though the Japanese administration was thus rather temporary, Yonuo is of the opinion that it nevertheless effected the abolition of the arbitrary division of the Naga hills by the British administration into administered and unadministered areas. The Japanese advanced without provisions and were left to live on what they could find on their way. Consequently they requisitioned everything that they could find in the Naga villages and paid for it with fake ten-rupee notes. The Nagas also were forced by the Japanese to work as porters and guides for them, or were locked up so that they were not in a position to warn the allies. If there was any suspicion of collaboration with the British, the Nagas were tortured and killed. Many villages were destroyed in the heavy fighting, the granaries burnt during retreats, and bombardments did not discriminate between civilians and combatants. The Nagas took refuge in the jungle.[139]

To the Allies the Nagas served as stretcher-bearers,[140] and porters,[141] and the British officer in command afterwards praised the Nagas:

> Despite floggings, torture, execution, and the burning of their villages, they refused to aid the Japanese in any way or to betray our troops. (. . .) they guided

our columns, collected information, ambushed enemy patrols, carried our supplies, and brought in our wounded under the heaviest fire. . . .[142]

In the battle of Kohima, the DC Charles Pawsey seemed to have been instrumental in gaining the support of the Nagas.[143] The *dobashi* Kosazu of the village Kigwema later told Archer that Pawsey, prior to the Japanese invasion, had ordered the Nagas to kill as many Japanese as possible:

> . . . I asked if any Japanese heads were taken in the fighting. Kosazu then explained that when the war approached the hills Pawsey issued an order urging the Nagas to kill all the Japs they could, but forbidding them to take their heads. Instead of this he but authorised them to remove a finger and an ear (Pawsey tells me that was done to avoid reprisals). Following this announcement, Whilie Angami, a Naga of Kigwema killed two Japs but he is the only member of the village who did so.[144]

The allies considered the hill tribes of the Indo-Burma region as brothers in arms, and the Nagas as their most faithful.[145] Yonuo writes that many Nagas helped the allies, hoping to receive something in return in the future.[146] This is definitely an allusion to promises for independence, which later on, when not realised, were perceived as a betrayal of the hill tribes in general and the Nagas in particular, especially by the British who had served during the war in the Naga hills.[147] That there was not always enthusiasm on the part of the Nagas to get drawn into the war more than was necessary, may be seen from Bower's description of how she convinced a group of Nagas to fight for the allies: at first they did not really see why they should do this for the British, but then gave in reluctantly to Bower's mixture of promises and blackmail.[148] The cooperation of the Nagas with the allies could anyhow not have been too ambitious, for the latter were entirely in the dark about Japanese movements and positions,[149] which would confirm what I was told by T. Muivah who grew up and experienced the war in Tangkhul area, northern Manipur.[150] This view, though, is challenged by Yong Kong, who aged roughly 15 at that time and living in Mokokchung, had two brothers in the Labour Corps working on the Imphal road, and who insists that the Nagas from the NHD supported the British war effort a hundred per cent.[151]

The end of the actual fighting left the Naga hills as a transit and rest area, and for the sake of the reconquest of Burma, the lines of communication through the Naga hills, especially the Dimapur–Kohima–Imphal–Tamu road, were improved to serve as support lines,[152] and Kohima remained a rest area for at least two divisions.[153] Several authors see the Second World War as the central and most traumatic experience for the Nagas since the British conquest of the Naga hills: '. . . it was the Second World War which had propelled psychological cataclysm far beyond its confines than anything that had taken place during the British rule for about 70 years'.[154] And:

> The large-scale contact with British, Indian and Japanese soldiers, over a period of some months, touched off a revolution in the minds of the Nagas.

A window was opened to the outside world, and through it blew in the winds of change that disturbed a stagnant life and wafted in new ideas and concepts.

It kindled a new awakening among them. It brought to them new ideas of living and new concepts of freedom. Their social outlook underwent change. It all generated a mental ferment and restlessness among the post-war generations of Nagas.[155]

Nibedon, though writing rather less metaphorically, saw the war as having achieved no less a consequence than the Nagas' entry into history: 'No, not a single Naga remained entirely unaffected. . . In fact, there was utter chaos in the tribal societal fabric . . .[the Nagas] . . . were plummeted into history.'[156] A window was torn open and the wind of destruction came in, but not due to some supra-history, but because of the affairs of others. Rustomji, who after the Transfer of Power often had the opportunity to talk to Nagas, due to his position as adviser to the governor of Assam in tribal affairs, writes that the Second World War and the extensive destruction of their country, above all, gave rise to the conviction among the Nagas that they wanted to be left alone.[157]

After the war the British started a programme of reconstruction. Temporary business transactions with the allies and the Japanese, together with compensation paid for services provided during the war, raised the standards of living in the Naga hills far above other hill tribal areas in the Northeast, and gave rise to a petty bourgeoisie among the Nagas. The contact with numerous nationalities, about which the Nagas beforehand had only heard, made the Nagas perceive themselves as part of a larger whole. Military requirements brought an immense improvement of the lines of communication and '. . . transformed tremendously the economic, political, social, moral and cultural life of the Naga people.'[158] The massive confrontation with the outside world put their traditional way of life in question, resulting in '. . . synthesizing western life into all aspects of their life.'[159] An increased interaction among the Nagas themselves, and their shared experience, made them forget their old feuds and made them start talking in terms such as 'unity' and 'nation'. The inscription honouring the dead of the battle of Kohima reads as follows: 'When you go home tell them of us, and say for your tomorrow we gave our today'[160] for Yonuo it mirrors '. . . the sentiments of the Nagas of sacrifice their life for the sake of the nation, rising above the narrow bounds of selfish ends.'[161] Thus, while the Second World War is seen by most authors as a collective trauma for the Nagas, which destroyed their supposedly traditional life, Yonuo is of the opinion that the war, though not being the father of the Naga nation, was definitely its midwife.

I have tried to sketch the war-time Naga hills, since I am convinced that it was this common experience and endurance on the part of the Nagas that made the majority of them for the first time receptive to whatever political programme their small elite might have had. Prior to this cataclysm, talks of unification, self-determination, etc. must have appeared as utterly irrelevant.

Conclusion

The partial subjugation of the Naga hills had been carried out for reasons lying beyond them. Consequently, the administrative set-up was limited to the minimum, thus the categorisation of the hill tribes as 'Nagas' by the British could not take hold among the majority of the Nagas, and only made its impact on a comparatively small elite. In their process of ordering and categorising the population into tribes, the colonial masters tried to orientate themselves along the line of existing structures. The *dobashis*, the cultural interpreters and political envoys, played an advising, if not, decisive role. The result was the strengthening of already existing units of identification and organisation, possibly with a reifying tendency, but not superseding those units of the lower order. A supporting role, as will be shown elsewhere, was played by the language policy of the missionaries, and by the educational and church structures, created and maintained in the main by indigenous people. This, together with the rudimentary administrative structures, presented a much wider framework, inside which a more closely knitted network constituted the field of action for the newly emerging elite among the Nagas. In their intercourse with British missionaries and plainsmen, this elite started to see itself not only as members of different tribes, but most probably also as members of the Naga people. This was definitely the case after thousands of Nagas had served overseas in the war zones of Europe and the Middle East. Not only did it give these men a wider vision of themselves, but it also placed that vision in a broader context. However, until the end of the 1920s this new Naga elite was also aware of the fact that the overwhelming majority of their people, far from seeing any necessity to unify, was not even aware of that question. Moreover, this elite, despite what they had witnessed, may have believed that there still was the possibility of a return to a life outside the worldwide state system. This all changed when the Naga hills themselves became the forward base, front line, and battlefield of the war in the east in the Second World War, by the connection of the Naga hills with the wider region, accompanied by the rapid improvement of the lines of communication, the fast-moving penetration of the hills themselves, and the flood of people and armies of all kinds. Moreover, the battle of personnel and *matériel* also must have revealed to them their absolute powerlessness against states that could employ, move, and if necessary, designate to wholesale destruction. Notwithstanding, the fact that the Japanese had been temporarily victorious, and had had the British on the run, demonstrated that the white man was anything but invincible and damaged his image beyond repair. This was the beginning of the end of European colonialism in all of South and Southeast Asia. Having said this, we may conclude that while colonial administration and Christianity delivered a small elite, it was the Second World War that widened political consciousness among the population.

5   India's nationbuilding and the Nagas, 1947–64

Introduction

This chapter sets out to shed some light on the actors in the Nehruvian era, in order to explicate in detail that, despite claims at the centre for unity in diversity, the policy was to pursue unity violently and eradicate diversity. In the case of the Nagas, the initial strategy was to give verbal assurances about constitutional safe-guards, but not implementing them. That was to ensure that the Naga hills, as a separate unit, would cease to exist following the first post-independence decade. Once the Nagas protested, the Indo-Assamese agents sent out contradictory signals of appeasement and imposition, not allowing for a clear counter-position. When the Nagas finally returned to their original demand for immediate independence and continued to insist upon it, the Assamese administration sent its paramilitaries to make the Nagas change their minds. This terror campaign backfired and Shillong had to ask Delhi for the assistance of the Indian army that was subsequently committed to it by Nehru. The Indian army, unable to break the resistance and itself hard pressed, started a genocidal campaign that also did not achieve the objective. Thus, the GOI, via its intelligence bureau, created, with the cooperation of some Nagas, a pro-Indian faction that was to head a future Naga unit which, soon after, was transformed into a state of the Indian Union. This move was destined to split the Nagas. As this also proved to be ineffective, Nehru, in the last month of his life, allowed for some initiatives that resulted in a genuine cease-fire which, though not ending the war, was to give the Naga population some breathing time.

The Indo-Assamese protagonists' stand vis-à-vis the Nagas was not different from the one we have encountered among the British in chapters one and three. They agreed on the same policy of state terror that made the Indian army into the main Indian agent in the Naga hills. Yet there was a crucial difference between the former British empire and the newly independent Indian state: imperialism had lost its legitimacy, and the doctrine of self-determination and democracy demanded a voluntary union of equals.[1] This being so, neither formal nor informal imperialism was left as a choice and nation-building had to be the order of the day, necessitating the total penetration of the projected territory and population. When the latter, how-ever, proved highly recalcitrant, the Indian state resorted to terror, and then to violent repression, to achieve its aim.[2]

Nationbuilding

The initial aim – to create the independent India as a decentralised polity with autonomous states – was dropped when the Muslim League and Congress were competing for power. Moreover, the carnage of partition, the resistance of some princely states and the weakness of Congress in the periphery provided the impetus to create a strong centralised state, which was in any case favoured by Nehru and a section of the Congress leadership.[3] The states thus became functional to the whole.[4] Though all the powers enabled the centre also to respond flexibly to demands for provincial and regional autonomy,[5] mainly it provided the centre with the power to impose its will on the states.[6]

In India, the major tool for nationbuilding on the periphery was the Indian army. The post-Transfer of Power Indian army fundamentally resembled its imperial predecessor. One difference, however, was that army personnel was now to be recruited proportionately, in such a way as to represent the nation as a whole. This new concept of aspired, representative constitution of the army was thus intimately connected to nationbuilding and national identity and became one of the main reasons to fight for the new national Indian army.[7] One of the legacies of the *raj*, however, was the omnipresence of the military, especially in its role upholding internal security. While this was generally opposed to by post-independence Indians and especially by their government, it was not the case however, for the periphery where the military continued to play its traditional role. Indo-Pakistani hostility and the perceived threat posed by China prevented a reform of the armed forces, since in times of crises the civilians had to rely on the military, making it easy for the army to withstand any attempt to reform.[8] Though politicians and the civil service successfully curbed the military's part in the decision-making process,[9] where it was deployed and in command, such as in the very peripheral Naga hills, the army still had a free hand. This remains disturbingly true until today.[10] Then, it meant that a young and inexperienced officer corps,[11] probably eager to prove itself and earn its merit, found itself in charge of a major crisis in nationbuilding. Despite continuous affirmations of its professionalism and striking power, the reality was probably closer to an ill-equipped[12] and ill-trained force, clearly demonstrated by the contemporaneous debacle in the Indo-Chinese war.[13] This rout by the Chinese, however, unleashed a military build-up that bore fruit toward the end of the 1960s. It perhaps explains GOI's assent to the ceasefire in the Naga hills and the proceedings of the peace mission as providing a breathing space to regroup and build up its military potential and capability, in order to relaunch subsequent assaults on the stubborn *junglis*[14] with even greater vigour. Thus, for example, in 1961 *The Times* correspondent wrote:

> The Indian Army was committed soon after the underground had struck its first blows against the administration. The Army's natural strategy was to attempt to wipe out guerrillas as quickly as possible.
>
> Villages thought to be supplying and supporting the underground were heavily punished or, if persistent, razed after their inhabitants had been

brought together in stockaded centres to be held under guard. The guerrilla forces were also vigorously harried.

In the recollections of the Army officers and some officials those tactics brought the underground to its knees, and they grumble now that they were cheated of victory and condemned to a long and frustrating campaign by the Government's 'Gandhian' hankering.[15]

Being humiliated by the Chinese was one thing, but being humiliated by the Nagas definitely smacked of a 'myth of the stab in the back' and called for rectification as soon as possible. However, before this could be done, the Indian army had to fight the Indo-Pakistani war of 1965, and had to crush the Mizos in 1966–7, both campaigns possibly contributing to the explanation why the ceasefire held for so long in the Naga hills. When then the army was again unleashed into the Naga hills it was better equipped and staffed but surely not better suited to fight a guerrilla war. Even today, though having been deployed for more than five decades, mostly in operations against fellow-citizens, the Indian army still considers its main task as the territorial defence of the union. As a consequence, it behaves in its counter-insurgency operations as what it is – a land army that moves in massive force against an enemy, and even today can not be convinced of the impracticality of this approach in a guerrilla war, let alone in low-intensity insurgency.[16]

Greater Assam

Assam in the late 1940s and early 1950s was of only marginal interest to Delhi, and India's Northeast Frontier policy was determined by her considerations for her own defence against Communist China and Nepali Communists.[17] This was even more so with the Naga hills.[18] General questions in the *Lok Sabha* in 1951 on the potential of the NHD for mineral wealth and agriculture, and in 1952 on the eradication of headhunting in the Naga tribal areas via development schemes, indicate that the Nagas did not yet pose a political problem for the central administration.[19] Furthermore, the short discussion in the *Lok Sabha* on 25th May 1951, on communications in the Naga hills, supports statements made by two of my interviewees that in the initial post-independence period nothing much had changed in the Naga hills, rather that the Nagas were administering themselves for the time being.[20] For although Assam was now in charge of administering the NHD, and the governor of Assam in charge of the Naga hills tribal area as agent of the president of India,[21] initially, neither had the means nor the manpower effectively to implement the duty associated with the office. Contrary to that there are statements in the literature that suggest the build-up of the Assamese administration immediately after the Transfer of Power.[22] Yet these will have referred to 1948 or even 1949, and not 1947. What might have changed on the ground, we will try to unravel closely in the next chapter. Here it is important to note that, although it had been brought to Nehru's attention that the Nagas were dissatisfied with the neglect of their point of view, the incorporation of the hill areas was left to the Assam administration. The Assamese themselves were for a long time fighting Bengali dominance and demanding *swaraj* for Assam, independent from India. The quest for preserving Assamese identity turned into one of building a Greater Assam by an Assamisation of the hills, triggering in turn a chain reaction of independence demands from the hill people. At the end of the British *raj* literally everyone in and around Assam wanted independence. The Nagas were by no means an exception, but maybe the most stubborn. Most of the different hill and plains people gave in to Congress for the time being, but the post-independence history of the Northeast shows that this was on revocation. However, the Assamese elite, who had been dominated by caste Hindus previously, under the Ahoms, then organised themselves in Congress, and decided for several reasons (among them the fear of Pakistan and Communism) to remain within the Indian Union.[23] The Assamese had long viewed the exclusion of the hill regions from the administration of Assam as a devious divide-and-rule device on the part of the British.[24] The Transfer of Power brought the opportunity to reverse this. Now the Assamese wanted what they saw as a political, cultural and administrative reunification of the hills and the plains as quickly as possible. The moment was there to build a Greater Assam, including the hill regions reaching until the international borders of China, Burma and East Pakistan.[25]

Hostiles

The first incident to give the Naga hills national public attention was when in March 1953 Nehru,[26] together with his Burmese colleague U Nu, toured the Indo-Burmese border region, primarily '. . . to study personally the law and order situation in the frontier areas.'[27] The source of the situation was the movement of 'dacoits' and 'lawless elements'.[28] When Nehru and U Nu visited Kohima, about 3,000 Nagas left the reception ground as a protest against Nehru's refusal of their demand for independence.[29] An unmatched re-narration of the humiliation of Nehru, who had been the darling of the masses, is given by Gita Mehta:

> The airplane landed, a great white bird with the symbol of the Indian nation, Emperor Asoka's pillar of truth, blazoned on its side. Would the child-like tribals be frightened by this miracle of aerodynamics descending from the heavens with its cargo of democratic divinity? Would they run for cover? But no, they were standing steady under quivering head-dresses watching aircraft personnel leaping out to fix the steps for the Prime Minister's descent, as the press photographers pushed forward for a clear view through their lenses.
>
> Finally the great man himself appeared – to be received by a reverence so profound that even the accompanying journalists were silenced. Possessing a sense of history, the leader solemnly descended the aircraft steps, assuming this warlike people wished to give him a colourful guard of honour.
>
> I suppose they did. Because as soon as he was on terra firma, they all turned with regimental precision and lifted their colourful sarongs. The Prime Minister of India found himself taking the salute of hundreds of naked tribal behinds.[30]

It was thereafter that GOI gave Assam's chief minister Bishnuram Medhi a free hand for a tougher policy.[31] However, the first incident that drew the attention of the international press and of Delhi was the attack on Yimpang in which 57 people were killed and was portrayed as the result of an inter-village feud between the former village and another one named Pangsha.[32] When in late April 1955 reports came in to Delhi saying that troops were being dispatched to Tuensang, the official explanation was that they were sent there to hunt 'subversive elements and restore order'. The Assam Rifles obviously had been attacked.[33] A month later A. K. Chanda, deputy minister for external affairs, admitted in the *Lok Sabha* that it was separatists who had assaulted another village on the grounds of its cooperation with GOI.[34] In July Nehru, in his double functioning as prime minister and minister of external affairs, admitted that some areas in the Northeast Frontier Area (NEFA) had been declared disturbed, but could not say whether the armed units operating there were the paramilitary Assam Rifles or the regular Indian army. When asked about the possible reasons for the unrest, Nehru suggested it was the Nagas of the adjacent NHD who were inciting the villagers in Tuensang.[35] The central government had to rely for information on the remote Northeast's local administration.[36] Two weeks later parliament was informed that the regular army was not yet involved in any fighting and was only performing garrison duties in Tuensang. Nehru referred to petty incidents.[37] A week later it became evident that Burmese security forces were cooperating with their Indian colleagues in fighting 'hostiles' which, according to Nehru's information, were estimated at being between 400 and 500 strong.[38] All the efforts to portray what was going on in Tuensang as a series of petty incidents were contradicted when details arrived that the political officer of the NEFA administration had asked the army to assist the local administration, and GOI had assented to post one battalion in the southern sector of the Tuensang division.[39] By the end of that month, finally, *The Express* had news that the Nagas were fighting a war of independence, and that Nehru had sent in 'steel-helmeted troops'; further, that the Nagas had proclaimed a republic and had elected 'Hong Khin' as head of state. Nehru, so *The Express* continued, had asked Burma for help and the Burmese military had launched operations against the Nagas. Casualties were mounting on both sides.[40] As early as September 1955 onwards, regular troops had been also sent into the NHD and were engaged in regular fighting.[41] By late December 1955 the official number of casualties on the Naga side was 258 killed and 68 wounded since the beginning of the fighting.[42] That one would have expected the ratio between killed and wounded the other way around, is a phenomenon that we are to encounter again. The parliamentary secretary of the external affairs ministry, Hazarika, told the *Lok Sabha* that the 'disorders had arisen from the demand by rebel tribesmen for an independent State'; further, that the above-mentioned casualties had occurred 'while Indian troops were restoring order recently in the Naga tribal area of India's north-east', but 'that the situation had improved considerably'.[43] The situation, according to GOI representatives' descriptions would continue to improve over the following years, and would be part of a strategy to play down the scale of the fighting and destruction. Those who demanded independence had to be only a few, and were singularly responsible for the fighting; they and their demand were defamed and ridiculed as 'misguided', 'extreme', 'hostile', 'terrorist' etc. The overwhelming majority of the Nagas had to be protected from them by Indian troops. Thus, by the end of 1955, eight years after the Transfer of Power, the fighting in the Naga hills, whether in the district or tribal area, had made its way into the consciousness of the decision makers in the Indian capital as a minor but persistent threat to India's newly won territorial integrity.

By April 1956, according to the press, three battalions of the regular Indian army had already been deployed to the Naga hills, to an area which then held approximately 350,000 inhabitants.[44] It had by then been understood in Delhi that measures, previously undertaken by the GOI to hasten civilisation in the Naga hills, were taken as aggression against their way of life by the Nagas and thus could be exploited by the 'extremists.' The desire for independence arose, according to 'observers', due to the suspicion that was felt toward the Assamese, and Phizo wanted to form a separate state out of all the hill districts. Delhi saw that the unification of all Naga territory had a case, further that its administration could be conducted by elected leaders. Once violence had stopped these were matters that could be negotiated, although Nehru made it clear that independence was out of the question.[45]

Despite the repeated incantations of an improved situation, at the beginning of May 1956 details were received of a battle between Indian security forces (ISF) and 200 rebels armed with machine and sten guns, as well as with regular rifles, near Kohima (where the Indian army had its headquarters), during which 30 rebels were killed. The Indian army ultimatum to surrender all arms by 3rd May had run out and now a full-scale military campaign was expected.[46] A day later it was reported that, since mid-April, more than 100 rebels had been killed and many more wounded, and that 14 villages had been burned down by the rebels. Nehru stated he had no information about any assistance by Pakistan or any other foreign government in support of the rebels, and denied that the rebels had gained control over any territory.[47] On government side, 17 people had been killed, 30 wounded and 5 were unaccounted for. Nehru signalled his government's readiness to grant a wider autonomy to the Nagas on the condition of the cessation of violence.[48]

It was the Indian member of parliament (MP) Joeshwar Singh who called into doubt all affirmations that the insurgents were but a few and certainly soon would be part of the past. Singh held first-hand information, since he had been held in captivity by the Nagas, and after his release stressed that there was no way of playing down the situation since, despite the Indian troops having their headquarters in Kohima, the stretch between Kohima and Khijuma, near Mao in Manipur, on the Dimapur-Imphal road, was effectively under Naga control. Singh's evidence was further corroborated by the fact that India continued to move Indian army reinforcements into the Naga hills. Delhi now clearly saw the Assamese civil authorities as being responsible for the trouble in the first place, and for the prospect of its protracted nature. Still, the army had problems finding its way around, distinguishing friend and foe, and building up an intelligence network. This was also blamed on the basic mistrust by the Nagas of the Assamese.[49] The Assamese clearly fulfilled a scapegoat role, in the absence from the narrative of the British and missionaries.

Hitherto, GOI had to rely for information on the provincial administration and its agents or on the Indian army personnel deployed there. It thus could very well have been the case that the information reaching Delhi was tailored for provincial or institutional interests. Although, by the end of July 1956 the minister for home affairs, Dattar, had visited the Naga hills, and had met, among others, the governor and the chief minister of Assam,[50] it is still to be assumed that he relied for the organisation and course of his visit on the men on the ground. The army was now in command of the area, but was hindered in the progress of its operations by the seasonal monsoon in the already difficult terrain.[51] The chief of army staff had toured the Naga hills in the previous June to assess the situation.[52] Shortly afterwards, with nearly a month's delay, the *Lok Sabha* was informed of an attack by Nagas, carried out in the middle of July, on a railway station in the Sibsagar district and the damaging of a railway bridge with the likely intended consequence of disrupting train services.[53]

Then from September 1956 onwards voices were raised, publicly suspecting that GOI might deny access to foreign journalists not so much because it held foreigners (the British and missionaries) responsible for having instigated the unrest in the first instance, but rather '. . . due to an unwillingness on the part of the Indian government to have their actions in that area exposed to world opinion?'. This was suggested by Graham Greene, who pretended to have applied in vain for a visa and come across a significant justification for the denial:

> An official at the High Commissioner's Office in London has informed me that no permits to this area have been allowed for many months past and that there is no chance at the moment of my receiving a permit. I suggested that an Indian writer would not be forbidden access to Cyprus, and his reply was that the case was different – Cyprus was 'colonial territory,' a new definition of colonialism, an area open to world opinion.[54]

Indeed, for the Naga hills, the previously so much criticised and denounced *Bengal Eastern Frontier Regulation 1873,* and the *Chin Hills Regulation 1896,* had been reactivated, this time to keep out the international press.[55]

In October the Assam government again predicted an early successful conclusion of the 'police action' with the end of the monsoon and the ensuing offensive just around the corner. This notwithstanding, the special correspondent of *The Times*, who had come as far as Shillong, was even declined permission to visit Kohima, despite him agreeing to close supervision. The officials, it appeared, were by now in a belligerent mood:

> This new-found confidence about the military situation seems to have banished finally any leanings towards a 'negotiated' settlement. 'Phizo is a madman and has simply got to be smashed,' an Indian official said. 'He is so completely obsessed with the idea of independence that there is no further purpose in talking with him.' In the same spirit, references to the Naga 'rebellion' are now somewhat frowned upon: the present events are described as 'just a police operation against a band of terrorists'[56]

In the same month Nehru toured Assam for four days and discussed the state of affairs in the Naga hills with NEFA – officials and a delegation of Nagas from Mokokchung. Simultaneously the intensified military operations were announced as under way in the discussed area under the command of lieutenant general Thimayyas.[57] Nehru then, at a public meeting at Jorhat, called '. . . the demand for an independent Nagaland absurd. Nagas were as independent as other Indians and the demand therefore did not arise.'[58] In his speech he seemed to equate Naga independence with their continued preservation as museum pieces, and a merger with Assam, as he suggested for NEFA, seemed to amount to an arrival at modernity. Nehru, who as we know by now was in theory sympathetic to the tribals, could retain his sympathy only once the tribals followed his evolutionist world view and shed their past and differences. Nehru was not only incapable of understanding minority fears in terms other than as vested interests of a local elite, but he was also utterly exasperated at every insistence of difference that he saw as fissiparous manifestations of past backwardness, getting in his way of building a nation. Nehru, who was aware of contemporary literature on nation and nationalism, knew that the nation had still to be achieved, and partition painfully alerted him to its fragility and its potential for 'balkanisation'. From then it was his paramount task to fight off any attempt to leave the Indian Union.[59]

In December 1956 the guerrilla war, defying all avowals to the contrary, continued into the cold season, and it is the first time we find a reference to the so-called 'resettlement schemes': '. . . good progress had been made in many areas resettling villagers who had been driven away.'[60] A week later the army issued an optimistic all-clear for the Naga hills that betrayed the fact that the Nagas had fought in an organised way, that there had been no day in 1956 without fighting and that the Naga fighters had previously brought territory under their control. The army had established 20 bases and was perpetually patrolling the jungle paths, forcing the rebels to take recourse to guerrilla techniques.[61]

Divide-and-rule

In January of 1957 Naga snipers shot at trains passing through Assam, bordering the Naga hills, with the effect of suspending train services.[62] This might have been due to efforts to slow down troop deployment, since one week after the second general elections, Anthony Mann, for the *Daily Telegraph* reported from Calcutta that more than 30,000 Indian troops, at least one and a half regular divisions, were fighting the Nagas. Mann drew parallels to the Mau Mau in Kenya.[63] Zinkin in Bombay also wrote that the Naga hills had been turned '. . . into no man's land and guerrilla jungles . . .'. The military, he continued, permanently issued statements about the impending collapse of the uprising. Movement inside the Naga hills was only possible in convoys, and even the trains were interrupted in Upper Assam. Phizo, despite having a reward on his head, had managed to become a hero in the Naga hills, and so much so that Congress had not dared to contest elections there. The wider picture of the hills showed that, as a result of the general elections,

Congress had lost all contested seats in the hill districts. This was taken as an expression of dislike of the Assam administration by all hill people.[64]

In 1957 the central government took away control of the Naga hills from the Assam state government and sent in some administrators, considered as elite. Some Nagas were won over to cooperate and were named the Naga People's Convention (NPC).[65] The NPC on its part asked for the application of greater force against the Naga fighters. However, there seemed to exist some doubt in Delhi whether it was the right policy to rely on the NPC, since it was not clear whether it had the support of the majority of the Nagas.[66] In July 1960 GOI and the NPC signed an agreement by which the previous NHD and the Tuensang area was to form the sixteenth state of the Indian Union.[67]

The end of August 1957 saw large-scale army operations but no security in the Naga hills. The NPC in Kohima, having demanded separation from Assam and the unification of Naga areas under central rule, called the uprising a rebellion against the Assam government and stressed that there always was peace in centrally administered Tuensang.[68] A month later GOI declared an amnesty after a meeting between Nehru and a Naga delegation, consisting of nine Naga leaders, on 25th and 26th September in Delhi. Nehru told the delegation that independence was still not possible, but the constitution could be changed to meet their demands. He accepted the proposal of a merger between Tuensang and NHD into one unit within the Indian Union, administered by the governor of Assam at the behest of the president of the union and under the authority of the ministry of external affairs.[69] Nehru now fell in with the chorus blaming the British and missionaries for 'Naga troubles'. The former isolated them from the rest of India, allowing only the latter – who had spread hatred of the Indians – to enter the Naga hills, and:

> Some of the Nagas were converted to Christianity. . . . and were educated to some extent. Because of their education they became the leaders of the Nagas. One of the last acts of the British officials was to encourage these Nagas to claim independence.[70]

In parliament Nehru responded to questions on the agreement reached with the Naga delegation stating that it had been accepted by the NPC, i.e., that it had given up its demand for independence. Further, responsibility for the new NHD would lay with the ministry of external affairs, working in close cooperation with the ministry of home affairs and in consultation with the Assam government. Finally, previously convicted or detained persons had been released, and only a very few minor incidents of violence were still occurring. Yet no de-grouping of villages had hitherto been undertaken.[71] It was then the home minister Pant who introduced the Bill for the administrative unification of the Tuensang tribal area and the NHD in parliament and the motion was adopted.[72]

By May 1958 the Nagas seemed intent to carry their struggle into Assam. Armed Nagas operated in the districts of United Mikir, Cachar and Sibsagar and GOI declared the whole of the former, and parts of the second and third to be 'disturbed areas'.[73] When martial law was declared under the name of *The Armed Forces*

(Assam and Manipur) Special Powers Bill (1958), this was criticised by the members of the *Rajya Sabha* for its prolonged duration (without name and legalisation, martial law had been already practised in the Naga hills since 1956), or on the grounds that it might lead to loss of control over the military. But Nehru in his final statement in that debate made it clear that measures like these were the normal tools of any state, otherwise Fascism would be the inevitable outcome.[74]

In September 1958 news came through that Phizo had made his way to East Pakistan, and was for the moment in Dacca. It was evident that Phizo sought to relate his case to the outside world, but Nehru cautioned the *Lok Sabha* saying that Phizo had been hitherto unsuccessful, and that there was no danger that the issue of Naga independence would be taken up in the United Nations.[75] Later that month questions were answered by Lakshmi Menon regarding the number of casualties, and Menon, reading out an obviously prepared chart, divided into Nagas, Indian civilians, and Indian army personnel, killed, wounded or taken prisoner (respectively: 1207, 1235, 1686; 28, 36, 2; 162, 452, Nil), was confronted with the question why the numbers of killed Nagas and those wounded were about the same. One would expect the latter to be several times higher. Menon was not in a position to answer this question, signifying again that the central government was out of the picture and that developments on the scene were reported by the respective agencies, i.e., in this case by the ISF, especially the Indian army. Further, when it was asked whether listing 'Nagas' and 'Indians' meant that the former were not Indians, it was answered that the latter meant Indians other then Nagas, but when it became clear that the Nagas' list did not include any casualties of friendly Nagas, the matter was interrupted.[76] This illustrates the fact that the Indian state, when fighting another people, had to deny it even to itself, which in turn resulted in such surreal debates.

In October new raids by armed Nagas in Manipur were reported,[77] and although it is unclear where the author had obtained his information, a report by *The Times* special correspondent dating from the end of the month described a war-ridden and destitute country, in which the army did not know who was friend and who was foe, mostly the former by day and the latter by night:

> Unable to identify the enemy, Indian soldiers have killed several innocent people on the slightest suspicion. Several villages have been destroyed, and their inhabitants sent to live in bigger villages watched by the Army. But still the enemy remains intractable.[78]

International observers were still banned from verifying the positive picture painted by GOI on the developments in the Naga hills in the months preceding March 1959. The Nagas of 16 tribes had demanded to be united in one unit and that now had been achieved. They were now administered by a number of 'hand-picked' men of the Indian frontier administrative service, a branch of the external affairs ministry and thus removed from the Assam administration. Every year the equivalent of nearly one million English pounds was spent on welfare and economic development. New roads, hospitals and schools were built in collaboration with the 'peaceful Nagas'. Agriculture was again flourishing. Rebels were continuing to respond to the amnesty, and some of them had settled to a quiet life. Re-grouping of villages had been given up, and we may assume that this meant that de-grouping had been effected. Naga volunteers had been armed to protect the villagers from the rebels. Indian army forces had been considerably reduced. All in all, the problem looked to be solved, though it was admitted that there still remained approximately 2,000 – 3,000 rebels at large.[79] The next thing we hear is that six people died, among them four policemen, in an ambush by Nagas near Imphal around the beginning of November 1959.[80]

In 1960 Phizo had reached London, accused India of massive human rights abuses and demanded a fact-finding mission on the situation in the Naga hills. Two days after Phizo's arrival in London, the Nagas resumed their attacks in Dimapur area and interrupted the train services between Gauhati and Dimapur. The Indian defence minister Krishna Menon, then in London, denied all charges made by Phizo, that ISF were undertaking punitive expeditions including the systematic rape of women and the destruction of the crops.[81] At the end of July 1960 Phizo held a press conference in London where he repeated in detail his accusations that would meet the UN definition of genocide.[82] This clearly motivated GOI to do something to regain the initiative and so the foreign affairs subcommittee of the Indian cabinet decided to suggest the setting up of a Naga state as part of the Indian Union. Incidentally a Naga delegation had arrived in Delhi which was just demanding what the foreign affairs subcommittee had proposed.[83] On the first day of August and then again three days later, Nehru informed the *Lok Sabha* that his government had agreed to convey statehood to the former NHD and therewith fulfil the demands of the NPC as presented to him in the form of what would become known as the *16-Points-Agreement*. He further briefed the house that the new state would not be able to pay for its own administration and therefore needed to be heavily subsidised. Nehru had declined an offer by Phizo to cooperate, since he could not agree to his conditions for cooperation and due to Phizo's allegations against the ISF who, except in very few cases, had behaved 'according to high standards and high traditions.' Yet Nehru admitted, when asked, that Jayprakash Narayan had visited Phizo in his hotel, indicating some effort to find a common way. Finally, GOI had negotiated and found an agreement with the elected representatives of the Nagas, meaning the NPC. Some members of the house criticised the name 'Nagaland' of the new union state, finding it too 'outlandish', others asked how it possibly could be that citizens of India could have an agreement with their own government.[84] *The Times* speculated that this concession of statehood would give a strong boost to the demand for a *Punjabi Suba*. Phizo, on his part, had denounced the agreement as null and void, since the NPC was not representative, and before any agreement could be reached, a joint Indo-Naga commission would have to investigate the atrocities committed in the Naga hills and foreign journalists would have to be given free access.[85] The Indian correspondents in London, as well as Nehru, described Phizo as '. . . a sinister but slightly comic mountebank poohpoohing his activities . . .'. The continued ban on foreign journalists from the Naga hills led to the growing suspicion that GOI had something to hide there.[86] The whole chimera of control over and peace in the Naga hills became apparent when the minister of defence Krishna

Menon had to answer questions regarding the shooting down of an Indian air force plane there, bringing to the fore the struggle of the Indian army when, for example, its outposts were besieged in the rough terrain. It had to rely on fighter planes that in turn had to cover supply aircraft that dropped supplies to the beleaguered forces.[87] Obviously the Indian state in all its senses had not completely penetrated these hills, it even had problems holding its bridgeheads there. The increase in Naga attacks was interpreted by GOI as a sign of desperation in the face of the successful negotiations with the NPC, while they were most likely to convey the fact of their irrelevance to the political problem at stake.[88] The continued increase in fighting was admitted and at the same time downplayed by Menon and Nehru in the *Lok Sabha* by a demonstratively displayed nonchalance and a vagueness in their statements ('firing etc.'). It was not only to be made clear that this was to be handled by the military but also that the military had everything under control and therefore did not need closer scrutiny by GOI. Nehru further briefed the parliament that the elections to the interim body (on its way to Nagaland statehood) were nearly completed and that it soon would be able to function (as being advisory to the governor of Assam who was also to be governor of Nagaland). He also admitted that the NPC had asked for the inclusion of all Naga-inhabited land (Manipur hill-areas, Assam bordering Naga hills, parts of NEFA north to the Naga hills), but that GOI had not consented to that.[89]

Simultaneously, there were preparations under way to launch a guided tour to the Naga hills,[90] for the international press, which took place in December 1960. During this one-week tour the Nagas were, despite the close supervision and shielding of the journalists, repeatedly able to bring their demand for independence across to them, at the same time demonstrating their unbroken ability to strike at the ubiquitous ISF even at their stronghold Kohima.[91] Many of those who openly approached the journalists in this way were later reported to have been arrested.[92]

Phizo's renewed proposals, a referendum to assess the Naga population's satisfaction with union statehood, and as a political solution to the continuing war, a qualified sovereignty jointly guaranteed by India, Pakistan and Burma, which did not necessitate UN membership. GOI's reaction was to deny the possibility of negotiations with Phizo or any of his representatives.[93] Pressure mounted on GOI, exerted by officials, army and pro-Indian Nagas, to crush the Naga resistance by force.[94] Prior to this, the Reverend Michael Scott, who had helped Phizo to come to London, and had supported his cause since then, but insisted on not being his representative, had arrived in Delhi, and, although he had not been allowed to proceed to the Naga hills, had been given time to discuss Phizo's standpoint with Nehru.[95] Scott had already acquired a name as a fighter for the weak in Africa,[96] and later would be one of the members of the Nagaland peace mission. There are strong indications that GOI at this point would have been able to negotiate directly with Phizo who still commanded the overwhelming support of the Naga people. The granting of statehood, the declaration of an amnesty, the pouring in of funds, and the calling off of the army – all were done in order to create moderates.[97] In the end this divide-and-rule policy, with the full understanding that the overwhelming majority of the concerned population was averse to such a co-option and creation of a collaborative class, cannot be considered as successful, even when evidently succeeding in fulfilling the ultimate objective to keep the periphery inside the union, for it creates a low-level war zone.

Statehood and peace initiative

In February 1961 the minister of home affairs, Govind Ballabh Pant, admitted in the *Rajya Sabha* an intensification of rebel Naga activities on Manipur territory around the turn of the year, but denied that this indicated the Manipur Nagas' demand for inclusion in the future Nagaland state.[98] In August 1961, the chairman of the interim body, Imkongliba Ao, was assassinated, and was succeeded by T. N. Angami.[99] The guerrilla war kept its momentum, troops continued moving in and this was interpreted by GOI as a sign of growing desperation on the side of the rebels. Thus the intensification of the fighting could be considered as an improvement of affairs, only the eradication of the 'hostiles' had not yet been effected. When pressed, they escaped into Burmese territory. In this way 1961–2 witnessed the absurdity that the escalation of the war was portrayed as a positive development, with its solution always around the corner.[100]

The wider context showed continuous proof of discontent with the federal set-up. The granting of statehood to the Nagas and the decision to declare Assamese an official language lent renewed vigour to the by then already long-standing demand for a separate state by the northeastern hill people, who accused the Assamese administration of aiming at dominance.[101] Support for the picture of a region in which frustration was the main growing factor is lent by the former US ambassador to India, J. K. Galbraith, who was able to visit parts of the Northeast in May 1962 and reported about it in one of his letters to Kennedy:

> My recent travels have taken me up along the Chinese frontier and back to the Burma border. In addition to their better-publicized problems with the Chinese, the Indians are having very serious trouble in living with people within their own borders. This is an area with a large number of ethnically separate groups and all are unhappy in their present relations with the Indians. The Nagas are in open revolt and tie down a couple of divisions but they are only the extreme case. A half-dozen other ethnic or linguistic groups are asking what they can have in the way of independence, autonomy or self-determination.[102]

The internal pacification was accompanied by the external, and Nehru's aggression towards Goa finally shattered India's image as mediator and peace maker in the world, and vehemently brought to the fore the difference between discourse and action since independence:

> Indian military action to safeguard her own interests has never squared with her peaceful international protestations. Kashmir and Hyderabad asserted Indian rights against Pakistan in the chagrin after partition and

without consistent principle. Action against the Nagas, certainly in its early stages, was in no way conciliatory. Goa is a case of ruthless aggression.[103]

The start of 1963 was characterised by the build-up for a massive military campaign to be thrown against the Nagas.[104] According to a comment in *The Observer*, the Indian army, frustrated by the thrashing it had received from the Chinese, but now re-armed by the US and Britain, saw the Naga hills as a welcome training ground to lift the morale of the troops and test the new hardware. The task was the extermination of the Naga guerrillas.[105] At the same time Nehru declined the truce offered repeatedly by the Nagas guerrillas,[106] and Phizo's offer to come to India for talks.[107] This scenario continued,[108] and Nehru, his military and his humiliated population seemed decided at least to bring the Naga campaign to a successful conclusion.[109] GOI went ahead with threatening the Naga population with holding it responsible *in toto*, in case the rebels should not respond to its amnesty offer.[110] Phizo, from London, appealed to the UN to halt the build-up of attacks by the Indian air force, and the ongoing arrangements for putting the populations of 700 villages into concentration camps.[111] At the same time Phizo signalled the Nagas' willingness to accept the verdict of plebiscite, even when carried out under Indian military occupation.[112] The resettlement scheme was confirmed by *The Guardian* that the GOI planned to regroup about 700 villages into '. . . 200 self-sufficient centres to afford greater protection to the people.' The aim was the separation of the fighters from the villagers, the wording '. . . the complete transfer of people from scattered villages to big centres to be raised overnight with full civic amenities' evokes the picture of holiday resorts. However, the report further recorded an intensification of the fighting.[113] The amnesty offer proved to be a failure and the violence was also carried into Manipur. GOI now demanded an unconditional surrender,[114] and the Indian press called for no mercy towards the 'hostiles'. In the meantime it had become known that Nehru had secretly sent his parliamentary secretary S. C. Jamir to London in order to meet Phizo.[115] Nothing, however, came of it, and with the inauguration of the Nagaland state on December 1st 1963 the road was closed for further negotiations with the guerrillas.[116]

The international press was banned during the elections for the new Naga state assembly and they were, according to eyewitness accounts, not only held under close military surveillance, but also accompanied by severe military repression.[117] Then Nehru, in his very last months, reopened the negotiation process in giving his go-ahead to a peace initiative of the Naga Baptist missionaries, the formation of a peace mission that included the foreigner Michael Scott. This initiative would, via the cessation of hostilities,[118] lead to a lasting ceasefire, that for several years brought a lull to the Naga hills.

Conclusion

For Nehru and the Indian National Congress the incorporation of the periphery was a given. For this a near-total consensus prevailed among the Indo-Assamese decision makers and agents, to continue the old garrison state of the dead *raj*. Nehru's pose as, and speech of, a freedom fighter, and the euphoria of a post-colonial and self-determined world had,[119] for quite some time, obscured the survival of the 'garrison state' that now had to fight more viciously than ever. This was so because by then any form of imperialism had lost its legitimacy and concomitantly the idea of self-determination had firmly taken root among the populations the Indian Union set out to subjugate, strengthening their resolve to resist and making any war into a people's war. As a consequence, the 'garrison state' now had to fight the people as a whole, and since it had to pretend to fight on behalf of the very people it was actually fighting, it had to employ terror to deter and criminalise those who resisted.[120] Finally, the resistance of the peripheral people against being included into the Indian Union embittered the Indians, who, after their own long subjection, now took it personally and would not allow anyone to endanger their nationbuilding.

6   The Nagas' war

Introduction

In this chapter, written from the perspective of the Nagas, we will provide evidence that the newly independent Indian state was not exceptional, but conformed with the nation-building policy of many post-colonial states that used massive force with utter brutality to eradicate resistance.[1] Initially it was Assamese expansionism that had already employed terror; this, in turn, made Nehru send the Indian army into the Naga hills which unleashed a ruthlessly brutal military campaign. The Nagas, faced with this onslaught, united to an unprecedented degree, and from then on thoroughly considered themselves as a nation. The Indian 'Other', the enemy, trying to define the Nagas by violence, served as the negative against which unification could be defined.[2] Christianity, far from being a prime mover itself, was employed as a means for mobilisation and unification.[3]

The Nagas were living in a terrain that was difficult to access, and even under British imperialism were only very lightly administered. Upon the departure of the British there existed a small western educated Naga elite. The majority of the Nagas were by then not affected, and in general were neither aware nor did they care, since they lived their life relatively undisturbed, and so did not anticipate any radical changes, if they were aware of any to come at all. This was not much different on the plains, where also the great majority of the people were unaware of the political developments. The main difference in the hills was that any kind of feudalism was consciously rejected; prevalent there was a high political participation in opposition to subordination, an ethos of freedom not known on the plains. However, the educated elite of the Nagas, always in contact with the more traditional leading figures of the different Naga groups, now entered the political process at the worst of all times. The British, trying to uphold the image of an ordered retreat, muddled through as fast as they could, and on their way out, tried to advise the Nagas to remain within the Indian Union. The Indian political elite for its part, inherently split, and in its respective groupings only loosely structured, sent off different and contradicting signals. The Nagas then came around from their demand for immediate independence to one accepting an interim solution, a scheme that had even been suggested by Nehru himself in one of his publications as late as 1944. However, the Nagas, who again received different and conflicting responses, were signalled and assured in their demand, requested to await further negotiations, and, in the end, simply ignored. The Indian state and its agents began its incorporation of the Nagas and their territory. This was the first time the Naga population in general came into direct and lasting contact, not only with this new state and its agents, but for the first time at all with any foreign agency that tried to actually govern them. In the main, the imperial predecessor ruled through the indigenous structures, was rarely present, and for years the British were not seen at all in the villages . But now the Nagas were confronted with the will and actions to effectively incorporate them into the economy and administration of the new polity. As a rule the Assamese and Indians regarded them as inferior; their language and way of life were considered something to be overcome and changed into that of the dominant group, or were not even considered as being capable of assimilation and relegated to the lowest layer of society. The Nagas had to realise that the legal safeguards of their rights were null and void in the reality of state incorporation. Local communities reacted to that in defence of their self-esteem and perceived right to their way of life by either non-cooperation and/or threatening and/or attacking the agents of the new state with words or deeds. The elite, partially engaged in renegotiating their political leeway, was also busy in trying to mobilise and unify those who were perceived as being the bearer of their identity, and to value it positively, in face of all the derogation.[4] It now came to the trajectory towards protracted warfare, as has been sketched in the introduction, and it was this ongoing war of the Indian state against the Nagas as a whole, already under Nehru's premiership, that cemented the Nagas into a nation using Christianity as a distinguishing unifier and determined to fight off of what they saw and still see as an invasion of their land.

Finding one's stand in post-imperial Asia

Thus, in order to understand why the majority of the Nagas supported the guerrilla war, we have to uncover the responsible factors affecting the majority of the people over a considerable period of time. However, the incidents in the Naga hills before and after the Transfer of Power are anything but well documented. This is due to at least three factors. First, the Indian government's success in shielding off, denying and defying its agents' conduct there; second, world opinion's general indifference to the Nagas' fate; and finally, the Nagas' unwillingness to document something that is so obvious and so emotionally important to them in a detailed and systematic way. Horam writes that a reconstruction of the exact course of events proved difficult, since there was rarely any material available concerning this period, and since most of the participants are dead and if they had produced written material, it was lost or destroyed in the fighting of the following years.[5] This notwithstanding, the material I have laid out here should sufficiently support my argument, but can only be considered as the beginning of further examination of that rather under-researched field.

Again, notes taken, and documents written by British officials, as well the exchange of communications among them and others, or simply received and stored, as in our case by W. G. Archer, are for us, a major source of information on the developments in the Naga hills in the years around the Transfer of Power. We have evidence that in the first phase, when it had become known that the end of the *raj* was imminent, the Nagas were clearly poised towards regaining their former freedom. In this way, at the end of December 1946, Sa'adulla the former prime minister of Assam tells of a delegation of Nagas that had come to tell him that the Nagas were determined to become independent again following the British departure. They also told him that they had already conveyed this message to Bardoloi, the then prime minister of Assam, who had toured the Naga hills during the previous month. Sa'adulla quoted one of the leaders as saying the following:

> We fought the British in 1879 and we will fight anyone who attempts to rule over us. The British conquered our country by force of arms, now that they are going to quit, the land is ours, and we propose to govern the hills as best as we can.[6]

Though it is not specified who the Nagas were, except the reference to them as 'leaders' on the basis of the quote, we might well assume that they came from Khonoma. A further indicator for this is that Archer, in succession to the above, has added a quote by Pawsey who must have said that it was the Christian clan of Khonoma that was in favour of complete independence, that another of the Khonoma clans was indifferent and the third against independence.[7]

The NNC, so Archer wrote at the end of 1946, was almost exclusively composed of government servants and by then the only political mouthpiece of the Nagas. Hitherto Pawsey, the DC, had always been consulted by the NNC for advice but this had become a problem for him under the new political situation. Archer understood the demand for complete independence as a tactical, bargaining point, starting with independence but aiming at effective autonomy. The approaching end of British rule had surprised everyone. The NNC thereupon instantaneously materialised, and in Archer's view, the absence of Pawsey (on leave) was given as the reason for the lack of unity among the Angamis, who had split into western, eastern and southern Angamis.[8] However, Archer's view of the affair was most likely tailored to the British view. The data suggests that it was more likely the following: the Nagas hearing of the imminent departure of the British decided again to be independent, since they had been before. Then it had been the British officers who had talked them into changing their stand, and so the Nagas agreed somehow, but not unanimously, on the interim solution by February 1947. This in turn was portrayed by the British as Nagas' traditional divisiveness.[9]

On 13th January 1947 Archer tells us something about Kevichusa Angami who came to tea. Kevichusa had served as sub-deputy magistrate and in this position had been transferred 17 times; until 1942, he had always had been posted outside the Naga hills. He had thus, as had many others of the Naga elite, a clear idea of the Northeast. Kevichusa told Archer that hitherto all work had been done by the tribal councils, and that it was only for the cabinet mission that the NNC had been founded.[10] He continued to tell Archer about the ongoing divisions among the

Nagas. Khonoma and the Western Angamis, for example, were in favour of complete independence while the rest were not sure whether this could be achieved. Simultaneously no one had faith in the guarantees given by the Indian National Congress after Nehru's directive to the governor of Assam to remove the *Chin Hills Regulation* negated that. The NNC was about to protest but faced the problem that nearly all its members were in government service and thus blocked from political work. Another point of concern was the lack of any Naga representation in either the constituent assembly or the advisory committee; this made the Nagas fear that the constitution would consequently not take their needs into consideration.[11]

By February-March the NNC sent a memorandum to the British prime minister, with copies to Simon and Churchill, asking to set up a 10-year interim government, during which they could develop themselves politically and decide afterwards whether they would prefer complete independence or some arrangement with the Indian Union. The British in Delhi and London, however, had decided to ignore the NNC.[12] The NNC also wanted to represent the tribal areas, i.e., the by then still unadministered part of the Naga hills, yet were discouraged from doing this by Archer. This had been so since the constitutional adviser Rau had recommended to Mills to treat the excluded and tribal areas as separate cases.[13] While the Nagas frantically worked for a unified stand, British and Indians now both suggested separate solutions and stressed the Nagas' divisiveness.

On April 11th the NNC met to choose five members that should start to work on a draft constitution for the Naga hills. One of the appointed members was Mayangnokcha and the work on the constitution was to begin on May 1st in Kohima. By then the '. . . solidarity of the Naga Nation . . .' had been decided by the NNC as '. . . its ultimate goal.'[14] Three days later Aliba Imti was nominated instead of Mayangnokcha. The Angamis, according to Pawsey, were afraid the Aos might go over to the Congress, and were increasingly annoyed by the Assam governor's appeasement towards Congress. Furthermore, it had already become clear that the subcommittee would not be able to go to Wakching to meet there the representatives of the tribes living in the tribal areas, hence they were asked to come to Mokokchung. The representatives were Hopongki for the Sangtams, Imlong for the Changs, and Chingkai for the Konyaks.[15] All of which were by then still completely independent.[16]

By 22nd April 1947 the constituent assembly informed the hill people of the decision to grant independence to India not later than June 1948 as announced by the British Prime Minister Attlee in the house of commons. At the same time, the coming of the subcommittee of the advisory committee to the constituent assembly was announced with the previously mentioned statement that they did not come with a pre-arranged plan, but at the same time clearly limiting the scope to a solution inside the legislation of the province of Assam.[17] This memo was not distributed to the tribal area, but forwarded to the '. . . representative people and bodies . . .' as the secretary to the governor of Assam Adams expressed it.[18]

The subcommittee on May 7th cancelled Mokokchung and Wakching, and announced its arrival at Kohima on 19th of May, staying two further days.[19] The

NNC, the same day, dispatched this information to the different tribal councils, and to Pawsey and Archer, and announced that all members were to come to Kohima on May 16th 1947.[20] A day later a provisional programme was formalised that showed the sequence in which the different people and parties were to meet the subcommittee[21] The tribal area groups like the Konyaks, Phoms and Kalyo Kengus could not be contacted and thus had to go unheard by the subcommittee. Yimchunger and Sangtams had drafted memoranda that could be presented, and the Changs were represented by Imlong. In general the restriction of the subcommittee's visit to Kohima seemed to limit the scope of representation considerably.[22]

On May 12th Archer conveyed his opinion on the position of the tribes in the hitherto unadministered tract (mentioned were the Phoms, Kalyo Kengyus, and Konyaks) to Pawsey, since they were unable to make themselves heard by the subcommittee:

> So far as I know the tribal areas (except the Konyaks) want to be an integral part of the Naga State and at the same time [underlining in the original] get lavish grants from the centre. The Konyaks aren't at all on grants they want to go on head-taking but have no objection to forming a single Naga unit provided the first two points are observed.[23]

Naga decisions were reached by consensus not by majority, so that might have been responsible for the conflicting conditions – if they were conflicting at all. A unified Naga state would have been possible, as would have been grants, if not from Assam, then from the centre, if simply to keep and help develop that area in exchange for the right to station troops at the border for strategic purposes. The question of headhunting (as shown in chapter two), intimately connected to that of political autonomy and power, as well as to the discourse on the tribes' right to independence, could have been safely left to the Nagas to sort out.

During the course of the first half of 1947, Archer believed he was witnessing an increasing demand for complete independence among the Nagas: the wish to get a pan-Naga state, including the Tirap frontier tract, the NHD, the Naga hills tribal area, and the forests that in the past had been transferred to the Sibsagar district. Archer felt a growing uncertainty about the intentions of the central government, which was showing an unwillingness to take into consideration any sharing of resources with Assam. He also remained unconvinced about the funding and control of a future Naga state, especially with hindsight to what had happened in the tribal areas.[24]

Overall the opinion among the Nagas at that point did have a propensity towards complete independence and the incorporation into this scheme of all Naga inhabited areas. But, a reluctance to any common solution with Assam, a growing distrust toward the forthcoming Indian government, and finally, for Archer, too much naivety in their belief of being capable of creating a viable state, persuaded Archer to remain inside the liberal tradition legitimising imperialism. The Nagas, however, although they had hitherto been only lightly, certainly not effectively, administered, had been viable before the British arrival, and they had no reason to believe they could not be so in the future. This standpoint was not, as Archer saw, a new development but simply a return to an earlier one.

By the end of June, Pawsey sent a message to Archer telling him, among other things, that the negotiations between Hydari and the Nagas were not going well.[25] In Archer's papers we find a draft of the *Nine-Points-Agreement* resulting out of these negotiations, that would have given the Nagas wide judicial, executive and legislative powers. It said the Nagas were to come under a DC appointed by the governor of Assam but otherwise were free to administer themselves what they could pay for themselves. Point six ensured the re-transfer of forests from Sibsagar and Nowgong districts back to the Nagas and to bring, as far as possible, all Nagas into one administrative unit for which this agreement then would be in force. These two points remain important demands of the Nagas until today. Point eight granted that both *The Chin Hills Regulations* and *The Bengal Eastern Frontier Regulations* would remain in force, and thus contradicted Nehru's former directive to the governor. Nehru, however, had sent Hydari, to the Naga hills with far-reaching powers and the order to achieve an agreement. The final point would develop into the main bone of contention between the NNC and the governor.[26]

The Naga representatives rejected the recommendations made by the subcommittee to the advisory committee, due to the fact that they did not treat the NHD as independent, but as part of Assam, with far-reaching powers for the governor of Assam, among them, for example, power to dissolve the NNC. Instead the Naga delegates referred to the agreement reached shortly before with Hydari and asked that it should be presented to the constituent assembly for acceptance as basis for future relations between India-Assam and the Naga hills. The subcommittee, chaired by Bardoloi, declined and referred to Attlee's statement in the House of Commons that the excluded areas would be part of Assam.[27] The incongruent policy took its toll and in mid-July the NNC had, according to Pawsey '... a minor split and the Extreme independent party have broken away.' Pawsey, to be sure, perceived this as a very positive development. For him those who had broken away were a tiny minority, led by the Merhema *khel* of Khonoma.[28]

On 30th July Archer received a confidential memo – sent from Adams (the advisor to the governor of Assam) on 18th July, and forwarded by Pawsey – in which he learned that Nehru had congratulated Hydari on his success in the negotiations at Kohima (and Imphal), and that Nehru had forwarded the papers (i.e., the *Nine-Points-Agreement*) to the constituent assembly and the state department, and though nothing had been decided yet, Adams was optimistic. Pawsey asked Archer to inform Mayangnokcha.[29] This contradicted the decision of the sub-committee, which had decided to ignore the agreement, and confirmed the confused state of affairs. In accord with that is Pawsey's observation on the Shillong administration that, around the beginning of August, descended into chaos, making it unlikely to receive any orders from that direction.[30]

Simultaneously, a Naga delegation had been in Delhi, trying to see Nehru, who referred them to Ramadhyani, who in turn refused to amend the ninth clause of the agreement with the same argument as the subcommittee, i.e., that all hill tribes should be receiving the same conditions. Nehru seemed to have said that the agreement was between the Nagas and the governor of Assam, hence only the latter was able to alter it. When on this point one Naga delegate stated that the Nagas then will have it their way, Nehru answered that, and now I quote Archer's notes '. . . India could not be split into a 100 pieces – Nagas got angry with him – Nehru said if they fought we all . . . [unreadable]'.[31]

On the very day India achieved her independence, Imti Aliba and Kumbho Angami, for the NNC, sent communication to Hydari, following a telegram dispatched the previous day, to stress again that the Nagas could only be part of the Indian Union if the *Nine-Points-Agreement* was accepted with the ninth clause modified.[32] This would leave less room for ambivalence and clearly conveyed the freedom to secede without actually naming it. Hydari refused the alteration of the ninth clause of the agreement with the following wording:

> I therefore propose that the wording of the understanding reached at Kohima which I have scrupulously followed and the substance of which has been accepted both by the Prime Minister of the Indian Union and of Assam should be maintained.
>
> I hope the Naga Leaders will accept this position. If they do not then I am afraid we must maintain the status quo until they do or until the constituent Assembly passes the Constitution Act whichever is earlier.[33]

Shortly before that, confusing the picture further, the Kohima and Kacha Nagas had declared their independence and left for Shillong, probably to see Hydari. The other Nagas, for the time being, were stuck with the *Nine-Points-Agreement* with the meaning of a ten-year interim period, that, as we have seen, had been declined by Hydari. On the very day of the Transfer of Power, the Indian ceremonies were boycotted by the Nagas in Kohima, instead a Naga flag was hoisted by Mrs Kevichusa and only taken down after Pawsey had convinced her in the course of long negotiations. The hauling down of the Naga flag, however, triggered the angry reaction of a Naga crowd. The civil surgeon, obviously Indian, hoisted an Indian flag outside his house which was immediately hauled down by the Nagas. Naga government servants refused to take the new oaths of allegiance. A day earlier the Khonoma group, according to Archer, had sent out telegrams to declare Naga independence, and Archer was not sure whether Pawsey had intercepted them all. Hydari then also revised his former decision and declared his willingness to accept the revised form of the ninth clause but stated it would not convey the right to secede from the Indian Union after the lapse of ten years. Finally, Khonoma seemed not to know, again, according to Archer, what to do after their declaration of independence and came round to agree to the ten-year interim period.[34]

In the ten days between August 24th and September 2nd Hydari propagated the fusion between hills and plains and Pawsey had set up a committee to work on a Naga constitution. Aliba Imti was angry with that and that Nehru had announced the *Chin Hills Regulation* – that controlled the movements into the hills – had been ended, without consultation with local authorities. Archer mused it happened for party political purposes.[35] Shortly afterwards, Aliba Imti enquired of Hydari whether his refusal to modify clause nine was his last word.[36] Three days later, Aliba Imti, in a communication to the chairman of the tribal council of the Aos, wrote that he had anticipated the resistance of the Indians towards the modification of the ninth clause of the agreement, and therefore he strongly advocated action:

> (1) Decision should be made in favour of non-cooperation with existing govt. (2) One month ultimatum be given to the govt. of India. (3) From the beginning of Nov. '47, the govt. servants of Naga people should be ready to lay down their pens.[37]

The same day Aliba Imti wrote to Nehru and insisted '. . . upon the recognition of our "Claim" submitted to you during our New Delhi discussion',[38] a reminder, so to speak, to Nehru, held in strong words, but also expressing awareness of the fact that Nehru also had other things (the Nagas were aware of the occurrences in Kashmir and Punjab) to do. The 'claim' Imti brought forward for recognition was the modification of clause nine.[39]

At the beginning of November, the NNC dispatched an *Ultimatum to the Government of India* that was addressed to Nehru. This paper gives us an important contemporaneous recapitulation of recent developments from the NNC's point of view. It said the NNC had submitted a memo to GOI on 19th February 1947, requesting an interim solution of ten years with an option to secede after ten years. Yet there was no reply, so after the lapse of three months they re-sent the memo with further details of the envisioned scheme, in essence demanding autonomy plus the option for independence after the interim had passed. The same memo was also submitted to the subcommittee with whom the NNC met on 20th May 1947. Yet the subcommittee had its own scheme and was not willing to go beyond it, hence the NNC rejected it. This resulted in the governor of Assam Hydari journeying to the Naga hills to negotiate with the NNC and the outcome was the *Nine-Points-Agreement*, without the amendment granting the right to secede after ten years, and thus not agreed unanimously by all Nagas. A minority still wanted to have this amendment made, and finally the NNC decided that it would have what in the end had already been the original demand. Furthermore the NNC had been threatened by the Indian leadership, and when the NNC asked for this amendment, its members received a disappointing treatment from Nehru and the Indian National Congress. This having been so, the document concludes, the NNC had no choice but to issue an ultimatum of 30 days to GOI, after which the Nagas would stop cooperating with India and would secede from the Indian Union on 6th December 1947.[40] Aliba Imti then informed the tribal councils that until an answer was received by GOI, people should be forbidden from working on tea-plantations or similar plains-holdings, and that Nagas living outside the Naga hills should be kept informed of the situation and were called upon to follow closely the developments between the Nagas and GOI.[41] Eleven days later an even more urgent telegram left the NNC office:

> 'National Council sits 26 Kohima. All members and public leaders must attend without fail. Situation very critical. Meeting may last days. Sd/Kumbho.'[42]

By the beginning of December 1947 the NNC seemed to have agreed on December 31st as the ultimatum to leave the Indian Union.[43]

In the meantime the governor of Assam assured the Nagas that the proposals to the constitutional assembly would be drafted in cooperation with the Nagas, and that a draft should be ready by 20th January 1948.[44] Six months later, on June 22nd 1948, a delegation of Nagas asked Hydari if the agreement was still valid and would be implemented. Thereupon Hydari and Bardoloi gave them written assurances that this had never been put into question.[45] Contrary to these assurances, the Assamese and Indians continued to build up their administration,[46] and by November 9th 1949, the chief minister of Assam, Gopinath Bordoloi, informed a NNC delegation that GOI never had accepted the Hydari agreement. This was taken by the NNC as a betrayal. Those inside the NNC, who had hitherto favoured an interim solution, now lost ground, and a clear majority now swayed towards immediate independence.[47] Alemchimba sees the NNC at this point unanimously behind the demand for independence.[48]

The takeover

In the previous chapter we noted the scant documentation of events from 1948 to 1955, when regular fighting had finally started. We have also learned there that the build-up of the Assamese administration effectively only started in 1950 or later. Then, however, the massive influx of foreigners that looked down on the Nagas as savages further aggrieved the Nagas and only strengthened their resolve to be independent. Only administrators who could be spared elsewhere were sent into the Naga hills, and those in turn tried to get reposted to the plains as fast as they could. The attempted incorporation of the people was accompanied by the attempted penetration of the land with the help of a massive material onslaught. *The Times* saw this in line with other post-colonial states:

> Like other newly independent countries, India was very keen to consolidate her territory and bring it under uniform administration. From Delhi, thousands of miles away, and from not-so-distant Shillong, administrators were dispatched to the land of the Nagas, where the British had mostly left the tribes to look after themselves. The task of the administrators (who had no knowledge of tribal society) was to raise the primitive Nagas to the level of the Indians, so that they could enjoy the same benefits as other citizens of the country. This miracle of transformation was to be accomplished as soon as possible so that the Nagas would cease to feel different from the Indians and would give up their demand for a separate homeland.[49]

Information abounds that the Nagas strongly resented the takeover of the Assam state administration and its officials.[50]

Of utmost significance was Zaphu Angami Phizo who, in June 1946, returned to Nagaland, and later on would become the 'voice of the Nagas'.[51] Although he had been exiled in London for some time, while he was alive he remained, for most of the Nagas, their only leader. Described as 'Moses of his people' or 'father of Naga nationalism', he unified the Nagas, who previously had been divided into clans and tribes, and he '. . . spelt out loud and clear what was in the heart of many Nagas, namely, an independent Naga nation.'[52] Phizo, who was born in Khonoma, was sent into an exile of his choice because of anti-British statements. He went to Rangoon. Phizo was made to understand that he only could return after the British left the Naga hills. When in 1942 the Japanese army and Subhas Chandra Bose's INA marched into Burma, the Japanese asked Phizo and his brother whether they wanted to cooperate with them, in return for Naga independence. Phizo agreed and consequently was admitted into the INA.[53] After the Japanese had been driven out of Burma Phizo became a British prisoner of war, and following his release in 1946, he returned to Kohima, where T. Sakhrie introduced him into the NNC. Sakhrie was then the general secretary of the NNC, and came from the same *khel* of Khonoma as Phizo.[54] The *khel* was that of Merhema, which had a long tradition of a dominant position in the Naga hills, as well as of resistance against outside forces.[55]

In 1948 Phizo withdrew from the NNC and founded the People's Independence League (PIL). He did this to consolidate his position as a leader, and to push the demand for a sovereign Nagaland that was to include the NHD, the Tuensang frontier area, but also all the other Naga-inhabited areas of India and Burma.[56] To build up a national consciousness, Phizo and his staff unceasingly toured the Naga hills, organised the youth in the Naga Youth Movement (NYM) and the women in the Naga Women's Society (NWS). In every village, people from all walks of life started party cells, to support the party and to which the villagers could come and discuss matters with the party workers. The councils of all levels (village, mountain chain or tribe) backed the party.[57] The same year Phizo was detained on grounds of anti-Indian subversive activities, and on his release unanimously elected President of the NNC on December 11th 1950.[58] Following his election he filled most of the important positions in the NNC with his own people from the PIL.[59]

In 1950 Phizo met Nehru and informed him about the decision of the Nagas not to join the Indian Union. Nehru rejected this claim, and at the same time began to claim the NNC only represented a small western-influenced minority, the overwhelming majority of the Nagas, however, resolutely wanted to be part of the Indian Union. Thus Phizo reached the decision to carry out a plebiscite.[60] In a letter to the Indian president, dated January 1st 1951, Phizo invited the Indian government to send observers to monitor the planned plebiscite.[61] GOI ignored the invitation; the plebiscite, however, commenced on May 16th 1951, and brought to an end in August of the same year.[62] It was carried out by the two youth organisations NYM and NWS, touring all villages. Voting was mostly by thumbprint, considered as being more meaningful and credible, and therefore meant to pre-empt possible accusations of fraud.[63] The plebiscite resulted in 99 per cent in favour of independence, weighed several kilograms and was sent to the Indian president.[64] GOI, in the end, refused to recognise the result, for Phizo and the NNC, however, it presented an unequivocal confirmation of their policy and a strong mandate for their mission.[65] In December 1951 a delegation of the NNC confronted Nehru with the result of the plebiscite. Nehru called the demand for independence absurd and warned the delegation about the possible violent result of their policy.[66]

The plebiscite showed for the first time the organising capacity of the NNC, which was demonstrated again during the general election of 1952,[67] resulting in a total boycott:

> . . . the government went ahead with the election arrangements and the entire election paraphernalia was made ready, electoral rolls were prepared, polling booths were set up, ballot boxes were made and Returning Officers were stationed. Nagas, on the other hand, were indifferent to the goings on and went about their daily work with studied calm and the whole election show proved to be a mockery as a result of the election that never was.[68]

On March 11th 1952 another delegation of the NNC, led by Phizo, set out to see Nehru, who then lost his composure, shouting at the Nagas that they would never get their own state. The NNC told Nehru that they were determined to continue their fight for independence through non-violent means, following the examples of Gandhi and Christ.[69]

The new chief minister of Assam, Bishnuram Medhi, openly propagated the Assamisation of all minorities, if necessary by force,[70] and he had the full support of the Indian foreign ministry.[71] Medhi's attitude towards minorities was well known throughout the hills, consequently, during his visit to Mokokchung in 1950 he was greeted by demonstrations.[72] In the aftermath of the 1952 elections boycott, following the last meeting with Nehru, the Nagas started their civil disobedience campaign; they refused to pay taxes, the *gaonburas* returned their red coats – symbols of their official function; government servants left their offices and students their schools.[73] To the Assam administration this was equal to an open rebellion, and it reacted with a massive deployment of armed forces into the Naga hills, convinced, according to the insider Rustomji, that these 'savages' would only understand the language of force.[74]

On October 18th of the same year, following reports that the Assam police had tortured a Naga boy to death, a demonstration was staged in Kohima, in the course of which one demonstrator was overrun by an Indian police officer and the formerly peaceful demonstration took a violent turn. During the ensuing fighting a highly respected Angami judge, who intended to arbitrate, was shot and killed.[75] Consequently the atmosphere was already heated between the Nagas and the government when Nehru and his Burmese colleague Thankin U Nu visited Kohima on the 30th March 1953. Yet this was exactly why the Nagas welcomed the visit. Representatives of all tribal councils and other leading personalities from all over the Naga hills came to Kohima. They saw it as a favourable opportunity to convey to Nehru their unanimous desire for freedom and drew up a memorandum.[76] The then DC of the NHD Barkati, however, did not allow them to present it to Nehru, or even to utter anything during the visit; they should rather be quiet and listen to what the two premiers had to say.[77] The Nagas assumed that Barkati's orders were

Nehru's, so they left the place chosen for the visit at exactly the moment when Nehru and U Nu appeared. Furthermore, as sign of their disapproval, the Nagas slapped their backsides while leaving.[78] Nehru was furious and held Medhi responsible for the fiasco, who in turn sacked Barkati on the spot.[79] Thereafter the Indian government decided to give Medhi a free hand and warrants were issued to arrest eight NNC-leaders.[80] Thereupon nearly the whole leadership of the NNC went underground, for the time being, and the Assam police shortly afterwards began to raid one village after the other.[81] The numbers of the randomly arrested, of the tortured and the sexually harassed and raped women increased.[82] More and more Assam police units were moved into the Naga hills,[83] and once in the country, they forced the population at gunpoint to carry their equipment, a practice legalised by the Assamese government in September 1953.[84]

All authors agree about the consequences of the police operations: for Alemchimba they were confirmation of the NNC-propaganda.[85] Panmei,[86] Luithui and Haksar[87] and Horam[88] see in them the reason why so many went underground and why the Nagas now, once and for all, developed '. . . a burning resentment against India and Indians . . .'.[89] The situation in the NHD, from September 1953 onwards, had already been characterised by the *Forced Labour Regulation* (issued in September 1953), and the introduction of the *Standing Order* from October 1953, that both took the jurisdiction out of the hands of the local councils; in new emergency laws; in thefts and looting committed by ISF of the houses, gardens, fields and firewood of the Nagas; in the treatment of the Nagas by the ISF; in the disrespect towards Naga traditions and religions; in raids on villages and the terrorising of the population; in the tearing down of house roofs, and the peeling of the bark from the trees, in order to kill them; in the torture of detainees, and the encouragement by the authorities to do so; and finally, in the order to the ISF to rape Naga women when and whereever possible.[90]

By autumn 1953 the Naga population had rallied behind the NNC, and the civil administration had collapsed.[91] By 1954 the underground had spread into the Tuensang frontier division (TFD).[92] India had already sent troops into this previously unadministered area in 1948, in order to build up its administration. The Nagas who were living there saw that as an invasion.[93] So it is not surprising that the propaganda of the NNC fell on fertile ground there. Phizo tried to win over the tribes and their chiefs of the TFD – the Konyak, Chang, Phom and Yimchunger – for the NNC. On September 18th 1954 he proclaimed 'The People's Sovereign Republic of Free Nagaland', with Hong Khin, as president. According to Nibedon, this government had the full support of the population of the TFD.[94]

In 1954 the Assam Rifles began to undertake comprehensive military operations in Tuensang. The paramilitaries used village rivalries[95] to portray themselves as ordering forces and the whole affair as an atavistic tribal war. On 7th of July 1954 a contingent of Assam Rifles surrounded the village of Chingmei and opened fire: 31 inhabitants survived with bullet wounds, the rest were killed, among them old people and children. On November 15th Assam Rifles-units raided the village of Yingpang, killing 60 men, women and children. Twelve days later the village Chingmei was bombarded again and this time completely destroyed.[96] In March

1955 units of the Assam Rifles were attacked in the TFD, as retribution for the destruction of villages in the Aghueto area. On 20th July 1955 a state of emergency was imposed in the TFD.[97]At this time the whole leadership of the NNC had resurfaced and was no longer underground; they denied having anything to do with the unrest. On August 15th 1955 Phizo and other NNC-members met Medhi in Shillong. They called upon the government to stop the fighting and handed over a declaration in which the NNC once more confirmed their commitment to non-violence.[98] The ISF brought the situation in the TFD under control,[99] for the time being at least.

At the beginning of 1955 a state of emergency was also imposed on the Mokokchung sub-district.[100] According to Yonuo a NNC-delegation met again with Medhi in October 1955, to discuss the possibility of a peaceful solution, yet without result since Medhi was determined to solve this by force.[101] If this is correct, then this meeting would have taken place after regular fighting had already started, and considerable acts of violence had already been meted out.[102] January 1956 marks the beginning of widespread armed conflict, and on January 31st of the same year a state of emergency was imposed on the whole of the Naga hills.[103] Nibedon saw the reasons for the uprising in the conduct of the Assam police and Assam Rifles units, who had been '. . . on a rampage . . .'[104] and had spread terror.[105] In this way they drove elite and the majority of the Nagas alike,[106] into armed resistance.[107] The Naga armed forces of the soon reached a strength of approximately 15,000 troops and overwhelmed the Assamese paramilitaries.[108] On March 22nd 1956 the NNC set up the Naga federal government (NFG) in Phensiyu, in the Rengma area, replacing the Hong Khin government. The NFG passed a constitution and declared Nagaland as a sovereign republic.[109] Nehru was outraged. In his eyes the Nagas were about to endanger the nation-building project that had just begun. He ordered the army to quell the uprising,[110] and on April 2nd 1956 Nehru handed over the responsibility for NHD to the army.[111] The army moved into the Naga hills and occupied the most important centres.

War

The village diary of Mokokchung tells a tale of a systematic terror campaign against the villagers at the hands of the paramilitary Assam police battalion starting with the destruction of houses and beatings on 26 April 1955; rapes on 14 May; destruction of 200 granaries and all of the fields in the same month; further destruction of the harvest on September 9; the rape of five women, including two aged 13 and 14 and beatings of a couple in the police station, leading to the death of the man in the course of the week. On 29 April the following year the Assam police battalion, now reinforced by the 9th Gurkha Rifles, set ablaze the whole village including the granaries; several villagers were arrested and severely beaten and two men, among them one 60 years old, were taken away and shot, their bodies were never handed over to their families. On 17 May 1956, a young man from the village was shot, as was one 13-year old girl on 14 July, and on 10 December, the Assam police battalion attacked the village, killed two boys aged 14 and 13, and injured one aged 15. The situation then worsened and became more comprehensive.[112] The report constitutes a meticulous description of human rights violations that even today are endemic in India, and part of a wider culture of violence in South Asia.[113]

From an autobiographical account of a member of the 3rd Gurkha Rifles, we receive additional evidence that regular troops had also been sent into the NHD as early as September 1955. The Gurkha and his colleagues were told it would only be for a few days, but in the end they stayed on for two years, and were involved in regular combat.[114] For *The Times*, fighting started in February 1956 with devastating effect:

> ... Indian troops and the rebel Naga tribes are now engaged in a game of death. Terror has paralysed life there. Fields lie fallow. In the orchards, orange trees are drying up for want of care and the ground is littered with decayed fruit. Most of the region's 350,000 inhabitants, whose villages have been regrouped, degrouped, and regrouped again, are destitute, living on rations the Indian troops give them every third or fifth day.[115]

However, despite these harsh measures, and despite the continuous influx of troops, not much had changed by 1958, since:

> ... the Indian Army does not know who is a loyal Naga and who is a rebel; they look the same. By day they are loyal, and by night they join the rebels, supply them with food and clothes, and tend their wounded. Unable to identify the enemy, Indian soldiers have killed several innocent people on the slightest suspicion. Several villages have been destroyed, and their inhabitants sent to live in bigger villages watched by the Army. But still the enemy remains intractable.[116]

It has to be stressed that we do not know on what basis these newspaper reports were written, whether they were based on accounts of eyewitnesses to whom the journalist had access or from where else he had his information. Until then only Nagas and Indians had access to the war zone. However, the more time progressed the more concerned the reports on the situation became. Further proof of the severity of the situation, and certainly contributing to its further deterioration, was the legislation of *The Armed Forces (Assam and Manipur) Special Powers Bill, 1958*. This, however, was simply a geographic extension of the previously granted special powers to the Indian army in the NHD in 1956. In 1957 it was extended to the combined area of NHD and Naga hills tribal area. Special powers meant in essence the declaration of martial law, and the bill of 1958 was simply the post-facto legalisation of an already established practice. That one normally does not have martial law on a permanent basis was noted back then by P. N. Sapru, during the debate in the *Rajya Sabha*: 'I can understand you having martial law and martial law is, after all, a temporary law. Martial law you don't have for three years; you don't have for two years; you don't have for a year.'[117] Further support is to be drawn from three case studies documented by IWGIA, telling tales of whole tribal populations going to live in the jungle form 1956 to 1959 in order to escape the Indian army, permanently on the run, malnourished and sick. By 1959 they returned, but still the work in the village and on the fields was done by women, children and elderly people while the men were fighting in the jungle until the ceasefire of 1964.[118]

Gavin Young of *The Observer*, who in early 1961 travelled illegally through the Naga hills with the Naga resistance, recorded some of the stories in which the Nagas told their reasons to fight. Young tells us the following about what was told him by a lieutenant P. Vikura from the Naga home guard:

> His face was impassive as he told me his story. His father had been bayoneted to death by Assamese riflemen of the Indian Army in 1956, and his mother gaoled. Vikura, who was eighteen at the time, was at school in central Nagaland. He and two hundred other students ran off into the jungle when the Indians began to organise Naga students into labour squads. He has been with the Home Guard ever since.[119]

While GOI, in its propaganda, played on incidents of conflict between single Naga villages, thus trying to portray a scenario of civil war in which the Indian forces would enter as arbitrating and finally ordering forces, in reality its agents and agency tried everything to bring about a field of infighting factions and irreconcilable standpoints. Gavin Young in 1961 talked to a young Naga who in the late 1950s was forced to join the village guards that were supposedly created to protect the Naga population from the 'hostiles'. In 1959, he and 58 others were commanded into a village suspected of collaboration with those demanding independence. In this operation he became witness to the lengthy torturing of five villagers. Furthermore, in an earlier operation conjointly with the Assam Rifles, he had to watch the repeated rape of a Naga girl and the battering of the male population ordered by an Indian officer. Thus, he later ran away to the Naga army, bringing with him six Indian rifles.[120]

By November 1960 access for the international press to the Naga hills was still denied, so when judging the situation there, Ursula Graham Bower, an anthropologist working among the Nagas during the *raj*, had to rely on Indian sources. Hence she was quoting the Indian journalist Easwar Sagar of *The Madras Hindu*, who had been able to tour the Naga hills for one week and whom Bower quotes with his description of reaching Kohima:

> The newcomer is instantly aware of the numerous eyes and ears which are sharply tuned to look for trouble: the vehicles in convoy with escorts out to front and rear, the soldiers in the road protection parties guarding the bad points on the route, the innumerable check-posts, the two sides of the road denuded of all trees and high grass which could provide cover for the sniper, the armoured cars which patrol the streets of Kohima . . .[121]

For Bower this was proof enough that the 'hostiles' were active at the very nerve centre of Indian power in the Naga hills, for which a small guerrilla force would suffice to keep the 30,000 Indian troops engaged. Furthermore, she tried to make sense of reports of outbreaks of violence in the very opposite and extreme corners of the Naga hills, the north-eastern among the Sangtams and in the south-western close to Tamenlong. For her these were expressions of dissatisfaction. Finally, she took from the Indian press the information about the 'grouping' of village populations into 'concentration camps' in which the detained people had to live on half rations. Bower at this point of time has understanding for the GOI's policy and applied measures.[122]

When finally a group of 12 foreign correspondents were allowed on a strictly guided tour for the international and national press into the Naga hills by the end of 1960, *The Times* correspondent understood from the omnipresent ISF and their patrolling in double strength, that the Naga army was still able to operate. Moreover, the 'overground' supporters were repeatedly able to approach the press corps with their statements, accusing the ISF of committing atrocities, denouncing the NPC of being Indian puppets, and reasserting their determination to achieve complete independence.[123] In a follow-up article *The Times* correspondent narrated how everywhere on their tour, despite close supervision by officials, the people told them of their wish to be free, and his conclusion was that all of them wanted to be as independent as possible from any country, and that the difference between those in the NPC and those in the NFG was one of degree, the former did not believe in the possibility of sovereignty, and thus tried to get as much independence inside the Indian Union, whereas the latter insisted on complete independence.[124]

The Observer correspondent, at this stage definitely anti-Naga, also testified how, despite all arrangements, the group was approached by pro-independence Nagas, for example Phizo's niece Beilieu and Lungshim Shaiza, a relative of hers. The DC Naga hills Ramunny finally conceded meetings between the journalists and the pro-Phizo group on the condition that the former would also see the NPC.[125] Knox, after his visit, was convinced that 90 per cent of the Nagas would opt for independence if asked.[126] He also seemed to see the necessity of some sort of inquiry into atrocities conducted by the ISF to appease the Nagas:

> Because the Nagas have long memories it may also be necessary to satisfy them by some sort of governmental inquiry into the past activities of the Indian security forces. Indian official records show 60 to 70 complaints of brutality over the past five years. All were inquired into and 24 persons punished. I have had access to the laboriously compiled, handwritten records of a single Naga village – Indian military unit and officers, places and dates, are listed – that make more than 70 such complaints.[127]

Indian officials seemed to have admitted that they aggravated the situation by considering and treating the Nagas as inferior,[128] and Young's description of part of his interview with the crew of the downed Indian air force plane in early 1961 is illuminating on what Indian army personnel might have had in mind when facing the Nagas. This holds true even when taking into consideration that it was conducted during Naga capture:

> 'I knew very little of the situation in Nagaland at that time,' Singha told me. 'In the I.A.F. we are not briefed on the Nagas – mainly, I suppose, because we are not expected to come into contact with them in the normal way.
>
> 'My impression was that the rebels were a handful of guerrillas or dacoits. I knew that some of them at least were Christians. But I found this difficult to reconcile with my belief (and that of the rest of my crew) that Nagas were head-hunters and even cannibals.'
>
> Naga officers (who are practising Baptists) shouted with laughter as Misra added, 'When we climbed out of the aircraft we didn't know how we would be received. I believed we might be eaten.'[129]

The Nagas on their part were aware of being looked on '. . . as colourful, semi-naked savages',[130] and this was so despite many of them being educated and having English as second language.[131] Gavin Young's description of the Indian army's inability to locate the captured Indian air force men demonstrates it was an occupational force in 1961:

> For more than seven months, Indian Army units in Nagaland (believed to comprise three divisions or 30,000 men) have been searching for the men in vain. All their efforts, including the use of military aircraft, have been frustrated by the extreme difficulty of operating effectively in such savage terrain against a well-organised, well-armed and determined Naga military force which seems to have the support of most Nagas civilians. It is this difficulty, too, which has baulked Indian attempts to end by force the Nagas' war for independence for their remote, land-locked country; a bitter, costly struggle which assumed nationwide proportions in 1955 and 1956 and which shows no sign of abating.[132]

He himself witnessed the scorched earth policy of the Indian army resulting in widespread destruction and food shortages and was told by a Naga:

> We want to be rid of these Indians once and for all, after all the crimes they have committed in our land. They say we are poor and backward and that they will bring us prosperity. We say, rather poverty and rags and freedom to choose our friends and allies than all the schools and hospitals in the world with Indian overlords.[133]

Evidence was relayed to Young showing that the Nagas had built up an effective parallel administration, that rested on voluntary support of the population. A not inconsiderable amount of funding was used to ensure the collaboration of parts of Indian officialdom:

A significant item in the Budget covers payments to Indian Civil Servants and soldiers, including officers. When I asked Naga officials if Indians did indeed accept bribes, they laughed as if the question was hardly worth answering. 'Some Indians who realise the true state of affairs sympathise with us. In some cases officers secretly tip us off before an attack and they have helped us in other ways. But they wouldn't dare express their views openly.[134]

Young starts the concluding part of his trilogy stating that Indian casualties in this war were '. . . three times higher than combined British losses in Cyprus and Mau Mau operations . . .' and by describing the ease with which Naga units were traversing the country even in 1961, unafraid of any Indian attack, well-armed with weapons and ammunition captured from the ISF.[135] Young, when travelling with the Naga soldiers through the Naga hills, came across villagers living in sheds in the jungle to either escape or avoid being put into one of the Indian-built concentration camps[136] and being coerced into labour squads for the Indians. The children especially, so Young witnessed, showed signs of malnutrition.[137] This information is important, because it has often been written that 'regroupment' and populations living in the forest had only been a feature of the very early years, i.e. 1956–7, and that thereafter the situation had improved considerably. Young's testimony from his peregrinations alone show, on the contrary, the Naga units moving like 'fish in the water', precisely due to having the support of the population. The Indian army, quite the reverse; owing to it being an occupational force, it was left with no choice, and continued to target the population, driving it from their villages and fields into the woods. On the other hand, the refugees Young had a chance to meet, were happy and unafraid, when coming across the Naga army that helped them with food and medicine. In the same vein, the Naga troops were welcomed by the large villages and the risk of hosting them willingly accepted. Young was given binoculars by his village hosts and shown Indian military posts that had been established in regular intervals on the prominent ridges, visible from the village perimeters. In addition, the Indian air force frequently patrolled the area. But again all this confirmed that the ISF were an alien body in a foreign territory with no connections to the civil population whatsoever, deepening the rift by perpetuating rampant human rights abuses.[138]

Young's series of articles precipitated a number of venomous letters to *The Observer* editor by readers of Indian origin that, among other things, blamed Young's report '. . . to be unduly elaborate and often obscene.'[139] However, Young in his retort to these letters clarified once more the Nagas' point of view as it had been relayed to him. He had been told by the Nagas that they had not started to fight for eight or nine years, and only did so when they were sure to be looked upon as only 'a batch of bandits.' Furthermore, they did not fight to achieve independence in the sense of achieving separatism, but independence understood by them as their traditional one, that they never had surrendered. Finally, according to Young's impression, though the Naga leaders were demanding complete independence, they were prepared to accept something short of it.[140] After the Indian government's version had also been published, which, of course, did not contain much new information but pretty much denied all Young had written,[141] Ursula Graham Bower set out again to sift the evidence. While she was proceeding in a very careful way, she, from her own experience and in the face of the Indian predilection to blame missionaries and British imperialists for the Nagas' recalcitrance, decidedly concurred with Young in his portrayal of Nagas' perception of their right to freedom:

> . . . one must again emphasise that the Nagas' deep-rooted desire for freedom, and their sense of 'apartness' from the plains people, is common alike to Christian and pagan. It reaches far back into history and long antedates both the missionaries and the British.[142]

This is in line with the argument I brought forward in chapter two that the hill people's perception of themselves, regardless of European imperialists' presence or absence, was a conscious distancing from the plains people, defined by their own free and self-determined way of life in contradistinction to the plains' feudalism. Coming back to Bower's effort to understand the state of affairs in the Naga hills from a distance via the available evidence, she draws a conclusion I would like to support:

> And now to consider the picture. In the first place, the official Indian view is that the backbone of the resistance has been broken and the guerrillas reduced to a minority, but the NNC's armed forces are well-organised, well-disciplined and well-equipped and, though nothing is definitely known of their numbers, 1,500 to 2,000 seems possible – the NNC claim many more. There is no sign of outside assistance, either in arms or money; morale is high; relations with local villagers seem good; both the guerrillas and their civilian supporters appear to move freely in spite of the presence of Indian troops, and underground and overground civilian 'hostiles' are active even in and about Kohima, as witness events during the recent Press visit. All this argues fairly widespread popular sympathy, and the minority, if such it is, is far from negligible.[143]

Her careful wording notwithstanding, she is likening the NNC to an iceberg and the NPC '. . . to a shallow-draught boat, with all its bulk above the surface and possibly not much grip on the water . . .'.[144]

The situation had not changed much in April the following year; 40,000 Indian troops, and that was the official number, were unable to win the war. Moreover, Naga leaders had obviously agreed to respect India's perceived strategic concerns and had offered free military passage in exchange for non-interference into the internal affairs of Nagaland. Guy Wint here saw parallels to British-Irish history, and that Britain back then, like India, missed the opportunity, and later was left with nothing.[145] This is to say, that even after seven years of fighting,[146] the door was not yet closed to a face-saving solution for both sides[147] that could not only have ended the war, but also would have avoided the consequences of its long-term continuation.[148] However, despite the heavy military presence in and around the Naga hills, 153 Nagas managed to reach East Pakistan almost unhindered, a distance of about

500 miles, with the main objective of countering India's propaganda maintaining that the majority of the Nagas wished to stay inside the Indian Union, and further, to give testimony about army excesses.[149] George Patterson, for *The Observer*, flew out to Pakistan to meet this party of Nagas. He was informed by the military Commander of the Naga forces, General Kaito, that the ISF kept 214 bases all over the Naga hills, and he gave the following description of the Naga army, that modelled itself on its opponent's predecessor and on the model of the opponent itself, and presents us with the picture of a regular army:

> Kaito estimated the Naga 'Home Guard' at 40,000 trained soldiers, in four divisions, each with its regional Commander. They had barracks and training grounds. Their military organisation and ranks, he said, were patterned on the British and Indian Armies, in which many of the Nagas had served. Their uniforms were Indian Army olive green, with Gurkha-type slouch hats and steel helmets. They had light arms and ammunition, but these had been of little use recently against the helicopter spotting and communication system of the reinforced Indian Army and jet bombing attacks.[150]

The Nagas relayed a series of instances of combat and successive Indian reprisals to Patterson that constituted war crimes of the worst category.[151] The number of casualties among the Nagas was put above 100,000, and four times the number, so Patterson quoted his informant '. . . Naga men, women and children are being held in 180 concentration camps and prisons in appalling conditions.'[152] This was followed by a plethora of rape allegations most inconspicuously committed in churches, or forced copulation at bayonet point of Naga men and women, all obviously designed to humiliate the Nagas where it hurt them most. Hence, included into the destruction of the villages and rice storage houses were more than 400 churches.[153] These reports render it comprehensible that the Indian campaign strengthened the case for Christianity in the eyes of the Nagas, and served as its ultimate catalyst among them, as is corroborated by the data. Patterson's report further bears testimony to a rather naive belief among the Nagas in the UN and its willingness to act on their behalf.

In many books on Naga modern history, written by Nagas and Indians, not only in official replies, do we find very general statements about the impeccable behaviour of the ISF, accompanied by reports on the excesses committed by it, which the Nagas would never forget nor forgive. This contradiction seems to indicate that even critical minds did not want to present themselves as unpatriotic prosecutors of the Indian *jawan*. Yet, what we get to know is enough to point towards a war of an occupying force against an occupied people. In the following we will see that the literature agrees with this judgement, even so, as a rule, it hastened to employ an appeasing tone and spread the blame equally on Nagas and Indians. Whether this was due to the acknowledgement of the continued power imbalance and the wish for further accommodation, or ascribable to the success of Indian propaganda, we are unable to say. This notwithstanding, even according to the then chief of the intelligence bureau and Nehru's confidant Mullik, it was the people of the Nagas fighting the ISF, making the massive presence of troops mandatory.[154] The army had orders to break the resistance of the Nagas, unofficially also that of the civil population.[155]

Scott, a member of the peace mission in the 1960s, was the only non-Indian and non-Naga, who could move officially and unhindered through Nagaland in the middle of the 1960s. He drove more then 3,000 miles through the Naga hills, visited many villages and talked to a lot of people.[156] Hundreds showed him their scars and crippling injuries and told him, that the ISF had attacked villages and suspended their inhabitants from the ankles and then beat them up.[157] Scott writes that he personally couldn't possibly verify all the accusations, but that everywhere he saw widespread destruction and heard personal accounts.[158] According to these accounts dozens of villages were raised to the ground, their populations driven into the jungle, their elders beaten up and tortured, churches desecrated by obscene actions and/or burnt down. Many Nagas were resettled, herded into overcrowded and unhygienic camps, where famines ensued, during which many of the children died.[159]

Maxwell, the *The Times* correspondent, was part of the mixed group of Indian and western journalists who were allowed on an organised tour into Nagaland. In a follow-up publication he wrote that he was secretly handed over a detailed list of cruelties committed by the ISF in a village. Later, one further such list reached him:

> . . . detailing the names of the victims, the nature of the ill-treatment (beating, rape and other sexual acts, torture by water or electricity, desecration of churches, and killings by bullet or beheading), dates, and very often the names of the units – even the individual soldiers.[160]

The meticulous listing of the excesses and what was known about comparable wars – in Malaysia, Algeria, Vietnam – was contributing, for Maxwell, to the credibility of the accusations. However, a final proof could only be brought about by an independent commission,[161] and this the Indian government refuses to allow to this day. Maxwell also reports on the Indian parliamentarian Lohia, who succeeded in 1956, despite the prohibition, to reach the Naga hills. He was arrested and deported. After his return he reported to the Indian parliament that the ISF would indulge in an '. . . orgy of murder . . .', of mass rapes, torture and massacres of the village population.[162]

Stracey, an Anglo-Indian, responsible in the 1950s and 1960s for the Nagaland forest administration, wrote about the situation there: '. . . the usual series of arrests, beatings and worse (. . .) along with burning of villages, destruction of granaries and orchards and lifting of livestock . . .',[163] and about curfews and *shoot on sight* orders.[164] Even though Stracey saw these measures as necessary,[165] he doubted that they would be successful:

> Destroy Nagaland, yes – by regrouping the villages so as to isolate them from contact with the hostiles, by filling the jails with suspects, by literally creating a scorched-earth peace – but end the movement . . . .[166]

His doubts about the success of all these measures were not nourished by the antagonisation of the population, which was to be expected, but by the inaccessible and uncontrollable nature of the border with Burma.[167] Rustomji confirms the resettlement of whole villages, the locking up and cramming in of whole parts of the population behind barbed wire, the scarcity of water, the absence of sanitation, medical facilities, schools or even real dwellings. This was done, according to Rustomji, to teach the Nagas a lesson, and the responsible authorities, with minor exceptions, did not see it as inadequate to lock away these 'primitives' or to transport them from one place to another like animals.[168]

India, as even pro-Indian Nagas agree,[169] led a '. . . full-scale war . . .',[170] '. . . short of an extermination campaign . . .'.[171] The result was the complete and utter antagonisation of the population,[172] hate of the ISF[173] and forced more and more people into armed resistance:

> . . . it is ironic but true that the very same Army which was in the Naga Hills to prevent insurgency drove so many Nagas to insurgency and rebellion. Before the Army stepped in, official callousness had done enough damage but the bunglings in the corridors of power were trivial compared to the pig-headedness of the Indian soldiers who became the most effective agents for recruitment of talent to the Underground ranks. Naga Nationalism, hitherto an embryonic concept, now became the obsession of almost every Naga. No longer was it possible to point out this or that village or tribe as agitators, for the entire Naga Hills from the Konyaks to the Zeliangs became the locus of agitation which had for its goal – Naga Independence. The Naga search for a distinct political and social identity had formally begun.[174]

Indian officers and politicians proclaimed for years that violence would be the easiest and fastest solution but again and again they were wrong. Different governors over 30 years stated they had solved the Naga problem. Yet this was always only:

> . . . the exhaustion following army repression (. . .). The violence of military operations on the other hand sows yet further seeds of discontent and bitterness, and no sooner have the victims of such violence recuperated than they take to arms again with redoubled vigour and the whole brutal process of repression and violence is started anew.[175]

In this way the war started in the middle of the 1950s, and continued until 1997, when it finally transformed into a low-level civil war that permanently threatens to relapse into a full-scale guerrilla war.

Conclusion

The Transfer of Power in India saw also the Transfer of Power in the NHD to the Indo-Assamese administration. One consequence of this was the influx of numerous tradesmen from the plains. Another consequence was the coming into effect of new laws, which brandished traditional usufructs as illegal. The theory of the sixth schedule was relating the protection of minorities. The reality of the conduct of the new masters spoke of chauvinism and indifference, of subjugation and colonisation, instead of equal rights, of assimilation into the lowest layer of Indian society, not of respect. We have seen that this is a common aspect of the nation building of post-colonial states, making the 'post-' invalid for the periphery.

The new administration penetrated now into even the most remote villages. Every Naga was from then on confronted with his categorisation as an inferior primitive, as someone who had no rights in what he had hitherto considered as his own country. Suddenly, the collective identity had for everyone noticeable consequences; the negative categorisation in concert with the exerted pressure to assimilate, served as catalysts for this very identity. Nehru's integration was perceived by the Nagas as invasion, and as insincere, as treasonable. Violent transgressions on the side of ISF, obviously in accord with official policy, further eroded any willingness to submit to Indian rule. By 1950 this had led all inside the NNC to a change of mind. An interim solution was now no longer considered as acceptable, the demand now was for immediate independence. The means to work towards this end, however, remained for the time being non-violent.

In order to refute the accusation that only a tiny western-influenced minority was behind the demand for independence, the NNC decided to conduct a plebiscite. The population were mobilised for that through the established party structures and voted against the new administration. It is questionable that the majority of the Nagas had already thought at that point in time in terms of 'nation' and 'self-determination'. More likely, they voted against what they perceived as an invasion by the Indians. Confronted with the plebiscite, Nehru categorically ruled out the possibility for self-determination. The answer of the NNC was to employ *satyagraha*, the strategy of non-violent non-cooperation the Indian National Congress itself had used against the British. GOI, however, busy with the fallout of partition and with Kashmir, delegated the Naga question to the Assamese state government. This government saw the Nagas as a horde of savages who would only understand the language of violence, and consequently started a campaign of terror to show the Nagas their place. Jenkins has demonstrated that a state, which during the incorporation of a region continuously falls back on violence, will fail to establish its monopolisation of violence.[176]

The reasons for the protracted guerrilla war were rooted in the Indian state's massive use of violence, annulling Gellner's 'weakness of nationalism',[177] the upholding of it in the face of overwhelming force, ample proof, according to Walker Connor, of the collective will and consciousness of a people, finally forced together by the Other's scorn and use of force.[178] Without this long, drawn-out war and intimate threat, the local Naga groups, though acknowledging relatedness, would certainly have chosen to remain politically independent from each other. Their unification may be likened to the process Linda Colley has described for their former imperial rulers, for whom permanent warfare with the outside was the main unifying factor.[179] But other than with Britain, the successive unification of the

Naga people seems to have been a more egalitarian process. Similar to Britain, religion was to be the nation-builder, but as a function not as a factor. In other words, the war forced upon the Nagas by Nehru served as a catalyst for the Naga nation, and of developing it into a Christian one. India, from the very beginning, used force to coerce the periphery.

7 Divide-and-rule

Introduction

Central leadership and mainstream intelligentsia have inherited the colonial mind-set with its concepts and categories of disregarding the common will and thinking mainly in terms of security and policing, wanting to settle any disagreement by force. Further, the Indian state's elite's self-perception as nation(state) sees every-thing in relation to the perceived Indo-Aryan-Dravidian heritage and consequently takes the tribals as the Others that are non-intelligent, don't know what is good for them, and have an existence only in relation to India and possess otherwise no territoriality.[1]

We have, in chapter five, established the factual imperial continuation in the case of the post-European maritime colonial Indian state. The Nehruvian discourse and the hopes for freedom obscured this for a while from the eyes of most of the protagonists and observers. The chant of the 'tryst for freedom' and 'unity in diver-sity' mesmerised even the victims for a while. Yet, the centralist and power-political quality of the Indian state became visible for most with Indira Gandhi establishing herself and her sons at the seat of the new empire trying to eradicate each real and imagined challenge to her power. The end of retaining power justified all means.[2]

The periphery, like the Northeast or even more so the Naga hills, were of little relevance to the power holders in Delhi. This remains the case until today and is one of the most crucial factors when trying to make sense out of the political history of this afflicted region. What emanates and takes shape from the acts and initiatives of successive governments in Delhi and their agents on the ground in the Northeast is the one paramount objective to keep the Northeast within the union. And as had become clear in the 1950s that force alone could not achieve this, one resorted to the old imperial device of divide-and-rule. And one was successful. What can be witnessed today is an atomized region, caught in countless fratricidal fights of all kinds – a mutually antagonized diversity of hatred, impossi-bly to be reconciled, since rapprochement anywhere will surely create violent opposition alongside it. But before we take a closer look at the realities of the Northeast itself let us first see 'How wars are got up in India,[3] in ever greater numbers.

Ceasefire – Shastri

Despite the deployment of 40,000 regular troops in the decade from 1954 to 1964[4], and the full-scale war against the Nagas for these ten years[5], the Nagas still retained their ability to hit hard. This and the rout at the hands of the Chinese may have contributed to Nehru's willingness to accept a ceasefire to allow for negotiations. And Shastri, Nehru's successor, was set for peace[6], and authorised the governor of Nagaland to negotiate a ceasefire agreement with the NFG. The ceasefire was to be the prelude to talks that would settle the Naga question.[7]

On 18th August the NFG accepted the ceasefire proposal to suspend all military activities from midnight 5th September onwards as did the Indian army.[8] Shastri, who had defied sharp political criticism to enable this ceasefire,[9] publicly welcomed it on 6th August.[10] A week later, on 14th September 1964, the preliminary discussions started at Chedima, a village near Kohima, including representatives of the Baptist Church Council and B. P. Chaliha, the chief minister of Assam and Reverend Michael Scott as members of the unofficial peace mission,[11] only to be broken off nine days later, on 24th September, due to the NFG's refusal to accept Shilu Ao's (chief minister of the Nagaland state government – NLSG) participation as delegate.[12] However, by the end of the month the NFG had accepted the NLSG as party to the talks and so this obstacle had been overcome for the moment.[13] And of course immediately afterwards the GOI was criticised for the way the negotiations were carried out, especially that the wording, symbols and proceedings conveyed too much legitimacy to the Nagas, that they evoked negotiations between two nations, not between one government and some rebels. For example A. B. Vajpayee asked why a white flag and not the Indian flag had been hoisted at the location where the negotiations took place. These kinds of questions were posed incessantly and only intensified in their fury over time.[14]

The talks seemed to have been held in a two-week pattern. From the middle of October onwards the different participants and parties began to expound their views. Narayan made it clear that independence or secession could not be considered as an option. Gundevia, as representative of the GOI, stated that should the Nagas put down their arms, the ISF would restrain itself to patrol the international borders. The leaders of the NFG, for their part, spoke of disarmament and nonviolence. Then the talks were adjourned[15] and the ceasefire was extended until the end of the year to grant time to formulate new and consider old proposals.[16] National politics was then dominated by a severe food crisis that put the new administration under considerable pressure.[17]

The affairs in the Naga hills once again triggered lively debates in the Indian parliament. The minister of foreign affairs, Swaran Singh, and the minister of defence, Y. B. Chavan, were exposed to criticism that included points that were always raised, namely that the Nagas were being dealt with under the foreign ministry and not as they should, under the home ministry; that a foreigner, in the person of the Englishman Scott, had been admitted to the talks; and of course the recurrent statements that the Nagas were Indians and nothing but. Of particular interest at that time were the knowledgeable comments of the MP for Gauhati, Assam, Hem Barua that 1,300 Naga troops were momentarily on their way to East Pakistan via Burma and that he himself had met two NFG leaders who had assured him that they would be satisfied with a status like Bhutan or Sikkim had. Singh's answer was an insinuation that the Nagas did not really know their present statehood status.[18]

Reports in the press indicated that the Indian delegation had been willing to discuss more than union state status with the NFG, but had to deny it,[19] and the prime minister was under renewed pressure to end the negotiations and to solve the Naga problem by force once and for all: 'There is a widespread belief in India that the Nagas' resistance would have been broken long ago if the Indian Army had not been hampered by orders to behave with restraint.'[20]

The most important outcome of the ongoing negotiations, though, was the continuous extension of the ceasefire. When reading the reports, one gets the impression that far more than the mutually irreconcilable standpoints – here the offer for maximum autonomy, there the demand for complete independence – there existed an inability to effectively communicate.[21] Soon enough this was confirmed by one of the contemporary actors, Scott, who stated that both sides had agreed on negotiations on the basis of mutually exclusive understandings of them – one said the Nagas were part of India, the other the Nagas were not and the latter could not see how they now, after having fought for more than ten years, could agree to the former.[22] In the Indian capital no one really supported the idea of Naga independence[23] and Scott, who had travelled to London for a stomach operation, gave *The Observer* his view on the Indian establishment's stand towards the Naga question and what he believed was at stake for India:

> India's Prime Minister, Mr Shastri, has a sincere desire to find a peaceful settlement, but he is beset by self-interested groups who thrive on a misinformed public opinion whose image of the Nagas as a fierce, headhunting people, hostile to India, has been built up by one-sided reporting of the struggle.
>
> Then there are the newly emergent nationalists who claim to stand for what they call the integrity of India, even if this means the destruction of villages and the harassment of defenceless women and children. (. . .)
>
> Far more than her Press or politicians realise, India's position in the world, especially in South-East Asia, depends on her ability to solve the problem, which is costing her even more in money, manpower and prestige than the disputes over Kashmir and the Rann of Kutch. India, in fact, is facing the test of her ability to stand by the principles which have entitled her to leadership in the world – in particular, the toleration of varying racial groups and minorities.[24]

Scott here, either strategically or sincerely, showed himself as an admirer of Indian politics, but made it clear that his continued admiration would depend on the way India would bring the Naga question to an end.[25]

The threat of renewed hostilities with Pakistan, and the same looming on the horizon with the Nagas, led Narayan and Chaliha to impress upon Shastri to allow Phizo to come to India, for without the president of the NNC a real solution to the problem could not be achieved. Narayan's and Chaliha's '. . . declared aim was to get the peace talks taken away from cautious and pedantic bureaucrats and lifted to a high political level.'[26] Chaliha urged Phizo to come to India and to partake in the negotiations; according to Chaliha, Shastri had given Phizo repeatedly assurances of safe conduct in case he returned.[27] Shastri was eager to continue the ceasefire, but, so the *Far Eastern Economic Review* reported, could not grant independence, referring to the usual Balkanisation argument: '. . . because the right of secession was specifically excluded by India's constitution-makers to safeguard the country's fragile unity. If it is conceded to Nagaland today, how can it be denied – the argument runs – to other areas.'[28]

Ceasefire – Indira Gandhi

The peace mission had arranged, again with Shastri, for direct meetings between the NFG and the prime minister of India, in which now the new prime minister, Indira Gandhi, took part on 18th and 19th February 1966. The NFG delegation consisted of Kugato Sukhai, prime minister of the NFG, Imkongmeren Ao, vice-president of the NNC, still the parental organisation, and Isak Swu, the NFG's foreign minister.[29] Indira Gandhi met the NFG despite heavy criticism from all sides.[30]

Then, in early 1966, a new front was opened in the Northeast: the Mizos started their uprising and attacked treasuries and armouries of the Indian state. In parliament the official number given of the strength of the Mizo National Front was that of 10,000 armed men of the Mizo National Front carrying out this attack, with many of those ex-army or Assam Rifles servicemen. The Mizos also were allegedly supported by Pakistan with arms and training and had, due to their socio-cultural affiliation, close connections with groups in Burma. It is further intriguing to note that the MP Swell reminded his colleagues in the *Lok Sabha* that the Mizos also had wanted independence at the time of the Transfer of Power and that since then nothing had been done about it,[31] or to phrase it differently, that the demand had simply been ignored. Among the Indian elite, though, it was felt even more strongly that the soft handling of the Naga question by the GOI had encouraged the Mizo insurgents.[32] The attacks of the Mizo National Front covered the whole Mizo district and were carried out in a well-planned, systematic manner. The Indian army took over command and imposed a curfew. *The Times* indicated that there existed a standpoint not to negotiate on the Indian side.[33] From now on we have to keep the Mizo battlefield in mind when trying to make sense out of our Naga case, since one consequence for the moment was a hardening of the Indian stand and the threat of a breakdown of the negotiations. 'Balkanisation' was one expression, 'power vacuum' another,[34] but the ceasefire with the Nagas must also have been a relief for the Indian army, for it did not have to fight on two fronts in the Northeast.

The ceasefire notwithstanding, fighting broke out in northern Manipur between ISF and the Naga army and Scott warned of the detrimental effects of the divide-and-rule policy of the GOI creating mercenary groups in the Naga hills under the pretext of protection of the villages.[35] Yet, despite this, a new round of talks was held in Delhi between Indira Gandhi and the NFG–delegation in the presence of the two remaining members of the peace mission, Chaliha and Scott, on 9th April in Delhi. The NFG criticised the GOI for aimless talking, but at the same time signalled its willingness for the continuation of the negotiation process; the prime minister said afterwards that it was good to go on talking. A new round of talks were scheduled for the following week.[36]

However, the second half of April 1966 saw two bomb attacks on trains close to the Nagaland state border in which nearly 100 people were killed and many others injured.[37] A consequence of this might have been that the GOI resolved to expel Scott from India, a decision that was welcomed with cheers in the *Lok Sabha*, and, together with the resignation from the peace mission also of Chaliha, ended the Peace Mission. However, the GOI announced its intent to continue its talks with the NFG but stuck to its no-negotiating stand in relation to the Mizos. Nagas and Mizos, in the meantime, joined forces, according to *The Times*, as 2,000 Nagas crossed into the Mizo hills.[38] Cyril Dunn of *The Observer* saw a growing cooperation between Nagas and Mizos and East Pakistan and reminded the reader that the GOI had other more pressing problems at the time: Pakistan, the criticism inside the party due to the famine throughout the country, the challenge to Indira Gandhi by Moraji Desai and the upcoming general elections.[39] This was a reminder of the marginality of the Northeast for Delhi.

After he had been expelled from India, Scott, broke, as he put it, his '. . . silence . . . in the hope of being able to help to bring about a peace.'[40] But the chances for peace, in his eyes, were rather small. Scott retells the story of the Nagas as it had been relayed to him. We remember, for many months, Scott was able to traverse the Naga hills unhindered and was free to form his own idea of what was going on. So the important aspect of his article for us is that Scott saw it as of utmost importance to have an impartial inquiry into the innumerable crimes committed by the ISF during the past 15 years. He even tells therein that Nehru, just before he died, had agreed to that.[41] We know now from many other post-war, -genocide, -dictatorship etc. examples of the world that a rigorous investigation into past wrongs and their publication is a necessary condition for the possibility of a future peace, otherwise violence will further be used and accepted as a natural conflict-solving means.[42] And of course we also know now that was exactly what happened and still happens in the Northeast. At the same time Scott had an intimate interaction with Indian decision makers on all levels and returning to the end of his article, he delivers his assessment of the current situation and a prognosis of what was to come:

Peace mission futile

The conferment of statehood within the Indian Union in 1963 failed to gain Naga political support. It always depended on the active presence of the Indian armed forces for its maintenance.

I have been slowly and reluctantly driven to the conclusion that the Government of India has never taken seriously the problem of negotiating a political settlement with the Nagas.

The unwillingness of Delhi to acknowledge that a people which had kept up their fight for some ten years in the jungle had earned any right to decide their own future 'of their own volition' rendered the peace mission's effort futile.

(. . .)

The Government of India accused the Naga federal army of violating the ceasefire agreement by sending thousands of men for training and to collect arms in East Pakistan. The Nagas counter-accused the Indians of cynically using the ceasefire to consolidate their military posts outside every important village, to build a permanent barracks and cantonment outside the Naga capital of Kohima, to reconnoitre the underground army's camps from the air and on the ground, to improve greatly their military communications, and to construct an enormous new prison.

Plans to uproot villages

It is a certainty that if no generous political proposals are made, and if the terms of a durable peace are not agreed, then another bloodbath in Nagaland is inevitable. Plans exist for the uprooting of all the villages and for re-grouping the population in vast concentration areas, where they would be permanently under guard and dependent for food on the Indian Government. These plans would already have been carried out if the peace mission had not been called into being in 1964 by the Baptist Church to try to find some other solution.

If all negotiations break down and the fighting is resumed, it may pose very grave problems for India and for her friends. Disaffection could easily spread into the other hill areas of Assam and the North East Frontier Agency.[43]

This is, as we know today, what happened. Two weeks later Scott, specified this and pointed out those he believed as actively opposing a peaceful solution as the personnel of the home ministry, especially home minister Nanda, and the defence ministry, led by Chevan and earlier by Krishna Menon.[44] And in two successive years, Scott blamed the Indian diplomacy for building up their armed occupation in the Naga hills, and playing for time with the understanding that the Nagas in this way would sooner or later come to accept '. . . that they are Indians – which, according to my observations, the Nagas would almost to a man stoutly deny.'[45] Concomitantly, in the wider Indian arena, the Sikhs' demand for self-determination had resulted in the Indian state arming itself with a new, what *The Observer* called, martial law, 'The Unlawful Activities (Prevention) Ordinance, 1966', that outlawed, in word, deed or script, all that aimed at secession.[46] The new law was aimed more at the electorate than at the Sikhs, since the next general elections were around the corner and the administration wanted to signal its tough stand towards secessionist elements.[47]

On 11th August 1966 the third meeting was held between Indira Gandhi and the delegation of the NFG during which again mutual assurances of a continued effort for a political solution were made, despite irreconcilable standpoints. And while the NFG asked for international mediation, the GOI wouldn't accept it.[48] On 27th October, in the fourth meeting between Indira Gandhi and the NFG, they agreed on an extension of the ceasefire until 15th December. Indira Gandhi, so *The Times* maintained, had to remain silent on the fact that the Nagas always demanded independence, otherwise she would have been pressurized to end the talks and to finish the Nagas' resistance in a quick campaign.[49] The NFG delegation didn't see any progress, but did not want to abrogate the ceasefire either.[50] Thus, the fifth meeting in the course of a year came to nothing. The following day, and maybe this was a consequence of the Nagas' adamant insistence, the minister of state Dinesh Singh offered them complete autonomy, apart from defence, external relations, communications and currency, but the Naga delegation declined, since this would be inconsistent with complete independence, pointing out once more that the Nagas never were part of India. However, both sides signalled their willingness to continue the ceasefire and the talks. The interlocutors of the GOI were to be Dinesh Singh and Z. Ramyo, a Nagaland MP.[51]

Meanwhile, in the Mizo hills, the Indian army had commenced to resettle around 60,000 Mizos into a so-called 'special security belt' and to put them into a kind of camp as part of an attempt to crush resistance. Further, the people of later Meghalaya, the Khasis and Jaintias, asked for separate statehood. As general elections were impending, the negotiation strategy drew acerbic criticism from Indian nationalists. On 5th January NFG representatives met again with Indira Gandhi. The representatives of the NFG under the leadership of the prime minister Kughato Sukhai went home to the Naga hills with the offer for special status in their briefcases and an overture by the chief minister of the Nagaland state I. N. Angami to accommodate the NFG leaders in his government and with the understanding that official talks would be resumed in March or April. What the elite of the capital thought of the whole process is handed down to us by *The Observer*:

> The entire position is summed up by a quip going the rounds among Delhi's officials: 'The Nagas want to be like Sikkim, Sikkim wants to be like Bhutan, Bhutan wants to be like Nepal, Nepal wants to be treated like China, and China wants to be looked on as God Almighty.'[52]

Nothing describes better the mixture of hurt pride and hubris of the neo-colonial Mandarin. The GOI then announced a plan to reorganize Assam into a federal state to accommodate the long-term frictions between hill and plains people. The details were still to be clarified but projected was a kind of sub-federation.[53] This plan was opposed by the plains people who preferred complete separation to partnership. The 'All-party hill leaders' conference' on the other hand could not agree on a common position, for the Mizos wanted their own state and so did the Mikirs, only the Khasis and the Garos agreed on sharing one.[54]

At the beginning of April the Press Trust of India reported that 300 Nagas had made their way to China through Upper Burma. Further, that Nagas and Mizos were cooperating in Manipur where, on 4th April, Nagas raided a Manipur Rifles camp.[55] Mid-April 1967 brought the official confirmation from the Chinese that Nagas had gone for arms, ammunition and training to China, and that the Burmese had tried to stop them passing through their territory.[56] An ambush by Nagas on a party of the Central Reserve Police Force in northern Manipur, in which 23 members of the latter were killed, triggered heavy criticism and calls for the talks from MPs to be cancelled. When Chavan, however, added that the ceasefire had brought real peace to the Nagaland state for the previous two and a half years, this was countered by Hem Barua, an MP from Assam, with the remark that this peace inside Nagaland was bought with the Nagas having exported their activities to Assam and Manipur. This was downplayed by Chavan.[57]

When the reorganisation of Assam was on the agenda of the *Lok Sabha* around the middle of July, the worries of the MPs – about the rapprochement between Pakistan and China, bombings of trains in Assam, armed collaboration between Nagas, Kukis and Mizos in Manipur, Assam and later Mizoram and trouble in Kashmir – formed the backdrop to these discussions and were expressed, among others, by the Assamese MP Hem Barua. As usual the instability of this border region was bemoaned together with the inadequate policy of the government and it was unclear whether the ceasefire was to be extended to Manipur or not. Jamir, the MP from Nagaland, was in favour of such an extension, justifying this by portraying the positive effects it had in the Nagaland state. In general this time the MPs were in favour of a sympathetic approach towards the people in all border regions, otherwise, so it was feared, the whole stretch of border region would end up in arms, supported by Pakistan and China. It was also admitted that it was deplorable that there was no differentiation between combatants and civilians during military operations in the border zone and that as a consequence of this it was no wonder that the people supported or even joined the insurgents. So, the tenor was this time sympathetic and in favour of negotiations[58] only to ask for firm action again six months later.[59]

Meanwhile, the 'bitter war', as it was called by Peter Hazelhurst, between the Indian state and the Mizos went on and Hazelhurst compared the tough manner of the fighting with the early phase in Vietnam.[60] What was more, towards the end of September 1967 the bitter antagonism between hill and plains in Assam became manifest when the hill districts demanded a separate statehood. Manipur and Tripura already had union territory, and Nagaland statehood status, hence, if granted to the other hill areas too, according to Inder Malhotra, this would '. . . cause the plains people to raise hell.'[61]

Towards the end of the year the Burmese and the Indian governments started to talk about the situation along their common border. The talks between the GOI and the NFG had broken down and Phizo informed *The Observer* that the Indian army were preparing for war as were the Nagas. Thus, with the Nagas threatening to resort to fighting again, the Mizos already up in arms and the Khasis and Jaintias more forcefully pressing for their own state, in addition to the confirmation of Chinese support to the Nagas, it made complete sense for the GOI to exchange views with the Burmese neighbours:

> The spreading demand for separate States among the hill peoples comes as a direct challenge to the authority of the Central Government in one of the country's most sensitive areas. It is also feared that the recent links established between the Nagas and the Chinese, and vitriolic anti-Indian propaganda by the Chinese radio and Press, may result in Chinese aid to the Nagas becoming something more than vocal.[62]

That fear was aggravated by the fact that in January 1968 the Chinese infiltrated Upper Burma to support the rebel groups based there, namely the White Flag Burmese Communists, the Kachin, Karen and the Shan.[63] India's home secretary, Y. B. Chavan, on 19th March in the *Lok Sabha*, accused China and Pakistan of supplying arms to the Nagas who in turn supported the left-wing Communist Party of India (Marxist) that wanted to take over power in Assam. The fear of losing not only the Naga hills grew.[64] Now the unrest had reached a threatening dimension, at least in the eyes of the Indian MPs and their home secretary, from Southern China into Northern Burma, the Indo-Burma border, the Naga and Mizo hills, Manipur, East Pakistan and even the heartland of Assam.[65]

The Indian army had since 1st February resumed military action with an assault on the Naga army headquarters at Toloi. This was done despite the ceasefire that was to have been in operation until at least 30th April. The Indian army moved through the hills in battalion strength to conquer all Naga army posts, but these evaded the attacks and continued to rebuild. Renewed full-scale war again seemed likely.[66] At the same time serious fighting broke out between Mizo units and those of the ISF south of Shillong. Mizos and Nagas united under Chinese influence, according to *The Times*, the whole border being in a state of unrest and the ISF stretched to the limit. The Khasis and Garos, in form of the 'All-party hill leader's conference' seemed on the verge of following the example of the Nagas and Mizos, while the Assam Congress for its part threatened that, in the case of any state reorganisation, Assam would turn into another Vietnam.[67] Contributing to the ferment were pro-Chinese Assamese communists who, with the help of the Nagas, tried to topple the Assam government, but the coup was thwarted and the men arrested.[68] This was why the GOI official L. P. Singh flew to Assam, Nagaland and Manipur to study what the hawkish Hem Barua described as an explosive anti-Indian feeling: 'The whole of the eastern frontier including Assam, Nagaland and Manipur is in ferment and there is an anti-Indian feeling and there is an anti-Union-Government feeling growing in that part of our country.'[69]

The clashes between the Naga army and ISF increased in number and intensity over the next month, while more Nagas went to China for training, where already more than 1,000 of them had been instructed.[70] This notwithstanding, the next round of talks between the Naga resistance, peace mission and GOI representatives was held at Dimapur during which one agreed on an extension of the ceasefire until 31st July.[71] Naga elders cabled Phizo to authorise him to find an agreement with the GOI. Phizo still believed in third party mediation and the GOI for its part declared it would not negotiate with Phizo and that he would not be allowed into India. Meanwhile the GOI increased the pressure on the Nagas to drop their demand for independence, and sent even more troops into the Naga hills to clear the jungle in anticipation of future military operations.[72] Indira Gandhi postponed the reorganisation of the Northeastern states, as the Assamese Congress government still vigorously opposed this.[73]

The NFG now was unanimously and openly in favour of Chinese support and Khugato Sukhai said that India acquired arms from the USSR and the Nagas from China. The GOI, according to Malhotra, would not be able to tolerate this considering Kashmir and Assam.[74] And it did not: Indian troops killed around 200 Naga soldiers when, returning from China, they tried to re-enter the Naga hills. Casualties on the Indian side were not announced. For weeks patrolling had been stepped-up and Chinese broadcasts encouraged the Nagas to keep up their fight.[75] A week later, the first major battle between the Indian army and Naga army was fought close to Kohima. While Malhotra and Dunn agreed that the first attack was launched by Indian troops – Dunn estimated them at around 3,000 – the latter saw this as violation of the ceasefire terms, while the former took it as justified reaction to the Naga arms build-up with the help of the Chinese. According to Malhotra, the Nagas were routed with the help of helicopters; Dunn, also referring to Indian reports for support of his view, told of a complete rout of the Indian forces with hundreds of them killed. *The Times*, claiming to have debriefed Indian journalists returning from Nagaland in Shillong gave the number of Indian soldiers killed as *c*.90, while the official number was 29. Dunn's report was written with several weeks delay.[76]

The Council of the People of Nagaland voted for the continuation of the ceasefire. Around the same time the Indian army launched its 'Operation Freedom' – the attempt to evict Naga army units by burning down villages – according to Michael Ross, the Naga army on its part saw this as the attempt to bring about an abrogation of the ceasefire and continued to evade the Indian army.[77] *The Observer*, by then accused by the GOI for interfering in internal affairs and being partisan towards the Nagas, replied to these charges as follows:

> India – the inspiration of Gandhi and Nehru – cannot expect to escape world censure if it should commit itself to naked repression involving mass killings – frequently the 'final solution' of governments faced with implacable minorities determinedly struggling for their rights.[78]

B. K. Nehru's transfer to the Northeast as governor of Assam, and thus responsible for dealing with the Nagas and Mizos, showed for one the seriousness of the situation, but also the way the Indians wanted to solve it: '[B. K. Nehru] has publicly threatened that the Indians might have to risk "a million casualties" in order to deal with the Nagas . . .'.[79]

In September 1968 the plan to carve out a new autonomous state within the state of Assam was announced to cover the Garo, Khasi and Jaintia hills; the Mikir and North Cachar hills would be given the option to join later. This was the first step towards the later formation of the state of Meghalaya. Effective administration would be put into the hands of local leaders, while law and order remained with Assam.[80] From the following month Indira Gandhi tried to profit from the contemporary inner-Naga split and followed a tough policy, extending the ceasefire never longer than four weeks. In this she had been advised by B. K. Nehru.[81] By Mid-November 1968 it was estimated the Indian military build-up in the Naga hills was at a rate of 100–200 transport lorries a night. The concern was to prevent the re-entering of the Naga units returning from China via Burma into the Naga hills.[82] And two months later the Indian army in some areas already outnumbered Naga villagers. Cyril Dunn suspected the troops were there above all to force the Nagas to vote in the general elections in February 1969.[83]

Indira Gandhi met the Burmese leader General Ne Win to discuss the security situation on their common borders that was characterised by the resistance of the local Kachin, Shan and Karen populations on the Burmese and the Nagas and Mizos on the Indian side. Intensive military operations were reported to have been carried out in the Naga hills in an effort to apprehend the returnees from China. At the same time the Soviet Union offered military support for India for the security of the Bay of Bengal.[84] Swaran Singh, the minister of defence, reported to the *Lok Sabha* the successful operation leading to the capture of Mowu Angami and his men and the mopping up operations that were under way chasing Issak Swu's men. He especially stressed the cooperation between the ISF, the NLSG, the local village guards and the villagers – all united in the effort to apprehend the returnees from China. For the defence minister this indicated a return to normalcy,[85] but this also could have meant a return to regular fighting. Inder Malhotra, to the contrary, lacking our retrospective wisdom, agreed with the defence minister in his assessment of the situation '. . . that the back of the Nagas' rebellion against the central authority in India has been broken.' Consequently the talks were suspended until the Nagas agreed to remain under India.[86] The ISF by that time put a shot Naga resistance fighter, by the name of Meludi, on display in the marketplace of the Nagaland capital: 'It is believed that Meludi's body was put on display to overawe the Kohima people in preparation for a public meeting the Indian authorities are planning.'[87]

Although two dozen enounters were admitted to by the defence minister,[88] it was not yet all-out war, but regular fighting for which the build-up had started in 1968. Debates in the *Lok Sabha* indicated that ISF personnel were killed in the Naga hills on a weekly basis, further, that the GOI had changed its strategy then, and that the negotiations were to be conducted now by the NLSG.[89] Despite this deterioration, Indira Gandhi visited Nagaland in September 1969.[90] The autonomous state of Meghalaya came into existence on 3rd April 1970 against the opposition of the Assamese.[91] And Delhi was confident to have contained what it saw as a Naga revolt by 1971, moreover, Laldenga, the leader of the Mizo resistance, sought ways to surrender. The situation was complicated by the fact that the Naga resistance had moved to parts of Manipur, with the people in the state themselves seeking statehood.[92] Suddenly, the NLSG also demanded the inclusion of all Naga-inhabited land into the Nagaland state and threatened with disturbance if the demand was not met.[93]

The quality of India's federalism as a divide-and-rule device again became apparent in the discussion about the establishment of district councils in the Manipur hills, which were opposed by the responsible tribal representative who considered the scheme as merely a fig leaf to preserve plains' influence and interest in the hills via the quasi-dictatorial powers of the administrator resembling the former British DC. The reorganisation of the state of Assam providing for the states of Manipur, Tripura and Meghalaya and later for those of Mizoram and Arunachal Pradesh (via the intitial status of union territories) was nothing more than the upholding of the complete control of this area by the central government in the tradition of the British *Raj*.[94]

Indira Gandhi's final drive, Shillong Accord and the extension of the combat zone

The creation of Bangladesh after the defeat of Pakistan led to the seizure of Naga resistance fighters and their bases in former Eastern Pakistan. For *The Telegraph* this meant the death blow to Naga resistance as well as to the Mizo rebellion and to all other insurgencies in Northeast India in the wake of the strengthening success for India in this region.[95] The Indian army, victorious and with newly gained confidence, was now free to turn to the Naga hills, and according to *The Observer*: 'The Indian General Officer Commanding in Nagaland has recently warned the underground Home Minister, Mr Biseto Medom, that it would take India fewer than the 14 days needed for victory in Bangladesh to impose final defeat on the Nagas.'[96]

As a forerunner to this 'final drive', the military – according to *The Observer*, that had as its source Phizo – engaged in attacks on the civil offices of the NFG and its personnel, including killings, public display of maltreatment and harassment of the ordinary population, all in order to intimidate the people to give up their support for the resistance. [97] Since we lack independent reports of what happened, little is more informative on, and symptomatic for GOI's policy in the Northeast or dissident areas in general, than the debates around the Armed Forces (Assam and Manipur) Special Powers (Amendment) Bill, amending the bill of 1958 and extending it to the whole of the Northeast, giving the central government, via its executive governors in the states or its administrators in the union territories, the power to declare any territory as disturbed, equivalent to a declaration of martial law. The bill was opposed by the MP Nagaland, Kevichusa, stating that the bill had already been continuously in force for 14 years and was now supposed to be given permanency. The MP Dutta, Tripura West, opposed it as well, because the bill for him revealed the basic fact that the '. . . mentality of the British raj [was] inherited by the Congress rulers.' In a similar manner for the MP from Contai, Guha, the bill demonstrated the totalitarian mindset and intentions of the ruling Congress party. However, the bill was passed,[98] and with it martial law and military rule were legalised in the Northeast, as they would be later in the Punjab and in Jammu and Kashmir.

The GOI seemed to be resolved by September 1972 to unilaterally end the cease-fire, outlaw the Naga bodies of representation – the NNC, NFG and the Naga Federal Army – and reinforce its armed presence in the hills. This all was done '. . . to ensure the safety of life and property of the local people', announced the deputy minister in the home ministry, F. H. Mohsin, in the *Lok Sabha*.[99] The new policy of the GOI was generally described as a 'final drive', but the *Hindustan Times* suspected it was there to support the diminishing pro-Indian faction in Naga politics. Along with this ban, four extra battalions of paramilitaries had been transferred to Nagaland, although B. K. Nehru, the new governor of Assam, said the ending of the ceasefire did not automatically point to an imminent military campaign, but the home ministry in Delhi made it clear that it wanted to keep the momentum won through the victory over Pakistan and finally wanted to end the Naga's resistance.[100] And indeed, at the end of the month the Indian troops in Nagaland, then estimated at around 30,000 (always only a rough estimate), moved to occupy, it was said, all Naga villages in order to root out Naga resistance.[101] The military had the incentive for the following two years, as we will see in the following and final chapter.

And yet, though the Indian state made serious efforts to ensure a victory for the pro-Indian Nagas during the general elections of 1974, villagers were escorted to the polling stations where the troops outnumbered civilian administrators, non-Naga residents – including troops – were given the vote and constituencies were reorganised to ensure a pro-Indian vote, they and their allies were defeated and the majority of the vote went to the United Democratic Front (UDF), the overground support of the underground.[102] With the start of the dry season in August, Indian troops went on the offensive in the Naga as well as the Mizo hills,[103] a pattern we have already witnessed from the beginning of British interference in these hills.

By September 1975 even the Indian army admitted 'massive operations' in the Naga hills and announced a successful outcome in the near future, though this had been reiterated again since 1972. The Indian army claimed that its pressure had forced the Nagas to split up into small groups to avoid clashes.[104] In the budget discussion of 1976 the MP Dasarattha Deb, Tripura East, criticised the budget for spending disproportional amounts on police and jails as well as on those ruling elites in the Northeast that supported Congress and who in turn distributed the funds among their followers:

> . . . to create a local prop to the ruling Party in the State. The fact that President's rule had to be imposed over the State shows that the ruling Party can rule only through the Draconian powers given to the President by the Constitution. (. . .) . . . these so-called social and economic services of the State Government are utilised through a system of contractors and agents who amass money from these schemes while the vast masses do not get any benefit whatsoever.
>
> A very interesting thing is that most of the contracts and responsibilities are given to those who support the Congress Party.[105]

Dasaratha Deb continued to describe the government in Nagaland as a mere Potemkin village that should conceal the factual army rule:

> Nagaland practically has been under the military rule for a very long time and even today, the Civil Administration has no power at all. In fact, without the help of the army, the civil officers cannot move even a mile from the city. This civil administration is nothing but a show-boy and the actual administration is being run by the military there. This is the fate of the Naga people that they are being ruled by army men and not by civilians.[106]

The deputy minister in the ministry of finance, Sushila Rohatgi, saw this differently:

There [in Nagaland] is this atmosphere of they being a part and parcel of this country. (. . .) I can only tell this that this is a very sensitive area and the people, on their own volition have now decided to come out and to recognise the Constitution and to lay down their arms.[107]

And K. Brahmananda Reddy, home minister, retold in the *Lok Sabha* the course of affairs in the Naga hills as a success story: that the resistance was active in 1974 and 1975, that this was the reason why President's Rule was imposed on 28th July 1975 and that the pressure then meted out on the 'undergrounds' by the ISF led to a dialogue and ultimately to the signing of the Shillong Accord on 11th November 1975 with the following main provisions:

1 They accept voluntarily and freely the Constitution of India;
2 They agree to deposit the arms in their possession; and
3 They will in due course formulate some requests.

Reddy further said that there had been '. . . no violent incident after the signing of the Accord of 11th November, 1975.'[108] He argued against any elections being held and for an extension of president's rule under article 356 of the constitution for another six months. He saw it as necessary '. . . that the Nagaland problem is settled once for all.'[109] Again, it was Dasaratha Deb from Tripura East opposing the government and confronting it with his version of a violent removal of a legitimate state government, bringing back to attention that the question of the Naga hills was also part of the power struggle at the centre:

We have seen that the provisions under Article 356 of the Constitution are abused by the ruling party. The provisions are there just to keep the ruling party at the Centre in power very conveniently. Otherwise in a normal way they would not be in power. We know how the President's rule was imposed in Nagaland. (. . .) Every one of us, in this House, knows how the Ministry led by Mr. Vizol was toppled. At that time five M.L.As of his party were kidnapped by the army men and therefore, he lost the majority in the Assembly. After that, Jasokie's Ministry which was supposed to be loyal to the ruling party in the Centre, was installed but only lasted for 11 days and then the President's rule was imposed.[110]

Deb acknowledged the peace accord but demanded elections in order to democratically legitimise the process. He continued to condemn the corruption that was practised as a divide-and-rule tool by the government, dampened the optimism about the surrender in personnel and arms, since the numbers were negligible and moreover, bought with excessive amounts of money (100,000 Rupees for a weapon). Deb demanded the installation of a true, civil administration and described the existing situation as leaving the people the choice between a rock and a hard place:

You have to establish civil administration there. You know there were three authorities earlier operating in Nagaland. The *de facto* authority is the army.

The *de jure* authority is the civil administration, but it has practically no power. The third is the underground Nagas. The Naga people have to submit to these three authorities. If some rebel Naga comes and says, 'Pay this tax', they cannot afford to refuse because otherwise they will be beheaded. If an army man demands something, they cannot refuse. If an army man goes to a village and says, 'Give me a beautiful girl to enjoy', the poor villager has to offer a girl.[111]

Deb went on stating that it was a mistake to try to rule the Nagas by force and bribe the leaders into collaboration and warned that peace could not be established like that.[112]

The context for this was the emergency Indira Gandhi had declared in June the previous year, thus the discussion included this larger frame. Instructive again was the acknowledgement of wrongs done to the Nagas at the hand of the GOI, the army and the ISF by Ranen Sen from Barasat, but who at the same time justified these with the foreign conspiracy that was behind the Nagas' desire for self-determination.[113] President's rule was extended for another six months,[114] as it was again in August (with effect from 26th September onwards) yet this time without opposition.[115] After Indira Gandhi's short fall from grace, the India PM Moraji Desai met Phizo in London in June 1977. The meeting ended in a debacle and the strengthening of the irreconcilable standpoints.[116]

The general elections of January 1980 provided Indira Gandhi's Congress Party with majorities nearly everywhere except for a few states – among them Kashmir and Nagaland – where regional parties won the day.[117] Kaufman spoke of Indira Gandhi as having become '. . . once again . . . the absolute ruler . . .', or '. . . the unchallenged ruler of India . . .' that is '. . . totally in command'. In command of India, of her party . . .'. Being aware that it was her victory and that Congress depended on her, Kaufman, chief of *The New York Times*' New Delhi bureau, asked rhetorically how it could be that such a vast country was dominated by parochial gossip, by a dynasty, and answered it by likening her to the '. . . mother goddess . . .', that is having a '. . . mythlike quality . . .', acquired by being the daughter of Jawaharlal Nehru, himself being the son of Motilal Nehru, by Indira Gandhi having had personal contact with Gandhi and even bearing his name, that she knew Tagore and '. . . always witnessed history from a front-row seat.' And that is why she then prepared her son Sanjay to be her successor.[118] This dynastic rule was bemoaned by Rushdie, who also reminded us that it was Indira Gandhi herself who played on the cult of the mother goddess and myth;[119] and Indira Gandhi's megalomania that India owed its freedom to her father and that therefore she owned India, was witnessed by Gita Mehta.[120] What followed from that? One question is whether the masses really saw her as rightful leader or whether they were coerced and coaxed by Congress bullies into voting for her?[121] The other, and for us more relevant, question is, how this absolute power at the centre arrived at the periphery? Kaufman assessed it such: '. . . most importantly, what she had established in the first two months is that what now matters most in India is the wishes, hopes, whims, likes, dislikes and fears of Indira Gandhi.'[122] meaning absolute power, which her father had already, although hers must have surpassed his due to the greater means provided to her state machine by technological advances. So whatever happened on the periphery would have been directed by her and her courtiers. To understand Nehru and his daughter then, is to understand much of the politics of post-independence India. Kaufman might have agreed to this by calling India '. . . despite its democratic framework . . . very feudal . . .' and gives us an example of it stating that Indira Gandhi stopped the construction works for the Asian Games to be held in India in 1982 with only one phone call, after she had read an unfavourable article about the consequences of them: 'It is all really very feudal. (. . .) In one sense she heads a government, but in another she dominates a court. With boundless energy, she entertains petitions from the citizenry, who sometimes seem more like subjects.'[123]

This was the reason why she could continue to talk with the Nagas despite scathing criticism, and for the very same reason she could unleash her armed forces without restraint against professed citizens of India. Kaufman again cites voices and instances of her ability to communicate with the masses and her lust for power on the one side and her being without a programme on the other,[124] or one might assume that the programme was to come to and stay in power. For this, so Kaufman said, she had purged her party of any potential rivals.[125] This assessement of power centralisation, and increasingly authoritarian, autocratic and feudal outlook is confirmed by Indira Gandhi's biographer Katherine Frank, and one of her closest advisers P. N. Dhar.[126]

From the late 1970s onwards, vehement opposition toward the politics of the central government reached the core of the Northeast, Assam. Protests of tens of thousands against immigration from Nepal, Bangladesh and West Bengal were reported from there. The crowds defied curfews and Assamese leaders were arrested.[127] The agitation was described by Kaufman as basically one '. . . between indigenous hill peoples . . . and the largely Hindu people of the plains.' Fear of being outnumbered and disempowered, according to Kaufman, hindered the Northeastern people from joining the Indian mainstream:

> For more than six months, a student-led movement in the state of Assam has demanded the expulsion of outsiders. In the course of the agitation, elections had to be cancelled and the flow of oil from the state, the source of about 30 percent of India's petroleum, had stopped. In the state of Manipur, guerrillas have attacked army buses and Government banks. In the states of Meghalaya and Tripura, university students have taken up the cry of 'Foreigners out!'[128]

The resistance in Nagaland and Mizoram was reported as 'dying down', and the Chinese had cut their assistance. Delhi, according to Kaufman, had never been really concerned about the Nagas' or the Mizos' rebellions, and if then only once the Chinese had got involved. However, while there the struggle abated, so-called tribal groups elsewhere in the Northeast, under pressure from immigration, fought back, often violently, which ironically was portrayed again by Delhi as success of its own policy to empower the tribal people, thus the attacks were seen as sign of progress.[129]

The beginning of 1983 saw mass killings of immigrants in Tripura and Assam.[130]

The violence was consciously triggered by the insistence of Indira Gandhi on elections and the call for boycott on the other. And Delhi seemed more annoyed by the international media coverage than by the fact itself. The larger context was the granting of regional powers in all the peripheral states during the state elections of 1982, leaving Congress in control only over the 'Hindi-speaking heartland'.[131] Troops were sent into Assam to take control, as they had been sent into Nagaland in the 1950s, into Mizoram in 1966, into Manipur in 1978 and into Tripura in 1980.[132]

Look East Policy

Rajiv Gandhi, following the assassination of his mother, spoke of 'revenge' by staying united against those who intended to split an 'unusual' country, employing the rhetoric of exceptionality, of being the chosen people by being peaceful while those working to break away from the union were described as violent. Elections were coming up and scheduled for the end of December.[133]

The end of fighting in Mizoram and the prospective political settlement due to renewed negotiations between GOI and Laldenga's Mizo National Front would enable the government to transfer large numbers of troops to fight separatists in Tripura, Manipur and Nagaland.[134] By December 1985 the armed groups in Tripura, Manipur and Nagaland had stepped up their military activities. If we take Steven R. Weisman's quote of a senior government official as indication then Delhi on its part responded with its usual arrogance: 'Delhi is not ruthlessly crushing these groups today, but if Delhi wants, Delhi can crush them. We are looking at it as a minor law-and-order problem.'[135] The peace accord between Laldenga and Rajiv Gandhi elevated Mizoram from union territory to a state with Laldenga as the new chief minister.[136]

In autumn 1988 the elected state governments of Mizoram and Nagaland were dismissed by the centre and presidential rule declared. This was done in Nagaland because the elections resulted in the defeat of those loyal to Delhi. Earlier, in August, the war in Tripura had been ended by an agreement between the GOI and the Tripura National Volunteers.[137]

The NSCN (K) (Khaplang), a faction of then dominant Naga resistance group, having been formed after the surrender of the old resistance cadre in the Shillong Accord, supported United Liberation Front of Assam since the early 1990s, facilitating among other things contact with the Myanmar-based Kachin Liberation Army for arms and training. ULFA peaked during the early 1990s and until 1997 the whole of the Northeast was in the grip of the battle between ULFA and the ISF. This changed with the new government of I. K. Gujral and his home minister Indrajit Gupta who established an effective central command for the different security agencies. In addition to that, due to the criminalisation of ULFA, it had lost its popular support.[138] The case of how the army dealt with surrendered ULFA-fighters in Upper Assam demonstrated that in essence the army acted not on its own volition but on behalf of the centre, and in this case following orders of the Ministry of Defence (MOD) under Georges Fernandes, independent of the state government.[139]

Throughout the whole of the 1990s the situation in the Northeast was defined by the war between ULFA and the ISF, but toward the last quarter of the 1990s, ULFA caved in, just at the same time when GOI and NSCN (IM) signed their ceasefire agreement.

The geopolitical position of the GOI in the Northeast had improved by the mid-1990s. This was mainly due to a rapprochement between India and China, closer collaboration with Myanmar and the election victory of the pro-Indian government of Sheikh Hasina Wajed in Bangladesh in June 1996. The prime minister, Inder Kumar Gujral, used this advantage to offer unconditional negotiations to all groups.[140] This external advantage was still threatened by the internal enemies, since ULFA retained its capacity in Assam to bring '. . . the state to a standstill . . . affecting the whole of the Northeast.'[141] This disadvantage may have contributed to the realisation that the policy of the GOI towards the Nagas until the end of the 1970s had been stubborn, arrogant and insulting. It was only the administration of Narasimha Rao that established contact with the NSCN (IM) via its intermediary Rajesh Pilot with the aim of meeting for negotiations. The GOI had possibly been pressurised into it by the army command that complained about mounting casualties and the continuing reports by the UN Human Rights Commission of atrocities committed by Indian government agencies in the Northeast. However, this policy of rapprochement had been followed up by the Gujral government and resulted in the ceasefire agreement of 1st August 1997. Yet, the *Economic and Political Weekly* saw three obstacles on the way to peace: first, Indian intelligence agencies had created many factions in the Northeast and would lose their clients if peace should come about; second, the NLSG, also created by the GOI, prospered greatly from the status quo and notably from drug trafficking, and third, a heavily factionalised Naga society itself.[142]

The new minister of defence Georges Fernandes visited Nagaland stating his concern about the security threat posed by China, especially on the grounds of its military presence in Myanmar's ports and therewith in the Indian Ocean, and its nuclear collaboration with Pakistan. A Calcutta-based correspondent of the BBC said that '. . . Fernandes' previous support for the democracy movement in Tibet could affect relations with China . . . .'[143] So shortly after the elections, a visit to the Naga hills and his concerns about China plus his convictions towards Burmese and Tibetan freedom movements might have had a profound effect on GOI's policy towards the Nagas.

By May 1998 the new government had appointed its negotiator, Swaraj Kaushal, former governor of Mizoram, to resume talks with the NSCN (IM) that had been interrupted because of change of administration.[144] At the end of June 1998 an Indian delegation led by Swaraj Kaushal had met with the leaders of the NSCN (IM) in Bangkok for a new round of talks to end the war.[145] And by the end of June 1998 GOI announced the extension of its ceasefire with the NSCN for another year.[146] Georges Fernandes was well known for his support of the democracy movement in Myanmar as well as his support for Tibetans and his damnation of the Chinese threat. The MOD under him had told the central command of the ISF in Northeast India and in the Bay of Bengal not to interfere with the flourishing arms

trade there. It had been the case that the central command had become very successful in disturbing the arms runners and had even caught the research and
analysis wing arranging arms to be delivered to the NSCN (K) faction and the Chin
National Army (CNA) in Burma. The article assumes that the research and analysis wing was doing this to support oppositional forces in Myanmar but '. . . destabilising an already volatile . . .' Northeast.[147] But while the author is at a loss to make
sense of this, for us it becomes evident here that destabilising the Northeast is keeping it divided and keeping it not only inside the Indian Union but also lucrative for
numerous cynical political entrepreneurs.

GOI allowed the top echelon of the NSCN (IM) to return to Nagaland '. . . to
consult tribal groups, churches and non-governmental organisations, as well as
local political leaders.' In return, the NSCN (IM) promised not to interfere with the
general elections this time although they continued to consider it as an 'imposition'.[148] And by the end of July 1999, Prime Minister Atal Behari Vajpayee sacked
its previous interlocutor Swaraj Kaushal and replaced him with K. Padmanabhaiah.
Kaushal in turn accused Vajpayee of ignorance towards the problems of the
Northeast.[149]

By April 2000 the peace process seemed to collapse. According to *Frontline*, the
UF government in 1997 stressed federalism and thus initiated the peace process, the
BJP, however, returned to the politics of centralisation. Yet, by mid-1999 both
NSCN factions agreed to stop internecine fighting and with the attempt on Jamir's
life in December 1999 the situation deteriorated. Jamir blamed IM for it, IM
claimed Jamir staged it himself to torpedo the peace process. Further, Muivah's frequent contacts with Pakistan's ISI annoyed the Indian security and intelligence
establishment as well as the union home minister and they tipped off the Thai
authorities who arrested Muivah twice in Thailand on the charge of travelling with
fake passports. In the meantime negotiations were held between NSCN (IM) and
GOI representatives in Bonn, Germany on 31st January 2000. *Frontline* concluded
that neither Jamir nor the Indian intelligence agencies had any use for peace and
that under a BJP administration both had gained more influence.[150] However, after
the release of Muivah from jail and the extension of the ceasefire the only contentious issue remained the extension of the ceasefire area to all the areas of the
Northeast in which the NSCN was functional. This however carried the danger of
legitimising Nagalim, i.e., the inclusion of all Naga-inhabited territory into one
administrative unit, and for this reason met with heavy opposition from the affected
state governments.[151] In addition to that, the NSCN (K) had entered into an informal ceasefire with the ISF, which was formalised when the GOI and the NSCN (K)
officially agreed on a ceasefire on 28th April 2001. The general secretary Kitovi
Zhimomi made it clear that they would accept any agreement entered into by the
NSCN (IM) group, but doubted that they would give their consent to anything
inside the Indian constitution.[152]

In January 2001 the home ministry announced its willingness to extend the
ceasefire to the whole of the Northeast, but hastened to add that it didn't want to
force the respective state governments to do so.[153] In Manipur, 16 people were
killed when police fired into a crowd of 50,000 protesters that burned the state

legislature in protest against the state's ceasefire with the NSCN (IM).[154] The Nagas of Manipur, however, in the form of the United Naga Council of Manipur, the Naga Women's Union and the All-Naga Students' Association, warned the home minister Advani not to give in to the protests, since they only were confined to the valley and that the Nagas of the hill areas of Manipur were all in favour of it.[155] The government finally gave in to the ongoing protests and reversed its decision to extend the ceasefire to areas outside the Nagaland state. The protests were staged out of fear that the extension of the ceasefire was a first step towards the territorial extension of the Nagas,[156] and also due to the fear of a breakup of the state of Manipur.[157] Yet it seems that the GOI did not really reverse the extension, since two years later *The Economist* states it as a fact.[158]

Meetings between the new representative of GOI, K. Padmanabiah, and the general secretary of the NSCN (IM), Muivah, from 9–11th July in Amsterdam, Netherlands and from 21–23rd September 2002 in Bangkok, Thailand largely produced a mutual agreement '. . . to extend the ceasefire for another year, with effect from 1 August 2002'. This notwithstanding, Muivah declared that the ceasefire was a sham, that the AFSPA was still in force, that there were numerous violations of the ceasefire and threatened to fight back.[159]

By the end of November 2002 the ban on the NSCN ended and the GOI announced it would not be renewed to allow its leaders to return to the Naga hills to continue peace talks.[160] Consequently, in January 2003 Muivah and Swu went to Delhi for discussions with Prime Minister Atal Behari Vajpayee. State elections were scheduled for February in Nagaland and two other Northeastern states. The *Economist* counted 58 insurgent groups in the Northeast and quotes the Indian army as having admitted to having lost more soldiers in the Northeast than in Kashmir.[161] According to Misra there had been a deadlock in the peace process that was broken when Muivah and Swu also came to Delhi for discussions with Delhi's political establishment, which, for Misra, signified a sea change in the perception of the Naga question held by Delhi's political elite. Naga and Indian decision makers have realised that the solution had to be a political, peaceful one.[162]

Conclusion

Subash Gatade, writing on the situation in 2004, says that the Northeast had been under military rule based on martial law since at least 1958. This long span of time has led to an excessive militarisation there and brutalisation to the degree that rape, torture, killings, disappearances etc. are therefore considered as normal, although elsewhere something anywhere near this would certainly be regarded as totally intolerable.[163] Roy Burman, an anthropologist working on the Northeast for decades and with close ties to leading mainstream Indian societal and political circles, also states that martial law has failed to combat insurgency and should be repealed at last. That the Indian state refuses to do so, Burman ascribes to ignorance, arrogance and the willingness to act irresponsibly out of political expediency, though he warns: '. . . there can not be any state security without human security.'[164]

For Bimol Akoijam, a Manipuri whose state was threatened to become truncated, it is the Indian's elite's colonial mindset obsessed with '. . . the nation's "security" in the region' that led to the negotiations with the NSCN (IM). This is exactly because the NSCN (IM) is 'militarily' the 'largest' and 'strongest', thus fitting the thinking of the Indian elite that is framed in a violent language and thus has no qualms contemplating to sacrifice Manipur's integrity and to disregard '. . . the socio-political and economic bases of different ethnic groups and their insurgencies.'[165] Similarly, J. K. Dutt describes GOI's policy towards the Northeast in general and the Nagas in particular as being characterised by indifference and arrogance all the way. Further, that the peace process was a step in the right direction, and that if an agreement could be reached it would become of central importance to the whole of the Northeast by way of providing the model for the whole of it.[166]

Monirul Hussain describes GOI's policy towards the Northeast since Indira Gandhi's power politics as bad or better no-governance, characterised by the absence of democracy and as institutionalised corruption, crime and violence. In his own words it was: '. . . sordid politics of northeast devoid of democratic and human content.'[167] That the situation became worse with time is indicated by the fact that since the end of the 1990s death squads started to operate in Assam and secret killings became a regular feature. The picture is completed by drugs, poverty, dependancy, frustration etc. and paid salary in the public sector becomes news. Thus the whole of the Northeast is in a shambles, the situation in Nagaland, though, has improved due to the ceasefire and the parallel polity that the NSCN has built up there and which the Indian state tolerates. And finally, Hussain agrees with Dutt that whatever solution will be found to the question of the Nagas, it will be the blueprint for the rest of the Northeast.[168] Gautam Navlakha, too, blames GOI's insensible approach towards the Naga hills right from the start in 1947 for '. . . the horrible suffering . . .' and waste of potential there. He gives us another possible reason for GOI's willingness to negotiate with the Nagas in the former's desire to establish economic ties with Southeast Asia and to counter China's influence in Myanmar. Navlakha counts the IA as supporting a negotiated peace, but warns that elements in GOI averse to negotiations could exploit the NSCN (K) to sabotage the peace process. However, the new Look East Policy, necessitating a pacified and collaborating Northeast that could facilitate economic transport corridors is the most likely single reason explaining GOI's willingness to enter into a trade-off with the Nagas to expand into SEA.[169]

If this were so, it should show the irony of history that the very same intentions – counter the influence of an imperial competitor and to render possible trade opportunities – were the main incentives of India's predecessor to subjugate the Naga hills in the first place. We have established, in chapters one and three, the fact that the Naga hills had only been collateral damage to a wider imperial project and were thus only partially subjugated. That the chances for peace and more self-determination come now in the same guise of geopolitical and economic calculations point towards a geographical and structural continuity that inspires hope that the Nagas could turn from victims of the global state formation process finally into respected partners in a truly post-colonial globalised world that cherishes economy over statism.

It is this hope that speaks out of Sanjib Baruah's last chapter that is consequently titled 'Beyond Durable Disorder: The Look East Policy of Northeast India',[170] but this prognosis is countered by Christophe Jaffrelot. He writes that the consensus among the Indian political elites on the need for this Look East Policy stems in the main from the desire to strengthen Asianism that is anti-West, and more important, is fed by the conviction that India lies at the centre of Asia, especially of 'Farther India', i.e. Southeast Asia. Also that this Look East Policy is one way to regenerate India, to come again rightfully into its own. Thus the desire for partaking in an Asian miracle, is solidly embedded in an outlook that is defined by geopolitics, security concerns,[171] and yet an aggressive nationalism. So I would have to agree with Bimol Akoijam, that the negotiations with the Nagas are conducted with a colonial mind obsessed with its own perceived (in)security. And it is no mere chance that Michael Scott, an erstwhile admirer of Indian politics, came to the conclusion that the Indian elite did not negotiate to come to any real result but to win time, to divide and rule, as imperialists do.

8 From nation to civil society

Introduction

To render plausible the atrocious conditions of life under martial rule in the Naga hills for decades, one does well to remember that summary arrests, detention without trial, encounter deaths, torture and random killings of the powerless and poor by the police and other state agencies are normal features of everyday life in mainland India[1] and not, and this has to be stressed, a peculiar and exclusive feature of the periphery. To the contrary, existing – and at the same time denied – violent state politics mutually depend and reinforce each other. Thus, the periphery may as well be in the centre of the Indian capital New Delhi: the peripheral in India is the powerless and she gets targeted with traditional brutality that, the longer it is tolerated and denied at the same time, will increase in brutality.

The scandal of the continued existence of the AFSPA, today applicable to all Northeastern states, is a martial law historically based on British wartime legislation. The agitation of the population against it in Manipur in 2004 and the iron fist handling of the new administration under Manmohan Singh that was no different from its predecessors, brought even Indian mainstream magazines to the conclusion that such a policy will drive people to demand freedom that beforehand did not want it at all, and will drive a civil society underground that once stood for political dialogue.[2]

The kind of war that lasts, stop and go, for such a long time in the Naga hills, and the well directed efforts of GOI's intelligence agencies, finally fragmented a once-united resistance into a plethora of standpoints, interests and mutual grievances. They themselves are further embedded in the wider field of the Northeast that is equally fragmented and are complemented by a multitude of state agencies with whom they enter into all sorts of relationships, simply because they have been sharing now for such a long time the same physical space. And for all participants in this mazy entanglement, violence has become the quasi-natural conflict-solving means. And there lies the Gordian knot. Take out violence and the threat of it and the traditional pluralism of the Northeast may become vibrant and creative again. We have seen in the previous chapter that our hopes may be misplaced on the Indian political elite, but in recent years there are signs of hope that local civil societies are determined to leave the vicious circle of violence and counter-violence.

Talking is better than fighting

At the end of 1963 the Indian army still practised what was euphemistically called regrouping of villages.[3] This notwithstanding, the first elections to the Nagaland state assembly were scheduled for 10th January 1964. The resistance had signalled that they planned to boycott them.[4] We have already learned that the plan to hold elections was heavily criticized by Reverend Michael Scott in London as a divide-and-rule device, and even Indian MPs argued that a lasting solution of what they considered as conflict could only be found in a negotiated solution that included the 'rebel leaders'.[5] However, the elections were carried out and[6] were embedded in what *The Observer* called '. . . serious military repression . . .'; the whole election process was monitored by two mountain divisions of the Indian army, in whose hands the ballot boxes remained and to which the voters were escorted by soldiers. The outcome of the elections – 33 of the 45 seats for the GOI-supported Naga National Organisation and 12 for the instantly created Democratic Party – thus loses some of its meaningfulness in hindsight. More so, when we look at the reports that were played into the hands of *The Observer* with full details of names and places, but which were, for the sake of the safety of the eyewitnesses, kept anonymous:

> One eyewitness reports: 'On January 20, the Indian Army went to a village (name given) and burnt down 12 houses. They shot and killed one man and took away the whole male population. Some shots were herd at a distance, and some more must have been killed.'
>
> According to another eyewitness: 'On December 4, three villages (names given) were burnt and the population were badly beaten. Women and children were not spared. A one-year-old child was snatched from its mother and its hands broken in two. Five people were beaten to death. They were chosen because they are influential men in their society.
>
> 'We felt particularly sorry about Mr R. He was first severely tortured, then beaten again, his flesh was cut into small pieces and he was forced to eat these. There was hardly a place in his body not pierced and bayoneted.'[7]

After ten years of war, it is important to remark that the Nagas were divided only into two camps with overlapping relations and all were interested in a genuine ceasefire. This is also highlighted when we consider that, around the beginning of July, the NLSG was willing to resign to pave the way for direct negotiations between the NFG and the GOI, '. . . because we are sick and tired of killing,' as the chief minister of the NLSG had told Paga Jamir, the only Naga MP in Delhi who functioned as envoy between Delhi and Kohima.[8]

At the beginning of May the command of the Indian army agreed to the suspension of hostilities and the Indian authorities supplied vehicles and authorisation to the peace mission.[9] Towards the end of May the peace mission met leaders of the resistance to discuss the ceasefire proposals worked out together with the Nagaland state authorities. From those local officials the peace mission was authorised to move freely in distinctly white-painted vehicles in the Naga hills. Consequently, the peace mission had no problem whatsoever making contact with the resistance that itself had developed a complex parallel administrative structure of civil and military cadres.[10] The Nagas also refused to disarm as long as the ISF remained in their territory and kept up their demand for complete independence in public,[11] while some of the NFG leaders in more private conversations seemed to signal that they would be satisfied with a status similar to Sikkim or Bhutan. At the same time Naga troops were on their way to East Pakistan via Burma, showing that the Nagas did not trust the GOI.[12] And Cyril Dunn, at the end of 1964, summarized the view of the 'Naga underground' as: '. . . armed resistance to what they consider unlawful occupation of their land by the Indian Army.'[13]

On 21st January 1965 the informal talks between GOI and NFG representatives were resumed at the peace camp Chedema. The immediate objective was to agree on an extension of the ceasefire. Neither side had yet said yes to the peace mission's proposal: the GOI should recognize the Naga's right to self determination who in turn were to voluntarily join the Indian Union. The NFG had referred that question to their parliament. The opposition party in the Nagaland state assembly, which was understood to be the above-ground political wing of the NFG, had already urged for an extension of the ceasefire, as had done the gathering of Sema chiefs and the leaders of the Baptist Church in Nagaland.[14] And indeed, the leader of the GOI delegation, Gundevia, announced that the ceasefire was extended until 6th March.[15] The elders of the Konyak tribe passed a resolution that called for a political settlement on the basis of the proposals made by the peace mission. This decision had been reached at a meeting of about 500 representatives of that tribe and had been held in response to a call from the finance minister of the NLSG, which the NFG did not recognize, so the influence this decision had is not clear. Clearly, however, the delegation of the GOI did refuse the proposal of the peace mission, since it referred to the then situation as having arisen out of an act of conquest. Further talks were to be held on 23rd February 1965.[16]

The beginning of February corroborates the suggestion that back then a truly voluntary union could have been the path to a lasting peaceful solution. The NFG demanded a plebiscite to be held and offered that once the decision to remain or secede was left to the Nagas, they would keep the option open for a kind of association that would ensure good neighbourly relations. This suggestion coincided with an all-party delegation from the *Lok Sabha* to the Naga hills to see the situation for themselves. For this occasion thousands of Nagas gathered in Kohima, among whom were about 1,500 NFG troops,[17] a truly surrealistic picture to imagine: the senators of the empire visit the embattled province in which a volatile truce allows a mutual glance between them and the warriors of the insurgent province.

A little later, when the talks were stalled due to the irreconcilable standpoints, Kevi Yallay flew, with consent of the GOI, to London to meet his brother Phizo who, though in exile, commanded the political authority of the Nagas, to save the volatile peace: '. . . since September the Nagas have been leading a relatively peaceful life, though India still maintains military posts outside many of their villages. It is supposed that most of them wish this peaceful state of affairs to continue.'[18]

Scott travelled to London for a stomach operation and gave *The Observer* his view on the changed situation for the population in the Naga hills. Scott's recollection is important in several ways: first, it gives us a rare glimpse of the state of affairs there by an outsider; second, it may illustrate that the Nagas upheld the negotiations, because it suspended, if only for the moment, the miseries of war in their hills:

> For the first time for ten years in the ceasefire area, neither villages nor crops have been burned. For nearly a year the children have been going to school. There has been no curfew in the towns. Health officers, mobile units and even district officers of the Indian-supported Government of Nagaland can travel in the forest and through the villages. Twenty-nine new hospitals, dispensaries and schools have been built and now only await doctors and nurses and teachers to staff them. New roads are being built and water pumped to the villages on the tops of the hills.[19]

Two months after Indira Gandhi had taken office Indian army units were fighting a fierce battle with *c*.200 Nagas armed with machine guns, mortars and rifles.[20] Moreover, the negotiations between the Nagas and the administration under Indira soon became mere time-winning devices devoid of any real content and though it seemed that the NFG, as part of the NNC, at that time would have settled for something like the status of Bhutan, it is unlikely that the GOI seriously considered this as an option. By early 1966 the peace process was dead, though the Nagas were reluctant to return to war again,[21] despite attacks on their army by the ISF and the creation of village guards recruited from criminals and those lured by money and an easy life.[22]

What it was that the Nagas avoided can be deduced from the contemporary case of the Mizos, where the foreign secretary of the newly created government of Mizoram, Hminga, accused the Indian army of an all-out war against his people in general,[23] confirmed by Indian officials:

> Professor Swell, M.P., and Mr. Nichols-Roy, of the Assam State Assembly, members of the all-parties hill leaders' conference from Assam, tonight reported to journalists in Delhi on their visit to the Mizo hills at the beginning of this month. They said that practically the entire population in the Mizo hills was under what amounted to village or house arrest. No movement was allowed without special permission, which was always difficult and sometimes impossible to obtain.
>
> Villagers had been unable to go on with their slash-and-burn system of cultivation, with the consequent danger that they might miss the planting season. Informal martial law prevailed, with the civil administration either paralysed or subservient to the Army.

VILLAGES BURNT

The observers recounted in detail, with names and places, instances of beatings and rape by members of the Indian security forces, which comprise the Assam

Rifles as well as the Regular Army, against peaceful and loyal Mizos, and said they had given evidence that the troops were burning whole villages in retaliation against the rebel presence, suspected or demonstrated. They also confirmed that the Indian air force had been used in ground support attacks against the rebels during the uprising at the beginning of March – which had been denied at high level in the Indian Government, and admitted only under strong pressure in the state capital.

Destruction and misery for the peaceful population is inevitable as a consequence of guerrilla warfare, and nobody can blame the Indian Government for reacting with force and determination against the armed revolt of the Mizos last month.

Professor Swell and Mr. Nichols-Roy made it clear that they were not criticizing the Army as a whole or subscribing to the thought that secession could be allowed, but they gave a warning that even those that had opposed the Mizo National Front, which led the uprising, were now turning against the Indian Government because of the methods the security forces were using. They suggested an early conference of leaders of hill people, which would include the Mizo National Front. If an apolitical solution was not sought, the situation would be out of control.[24]

While in the Naga hills, the loyalist NLSG of Shilu Ao was overthrown in the Nagaland state. Six out of the nine members of the government had already resigned before a motion of no confidence in the Nagaland state assembly succeeded on that day, when only 6 out of 46 assembly members voted for the government. GOI thus lost its ally in the Naga hills and it was speculated that tribal rivalries were behind the no-confidence motion, since Shilo Ao had been accused of favouring his Ao tribe.[25]

When discussing the Northeast in the *Lok Sabha*, it was unclear whether the ceasefire was to be extended to Manipur or not. Jamir, the MP from Nagaland, was in favour of such an extension, justifying this by portraying the positive effects it had in the Nagaland state.[26] As to support this argument, heavy fighting was reported from Manipur, near the Burmese border and about 65 miles from Imphal in which 20 soldiers were killed and their opponents, around 300 unspecified tribesmen, were also believed to have suffered heavy losses.[27] Though the talks between the Nagas and the GOI did not show any progress, were interrupted in October 1967, and the ceasefire due to expire at the end of January, the Nagas wanted a six-month extension, in order to secure Chinese support in case the talks failed, so Malhotra assumed.[28] The Naga resistance was now under the control of those in favour of Chinese arms and support. Furthermore, the majority of the Nagas began to oppose further talks with the GOI.[29]

Consequently, on or around 6th June 1968 the first major battle between the Indian army and the Naga army was fought close to Kohima. While Malhotra and Dunn agreed that the actual attack was launched by Indian troops (Dunn estimated them at around 3,000) and saw this as violation of the ceasefire terms, Malhotra took it as justified reaction to the Naga arms build-up with the help of the Chinese.

According to Malhotra the Nagas were routed with the help of helicopters, while Dunn, referring for support of his view also to Indian reports, told of a complete rout of the Indian forces with hundreds killed. *The Times*, claiming to have debriefed Indian journalists returning from Nagaland in Shillong, gives their number of Indian soldiers killed as *c*.90, while the official number was 29. Dunn's report was written with several weeks delay.[30]

Following the battle the Naga commander-in-chief, General Zheto, was arrested by his predecessor General Kaito, as was another brigadier and several other dignitaries of the NFG. Malhotra ascribes this to an inter-tribal power struggle.[31] Hazelhurst's report on this incident suggests a division between Nagas negotiating with the GOI and others who used the old Stilwell Road across Burma to China to get arms and training from there. Hazelhurst called the latter the militant wing that also had established ties with Naga rebels on the Burmese side as well as with the Mizos.[32] Approximately 600 Mizo and Kuki guerrillas also tried to cross into Burma to reach China, while another Mizo group was already on the way and had encounters with the Burmese military,[33] conveying and illustrating the relief of resistance formed as a crescent at the easternmost part of Northeast India.

The Naga hills were off limits for foreign journalists, so for independent eyewitnesses we have to rely mainly on journalists that went there without the consent of the GOI. One of these was Michael Ross who relayed to us his insights gathered there in June 1968. He spoke of the danger of a renewed open war between the Indian state and the Nagas and attended a gathering of several thousand Nagas of different tribes in the vicinity of Mount Japfu, an assembly that was obviously there to discuss the challenges of the present and the immediate future. There were questions about how Chinese communism could be reconciled with Naga Christianity, the answer was that there was nothing to be reconciled, since the Nagas were in no danger of being converted to Communism. The next question concerned the extension of the ceasefire, and though the general mood was against such an extension since the negotiations brought no progress, nevertheless it was agreed in favour of it plus the demand for independence verified by an internationally controlled plebiscite.[34]

Ross was also provided insight into the workings of the Naga power structure. The Tata Hoho, the Naga parliament, had been suspended in October 1967 and the government rested with the president of the NFG, Mhiasu, and a body of seven men on whose advice he relied. The vice-president was Imkongmeren, and the executive secretary Ramyo; all were determined to fight again, if necessary, but neither of them wanted to join their fight for freedom with those of the neighbouring groups. Not with the ones inside Northeast India, since they at some stage or other had accepted the Indian Union and had even fought against the Nagas. and not with those Nagas on the Burmese side, since this would force the Nagas to fight on two fronts, though for the future a confederation with the Nagas, Shans and Kachins on the Burmese side was considered. Regarding the arms of the Naga army, whose source put such an outrage to the GOI, Ross was astonished to find out that, though many soldiers had indeed been to East Pakistan and acquired weapons there, most of their arms and uniforms came from Indian traders or even Indian soldiers who freely sold theirs to their adversaries, a matter simply of price rather than of principle. This pragmatism was mirrored by the membership of about 1,000 Nagas in the civil service and 2,000 Nagas in the Nagaland armed police under Indian military orders, as well as 46 Nagas as members of the Nagaland state assembly, to which Ross gave the qualifier 'puppet'. These Nagas working for India were in danger of being taken as collaborators by some, but most others saw them still as part of themselves and were sure they would come over, if war broke out again. Ross found all Naga leaders supporting the demand for sovereignty, and was told that the talks with Indira Gandhi were characterised by her lack of time and tells us that Phizo favoured a peaceful solution.[35]

While the Mizos had been fighting for two years, the Nagas had supported them with arms and contacts as they did the Kukis in Manipur and held contact via the Burmese Nagas with the pro-Chinese White Flag communists in the Kachin province in Burma. The ceasefire was in jeopardy while the talks were in deadlock and the Naga general Thinoseille had erected his army camp next to the headquarters of the Indian army in Nagaland.[36] We have learned in the previous chapter that while the Council of the People of Nagaland decided in a vote for the continuation of the ceasefire, the Indian army started its 'Operation Freedom' which the Naga army tried to evade.[37]

In October General Kaito was murdered in Kohima. His brother Kugatho Sukhai, a former prime minister of the NFG kidnapped. Kaito and Sukhai belonged to the top echelon of the Nagas until 1967, were part of the Sema tribe and were against turning for assistance to China on grounds of their Christian faith. The new leadership of the NFG – Mhiasu Angami, president and Z. Ramyo, home minister – were from the Angami tribe and in favour of turning to China for support. At that time 1,500 Nagas were on their way back from China and 2,000 were still undergoing training there. So it could have been a decisive moment for both camps. Phizo, however, denied that there existed an ideological plus tribal conflict between Semas and Angamis, since leaders in the NFG usually came from both tribes and creeds.[38] And the Nagas considered this merely as a personal power struggle, meaningless for their movement and expected in a country that for such a long time lived through upheavals.[39]

With Burmese cooperation Mowu Angami and 200 of his men were arrested by ISF on their return from China. 1,000 more Naga forces were trying to enter the Naga hills under the political leadership of Isak Swu and the military leadership of Brigadier Thieno Seilie.[40] Intensive military operations were reported to have been carried out in the Naga hills in an effort to apprehend the returnees from China,[41] indicating a return to regular fighting. However, contradictory messages continued: the Indians claiming to have broken Nagas' resistance, the Nagas claiming that Mowu had not even been apprehended and that in the two dozen encounters hitherto, also admitted by the Indian defence minister, 800 to 1,000 Indian troops had been killed, which of course was not admitted by the defence minister.[42] It is only clear that this meant heavy fighting in the Naga hills, or, that the build-up that started around a year ago and the occasional encounters had not resulted in regular fighting until March-April 1969. The doubts expressed by Phizo on the truth of the statement that the Indians had captured Mowu might have been motivated by the desire to force the Indians to allow Mowu to be visited by some member of an independent body, for example the Red Cross, or to get Mowu out of interrogation and into an open court. The Indians claimed to have detained Mowu in the Red Fort in Delhi.[43] Soon later Phizo admitted the fact that Mowu had been caught due to information given to the Indians by dissidents whose leader was Kughato Sukhai and with the active help of colonel Zuheto who, according to Phizo, went to the border to detain Mowu. According to Phizo, this made the fight more difficult, but did not mean the end to it.[44]

The NFG announced the replacement of Mowu Angami by Thinoselie M. Kayho as commander-in-chief and the *Hindustan Times* reported that the Sukhai faction moved its camp close to the Indian troops for protection from feared NFG attacks.[45] The MPs of the *Lok Sabha* discussed the situation in Nagaland that was already characterised by three ambushes on the ISF at the beginning of August. These must have been the first acts of offensive attack on the part of the Nagas, since the Indians discussed whether it was a breach of the ceasefire or not and since we know that fighting had occurred often during the previous one and a half years we must conclude that then the initiative had always been with the ISF.[46] Yet, with the fourth encounter happening in the first week of August, the Nagas' 'offensive' seemed to threaten the ceasefire by provoking the ISF into open war.[47]

Major Melvin Kiesel, an US foreign area specialist on South Asia (who had previously been assigned to Vietnam), later attached to the US Defense Attaché Office, New Delhi, estimated the Naga fighters at more than 10,000 and the Indian troops stationed there he described as '. . . a heavily reinforced division . . .'.[48] The closure of camps in the Chittagong Hill Tracts of East Pakistan worked to the disadvantage of the Nagas. These had been used by the Nagas since 1962 due to the rebellion there, the difficulty to reach Yunnan via the long tedious route through a hostile Burma, and the dissatisfaction with the China-Pakistan connection in general. This may have led to the formation of a third political party in the Naga hills in 1969, the United Front of Nagaland, that received support from the underground NFG especially in the 1971 mid-term elections and thus landed a surprise victory over the ruling Naga Nationalist Organization. Kiesel saw this as indication that the armed resistance was on its way to a more moderate stand. The internal power struggle, however, seemed to have been decided in favour of those called 'extremists' by Kiesel. Kiesel hoped that Indira Gandhi, having achieved a position of strength after her election victory in 1971, might have been able to make the concessions necessary to defuse the situation, that were: '. . . the creation of a Naga Supreme Court, the appointment of a State Governor, and the removal of the Indian Army from the state.' On the last point in particular all Naga groups, including the NLSG, were united. Furthermore, all Nagas – especially those in Manipur – were pressing for the demand for the integration of all Nagas into the Nagaland state. Kiesel warned that delay in these matters would only result in further guerrilla violence, that, in his estimation, the Nagas could keep up for a long time to come, due to a number of factors that all played in favour of this kind of resistance: the terrain, the history, the bonds by family, religion, history and fears etc. Kiesel, in this way, clearly advised a concessional and conciliatory policy at the end of 1971.[49]

War, Shillong Accord and reorganisation

Confronted with the loss of bases in former East Pakistan and the predictions that this meant an end to the Naga and Mizo resistance, Phizo in London was quick to state that the struggle would continue.[50] Information conveyed by Phizo to *The Observer* spoke of attacks on the civil offices of the NFG and its personnel, including killings, public displays of maltreatment and harassment of the ordinary population, all in order to intimidate the people into giving up their support for the resistance. This happened for the whole of the first quarter of 1972 and was part of the GOI's 'final drive' against Naga resistance.[51]

Around the same time Nagas were still returning from China and entering Manipur, the resistance's activities seemed to have shifted towards the south of the Naga hills, i. e. to North Manipur. The hills surrounding the Manipur valley were, and are still, inhabited by groups that see themselves as Nagas. *The Observer* gave the number of Indian troops in NL at around 40,000, and that the mood in the population had definitely swung back towards demanding independence or something close to it and that the GOI should take up its negotiations again with the NFG. This had also been propagated by the biggest demonstration thus far, in which predominantly villagers proclaimed on placards that their women were being harassed by Indian troops.[52] Yet, GOI now was set for war and the assassination attempt on Hokishe Sema was used as a pretext to outlaw the NNC, the NFG and the Naga army.[53]

To mark the publication of Neville Maxwell's *India and the Nagas*, Patrick Montgomery, the secretary of the Anti-Slavery Society, retold the modern history of the Nagas in *The Times*, also describing recent developments since August 1972, when GOI redirected its troops from newly founded Bangladesh to Nagaland:

> . . . now to be pacified for good. A long-term road-building programme is far advanced; strong reinforcements have brought the Indian garrison to an estimated 100,000, and now large tracts of forest are being burned, presumably as a prelude to the destruction in detail of the Nagas still to resist.[54]

A depiction reminiscent of the 1880s – the penetration of the hills with lines of communication, the destruction of the forest that could serve Naga resistance as cover, the dramatic build-up of troops – were the harbingers of the coming offensive. As had been demonstrated in chapter six the strategy of the military campaign in these wars against fractious populations consisted in the main of tactics of terror:

> The reports which have reached Europe over the years from Federal sources would be hard to credit were they not in great detail, giving names, ages, dates and places, and did they not conform to the pattern known to Scott. One incident became so widely known that to preserve the credibility of the puppet government that government's own newspaper published the story. This named an Indian company Commander who with some of his men raped four Naga girls in their village church.[55]

The Observer likened India's policy to former and contemporary forms of colonial subjugation. Even the NLSG admitted that the villagers supported the NFG which in turn made them into the natural targets for the ISF '. . . in lieu of the elusive Federal forces . . .' and taking Maxwell's report as source said that the GOI had unilaterally broken the ceasefire and:

> . . . that the Indian Army has returned to the violently repressive but unsuc-cessful methods it tried in 1957–58. Villages suspected of supporting the guer-rillas are being burned with their standing crops and granaries, villagers beaten and tortured, the women raped. The report includes a detailed account of 147 acts of cruelty committed since September 1972 – 47 of them in one day in February 1973 when the 7th Jat Regiment attacked Sakraba.[56]

The general elections of 1974 dismissed Hokishe Sema and his Naga National Organization, and Vizol and his UDF were voted to power in the Nagaland state. Vizol's UDF was the overground support for the underground, because the NFG and its armed wing, the NFA had been banned, as had been Phizo's NNC. The UDF stood for the resumption of negotiations between the NFG and the GOI, i.e., for a political settlement of the Naga question. The outcome of the vote as being pro-Naga underground was the more astounding, according to the Bombay *Economic and Political Weekly,* since several measures were undertaken to ensure a pro-Indian result: villagers were escorted to the polling stations where the troops out-numbered civilian administrators, non-Naga residents, including troops, were given the vote and constituencies were reorganised to ensure a pro-Indian vote for Hokishe Sema, but the Nagas must have voted unanimously for Vizol to prevent this, using the vote as an anti-Indian demonstration.[57] Later, with the start of the dry season in August, Indian troops went on the offensive in the Naga as well as the Mizo hills.[58]

By September 1975 even the Indian army admitted 'massive operations' in the Naga hills and announced a successful outcome in the near future, though this had been reiterated since 1972. The Indian army claimed that its pressure had forced the Nagas to split up into small groups avoiding clashes and was by then concentrated in the Eastern Naga Revolutionary Council area in Konyak terrain bordering Burma, i.e., northern Naga hills. 200 armed Nagas under Muivah and Vedai had been going to China for training in January 1975 and were about to return to the Naga hills.[59]

The Shillong Accord in November 1975 marked a temporary breakdown of Naga resistance and its further compartmentalisation. For Hazarika, the ceasefire in the 1960s triggered the development of Naga factions into pro- and anti-Indian. The Shillong Accord of 1975 then produced the National Socialist Council of Nagalim (NSCN) in 1980, since the NNC was part of the Accord. The NSCN was led by Muivah and Swu and both, right from the start, established contacts with human rights groups in Europe, Southeast Asia and the United States.[60] By 1984 the NSCN, with bases mainly in Manipur, the neighbouring Somai tract of Burma, in Bangladesh and in the Tirap district of Arunachal Pradesh, lying to the north of

Nagaland, had already become the most active resistance group. The north of Manipur saw most of the fighting and Hazarika pictured life in Imphal, the capital of state, as a besieged one:

> Paramilitary troops armed with automatic weapons and equipped with radios continuously patrol the streets of this capital of the northeastern frontier state of Manipur, searching for insurgents fighting for independence from India. Posters of 'wanted criminals' with photos and rewards are plastered at street corners, bringing to mind Hollywood westerns.[61]

What Hazarika conveyed is the picture of a region in which many have acquiesced to the superior means of power of the Indian Union, but also that many have not, and that actually the area caught in violence was growing not shrinking, despite the mantra of the authorities that an end to violence was just around the corner.[62]

Later, clashes between the NSCN on the one side and the Burmese army and local population on the other, on Burmese territory across the frontier from the Tuensang district, were reported in which 300 local villagers and 40 NSCN cadres were killed. The reason given was the refusal of the residents of Mutang to give assistance to the NSCN and the retaliation for the killing at the hands of the inhabitants of the village Konwa. The number of the NSCN army is given as being around 3,000.[63]

By December 1985 the armed groups in Tripura, Manipur and Nagaland had stepped up their military activities.[64] After 20 years of fighting, the war in Mizoram ended after an accord was signed between Rajiv Gandhi and Laldenga who had been in jail for most of the 20 years. The troops, no longer needed in Mizoram, were thought to have been redirected to Manipur and Nagaland.[65] In September and August 1988 the elected state governments of Mizoram and Nagaland were dismissed by the centre and presidential rule declared. This was done in Nagaland because the elections resulted in the defeat of those loyal to Delhi.[66] In 1988 the NSCN split into NSCN (Isak-Muivah) and NSCN (Khaplang), after the latter had tried to assassinate the former. Since then mutual killings were the order of the day and both groups practised what Hazarika called extortions.[67] In the middle of August 1990 the ULFA, the United Liberation Front of Manipur and the NSCN (K) reached an understanding to coordinate their military operations.[68] Yet, different groups also turned increasingly against each other, internecine fighting began to gain pace.[69] In neighbouring Assam, due to mounting military pressure, ULFA signalled its willingness to negotiate a peaceful settlement. This was also intended to remove direct rule by centre and the de facto martial law to which the state was subjected.[70] By December 1991 ULFA announced a unilateral ceasefire, which was considered to be a result of the relentless campaign of the Indian army and its divisions inside ULFA.[71]

In May 1993, the NSCN (IM) had renewed its activities in the Manipur-Myanmar border area. At the same time fighting between the Tangkhul Nagas and the Kukis had started. Hazarika described the NSCN (IM) as dominated by Tangkhuls and the Kukis as their traditional rivals.[72] A particular instance of brutalisation in the Naga-Kuki fight was the attack by the NSCN (IM) on the Kuki village Zaupi in Manipur, where they '. . . lined up the men and shot them.'[73] The Nagas saw the Kukis as government informers, settled there first by the Meitis and then by the British and ordered them to leave the region. The Nagas had taxed the Kukis, but they took the opportunity of the split in the NSCN, and refused to continue to pay taxes. The Kukis received support from the Kuki National Army. In the above mentioned massacre 90 Kuki men were killed, and in the ensuing revenge and counter-revenge villages were burned, thousands fled their homes and an additional 150 were killed. The death toll of the previous 10 months was numbered at more than 1,000 Nagas and Kukis, while all but 50,000 had fled their villages. The fight is also seen as one of control over the '. . . profitable smuggling of timber, gold, arms and heroin.' as a major means of financing their guerilla wars. [74]

The second half of 1993 revealed an increase of operations in scope and territorial expansion of the NSCN (IM) against the ISF and its rival faction NSCN (K) (who by now supported the Kukis). The NSCN (IM) group, from its former stronghold in North-Manipur, encroached into northern Nagaland, into the districts of Mokokchung, Zunheboto and Wokha and managed to ambush ISF personnel and relieving them of their weapons on a regular basis. This demonstrates an operational area covering Manipur's districts of Tamenglong, Ukhrul and Senapati and Nagaland's districts of Kohima, Mokokchung, Zunheboto and Wokha. Before this renewed and growing confrontation with the Indian state, everyday life in the Naga hills had been characterized by violence once more:

> Over and above these isolated incidents in remote areas is the daily reality of life in Dimapur, the headquarters, no less, of three corps of the Indian army, where a virtual free-for-all situation has been prevailing for years, and where every faction and sub-faction of the insurgents, genuine and bogus, as well as 'underground', and overground activists have been having a field day, openly collecting taxes and settling scores.[75]

At the end of February 1995 a train carrying troops was bombed, killing 25 Indian soldiers and critically wounding 30. The NSCN (IM) then had the incentive, controlling the highways into Manipur and training and arming the Bodo Security Force in Assam. A further complication was the situation caused by the Naga-Kuki fight, leaving 600 dead, and rivalries over control of the drug routes between insurgent groups that used them to finance their arms and organisation. The situation was further characterised by a tense military that whenever targeted ran amok against civilians, as it had done in Imphal shortly before, because it couldn't catch its adversary.[76] The mutual killing between Nagas and Kukis was ended due to the efforts of the women of both groups.[77] We will later hear more about the instrumental role women started to play in the peace process.

Sanjay Sangvai – who visited Nagaland in April 1996 as part of a group that intended to gather information on the Naga problem in general and the human rights situation there in particular – took note of four outstanding factors that for him at that time determined to a large degree Naga society: First was the egalitarian outlook of the Nagas, the second the relative prosperity, the third the determination to continue the fight for freedom and the insistence of being not Indian, and the fourth the ongoing human rights violations by the omnipresent armed forces of the Indian state:

> The continued presence of the armed forces, and the atrocities and violation of human rights by them has been the fourth aspect of the reality of Nagaland. Apart from the visible atrocities in and outside of the custody, of which there has been no dearth, the armed forces presence has itself made life abnormal. These armed jawans, insecure though they feel in this alien land, are every-where – in bazaars, chowks, on roads, highways. People, particularly girls, feel insecure and threatened. Any time a havaldar can nab you or shoot you, make the people run for their life and dignity. The Armed Forces Special Powers Act has further immunised them from the normal state administrative control, leg-islative and judicial accountability. The armed forces thus has been a state within state. The very presence of these forces, notwithstanding some gestures of goodwill and concern by the army and by some enlightened officials, con-tinues to antagonise the people. An avoidable bitterness about the state, about India pervades throughout the villages, and boardrooms of the intellectuals. The armed forces and their acts of omissions and commissions further alienate the Naga people . . .[78]

And Sangvai perceived, what he called '. . . an enlightened [Naga] intelligentsia . . .' that for the previous five years had made an effort to add to the discussion on Naga freedom, and besides the concern for human rights, that groups like the Naga People's Movement for Human Rights and the Naga Students' Federation high-lighted, considerations for: '. . . democracy, tolerance, participation, cultural iden-tity, restraints on consumerism and money culture along with saving the natural resources, [and the] indigenous knowledge system. All this is still in an incipient stage though.'[79]

Sangvai further established that the local government was not representative of the people but as part of a local profiteer class represented only by its own interests that coincided with those of the central government and the task of the armed forces on the ground was to protect these interests.[80]

In the beginning of 1997, while Bodo separatism was blamed for a bomb attack on a train north of Gauhati and Tripuri, guerrillas had killed 22 Hindu settlers, Naga separatists were reported to have killed three members of the NLSG on Christmas Day 1996, as well as having shot 30 bus passengers from the Kuki tribe.[81] Later that year there was evidence of an extension of the inter-tribal fighting into southern Manipur. The Kukis wanted to bring their related group of the Paites into their camp to counter Naga dominance. The Paites, however, preferred to remain neutral. The Kukis took this as taking sides with the NSCN (IM) and attacked them. The Paites retaliated in due course with the result of 100 dead, 300 houses destroyed and 10,000 homeless in the Churachandpur district.[82]

Ceasefire and civil society

On the eve of the agreed ceasefire between the NSCN (IM) and the Gujral administration four army personnel were killed and 15 injured in two attacks in the vicinity
of Dimapur. *The Indian Express* said that the NSCN (IM) dominated Manipur,
while the rival faction NSCN (K), opposed the ceasefire and controlled the
Nagaland state. Yet the ceasefire only covered the Nagaland state. The NSCN (K)
denounced the ceasefire as a farce and a ploy of the GOI to keep the Nagas
divided.[83]

The NSCN (IM) had by the middle of the 1990s established itself as the most
powerful organisation of the Northeast. So it was not accidental that it was this
organisation the GOI decided to negotiate with. But at the same time, it was also
acknowledged, that the Nagas were hopelessly at odds with each other; there was
the NSCN (IM), the NSCN (K), the Federal Group, the parental organisation NNC
and the NLSG. The NLSG in particular profited from the thriving drug trafficking,
which was vehemently opposed by the NSCN (IM). It had by then also become
clear that Indian intelligence agencies had worked towards creating as many factions as possible and was averse to any peaceful solution which would antagonise
their clients. In this way, the intelligence agencies, their clients, the officials of the
NLSG and the drug mafia were all opposed to non-lucrative peace. However, the
need for reconciliation and unification was obvious to the general population and
the church and the tribal leaders were already mentioned as being instrumental in
this respect.[84]

Another consequence of the ceasefire was the admission of a BBC team into
Nagaland. The impression the BBC got was that the IA had '. . . adopted a lower
profile . . .', at least in Kohima; the BBC obviously was not allowed to travel
widely, but witnessed even in Kohima that the ceasefire was deceptive – not less
than 120 people had been killed mostly in inter-factional fighting between NSCN
(IM) and NSCN (K). The Naga population, according to the BBC, saw this fratricidal war as serving Indian interests.[85] The call for a boycott of the general elections
1998 resulted in the resignation of several members of the state assembly, obviously due to threats from the separatists.[86] Yet a week later the NSCN (IM) agreed
to an extension of the ceasefire until April and declared it would not interfere with
the upcoming elections '. . . as threatened by its armed wing.'[87] However, as a result
of the boycott only Congress competed in the elections and accordingly won
unchallenged 43 out of the 60 constituencies.[88]

At the end of June 1998 the leaders of the NSCN (IM) met with an Indian delegation led by Swaraj Kaushal in Bangkok for a new round of talks to end the war,
but with no result.[89] The demands of the NSCN (IM) were the participation of the
prime minister in unconditional talks to be held outside India, as these were the articles of the ceasefire agreement. The NSCN (IM) furthermore signalled that it then
would agree to a status similar to the one of Bhutan and made it clear that the GOI
had already abrogated the agreement by not agreeing to talks at PM level and by
violating the ceasefire that initially covered all areas in which the NSCN (IM)
was active, while the ISF respected only the Nagaland state and had launched

operations in Arunachal Pradesh, Assam and Manipur. However, the NSCN (K) and the NNC announced their opposition to the ceasefire and the negotiations, invalidating their chances to achieve real peace, according to the magazine *Frontline*.[90] In November 1998 the IA suspended operations against the NSCN (K) and asked them to come forward to discuss the details of the implementation of the ceasefire.[91]

At the end of July 1999 the NSCN was blamed for an attack on the police in Assam, killing at least five.[92] At the same time the almost two-year-old ceasefire had a chance for renewal on 31st July, although Muivah made it clear an extension would depend on GOI's willingness to concede something in the direction of Naga independence. Simultaneously, the leadership of the NSCN (IM), with the blessing of the GOI, had officially come to the Naga hills for the first time in 33 years to confer with Naga tribal, church and civil society groups. In return the NSCN (IM) pledged not to interfere with the upcoming general elections, though they insisted that they saw them as being forced on the Naga people.[93] A month later, the NSCN (IM) carried out an attack on its rival faction, the NSCN (K), and killed three of its leaders. Chief Minister Jamir said this violated the ceasefire agreement.[94] Since the ceasefire the fratricidal war between the two NSCN factions had intensified and slowly the Khaplang group had been put on the defensive and only retained its hold on the very north of Nagaland, in the territory of the Konyak tribe, not represented in its rival NSCN (IM) and in Myanmar. This limitation in territorial extension in contradistinction to its rival group made it into a natural ally for other resistance organisations in the Northeast that had developed into opponents of the IM-group. The dominance of the NSCN (IM) made the other groups around it join ranks. And despite the complex picture it conveys to the outside, on the ground 'Everyone knows who is on whose side.'[95] The end of August 1998 saw renewed fighting between the two NSCN factions in Mokokchung town and area. The general secretary of the Khaplang group had been assassinated the previous week.[96]

The NSCN (IM) had by then established itself in Bangkok and had been tolerated by the Thai authorities. Yet, in January 2000, Muivah, arriving from Pakistan, was arrested by the Thai authorities and sentenced to a year in jail for trying to enter Thailand on a fake South Korean passport. He was first released and then rearrested when he tried to leave the country for Singapore on another fake passport on his way to a conference in the Netherlands.[97] Lawyers co-ordinated by human rights organisations stressed Muivah's importance for the peace process in Northeast India during his trial in Bangkok.[98] Back in the Northeast the NSCN (IM) boycotted the state assembly elections in the state of Manipur set for February 2000 and threatened to fine each village that allowed the vote to take place. The reason given by a NSCN spokesperson for its opposition to elections, was that '... they added a complication to the talks taking place between his organisation and the Indian government.'[99] However, elections were carried out and the governor Ved Marwah swore in a coalition government in which all but four members of the assembly held cabinet positions.[100]

In 2000 Muivah was described by Hazarika as the key figure of the NSCN (IM); he in turn described NSCN (IM), as the organisation accepted by the Nagas as their national organisation.[101] Moreover, Hazarika repeatedly named the NSCN (IM) as the mother of all Northeastern insurgencies, since it had trained many of these and possessed itself a powerful cadre and thus he considered it as the key to the peace process in the Northeast. The NSCN (IM) had originally negotiated with former Mizoram governor Kaushal; since 1997, with the GOI, mostly at The Hague in the Netherlands; and from 1999 onwards with the former home secretary Padmananabhiah.[102] While in jail Muivah had nominated Swu to continue the negotiations who in turn agreed with Padmananabhiah on an extension of the ceasefire. At the same time members of the Naga civil society exerted pressure on the two NSCN factions to settle their differences and thus face the GOI from a united and strong position. Most Nagas wanted unity. Everyday life was charac-terised by corruption, extortion, double taxing, kidnapping and violence, in which state governments and factions alike participated.[103] The code of conduct during the ceasefire was and is still today that the militants did not carry their weapons in towns and other mutually agreed places while the ISF remained in their barracks; complaints about violations of the ceasefire terms were followed up by members of a ceasefire monitoring cell. Hazarika stressed the severe pressure from the Naga civil society on the NSCN to continue the negotiations.[104]

However, the decades-long nightmarish reality and the disillusion that set in had brought about an outspoken Naga civil society that Hazarika wanted to see as a hopeful example for other regions afflicted by violence.[105] Similarly, Udayon Misra argued that, in contrast to the lively civil societies of Mizoram, Manipur and above all of Nagaland, the civil society of Assam seemed to have been silenced by 2002 in the face of intimidation, rape, torture, fake encounters and random killings. The Indian army, protected by draconian laws, acted as the principal agent of the Indian state and consequently both were seen increasingly as an occupational force and as abrogators of the rule of law and human rights. And Misra reminded his read-ers that the Indian state had failed in the same way in the Naga hills and that it had been the Naga civil society that stepped in instead to insist on a peaceful solution and was pivotal in bringing about the ceasefire as well as mediating arising con-flicts. Misra added that no group could afford to ignore the pressure of this civil society.[106] However, in 2002 internecine fighting was still being reported between NSCN (IM) and (K), and the former accused the latter of having the support of the NLSG and certain Indian paramilitaries.[107]

Despite the ongoing peace process, the 'ground realities' in the Naga hills were characterised by '. . . abductions, ambushes, looting, extortion and sabotage by sev-eral other insurgent groups . . .'[108] Yet, at the beginning of 2003 J. K. Dutt thought it possible that all the different Naga factions and civil society groups '. . . rally round the Nagalim issue and extend support to the NSCN (IM).' He explicitly mentioned the NSCN (K) group.[109] Dutt, as well as the *Economist* speculated that the Nagas might accept something short of independence but not within '. . . Nagaland's current borders.'[110] The Naga intelligentsia rediscovered the 16-Points Agreement stemming from 1960 as a starting point for greater autonomy that replaced the demand for complete sovereignty, although neither faction or part of Naga society and politics would relinquish the demand for Nagalim, i.e. the inclusion into one polity of all Naga-inhabited areas, and the granting of independence. In this there existed consensus,[111] but stubborn resistance to it in Manipur. However, Swu, after having been to Delhi for negotiations in Janurary 2003, declared peace, and the Indian Army admitted it had lost more of its men in the Northeast than in Kashmir. Peace, so declared the *Economist*, might be possible[112] though progress in the peace process remained elusive,[113] and the new Look East Policy was still conducted in the colonial mindset and garrison mentality. The GOI looks east still through the security lens, putting everything in military categories,[114] to establish 'Pax Indica': '. . . in the typical manner of the master-servant dialectic, while the periphery is turned into bloody and grimy indignity, the centre declines unawares through lofty rhetorical fog into a frightening brutality.'[115]

Rhetoric and discourse are not everything and have to be measured against actions and these show brutality as a regular feature and standard procedure, and once its agencies are brutalised '. . . the state cannot remain far behind.'[116] So, nothing new in the Northeast, except a pause in violence in the Naga hills, which, though, '. . . for many locals . . . is blessing enough.'[117]

Conclusion

That the arrogance and indifference of the Indian state's policy towards the Northeast has alienated its inhabitants to the degree that they don't consider themselves as Indians is by now widely agreed on.[118] So, the question remains, why are the Nagas willing to negotiate while most of the rest of the Northeast is in turmoil? While Nagaland state elections have to be understood in the context of tribal and political rivalry, as reflections of factional politics, the institutions of the Naga civil society have achieved the real extension of democratic space.[119] And it is in the pressure exerted by their own civil society, the Tata Hoho, the churches, and above all the Naga women's organisations, where we find the answer to the willingness to negotiate on the part of the Naga fighters. In recent years most authors agreed on the central and exemplary role that Naga civil society played in furnishing peace. For Misra this vibrant Naga civil society has its roots in the traditional power structure. The dominant role the women have therein is credited by Shimray to their traditionally strong position in their society and specifically to their role as mediators and peacemakers and as guardians of social values. For Misra it is also this traditional heritage that points the way out of the contemporary impasse. The very democratic structure of the different layers of Naga society and the democratic spirit of its personnel do not allow for totalisation under one organisation:

> Rather it would be a synthesis of the traditional and the modern, of divergent viewpoints and attitudes where the sanctity of both social and individual space of the different Naga tribes as well as the minorities would be ensured. This is exactly what the civil society groups led by the Naga Hoho have been trying to achieve.[120]

This could be the solution: we have the *genius loci* and the separation of powers of Montesquieu together with Kant's demand for evolution instead of revolution.[121] The absence of the feudal tradition and the stress on individual self-determination and personal pride among the people of the hills of Northeast India, that we have attested them in chapter two, now resurfaces as a decisive character trait of the local people to infuse their civil society to stand up to the GOI, its security agencies but also to their own armed groups in order to find a peaceful solution to the contemporary impasse. Though the odds are against them, since they are still too few and too unimportant for their mighty adversary, as is the whole of the Northeast,[122] they have already accomplished a lot. They have, for one, as we just have learned, widened the democratic space to manoeuvre, reduced violence through their pressure and brought attention to human rights violations. But above all, their main achievement is that the Nagas today are not looked upon as semi-rational savages, or *junglis*, as they were called in the Indian parlance until recently, but as courageous people that stood up, and still do so, to injustice and state terror and today inspire people elsewhere, at least in the Northeast, subjected to the same fate. Although the Nagas have not yet gained peace, they have attained recognition.

Conclusion

The aim of this work has been to demonstrate the continuation of two interrelated processes: that the continuing political divide between hill and plains people dates back to the pre-colonial period, and that this divide is rooted in the efforts to subjugate the hill people which has often promoted attempts to conquer them by force. That the hill peoples' resistance has resembled a movement for political independence is as such no mere accident of history. In other words, if instead of conquest by force mutual relations based on the principles of equality and voluntarism would have been offered, especially during the first two decades after India's independence, at a time when the ideology of imperialism had already been thoroughly discredited, then there would have been the possibility that the region might not have been torn by the kind of civil and 'nationalities' wars that afflict the region today. Such a post-colonial constitutional framework is more likely to have accommodated the demands of most of the nationalities in India's troubled Northeast region.[1]

The method chosen to demonstrate this argument in the case study of the Nagas was to render the respective historical agency meaningful by embedding it into a larger framework. This work therefore is very much anchored in the interplay and articulation of historical anthropology, history and political science. Since the British and Indians were more powerful agents, the chapters about them preceded those dealing with the Nagas: chapters one and three focused on the invasions by the British and chapters five and seven on the Indians'. The reaction of the Nagas to these incursions was dealt with in chapters two, four, six and eight. The initiative for conquest always lay with the British and the Indians. Yet, both had to adapt their strategies of invasion and occupation to the circumstances created by the Nagas.

While British imperial ideology drew its legitimacy from the proclaimed difference of the Other and from the right of conquest, the Other, once conquered, was not only allowed, but had to remain *different*. In the case of the economically unpromising Naga hills this meant that within certain limits the Nagas were allowed to handle their own affairs and encouraged to keep their identity. This helped the Nagas to come to terms with their subjugation and defeat. The independent Indian Union, on the other hand, was based on the negation of imperialism by the right to self-determination and was theoretically a voluntary union of people. Imperialism thus ends where consent starts. Since the Nagas refused to give their consent the GOI had to use force, which in turn only strengthened the Nagas' resolve to regain independence.[2]

The longer historical perspective might be summarised as follows: the pre-modern multi-centred world knew regional empires, states etc., but due to a lack of means of communication and control, in addition to shortage in manpower and surplus of land, the centres did not seriously try to subjugate inaccessible frontier areas that constituted a refuge for populations outside larger polities. When European states began to erect worldwide empires, many of these former regional empires and states turned into peripheral colonies from the perspective of the European metropolises. The frontier areas of these peripheries now were in many cases pacified, but not really integrated into the administration of the colonies, and when these colonies themselves returned from periphery to centre by regaining their independence, they in turn endeavoured to incorporate the former frontiers that represent the peripheries of today. In this way the former colonised periphery has transformed into a metropolis and now exerts imperial policy on the former frontier, its contemporary periphery. However, if empire was justified in the past, today most states aim to rule by the principles of self-determination and, at least in theory, the rule of law. The case of the Nagas demonstrates that imperialism and colonialism are very much a feature of nation-building in India.[3]

To recapitulate: the British 'military-fiscal state', itself a product of permanent warfare on a global scale with its rival France, acquired actual control over the East India Company's holdings in South Asia by the end of the eighteenth century.[4] The British possessions in India developed into state-like structures that were equally militarised, its personnel poised for conquest and thus were adequately described as 'garrison states'. When Burmese actions delivered the pretext for war the British invaded Assam, expelled the Burmese from there and thus came into contact for the first time with the hill people known to the plains people as 'Nagas'. Initially the British saw the Nagas as potential allies and described them neutrally, but when British interest directed itself at the hills, their inhabitants were suddenly portrayed as 'bloodthirsty savages' who had to be subdued for the sake of Assam and also their own. However, when several different strategies did not effect the subjugation of the Nagas, this objective was abandoned for more than a decade.

These people of the hills were conscious of themselves as politically different and as comparatively free in contrast with the people living in the quasi-feudal states of the plains. They also knew that they were militarily weaker and that it was only the difficulty of their terrain that protected them. Socially, they were organised in a multitude of polities, which were partially based on a mix of (strategic) kinship and territory, had a high military participation, a strong ethos on individual freedom and collective responsibilities, and cross-cutting ties between the different groups whose actual extent and quality still evades rigorous analytical understanding. Hence when the British invaded their hills the Nagas could rally, and also enforce strong support. They employed a mix of staunch resistance and conciliation, always with the understanding that the foreign conquerors would never stay.

From the middle of the 1860s onwards the British again started to encroach on and partially conquer the Naga hills; a process that dragged on into the twentieth century and was never completed. The motivations for this renewed move forward – a move that not only affected the Naga hills – were manifold and can be ascribed roughly to three reasons: the wish to distract from politics at home, the imperial ideology of late Victorian Britain, and the beginning of a new round of great powers rivalry.[5] None of these reasons actually demanded the conquest of the Naga hills that were of only marginal interest to the British. This explains the reluctant and partial nature of the conquest and defined the set-up of the administration as consequently very light. Moreover, in order to avoid problems experienced in other hill regions, the Naga hills were excluded from the administration of the plains and protected from unhindered immigration. When the British were eventually forced to leave India they did not – despite being conscious of the fact that hill and plains cultures were antithetical[6] – want a separate solution for the Nagas beyond the vague demand for the inclusion of some safeguards for them and other minorities in the constitution of the Indian Union. The Congress-dominated constituent assembly was determined to allow only nominal safeguards and projected the integration of the hill people via assimilation.

The light British administration notwithstanding, the opening up of the Naga hills had a devastating effect on the populations there, with resulting famines, forced labour, epidemics, loss of self esteem and value. In respect of their social and political identity formation it meant the widening of their horizon through heightened interaction among themselves as well as with an increasing number of Others. This process was, however, confined only to a small and western-educated elite that was predominantly trained by Christians, often Christian themselves, and employed in the service of the colonial government. Confronted with contemporary affairs and influenced by western ideas, this elite started to think about its people as a 'nation'. But the elite was an exception. For the majority of the Nagas it was only the Second World War that made them receptive to arguments of their elite that a life purely oriented at and dedicated to the locale was not possible anymore. The boundaries of the populations that were considered by the plains people as 'Nagas' had already been roughly defined before British arrival. The British were only left with the task to find out the basis of this categorisation and the finer divisions among these people themselves.

The hardening of these into national boundaries was realised by post-colonial policy. The agents of the newly independent India professed to respect the right of the Nagas to speak for themselves. This, however, was only liberal rhetoric. As a rule Indians and Assamese looked down on the Nagas as half-savage *junglis*, saw them as unintelligible forest dwellers that had to be ruled and Indianised, if necessary by force – the best language these savages understood. This attitude and objective was not uncommon in the post-colonial world. The GOI thus deprived the Nagas of any right that could have gone unchallenged and finally invaded and occupied their country. When the Nagas refused to obey orders or to cooperate, they were terrorised into submission. The Nagas retaliated in kind and Nehru sent the army in. From then on it was the Indian army that was the main nationbuilding agency in the hills. As Naga resistance persisted, the Indian state started to employ a second strategy: concessions, a share of power and funds to build up a collaborator class in order to divide the Nagas. The strategy which McGarry and O'Leary define as 'Hegemonic Control'[7] has divided Naga factions against each other. From the perspective of the Indian state, it has proven extremely successful.

It was precisely these short-sighted and very crude measures that antagonised the Nagas to the extent that they categorically refused to become incorporated into the Indian Union and became determined to keep fighting to regain their freedom, despite heavy costs. The modern Indo-Naga war is clearly a product of post-colonial politics and could have been avoided. There were several points and turns where Phizo signalled that the Nagas would accept something short of complete sovereignty. Nehru had the standing to push such constitutional arrangements through parliament, but it seemed not to have been within the scope of India's decision-makers' imagination. Rather than negotiate, India's political elite then and now were ideologically inclined toward expansion and domination, not accommodation.[8]

This imperial policy of the new post-colonial states is mostly termed nation building and has always contained the strategies of (state) terror and genocide.[9] And it was – and still is – these components of that policy that created at the peripheries a situation that nowadays is often described as ethnic or sub-national conflict, and the genesis of which might be described thus: an elite belonging to the majority population took over the imperial administrative unit from the departing colonial power. At this point the artificial connection was still visible and acknowledged. The minority elite was told by the majority elite that they would have the possibility to secede later, or they were made to give in through a mixture of promises and threats of violence. At this stage the policy of nation building set in; the attempt of real, effective physical-administrative penetration of the territory inhabited by the minority and seen by it as its homeland. Now every single member of this population experienced foreign rule personally. This experience was reinforced by the fact that the new masters generally looked down on them, a fact that made assimilation impossible. Their treatment as inferior Others at the hands of the representatives of the new state strengthened the We-feeling and sensitised each one for the political mobilisation of their own elite.

If at that stage the minority had not been treated in this blatantly derogatory way, there could have been a chance that they would have assimilated themselves into the majority population and thus become invisible. This was prevented by the jingoism of the new masters that often shows its face after prolonged periods of suppression and humiliation. Local communities reacted to that in defence of their self-esteem and perceived right to their way of life by either non-cooperation and/or threatening and/or attacking the agents of the new state with words or deeds. Their elite, partially engaged in renegotiating their political leeway, was also busy trying to mobilise and unify those which were perceived as being the bearer of their identity, and to value it positively in face of all the derogation.[10]

It was now up to the agents of the new state, who had just turned from servants into masters, to teach the recalcitrant population a lesson. Again, irrespective of the official propaganda by the centre, which either denied the existence of trouble at all, or if admitting it, denounced it as the product of foreign agents or the actions of mis-guided child-like fellow citizens in need of guidance, the agents on the ground were convinced that the targeted population understood only one language: force and violence. Terror and torture became part of a deliberate policy.[11] In the long run it served the determination to unite and fight back. The ensuing fighting developed into a full-scale war and more and more troops were sent into the periphery. Due to the superior firepower of the central forces the minority resorted to a guerrilla war in which it became difficult to distinguish between combatants and civilians. The state forces, seldom able to catch those who were ambushing them, redirected their reprisals against the whole population, and thus firmly established a regime of ter-ror out of their personnel's fear and to deter civilians from helping the guerrillas. Therewith they guaranteed themselves as being continuously seen as a foreign occupational power by clearly creating a them-us divide inscribed in violence, making sure that the bequeathed humiliations would always drive people into the forces of resistance. The experience of such violence, especially against non-com-batant elderly people, women and children, and the stories about it, constituted from then on an integral part of the social identity of the minority and of the history of this identity. It was this ongoing war against the targeted population as a whole that cemented the minority into a nation, determined to fight off of what they saw and still see as an invasion of their land.

The massive mobilisation and the acquaintance with the terrain often led to a situation where the security forces of the state came under pressure or even lost con-trol of the centres of the territory inhabited by the minority. Nonetheless, far supe-rior resources enabled the security forces to bring parts of the land, mostly urban centres, under their control again, if only during the day, by transforming them into fortresses. This marked the beginning of a war that neither side could win.

The right to self-determination, as already mentioned above, on which the inde-pendence of the new post-colonial states rested, made it necessary to deny resist-ance at all, to play it down or to criminalise it. This criminalisation of the defence of their country removed the minority from any possible application of international law that might have protected them in the ensuing war. This criminalisation of the whole population made it a target for the state security forces that unleashed a cam-paign describable as state terror and even genocide. This antagonised the popula-tion to the extent that they remained unwavering in their insistence of regaining their independence.

At the same time the occupational power tried to split the resistance, either with material rewards, blackmailing or by playing on internal differences. The longer the war of attrition lasted the easier this became. Such a division of the resistance, though – and it is now appropriate to change into the present – makes future solu-tions reached through negotiations increasingly unlikely, as this would mean betraying one's allies. Further reasons preventing a solution are the conflicting interests among the personnel of the different security agencies. Different agencies – army, paramilitary, armed police, police – entered into alliances or had business relations with sections of their opposition. Over time this creates an inextricable net of alliances, antagonisms and interests that makes a solution of the conflicts underlying the war nearly impossible. Caught in this web, the civil population grows increasingly disillusioned with their own resistance, but in the face of the invader has no choice but to continue to see it as their boys and girls.

With that a war zone has been established that carries its own dynamic. It presents a reality in which everyone has to accommodate herself, has to survive in it. Violence now presents the dominant way of solving conflicts and thus penetrates every aspect of life. War profiteers aside, any economic development worth mentioning becomes impossible. The social fabric gets destroyed, lack of perspectives lead to epidemic drug abuse and spread of HIV. The centre of the neo-imperial state plays on time. The consequences of the wars at the periphery are here only marginally noticeable or even may be used to distract from other problems.

I have attempted to sketch the development of a continued subjugation under post-colonial/neo-imperial conditions here. This line of argument has been accepted to be valid for many peripheries of Southeast Asia, though maybe not in this historical detail and rigour.[12] In South Asia, however, this is not the case, though the wars in the Naga hills, in Punjab, in Kashmir and in Sri Lanka alone developed roughly as outlined above.[13]

The political struggle of Nagas for autonomy helps put Kant's observation regarding the relative power of evolution over revolution in a South Asian context. In the end what changes is only personnel: the constellation of ideas remains.[14] This led to the continuation of colonialism in India, but there are signs that an evolution has happened recently, though only in the writings of the intelligentsia that is from this very periphery – the Northeast. At the same time Kant's insight plays in favour of democracy and peace, since the Nagas had retained their indomitable spirit of freedom untainted by feudalism. And it is exactly this lack of subservience that in the form of its vital civil society presses for reconciliation, rapprochement and above all for a peaceful society. This is by no means banal. If the sum of the individuals does not allow itself to be intimidated this poses an insurmountable obstacle for any form of totalitarianism that breeds uniformity and death, and works towards a diverse social and cultural universe that celebrates as it proceeds the spirit of life itself.

Notes

Introduction

1 To be fair, one has to admit that in recent years more voices are heard, mostly from the Northeast itself, that acknowledge the imperial politics of the Indian state. These are granted space in chapters seven and eight.

2 Uday Singh Mehta, *Liberalism and Empire: India in British Liberal Thought* (New Delhi, 1999).

3 Michel de Montaigne, *Essais* (Frankfurt am Main, 1998 [1595, 1802]), p. 526, Montaigne here refers to Plato for support of this. See also Immanuel Kant, *Grundlegung zur Metaphysik der Sitten* (Frankfurt am Main, 2007 [1786]).

4 Wassilij Grossman, *Life and Fate* (New York, 2006 [1959]); Isaiah Berlin, *The Crooked Timber of Humanity. Chapters in the History of Ideas* (London, 1990).

5 This was stated by Isaiah Berlin, 'Does Political Theory Still Exist?', in *idem.*, *Concepts and Categories: Philosophical Essays* (London, 1978), pp. 143–172 and demonstrated by Charles Taylor, *Sources of the self: making of the modern identity* (Cambridge, 1989).

6 Charles Taylor, 'Interpretation and the sciences of man', in *idem.*, *Philosophy and the Human Sciences: Philosophical Papers 2* (Cambridge, 1985), pp. 15–57.

7 John Dunn, 'The History of Political Theory', in *idem.*, *The History of Political Theory and other essays* (Cambridge, 1996), pp. 11–38.

8 Taylor, *Sources of the self.*

9 Richard Rorty, *Contingency, irony, and solidarity* (Cambridge, 1989) and maybe comes close to the demand for local concepts and categories that was made by Sumit Sarkar as well as by Dipesh Chakrabarty who otherwise disagree on everything else, see Sumit Sarkar, 'Postmodernism and the Writing of History', in *idem.*, *Beyond Nationalist Frames: Relocating Postmodernism, Hindutva, History* (Delhi, 2002), pp. 154–194 and Dipesh Chakrabarty, 'Subaltern Histories and Post-Enlightenment Rationalism', in *idem.*, *Habitations of Modernity: Essays in the Wake of Subaltern Studies* (Chicago and London, 2002), pp. 20–37.

10 Michel Foucault, 'Nietzsche, Genealogie, die Historie', in *idem.*, *Von der Subversion des Wissens* (Frankfurt am Main, 1987), pp. 69–90.

11 Christopher Bayly, *The Birth of the Modern World, 1780–1914* (Oxford, 2004).

12 That it is indeed possible to analyse while narrating when coming from the density of facts and abstaining from premature rationalizing, see also Tzvetan Todorov, *Facing the Extreme: Moral Life in the Concentration Camps* (London, 1996 [1991]).

13 Karl Löwith, *Meaning in History* (Chicago, 1949).

14 Like Sumit Sarkar does in his *Modern India, 1885–1947* (Delhi, 1983).

1 British imperial expansion and historical agency, 1820s–1850s

1 A. R. Radcliffe-Brown, 'Preface', in M. Fortes and E. E. Evans-Pritchard (eds.), *African Political Systems* (London and New York, 1987 [1940]), pp. XI–XXIII.
2 Prasenjit Duara, *Rescuing History from the Nation: Questioning Narratives of Modern China* (Chicago, 1995), pp. 22–23.
3 'Civilization' and 'Europe' by and large took the place of the term 'Christendom' to define the West against the rest. G. W. Stocking, *Victorian Anthropology* (New York, 1987), p. 11. About the properties of the concept: 'The notion of "wildness" (or in its Latinate form 'savagery') belongs to a set of culturally self-authenticating devices which includes, among many others, the ideas of 'madness' and 'heresy' as well. These terms are used not merely to designate a specific condition or state of being but also to confirm the value of their dialectical antitheses: 'civilization', 'sanity' and 'orthodoxy' respectively. Thus, they do not so much refer to a specific thing, place or condition as dictate a particular attitude governing a relationship between a lived reality and some area of problematical existence that cannot be accommodated easily to conventional conceptions of the normal or familiar.' Hayden White, 'The Forms of Wildness: Archaeology of an Idea', in Edward Dudley and Maximillian E. Novak (eds.), *The Wild Man Within: An Image in Western Thought from the Renaissance to Romanticism* (Pittsburgh, 1972), pp. 3–38, p. 4.
4 Tzvetan Todorov, *Die Eroberung Amerikas: Das Problem des Anderen* (Frankfurt am Main, 1985), p. 142 (my translation; French in the original: *La conquête de l'Amerique. La question de l'autre.*).
5 Ibid., p. 151.
6 Max Weber, *Gesammelte Aufsätze zur Wissenschaftslehre* (Tübingen, 1973), p. 594.
7 Todorov, *Die Eroberung Amerikas: Das Problem des Anderen*, p. 59.
8 Ibid., p. 65, (my translation).
9 John Brewer, *The sinews of power. War, money and the English state, 1688–1783* (London, 1989).
10 Michael Mann, *Bengalen im Umbruch: Die Herausbildung des britischen Kolonialstaates 1754–1793* (Stuttgart, 2000).
11 Douglas M. Peers, *Between Mars and Mammon: Colonial Armies and the Garrison State in Early Nineteenth-Century India* (London, 1995).
12 C. A. Bayly, *Imperial meridian: The British Empire and the World 1780–1830* (London, 1989), p. 105: 'New markets came as a result of war and empire; they did not apparently cause it.'
13 Linda Colley, *Britons: Forging the Nation, 1707–1837* (New Haven and London, 1992), p. 186, see also George Orwell, *Burmese Days* (Utrecht: 1967 [1934]), p. 174.
14 Peers, *Between Mars and Mammon*, p. 65.
15 Nicholas Canny, 'The Origins of Empire: An Introduction', in *The Oxford history of the British empire. Vol. 1. The origins of empire: British overseas enterprise to the close of the seventeenth century* (Oxford, 1998), pp. 1–34, pp. 7–9 and 15. See also Thomas R. Metcalf, 'Ideologies of the Raj', *The New Cambridge History of India*, Vol. III.4. (Cambridge, 1994), pp. 2–3.
16 Anthony Pagden, *Lords of all the world: Ideologies of empire in Spain, Britain and France c.1500- c.1800* (New Haven and London, 1995), pp. 20–23.
17 A. C. Banerjee, 'The East-India Company and Assam', in H. K. Barpujari (ed.), *The Comprehensive History of Assam. Vol. II. Medieval Period: Political. From Thirteen Century AD to the Treaty of Yandabo, 1826* (Guwahati, 1992), pp. 300–331, p. 300.
18 Ibid., p. 301.
19 Peers, *Between Mars and Mammon*, p. 57.
20 Ibid., pp. 147–149.
21 This was so, since gangs operating from EIC's territory were partially responsible for these, see Banerjee, 'The East-India Company and Assam', p. 306.

22 Ibid., p. 306–328. Under the command of Captain Welsh, 'Welsh's Report on Assam, 1794', in Alexander Mackenzie, *History of the Relations of the Government with the Hill Tribes of the The North-East Frontier of Bengal* (Calcutta, 1884), Appendix A., 377–394. That Welsh's expedition was instigated by the prospect for commerce, see A. C. Banerjee, *The Eastern Frontier of British India 1784–1826* (Calcutta, 1946[1943]), pp. 109–111.

23 Ibid., p. 330.

24 A. C. Banerjee, 'Internal Dissensions and Foreign Invasions', in H. K. Barpujari (ed.), *The Comprehensive History of Assam*, Vol. II., (Guwahati: Publication Board, Assam, 1992), pp. 332–352, p. 347.

25 Ibid., p. 351.

26 *Bengal Secret and Political Consultations* (BSPC), Vol. 320, 2nd January 1824 –27. February 1824, listed under Fort William 2nd January, Doc. No. 16, letter written by H. Gordon, Lieut. Dept. Staff to Captain Truman, commanding at the disputed island of Shapuree, dt. Dec. 13th 1823.

27 Ibid., listed under Fort William 6th February 1824, Doc. No. 6.

28 Ibid., dt. Budderpree, 25th January 1824.

29 BSPC, Vol. 321, 5th March 1824–9th April 1824, listed under Fort William, 5th March 1824, Doc. No. 1, dated 24th February 1824.

30 Peers, *Between Mars and Mammon*, pp. 145–146.

31 Ibid., pp. 150–152.

32 Ibid., p. 195.

33 Anthony Webster, *Gentlemen Capitalists: British Imperialism in South East Asia 1770–1890* (London, 1998), pp. 40–42.

34 Ibid.

35 Ibid., pp. 138–145. For a detailed discussion of Anglo-Burmese affairs, though it proposes a different conclusion, does support our argument with its data, see A. C. Banerjee, *The Eastern Frontier of British India 1784–1826* (Calcutta, 1946). Nirode K. Barooah, *David Scott in North-east India 1802–1831: A Study in British Paternalism* (New Delhi, 1970), pp. 63–87 and 230–231, shows that Scott, who was then commissioner of Koch Bihar, and later became agent to the governor general on the Northeast Frontier, and of whom we will hear more, might have been one of the main propagators for territorial gain and war with the Burmese, who in turn might have only wished to consolidate their provinces.

36 BSPC, Vol. 321, 5th March 1824–9th April 1824, listed under Fort William, 5th March 1824, Doc. No. 2.

37 Ibid., Doc. No. 4 and 5.

38 G. J. Bryant, 'Pacification in the Early British Raj, 1755–85', *The Journal of Imperial and Commonwealth History*, Vol. XIV, Oct. 1985, No 1, pp. 3–19, p. 3 and H. L. Wesseling, 'Colonial Wars: An Introduction', in J. A. de Moor and H. L. Wesseling (eds.), *Imperialism and War: Essays on Colonial Wars in Asia and Africa* (Leiden, 1989), pp. 1–11, pp. 2–5.

39 Major John Butler, *Travels and Adventures in the Province of Assam, during a Residence of fourteen years* (London, 1855), p. 106.

40 As had been done before with Scottish highlanders (as already remarked) and in the Bengal presidency, see Bryant, 'Pacification in the Early British Raj, 1755–85', p. 11.

41 India Political consultations (IPC) Vol. P/195/31, Doc. 112, listed under 1st Jan. 1840, Jenkins to Prinsep, dated (dt.) 6th Dec. 1839, includes copy of Bigge to Jenkins, dt. Mahojong 26th Nov. 1839, including copy of Bigge to Grange, dt. ibid.

42 Ibid. The two villages mentioned here must have been Mozema and Khonoma.

43 Ibid.

44 Ibid.

45 Ibid., Doc. 113, Prinsep to Jenkins, dt. Fort William (FW), 1st Jan. 1840.

46 IPC Vol. P/195/39, 25th May–15th June 1840, Grange to Bigge, dt. Summoo Guding, 16th Feb. 1840.

47 *Panjies* were sharpened bamboo sticks, stuck into the ground to hinder opposition progress or to cause injury.

48 Ibid., Grange to Bigge, dt. Sumoo Guding, 29th Feb. 1840.

49 Ibid., Jenkins to Maddock, Secy. to the Govt. of India in the Pol. Dept., FW, dt. 2nd May 1840.

50 Ibid.

51 IPC Vol. P/195/42, 20th July -3rd August 1840, Doc. 93, listed under FW, 3rd August 1840, Jenkins to Torrens, Officiating Secy. Govt. India, Pol. Dept., FW.

52 Ibid., Doc. 94, Torrens to Jenkins, dt. FW, 3rd August 1840.

53 IPC Vol. P/195/55, 12th–26th April 1841, Doc. 79, listed under FW, 12th April 1841, Jenkins to Maddock, dt. Gowhatty, 21st March 1841.

54 Ibid., Doc. 80, Maddock to Jenkins, dt. FW, 12th April 1841.

55 IPC Vol. P/195/56, 3rd–24th May 1841, Doc.105, Maddock to Jenkins, dt. FW, 19th July 1841.

56 IPC Vol. P/196/4, 13th–30th Dec. 1841, Doc. 95, listed under FW, 13th Dec. 1841, Maddock to Jenkins, 13th Dec. 1841.

57 IPC Vol. P/196/10, 7th March–30th March 1842., Doc. 39, listed under FW, 7th March 1842, Maddock to Jenkins, dt. 7th March 1842.

58 IPC Vol. P/196/4, 13th–30th Dec. 1841, Doc. 94, listed under FW, 13th Dec. 1841, Jenkins to Maddock, dt. 24th Nov. 1841 & IPC P/196/13, Doc. 12, listed under FW, 1st June 1842, a series of communications between Jenkins, Bigge and Gordon (the Gordon in charge of Nowgong, not the Gordon in charge of Manipur).

59 IPC Vol. P/196/29, 29th March–12th April 1843, Doc. 76, listed under FW, 12th April 1843, Jenkins to Bushby, dt. 19th March 1843.

60 As a more dated work, see Bryant, 'Pacification in the Early British Raj, 1755–85'. For a newer treatment of this topic see Mann, *Bengalen im Umbruch: Die Herausbildung des britischen Kolonialstaates 1754–1793*, pp. 213–259.

61 Morag Bell, Robin Butler and Michael Heffernan, 'Introduction: Geography and impe-rialism, 1820–1940', in *idem* (eds.), *Geography and imperialism 1820–1940* (Manchester, 1995), pp. 1–12. That the created knowledge was anything but exact, and a long way from qualifying as monolithic or even totalizing, but rather chaotic, see Matthew H. Edney, 'The Ideologies and Praxis of Mapping and Imperialism', in *idem, Mapping an Empire: The Geographical Construction of British India, 1765–1843* (Chicago, 1997). Edney here especially argues against Edward Said, whose view he sees as follows: 'The imperial power thus recreates the empire in its maps, subsuming all individuals and places within the map's totalizing image. Military conquest, geo-graphical conquest, and cultural conquest are functionally equivalent.' (24) But even Edney admits that the so created data was valid enough to allow for conquest and control (35).

62 And preparing their way towards qualifying as ethnic group, Jean and John Comaroff, 'On Totemism and Ethnicity', in *idem, 'Ethnography and the Historical Imagination.'* (Boulder, 1992), pp. 49–68. An ethnic group therefore is mainly one that lives in an unequal and subordinated position, by taking away their control over the means of production, defined and justified through cultural signifiers. Timothy Garton Ash, when writing on Bosnia and on the difference between a dialect and a language, quotes the linguist Max Weinreich, who said in 1945, that 'A language is a dialect with an army and a navy.' Timothy Garton Ash, *History of the Present: Essays, Sketches and Dispatches from Europe in the 1990s* (London, 2000), pp. 218 and 477. We may say a nation is an ethnic group with an army.

63 See again Bryant, 'Pacification in the Early British Raj, 1755–85.' The British asserted their control over frontier areas in which they were simply seen as another

competitor, moreover, they enforced a tighter control that hitherto had been exercised.

64 *India Political and Foreign Proceedings* (IPFP) Vol. P/196/63, 2nd–16th Nov. 1844, Docs. 74–76, listed under FW, 16th Nov. 1844.

65 IPFP Vol. P/197/2, 14th–28th Dec. 1844, Doc. 87, listed under FW, 28th Dec. 1844, Subassistant to Commissioner Golah Ghat B. Wood to Collector/ Assistant to Commissioner Nowgong Capt. P. Eld, dt. Golah Ghat 15th Nov. 1844.

66 Ibid., Doc. 88, Jenkins to Eld, dt. 20th Nov. 1844.

67 IPFP Vol. P/197/16, 23rd May 1845, Doc. 69, listed under FW, 23rd May 1845, Jenkins to Currie, dt. 3rd April 1845. This logic held whole populations responsible for the acts of their democratically elected governments, see also Docs. 70 and 71, the reports of Capt. Eld.

68 Ibid., Doc. 72, Currie to Jenkins, dt. 23rd May 1845.

69 IPFP Vol. P/197/19, 20th to 27th June 1845, Doc. 123, listed under FW, 27th June 1845, Eld, Principal Assistant to the Agent to the Governor General to Jenkins, dt. Nowgong 20th May 1845.

70 Ibid., Doc. 125, Jenkins to Currie, dt. Gowahatte 5th June 1845.

71 IPFP Vol. P/197/44, 5th–26th Sept. 1846, Doc 18, listed under FW, 19th Sept. 1846, Butler to Jenkins, dt. 29th May 1846 & Butler to Jenkins, dt. Now Gong 12th June 1846 & Doc. 17, Jenkins to Bushby, 19th August 1846.

72 Ibid., Doc. 19, Bushby to Jenkins, dt. FW, 19th Sept. 1846.

73 IPFP Vol. P/197/47, 31st Oct.–21st Nov. 1846, Doc. 18, listed under FW, 14th Nov. 1846, Jenkins to Butler, Principal Assistant of Nowgong, dt. 20th Oct. 1846.

74 Ibid., Doc. 42, listed under FW, 19th May 1849, Butler to Jenkins, dt. Nowgong, 17th April 1849.

75 IPFP Vol. P/197/47, 31st Oct.–21st Nov. 1846, Doc. 43, Jenkins to Butler, dt. Gowhatti, 2nd May 1849 & Doc. 44, Grey, Officiating Undersecy. Govt. India, FD, to Jenkins, dt. FW, 18th May 1849.

76 IPFP Vol. P/198/59, 17th–24th Nov. 1849, Doc. 156, listed under FW, 17th Nov. 1849, Butler to Jenkins, dt. Nowgong Assam, 9th August 1849.

77 Ibid., Doc. 157, Jenkins to Halliday, dt. Gowhatty 22nd August 1849.

78 Ibid., Doc. 171, Halliday to Jenkins, dt. FW, 17th Nov. 1849.

79 IPFP Vol. P/198/65, 4th–18th Jan. 1850, Docs. 85 & 133, listed under FW, 4th Jan. 1850; IPFP Vol. P/199/3, 19th–26th April 1850, Docs. 287, 277, 285, 278, 296, 294 listed under FW, 19th April 1850; IPFP Vol. P/199/5, 31st May–7th June 1850, Docs. 139, 141, 140 listed under FW, 7th June 1850; IPFP Vol. P/199/5, Doc. 145, listed under FW, 7th June 1850.

80 IPFP Vol. P/199/4, Doc. 13, listed under FW, 10th May 1850, Grey to Jenkins, dt. FW, 10th May 1850.

81 IPFP Vol. P/199/5, Doc. 144, listed under FW, 7th June 1850, Jenkins to Grey, dt. Gowhatty, 10th May 1850. Note that Jenkins reported before the request of the government could have reached him, showing him having been conscious that a report was long overdue.

82 Ibid.

83 Ibid., Doc. 148, Grey to Jenkins, dt. FW, 7th June 1850.

84 IPFP Vol. P/199/12, 23rd–30th August 1850, Doc. 68, listed under 30th August 1850, Jenkins to Grant, Secy. Govt. Bengal, Judicial Dept., FW, undated.

85 Ibid., Doc. 69, Extracts From Military Department, undated.

86 IPFP Vol. P/199/15, 11th–18th Oct. 1850, Docs. 88–90, listed under FW, 18th October 1850, communications between Jenkins, Butler, Grant and Grey.

87 IPFP Vol. P/199/17, Doc. 89, listed under FW, 8th Nov. 1850, Grey to Jenkins, dt. FW, 6th Nov. 1850.

88 Ibid., Doc. 144, Grey to Jenkins, dt. FW, 8th Nov. 1850.

89 IPFP Vol. P/199/21, 20th Dec. 1850, Doc. 303, listed under FW, 20th Dec. 1850, Lt. Vincent to Butler, undated.
90 Ibid., Doc. 308, Note by Officiating Under Secretary to the Government of India in the Foreign Dept., Grey, dt. FW, 19th Oct. 1850.
91 Ibid.
92 Ibid., Doc. 318, Minute by the Most Noble the Governor General of India Lord Dalhousie, dt. 20th Nov. 1850.
93 IPFP Vol. P/199/32, 21st–28th March 1851, Doc. 252, listed under FW, 21st March 1851, Minute by the Gov.Gen. of India Dalhousie, dt. 8th Feb. 1851.
94 Ibid., listed under FW, 21st March 1851.
95 Ibid., Doc. 1, listed under FW, 28th March 1851, Minute by the Gov. Gen. of India Dalhousie, dt. 20th Feb. 1851.
96 Ibid.
97 Ibid.
98 Ibid., Doc. 241, Grey to Jenkins, dt. FW, 21st Feb. 1851.
99 Bayly, *Imperial Meridian*, p. 105: 'New markets came as a result of war and empire; they did not apparently cause it.'
100 Colley, *Britons*, p. 186 and Orwell, *Burmese Days*, p. 174.
101 Peers, *Between Mars and Mammon*, p. 65.
102 Cited from Linda Colley, *Captives: Britain, empire and the world, 1600–1850* (London, 2002), p. 304.

2 The Nagas, the Angami case – polity and war, 1820s–1880

1 Ernest Gellner, *Anthropology and Politics: Revolutions in the Sacred Grove* (Oxford, 1995), p. 164.
2 S. Chattopadhyaya, 'Economic condition', in H. K. Barpujari (ed.), *The Comprehensive History of Assam, Vol. I: From Pre-historic Times to the Twelfth Century AD* (Guwahati, 1990), pp. 233–264, pp. 258–259.
3 Ibid., p. 161.
4 H. D. Sankalia and T.C. Sharma, 'The Prehistoric Age', in Barpujari (ed.), *The Comprehensive History of Assam, Vo. I: From Pre-historic Times to the Twelfth Century AD*, pp. 25–43, pp. 35–36.
5 H. K. Barpujari, 'Introduction', in *idem* (ed.), *The Comprehensive History of Assam, Vol. I*, pp. 1–24, p. 3.
6 Alastair Lamb, *Asian Frontiers: Studies in a Continuing Problem* (London, 1968), this and preceding quote pp. 40–44.
7 Anthony Reid, *Southeast Asia in the Age of Commerce, 1450–1680. Volume One: The Lands Below the Winds* (New Haven and London, 1988), pp. 17–18 and 120–124.
8 Anthony Reid, 'Introduction: A Time and a Place', in *idem* (ed.), *Southeast Asia in the Early Modern Era: Trade, Power, and Belief* (Ithaca and London, 1993), pp. 1–23, pp. 7–8. Reid refers here to Victor Lieberman, *Burmese Administrative Cycles: Anarchy and Conquest, c.1580–1760* (New Jersey, 1984), pp. 3–5.
9 Stanley J. Tambiah, *World Conqueror and World Renouncer: A Study of Buddhism and Polity in Thailand against a Historical Background* (Cambridge, 1976), pp. 112–113.
10 Ibid., p. 524.
11 Reid, 'Introduction: A Time and a Place', pp. 3–5.
12 See his two book-like articles: Victor Lieberman, 'Local Integration and Euroasian Analogies: Structuring Southeast Asian History, c.1350–c.1830', *Modern Asian Studies* 27, 3 (1993), pp. 475–572 and *idem*, 'Transcending East-West Dichotomies: State and Culture Formation in Six Ostensibly Disparate Areas', *Modern Asian Studies* 31, 0 (1997), pp. 463–546.

13 Bengal Secret and Political consultations (BSPC) Vol. 344, 5th January 1827 – 16th March 1828, Doc. No. 12, listed under Fort William 12th January 1827, from Grant to Tucker, dated Mannipoor, 20th December 1826.

14 BPC Vol. 126/64, 19th February – 12th March 1833, Doc. 76, listed under Fort William, 13th February 1833; BPC Vol. 127/35, 3rd January – 22nd August 1837, Doc. 4, listed under FW, 21st February 1837 and Doc. 6, listed under FW, 9th January 1837.

15 BPC Vol. 126/68, 30th May – 21st June 1833, Doc. 110, listed under Fort William, 30th May.

16 BPC 127/35, 3rd January – 22nd August 1837, Doc. 3, listed under FW, 21st February 1837, To D. Mungles, Secy to the Govt. of Bengal, Judicial Dept., FW. Extracts from the Proceedings of the Rt. Hon. the Gov. of Bengal in the Judicial Dept., dated 17th January 1837 (copies of certain correspondence about the inroads on the frontier).

17 Ibid. and BPC 127/32, 7th April – 27th September 1836, Doc. 20, listed under FW, 26th April 1836, dated 30th March 1836, Gordon acknowledged the receipt of a copy of the Proceedings of the Govt. of Bengal in which the incursions of Nagas into Manipur were discussed and BPC Vol. 127/35, 3rd January – 22nd August 1837, Doc. 3, listed under FW, 11th April 1837.

18 BPC Vol. 127/28, 7th January – 30th March 1835, Doc. 4, listed under Fort William, 13th March 1835.

19 BPC Vol. 127/35, 3rd January – 22nd August 1837, Doc. 1, listed under FW, 25th July 1837, dt. Cachar, 18th May 1837.

20 IPC Vol. P/195/3, 21st – 28th November 1838, Doc. 106, listed under FW, 21st November 1838, copy in a communication from Jenkins to Prinsep, dt. Assam, 10th Nov. 1838.

21 BPC Vol. 127/35, 3rd January – 22nd August 1837, Doc. 3, listed under FW, 21st February 1837; IPC. Vol. P/195/8, 16th January – 13th February 1839, Doc. 60, Copy of a letter from Jenkins to Lt. Bigge, dt. 18th Dec. 1838; IPC Vol. P/195/19, Doc. 56, listed under FW, 10th July 1839, Jenkins to Prinsep, dt. 20th May 1839, copy of Grange's report about his expedition into Angami territory, undated, sent by Lt. Bigge to Jenkins, dt. Nowgong, 8th May 1839.

22 IPC Vol. P/195/8, 16th January – 13th February 1839, Doc. 59, Jenkins to Prinsep, dt. 11th Dec. 1838. For a detailed discussion of the following decade, see Marcus Franke, *Identity, War and The State in India: The Case of the Nagas* (PhD-thesis, Hull, Dec. 2004), pp. 83–91.

23 See the following documents on the ensuing war: IPFP Vol. P/199/3, 19th – 26th April 1850, Doc. 287, listed under FW, 19th April 1850, Butler to Masters, Sub-assistant to the Commissioner Golaghat, dt. Nowgong Assam, 12th Feb. 1850; Doc. 277, Jenkins to Grey, dt. Gowhatty, 16th Feb. 1850; Doc. 278, Jenkins to Grey, dt. 21st Feb. 1850; Doc. 285, Jenkins to Butler, dt. 17th Feb. 1850; Doc. 290, Butler to Lt. Vincent, dt. Nowgong Assam, 15th Feb. 1850; Doc. 294, Jenkins to Grey, dt. Gowhatti, 25th Feb. 1850; Doc. 296, Jenkins to Butler, dt. Gowhatti, 24th Feb. 1850; Doc. 297, Grey to Jenkins, dt. FW, 22nd March 1850; IPFP Vol. P/199/5, 31st May – 7th June 1850, Doc. 139, listed under FW, 7th June 1850, Lt. Vincent to Butler, dt. Camp Mozumah, 6th March 1850; Doc. 140, Jenkins to Grey, dt. Gowhatty, 9th April 1850; Doc. 141, Butler to Jenkins, dt. Nowgong, 28th March 1850. IPFP Vol. P/199/4, 3rd – 23rd May 1850, Doc. 11, listed under FW, 10th May 1850, Jenkins to Halliday, Secy. Govt. India, FD, FW, dt. Gowhatti, 16th April 1850. IPFP Vol. P/199/5, Doc. 142, listed under FW, 7th June 1850, Jenkins to Grey, dt. Gowhatti, 25th April 1850; Doc. 145, Communications between Jenkins, Butler and Lt. Vincent, dt. between 16th of April and 6th of May 1850. IPFP Vol. P/199/4, Doc. 13, listed under FW, 10th May 1850, Grey to Jenkins, dt. FW, 10th May 1850. IPFP Vol. P/199/5, Doc. 144, listed under FW, 7th June 1850, Jenkins to Grey, dt. Gowhatty, 10th May 1850; no Doc. No., listed under FW, 12th July 1850, Lt. Vincent to Capt. Butler, dt. Camp Mozemah, 29th May 1850. IPFP Vol. P/199/12, 23rd – 30th August 1850, Doc. 66, listed under 30th August 1850, Jenkins to

Grey, dt. Gowhatty, 28th May 1850; Doc. 68, Jenkins to Grant, Secy. Govt. Bengal, Judicial Dept., FW, undated. IPFP Vol. P/199/17, Doc. 88, listed under FW, 8th Nov. 1850, communications between 20th Sept. and 22nd Oct.; Doc. 89, Grey to Jenkins, dt. FW, 6th Nov. 1850; Doc. 144, Grey to Jenkins, dt. FW, 8th Nov. 1850. IPFP Vol. P/199/21, 20th Dec. 1850, Doc. 303, listed under FW, 20th Dec. 1850., Lt. Vincent to Butler, undated; Doc. 304, Jenkins to Grant, dt. Gowhatti, 2nd Oct. 1850. IPFP Vol. P/199/28, 7th – 21st Feb. 1851, Doc. 195, listed under FW, 7th Feb. 1851, Fouqett to Butler, dt. Camp Mozemah, 12th Dec. 1850; Doc. 194, Butler to Jenkins, dt. Mozumah, 17th Dec. 1850; Doc. 248, dt. 5th March 1851. IPFP Vol. P/199/38, 11th – 20th June 1851, Doc. 95, Reid, Commanding Troops in Naga Hills to Jenkins, undated; Jenkins to Halliday, dt. Nowgong, 17th March 1851; Doc. 96, Grey to Jenkins, dt. FW, 4th April 1851 and Major John Butler, *Travels and Adventures in the Province of Assam* (London, 1855), pp. 179–211.

24 IPFP Vol. P/199/21, 20th Dec. 1850, Doc. 308, listed under FW, 20th Dec. 1850, Note by Officiating Under Secretary to the Government of India in the Foreign Dept., Grey, dt. FW, 19th Oct. 1850.

25 Ibid., refers to Doc. 303 of the same volume.

26 Indian Foreign Proceedings (IFP-P), Vol. P/1551, Jan. 1880, Doc. 330, Cawley to Colonel J. Johnstone, Political Agent Manipur, dt. Kohima, 28th October 1879, pp. 268–269.

27 Christopher Boehm, *Blood Revenge: The Enactment and Management of Conflict in Montenegro and Other Tribal Societies* (Pennsylvannia, 1984), chapter 3. That Boehm's book is both, a treatise of Montenegrin feuding and one on feuding in a comparative and theoretical way, see Keith F. Otterbein, 'Feuding – Dispute Resolution or Dispute Continuation?', in *idem* (ed.), *Feuding and Warfare: Selected Works of Keith F. Otterbein* (Amsterdam, 1994), pp. 133–146.

28 Thomas Gibson, 'Raiding, trading, and tribal autonomy in insular Southeast Asia', in Jonathan Haas (ed.), *The Anthropology of War* (Cambridge, 1990), pp. 125–145, pp. 140–141.

29 Janet Hoskins, 'Introduction: Headhunting as Practice and as Trope', in *idem* (ed.), *Headhunting and the Social Imagination in Southeast Asia* (Stanford, 1996), pp. 1–49, p. 2.

30 Ibid., pp. 18 and 40–41.

31 IPFP P/198/29, 10th – 24th June 1848, Doc. 97, listed under FW, 17th June 1848, Jenkins to Elliot, Secy. Govt. India, FD, dt. FW, 17th May 1848.

32 Julian Jacobs, *The Nagas, Hill Peoples of Northeast India: Society, Culture and the Colonial Encounter* (Stuttgart, 1990).

33 Richard Allen Drake, 'Construction Sacrifice and Kidnapping Rumor Panics in Borneo', *Oceania* 59, 1989, pp. 269–279, p. 277, cf. Hoskins, 'Introduction', p. 33.

34 Rosaldo, *Ilongot Headhunting, 1883–1974: A Study in Society and History*, p. 135–136 and passim.

35 Sandra Pannel, 'Travelling to Other Worlds: Narratives of Headhunting, Appropriation and the Other in the Eastern Archipelago', *Oceania*, 62, 1992, pp. 162–178, p. 173, cf. Hoskins, *'Introduction'*, pp. 33–34.

36 Hoskins, *'Introduction'*, p. 41.

37 Christopher Boehm, *Blood Revenge: The Enactment and Management of Conflict in Montenegro and Other Tribal Societies* (Pennsylvannia, 1984), pp. 40–41, 46, 72.

38 Rosaldo, *Ilongot Headhunting, 1883–1974*, p. 140 ff.

39 Boehm, *Blood Revenge*, pp. 43–45.

40 Rosaldo, *Ilongot Headhunting*, p. 168.

41 M. Fortes and E. E. Evans-Pritchard (eds.), *African Political Systems* (London and New York, 1987 [1940]).

42 Boehm, *Blood Revenge*, pp. 195–197.

43 Ibid., pp. 51–63, 85 and 187.

44 Ibid., pp. 187, 203–205 and 207.

45 Ibid., p. 114.

46 Ibid., pp. 119, 121–142, 144, 153 and 162–163.

47 Rosaldo, *Ilongot Headhunting*, p. 221.

48 Boehm, *Blood Revenge*, pp. 43–45, 48–49 and 184–185.

49 M. Fortes and E. E. Evans-Pritchard, 'Introduction', in *idem* (eds.), *African Political Systems* (London and New York, 1987 [1940]), pp. 1–23. Though, at least for the case of West Africa, Fortes and Evans-Pritchard seemed to have deliberately neglected the presence of states and empires to propagate their segmentary scheme, see Elizabeth Tonkin, 'Borderline questions: people and space in West Africa', in Hastings Donnan and Thomas M. Wilson (eds.), *Border Approaches: Anthropological Approaches on Frontiers* (Lanham, 1994), pp. 15–30, p. 21.

50 As Reid writes in another context, *idem, Southeast Asia in the Age of Commerce, 1450–1680. Volume Two: Expansion and Crisis* (New Haven and London, 1993), p. 122.

51 Ibid., pp. 263–265. In a similar vein Tambiah finds evidence that polities contemporary to Buddha could be '. . . better described as segmentary states with ranked lineages rather than as democratic and republican in Western terms.' Tambiah, *World Conqueror and World Renouncer*, p. 48.

52 Fortes and Evans-Pritchard, 'Introduction', pp. 17–23.

53 Tonkin, 'Borderline questions: people and space in West Africa'.

54 To be sure Visièr Sanyu, *A History of Nagas and Nagaland: Dynamics of Oral Tradition in Village Formation* (New Delhi, 1996) is a study in oral history of Khonoma and Kohima, but thoroughly lacks a critical interrogation of his findings. He neither cross-checks them with historical sources, nor does he (to any satisfying extent) embed them theoretically.

55 See István Kende, 'Terrorism, wars, nuclear holocaust', *International Social Science Journal* 110, 1986, pp. 529–538.

56 To name again Reid, *Southeast Asia in the Age of Commerce, 1450–1680. Volume One: The Lands below the Winds*, pp. 17–18 and 120–124 and Douglas M. Peers, 'Introduction', in *idem* (ed.), *Warfare and Empires: Contact and conflict between European and non-European military and maritime forces and cultures.* (An Expanding World: The European Impact on World History, 1450–1800: Vol. 24, Aldershot, 1997), pp. XV–XXXIV.

57 What was also one of the reasons for the easy conquest of Vietnam by the French: '. . . the court did not fully understand the intentions of the French, thinking that since they came from so far away they would be interested only in obtaining certain trade advantages rather than conquering the country and occupying it by force.' Ngo Vinh Long, 'Vietnam: The Real Enemy', *Bulletin of Concerned Asian Scholars*, Vol. 21, Nos. 2–4/April–Dec. 1989, pp. 6–34, p. 7.

58 Interview with Yong Kong, London, 7th August 2001.

59 Walker Connor, 'Homelands in a World of States', in Montserrat Guibernau and John Hutchinson (eds.), *Understanding Nationalism* (Cambridge, 2001), pp. 53–73, p. 60.

60 Ibid.

61 Ibid., pp. 58–60 and quote p. 72.

62 See for example Reid, *Southeast Asia in the Age of Commerce, 1450–1680. Volume Two: Expansion and Crisis*, pp. 89–90.

63 Thomas Gibson, 'Raiding, trading, and tribal autonomy in insular Southeast Asia', in Jonathan Haas (ed.), *The Anthropology of War* (Cambridge, 1990), pp. 125–145.

64 Friedrich Schiller, *Wilhelm Tell* (Stuttgart, 1979 [1804]), pp. 61–62.

65 Schiller, *Wilhelm Tell*, p. 15, italic in the original.

66 Like H. K. Barpujari is doing in his 'Introduction' to the first volume of *idem* (ed.). *The Comprehensive History of Assam. Vol. I: From the Pre-historic Times to the Twelfth Century AD* (Guwahati, 1990), pp. 1–24, trying to reconstruct the history of Assam with the anthropometric pseudo-science of so-called races, comparing hair

types and asking for genetic studies to clarify why, for example, the Nagas are not homogeneous (17). To use Assamese sources in relation to the Nagas is problematic, since in their histories two directly competing national narratives are meeting. We are warned when we see that someone still seriously refers to and uses anthropometric data, as we are when we read that writing and compiling this comprehensive history of Assam is a task of national importance as does Satish Bhattacharyya in his 'Publishers Note' (pp. V–VI) and H. K. Barpujari in his 'Preface' (IX–XII) to the above mentioned volume.

67 Y. L. Roland Shimmi, *Comparative History of the Nagas: From Ancient Period Till 1826* (New Delhi, 1988).

68 D. C. Sircar, 'Epico-Puraanic Myths and Allied Legends', in H. K. Barpujari (ed.), *The Comprehensive History of Assam: From the Pre-historic Times to the Twelfth Century AD* (Guwahati, 1990), pp. 81–82 and 88.

69 For this doctrine, mostly the German Romantic is blamed. See Isaiah Berlin's essays on the romantic school and on nationalism in his *The Crooked Timber of Humanity. Chapters in the History of Ideas* (London, 1990 [1959]) and on nationalism in his 'Nationalism: Past Neglect and Present Power', in *Against the Current: Essays in the History of Ideas* (London, 1997 [1959]). Berlin credits Herder with having created the basis for nationalist thinking.

70 Edmund Leach, 'Tribal Ethnography: past, present, future', in Elizabeth Tonkin et al. (eds.), *History and Ethnicity* (London, 1989), pp. 34–47, p. 43.

71 Charles Keyes, 'Presidential Address: "The Peoples of Asia" – Science and Politics in the Classification of Ethnic Groups in Thailand, China, and Vietnam', *The Journal of Asian Studies* 61, no. 4 (November 2002): pp. 1163–1203.

72 Frank Proschan, 'Peoples of the Gourd: Imagined Ethnicities in Highland Southeast Asia', *The Journal of Asian Studies* 60, no. 4 (November 2001), p. 999–1032.

73 Ronald R. Atkinson, *The Roots of Ethnicity: The Origins of the Acholi of Uganda Before 1800* (Philadelphia, 1994), p. 1.

74 Ibid., pp. 66–81.

75 Prasenjit Duara, *Rescuing History from the Nation: Questioning Narratives of Modern China* (Chicago, 1995), pp. 51–52. For bringing my attention to both, Atkinson and Duara, I am indebted to Proschan's article.

76 Ibid., p. 54.

77 Ibid., pp. 55–56.

78 Walker Connor, 'The timelessness of nations', *Nations and Nationalism* 10 (1/2), 2004, pp. 35–47, p. 46, note 9.

79 These are central statements of both Boehm's *Blood Revenge* and Rosaldo's *Ilongot Headhunting*.

3 Imperial conquest and withdrawal, 1860s–1947

1 A policy already criticised by a contemporary, see Richard Cobden, *How wars are got up in India: the origin of the Burmese war* (London, 1853). Besides Lower Burma, Dalhousie also had annexed Punjab, Oudh, Nagpur, Berar and Satara, in order to add '. . . profitable revenue-bearing territory . . .', see E. T. Stokes, 'Bureaucracy and Ideology: Britain and India in the Nineteenth Century', *Transactions of the Royal Historical Society*, Fifth Series, Vol. 30, London 1980, pp. 131–156, p. 153.

2 David Cannadine, 'The Context, Performance and Meaning of Ritual: The British Monarchy and the 'Invention of Tradition', *c*.1820–1977', in Eric Hobsbawm and Terence Ranger (eds.), *The Invention of Tradition* (Cambridge, 1983), pp. 101–164, p. 153ff.

3 C. A. Bayly, 'The First Age of Global Imperialism, *c*.1760–1830', *The Journal of Imperial and Commonwealth History*, Vol. XXVI, May 1998, No. 2, pp. 28–47. See

also Nicholas Tarling, *Imperialism in Southeast Asia: 'A Fleeting, Passing Phase'* (London and New York, 2001), chapters 1 and 2.

4 Andrew Porter, 'Introduction: Britain and the Empire in the Nineteenth Century', in *idem* (ed.), *The Oxford History of the British Empire, Vol. III, The Nineteenth Century* (Oxford, 1999), pp. 1–28. For the decisive importance of geopolitics in British Foreign policy, see also Ronald Hyam, 'The Primacy of Geopolitics: The Dynamics of British Imperial Policy, 1763–1963', *The Journal of Imperial and Commonwealth History*, Vol. XXVII, May 1999, No. 2, pp. 27–52. Marvin Swartz believes that from 1865 onwards the decision-makers of the British empire already saw themselves challenged by a new round of global competition, see *idem., The Politics of British Foreign Policy in the Era of Disraeli and Gladstone* (New York, 1985), pp. 6 and 12.

5 Cf. John S. Galbraith, 'British War Aims in World War I: A Commentary on "Statesmanship"', *The Journal of Imperial and Commonwealth History*, Vol. XIII, October 1984, No. 1, pp. 25–45, p. 25.

6 Ronald Robinson, 'Wm. Roger Louis and the Official Mind of Decolonization', *The Journal of Imperial and Commonwealth History*, Vol. XXVII, May 1999, No. 2, pp. 1–12, p. 9. Wm. Roger Louis and Ronald Robinson, 'The imperialism of decolonization', *The Journal of Imperial and Commonwealth History*, Vol. XXII, 1994, No. 3, pp. 462–511, p. 493. British military advisors, for example, were still around in India and Pakistan after the Transfer of Power. H. W. Brands 'India and Pakistan in American Strategic Planning, 1947–54: The Commonwealth as Collaborator', *The Journal of Imperial and Commonwealth History*, Vol. XV, October 1986, No. 1, pp. 41–54.

7 Hyam, 'The Primacy of Geopolitics: The Dynamics of British Imperial Policy, 1763–1963'.

8 John Benyon, 'Overlords of Empire? British 'Proconsular Imperialism' in Comparative Perspective', *The Journal of Imperial and Commonwealth History*, Vol. XIX, 1991, No. 2, pp. 164–202.

9 P. J. Cain and A. G. Hopkins, *British Imperialism, vol. I: Innovation and Expansion, 1688–1914; Vol. 2: Crisis and Deconstruction, 1914–1990* (London, 1993). Albeit heavily criticised for oversimplification and mono-causality by D. K. Fieldhouse, 'Gentlemen, Capitalists, and the British Empire', *The Journal of Imperial and Commonwealth History*, Vol. XXII, 1994, No. 3, pp. 531–541.

10 Swartz, *The politics of British Foreign Policy in the Era of Disraeli and Gladstone*, especially chapter 6, pp. 123–144.

11 R. J. Moore, *Liberalism and Indian Politics, 1872–1922* (London, 1966), passim. For the connection between democracy and racism in the 1860s and 1870s, see also Thomas R. Metcalf, 'Ideologies of the Raj', *The New Cambridge History of India,* Vol. III, 4 (Cambridge, 1994), pp. 56–59 and Hugh Tinker, *Viceroy: Curzon to Mountbatten* (Karachi, 1997), pp. 45–46.

12 Uday Singh Mehta, *Liberalism and Empire: India in British Liberal Thought* (New Delhi, 1999), p. 1.

13 David Cannadine, 'Empire', in *idem, History in Our Time* (New Haven and London, 1998), pp. 143–154.

14 John Darwin, 'Imperialism and the Victorians: The Dynamics of Territorial Expansion', *English Historical Review*, CXII (1997), pp. 614–642, p. 628.

15 Bayly, 'The First Age of Global Imperialism, *c.*1760–1830', p. 29.

16 Hyam, 'The Primacy of Geopolitics: The Dynamics of British Imperial Policy, 1763–1963', p. 32 and 38–39. About the paramount value of the *raj* for the British, in general see Benyon, 'Overlords of Empire? British "Proconsular Imperialism" in Comparative Perspective', pp. 168–169 and 173–175; in a financial context see Cain and Hopkins, *British Imperialism, vol. I: Innovation and Expansion, 1688–1914*, chapter 10, pp. 316–350; in respect of delivering the means to great power status, see D. A. Washbrook, 'India, 1818–1860: The Two Faces Of Colonialism', in Andrew Porter (ed.), *The Oxford History of the British Empire, Vol. III, The Nineteenth Century*

(Oxford, 1999), pp. 395–420, p. 419; or India's crucial importance for Britain's imperial defence, even after WW II, see Pradeep Barua, 'Strategies and Doctrines of Imperial Defence: Britain and India, 1919–45', *The Journal of Imperial and Commonwealth History*, Vol. XXV, May 1997, No. 2, pp. 240–266; and for a combination of these reasons, see Robin J. Moore, 'Imperial India, 1858–1914', in Andrew Porter (ed.), *The Oxford History of the British Empire, Vol. III, The Nineteenth Century* (Oxford, 1999), pp. 422–446, pp. 441–443 and Judith M. Brown, 'India', in *idem* (ed.), *The Oxford History of the British Empire, Vol. IV, The Twentieth Century* (Oxford, 1999), pp. 421–446, p. 426.

17 A. P. Thornton, 'With Wavell on to Simla and Beyond', *The Journal of Imperial and Commonwealth History*, Vol. VIII, October 1979, No. 2, pp. 175–185.

18 P. J. Marshall, 'The Transfer of Power in India: Lord Wavell and his Political Masters' (Review Article), *The Journal of Imperial and Commonwealth History*, Vol. V, October 1976, No. 1, pp. 331–334 and Tinker, *Viceroy: Curzon to Mountbatten*, p. 207ff.

19 But this did not mean that Labour was willing or even planned to surrender the rest of the empire, nor that it relinquished further imperial enterprises. Far from that, the imperial idea by then had firmly taken root among Labour. Kenneth O. Morgan, 'Imperialists at Bay: British Labour and Decolonization', *The Journal of Imperial and Commonwealth History*, Vol. XXVII, May 1999, No. 2, pp. 233–244.

20 Louis and Robinson, 'The imperialism of decolonization', pp. 464–466.

21 Mehta, *Liberalism and Empire: India in British Liberal Thought*, p. 39.

22 Summarised in 'Office Precis (1875)', in *India Foreign Proceedings – Political* (IFP-P), Vol. P/1035, August 1877, Doc. 127, p. 124.

23 Ibid., p. 125. On the other hand the British had other problems in the mid-1850s and after (the Mutiny in general and the wars with the Bhutanese and Mishmis in the Northeast), so that reports on the Nagas ceased for the time being, see Vols. Z/P/1775 and Z/P/1777, Indexes for 1854 and 1855.

24 See for example the following contemporaneous reports, demonstrating a decided interest in the region: Captain Henry Yule, 'On the Geography of Burma and its Tributary States, in illustration of a New Map of those Regions', *Journal of the Royal Geographical Society*, Vol. 27, London, 1857, pp. 54–108; General Sir Arthur Cotton, 'On a Communication between India and China by the Line of the Burhampooter and Yang-tse', *Journal of the Royal Geographical Society*, Vol. 37, London, 1867, pp. 231–239. J. Coryton, 'Trade Routes between British Burmah and Western China' *Journal of the Royal Geographical Society*, Vol. 45, London, 1875, pp. 229–249; According to Alastair Lamb, *Asian Frontiers* (London, 1968), it was the French challenge in Burma that contributed to the decision to annex Upper Burma in 1886 (p. 57).

25 S. Gopal, *British Policy in India, 1858–1905* (Cambridge, 1965), this quote p. 74; the paragraph is based on chapters 1 and 2, pp. 1–128. Yet the conclusions drawn in respect to the Naga Hills are completely mine, Gopal doesn't even mention them once.

26 IFP-P, Vol. P/1216, Jan.-Feb. 1878, Feb. 1878, Docs. 11, 32, 35 and 42.

27 Ibid., Docs. 74–76, dt. between 21st Jan. 1878 and 8th Feb. 1878, pp. 47–48.

28 IFP-P, Vol. P/1219, Doc. 29, T. C. Plowden, Officiating under secretary, Government of India (Offg. Under-Secy. Govt. India), foreign department (FD), to CC Assam, dt. Simla, 22nd March 1878, p. 44.

29 IFP-P, Vol. P/1551, Doc. 504, Telgram, Assistant Secy., Shillong, to Foreign Secy., Lahore, dt. 22nd Nov. 1878, p. 407.

30 IFP-P, Vol. P/1391, Dec. 1879, Doc. 533, Secretary of State for India, to Govt. of India, dt. India Office, London, 5th Dec. 1878, p. 572.

31 IFP-P, Vol. P/1551, Jan. 1880, Doc. 497, 'Notification – By Chief Commissioner of Assam.', dt. 14th April 1879, p. 392.

32 Ibid., Doc. 507, Ridsdale to Secy. Govt. India, FD, dt. Shillong 19th August 1879, pp. 415–419, p. 417.

33 Ibid., February 1880, Doc. 249, Telgram, CC Assam, Darjeeling, to Foreign Secy., Simla, dt. 18th Oct. 1879, 19h.39m: recd. 19th, 11–30 A.M., p. 223 & Doc. 253, Telegram, Viceroy, Simla, to Secy. of State, London, dt. 21st Oct. 1879, p. 223.
34 Ibid., Docs. 250 – 260 Docs. 275 – 335; ibid., March 1880, Docs. 575–582.
35 Ibid., April 1880, Doc. 220, Telegram, CC Assam to Foreign, Calcutta, dt. Dibrugarh, 29th March 1880, 6h25m, Recd. 11–45 A.M., p. 249.
36 Ibid., Doc. 616, India Office London, dt. 26th August 1880, p. 585.
37 IFP-P, Jan. 1882, Doc. 135, Memorandum on the Administration of the Naga Hills District. By C. A. Elliott, CC of Assam, dt. March 31st 1881, pp. 141–147.
38 Ibid., p. 141.
39 Ibid.
40 Ibid., p. 142.
41 Ibid.
42 This intelligence, regarding the natural conditions in the Naga hills, was then added to the existing knowledge of the distribution of the populations and their political organisation, including social and political geography.
43 Ibid.
44 IFP-P, Vol. P/1916, Jan. 1882, Doc. 135, Memorandum on the Administration of the Naga Hills District. By C. A. Elliott, CC of Assam, dt. March 31st, 1881, p. 142.
45 Ibid., p. 143.
46 Ibid.
47 Ibid., pp. 143–144.
48 Ibid., p. 144.
49 Ibid., pp. 144–145.
50 Ibid., p. 145, on this occasion he referred to the presence of a missionary of the American Baptist Society in Kohima, who obviously had not yet acquainted himself with the Angami language but Elliot was sure he would soon do so and was prepared to support him in the way it was sanctioned by the government.
51 '. . . to carry out a systematic record of the institutions which have hitherto existed among the Nágas – the village constitutions, the origin of clans, the laws of marriage, inheritance, and private rights in land and water, the superstitions, legends, religious belief, historical traditions, folk-lore, and the like.' Ibid., pp. 146–147.
52 Ibid., pp. 145–146.
53 Ibid., p. 146.
54 Ibid., Doc. 136, dt. Simla, 11th June 1881, p. 149, from Secy. Govt. India, Foreign Department (FD), to CC Assam. On the 2nd of October London was informed about the final selection of Kohima as the central military station for the Naga hills. Ibid., Doc. 137, dt. Simla, 2nd October 1881, from Govt. India, to Secy of State for India, London, p. 150.
55 IFP-P, Vol. P/1917, Feb.–Apr. 1882, April 1882, Doc. 207, from C. J. Lyall, Offg. Secy. CC Assam to C. Grant, Secy Govt. India, FD, p. 175.
56 Ibid., pp. 175–177.
57 *Proceedings of the Chief Commissioner of Assam* (PCCA), Vol. P/2183, Judicial Department, Doc. 7, dt. Shillong, 9th August 1884, pp. 11–17, p. 11.
58 Ibid., p. 13.
59 Ibid.
60 Ibid.
61 Ibid., p. 15.
62 Ibid., p. 16.
63 PCCA in the FD, Vol. P/2429, November 1885, Doc. 14, from DC of Naga hills (NH) to the Secy to the CC of Assam, dated (dt.) Kohima, 10th June 1884, pp. 16–17.
64 Ibid., Doc. 16, from Secy CC Assam to Secy. Govt. of India, FD, dt. Shillong, 22nd August 1884, p. 19.

65 Ibid., Doc. 15, from Secy. Govt. India, FD, to CC Assam, dt. Simla, 20th Oct. 1884, pp. 17–18.
66 J. P. Mills, *The Ao Nagas* (London, 1926), p. 404.
67 Shibanikinkar Chaube, *Hill Politics in North-East India* (New Delhi, 1973), p. 14.
68 Ibid., p. 25.
69 Ibid., p. 17.
70 *Government of India Proposals and Dispatch of the Secretary of State*, 1907, Vol. I.
71 Hermann Kulke and Dietmar Rothermund, *A history of India* (Calcutta, 1991 [1986]), p. 273.
72 *Report of the franchise committee, 1918–1919* (Calcutta: Superintendent Government Printing, India), p. 269.
73 Ibid., p. 2.
74 *Proceedings of the Government of Assam* (PGA), Vol. P/11738, Appointment and Political Department. Political-A. June 1929. Proposal for the formation of a tribal authority among the Lhotas in the Naga Hills district. Docs. 105–114, dt. between 15th December 1928 and 27th May 1929, pp. 1–5.
75 Kulke and Rothermund, *A history of India*, p. 274.
76 Nehemiah Panmei, Naga movement and its ramifications. In: R. Vashum, Aleube Iheilung u. a. (eds.). *Nagas at Work*. New Delhi, 1996), pp. 85–100, p. 87.
77 'Naga Memorandum to Simon Commission', dated 10th January 1929. Appendix I., in R. Vashum, Aleube Iheilung et al. (eds.), *Nagas at Work* (New Delhi, 1996), p. 151.
78 Ibid., pp. 151–152.
79 'Memorandum submitted by the government of Assam to the Indian statutory commission 1930', in *Indian Statutory Commission*, Volume XIV. London: Published by his Majesty's stationary office, p. 100.
80 Ibid., p. 101.
81 J. H. Hutton, 'Note, dt. Kohima 17th March 1928', in *Indian Statutory Commission*, Volume XIV, Appendix B, 1930, pp. 111–117.
82 *Report of the Statutory Commission*, Volume 1, Paragraph 94, quoted from PGA, Vol. P/11892, Political-A, September 1931, Government of Assam. The Governor in Council. Appointment and Political Department. Doc. 134, from W. A. Gosgrave, Chief Secretary to the Govt. of Assam to Secy. Govt. of India, Reforms Office, dt. Shillong, 29th July 1931, p. 2.
83 PGA, Vol. P/11892, Political-A, September 1931, Government of Assam. The Governor in Council. Appointment and Political Department. Doc. 134, from W. A. Gosgrave, Chief Secretary to the Govt. of Assam to Secy. Govt. of India, Reforms Office, dt. Shillong, 29th July 1931, p. 4.
84 Ibid., p. 7.
85 Ibid., p. 10.
86 Ibid., p. 5.
87 Ibid., p. 11.
88 Ibid., p. 4.
89 *Hutton Papers*, Tour Diaries, 26th July 1934.
90 M. Alemchimba, *A Brief Histrorical Account of Nagaland* (Kohima, 1970), p. 165.
91 *Parliamentary Debates*. Fifth Series – Volume 301 H.C., (London, 1935), 10 May 1935, columns 1343–1449.
92 M. Horam, *Naga Insurgency: The last thirty years* (New Delhi, 1988), pp. 40–41.
93 Asoso Yonuo, *The Rising Nagas: A Historical and Political Study* (Delhi, 1974), p. 133–139.
94 Extract from private and secret letter from Lord Wavell to Mr. Amery, dated 27th July, 1944, Oriental and India Office Library (OIOC): L/PJ/7/6787.
95 Extract from private and secret letter from Mr. Amery to Lord Wavell, dated 9/10th August, 1944, in ibid.

96 Amery to Field Marshall Viscount Wavell, India Office, 28 September 1944, in Nicholas Mansergh and Penderel Moon (eds.), *The Transfer of Power, 1942–7, Volume V, The Simla Conference: Background and Proceedings, 1 September 1944 – 28 July 1945* (London, 1974), No. 25, pp. 52–56; Field Marshall Viscount Wavell to Mr Amery, The Viceroy's House, New Delhi, 3 December 1944, in ibid., No. 128, pp. 263–264. Lord Pethick-Lawrence to Sir J. Colville, India Office, 24 August 1945, in Nicholas Mansergh and Penderel Moon (eds.), *The Transfer of Power, 1942–7, Volume VI, The post-war phase: new moves by the Labour Government, 1 August 1945 – 22 March 1946* (London, 1974), No. 66, pp. 153–154. Nearly two years later, some other solution under the central government was implicitly confirmed, among others, the Naga hills, since for one the economic development of those hills was seen as beyond the capacity of any provincial government, and the exploitation of the hill people, it was stated prophetically, following from an unprotected scheme, would trigger sustained resistance that would need a long time and considerable funds to quell, see 'The Tribes of the North-West and North-East Frontier in a Future Constitution. Note by Government of India, External Affairs Department', in Nicholas Mansergh and Penderel Moon (eds.), *The Transfer of Power, 1942–7, Volume VII, The Cabinet Mission, 23 March – 29 June 1946* (London, 1974), No. 15, pp. 30–35.

97 Summary of views of Sir O. Caroe and Sir A. Clow on the tribal question given to the Cabinet Delegation in discussions at the Viceroy's House, new Delhi on 28 March 1946, in ibid., No. 16, pp. 35–39.

98 Minutes of Meeting between Cabinet Delegation, Field Marshal Viscount Wavell and Mr Gopinath Bardoloi on Monday, 1 April 1946 at 4.50 pm, in ibid., No. 35, pp. 76–80 and Note of Meeting between Field Marshal Viscount Wavell, Cabinet Delegation, Mr Qaiyum and Sir M. Sa'adullah on Tuesday, 2 April 1946, in Ibid., No. 40, pp. 88–90.

99 Text of Sir S. Cripps' Press Converence given on 16 May 1946. The Cabinet Mission's Statement, in ibid., No. 305, pp. 595–599; Record of Meeting of Cabinet Delegation and Field Marshal Viscount Wavell on Saturday, 8 June 1946 at 4 pm, in ibid., No. 474, pp. 842–843; Record of Meeting of Cabinet Delegation and Field Marshal Viscount Wavell on 18 June 1946 at 10 am, in ibid., No. 559, pp. 967–969; Office Memorandum on the Advisory Committee on the Rights of Citizens, Minorities and Tribal and Excluded Areas, undated, in ibid., No. 614, pp. 1055–1057.

100 Cabinet. India and Burma Committee. Paper I.B.(47)14. Indian Policy. Memorandum by the Secretary of State for India, India Office, 6 February 1947, in Nicholas Mansergh and Penderel Moon (eds.), *The Transfer of Power, 1942–7, Volume IX, The fixing of a time limit, 4 November – 22 March 1947* (London, 1974), No. 355, pp. 628–630.

101 Lord Pethick-Lawrence to Rear-Admiral Viscount Mountbatten of Burma, India Office, 12 April 1947, in Nicholas Mansergh and Penderel Moon (eds.), *The Transfer of Power, 1942–7, Volume X, The Mountbatten Viceroyalty: Formulation of a Plan, 22 March – 30 May 1947* (London, 1974), No. 134, pp. 217–220.

102 Rear-Admiral Viscount Mountbatten of Burma to the Earl of Listowel, 24 April 1947, in Ibid., No. 210, pp. 399–402.

103 Sir A. Hydari (Assam) to Rear-Admiral Viscount Mountbatten of Burma (Extract), Government House, Shillong, 11 July 1947, in Nicholas Mansergh and Penderel Moon (eds.), *The Transfer of Power, 1942–7, Volume XII, The Mountbatten Viceroyalty: Princes, Partition, and Independence, 8 July – 15 August 1947* (London, 1974), No. 68, pp. 104–105.

104 *The Gazette of India Extraordinary*. Secretariat of the Governor-General (Reforms). Notification, New Delhi, the 14th August, 1947. The Indian Independence (Rights, Property and Liabilities) Order, 1947, in ibid., No. 471, pp. 713–720.

105 Private correspondence from Mills to Archer, dt. Shillong, 25th Oct. 1946, in *Archer Papers*, MSSEur F 236/80.

106 *Archer Papers* MSS Eur F 236/78, paper 2c, note, dt. 26th Dec. 1946.

107 A. R. H. Macdonalt, S. P. Lushai Hills, to the Secretary to the Governor of Assam, dt. Aijal, 14th Feb. 1947. In *Archer Papers*, MSS Eur F 236/78, paper 7.
108 Confidential. D. O. No: 58/47/C-621–23. Governor's Secretariat, to A. R. H. Macdonald, SP, Lushai Hills, Aijal, dt. Shillong, 23rd April 1947, in ibid., paper 30.
109 Confidential. S.O.No. A. 11/46. J. P. Mills, Office of the Adviser to the Governor of Assam for Tribal Areas and States, dt. Shillong, 16th April 1947, to G. E. D. Walker, Political Officer, Tirap Frontier Tract, in ibid, paper 13.
110 Ibid.
111 Memorandum. Most Secret and Personal. Mills to all P.Os and D.C. Naga Hills, dt. Shillong, 24th April 1947, in ibid., papers 32 – 34.
112 Ibid.
113 Ibid., papers 35–39. Draft attached to previous document.
114 Ibid.
115 Communication from Pawsey to Archer, dt. Kohima, 30th April 1947, in ibid., paper 42 and Secret D. O. No./3/C., C. R. Pawsey, Office of the Deputy Commissioner, Naga Hills, to J. P. Mills, Adviser to the Governor of Assam Tribal Area and States, Shillong, dt. Kohima, 30th April 1947, in ibid., paper 43.
116 Ibid.: Notes, paper 54, dt. 3rd June 1947.
117 Letter from Mills to Archer, dt. 15th June 1947, in ibid., paper 55.
118 Letter from Mills to Archer, dt. Shillong, 24th June 1947, in ibid., paper 56.
119 Copy of U. O. (Memo) No. A.11/46 dt. 8.7.47. from J. P. Mills, the Adviser to the Governor of Assam Shillong to the Governor's Secretary U/O, dt. Shillong, 8th July 1947, in ibid., paper 71.
120 Ibid.
121 Letter from Pawsey to Archer, dt. Kohima, 18th July 1947, in ibid., paper 72.
122 Letter from Archer to Mayangnokcha, dt. 23rd July 1947, in ibid., paper 75–76.
123 Letter from Mayangnokcha to Archer, dt. Mokokchung, 15th September 1947 & Communication to The President of the Naga National Council from members of the NNC, dt. Mokokchung, 19th September 1947, in ibid., unnumbered.
124 Letter from Mills to Archer, dt. Shillong, 4th August 1947. In: ibid., paper 84; Letter from Pawsey to Archer, dt. undated [sometime in October 1947], in ibid., paper 87.
125 Letters from Pawsey to Archer, dt. 24th October and 5th November 1947, in *Archer Papers* MSS Eur F 236/76.

4 The transformation of Naga societies under colonialism

1 The argument that Christianity was rather a function than a factor will be demonstrated in a separate publication.
2 C. A. Bayly, 'The British and indigenous peoples, 1760–1860: power, perception and identity', in Martin Daunton and Rick Halpern (eds.), *Empire and Others: British Encounters with Indigenous Peoples, 1600–1850* (Philadelphia, 1999), pp. 19–41. The less centralised, the harder these societies were affected by their incorporation into the global political economy of the empire (ibid.). Moreover, many epidemic diseases could not sustain themselves among relatively small and isolated tribal societies, i.e., they could not develop antibodies against them, so once exposed to them they suffered heavy epidemics, see Jared Diamond, *Guns, Germs and Steel: the fates of human societies* (London, 1997), pp. 203–205.
3 Crawford Young, 'Ethnicity and the Colonial and Postcolonial State in Africa', in Paul Brass (ed.), *Ethnic Groups and the State* (London, 1985), pp. 57–93, p. 74.
4 J. Iliffe, *A Modern History of Tanganyika* (Cambridge, 1979), pp. 323–324, cf. Terence Ranger, 'Kolonialismus in Ost- und Zentralafrika: von der traditionellen zur traditionalen Gesellschaft – Einsprüche und Widersprüche', in Jan-Heeren Grevenmeyer

(ed.), *Traditionale Gesellschaften und europäischer Kolonialismus* (Frankfurt/M., 1981), pp. 16–46, pp. 19–20, my re-translation.

5 Ranger, 'Kolonialismus in Ost- und Zentralafrika: von der traditionellen zur traditionalen Gesellschaft – Einsprüche und Widersprüche', p. 22–24; David Maybury-Lewis, *Indigenous Peoples, Ethnic Groups, and the State* (Boston, 1997), p. 53–54 and Young, 'Ethnicity and the Colonial and Postcolonial State in Africa', p. 75.

6 Young, 'Ethnicity and the Colonial and Postcolonial State in Africa', p. 74.

7 Edmund R. Leach, *Political Systems of Highland Burma: A Study of Kachin Social Structures* (London, 1964 [1954]), pp. XV, 279, 290–292.

8 Prasenjit Duara, *Rescuing History from the Nation: Questioning Narratives of Modern China* (Chicago, 1995), pp. 65–66.

9 Edmund Leach, 'The Frontiers of "Burma"', *Comparative Studies in Society and History*, Vol. 3, No. 1, Oct. 1960, pp. 49–68.

10 Young, 'Ethnicity and the Colonial and Postcolonial State in Africa', p. 85; Donald L. Horowitz, *Ethnic Groups in Conflict* (Berkeley, 1985), p. 75.

11 Richard Jenkins, *Rethinking ethnicity: arguments and explorations* (London, 1997), passim.

12 Young, 'Ethnicity and the Colonial and Postcolonial State in Africa', p. 76.

13 Ibid., pp. 78–79.

14 Andrew Porter, '"Cultural Imperialism" and Protestant Missionary Enterprise, 1780–1914', *The Journal of Imperial and Commonwealth History*, Vol. 25, No. 3, September 1997, pp. 367–391.

15 Horowitz, *Ethnic Groups in Conflict*, p. 66.

16 Ibid.

17 Ibid., p. 76. Yet was only consequential when improved communications and increased interaction made these boundaries effective and meaningful.

18 Ibid., p. 75.

19 Young, 'Ethnicity and the Colonial and Postcolonial State in Africa', p. 80.

20 Benedict Anderson, *Imagined Communities: Reflections on the Origin and Spread of Nationalism* (New York, 1983).

21 Sumit Guha, 'The Politics of Identity and Enumeration in India *c.*1600–1990', *Comparative Studies in Society and History*, 2003, Vol. 45, pp. 148–167, p. 155.

22 Ibid., pp. 162–163.

23 Ibid., p. 161.

24 Marshall Sahlins, 'Goodbye to *Tristes Tropes:* Ethnography in the Context of Modern World History', *Journal of Modern History* 65 (March 1993), pp. 1–25, pp. 4 and 7.

25 Possibly in the way of oral history as conducted in Uganda by Ronald R. Atkinson, *The Roots of Ethnicity: The Origins of the Acholi of Uganda Before 1800* (Philadelphia, 1994).

26 In societies in which the *morung* was an important institution, children aged between 6–12 years stopped sleeping in their parents' house, and instead moved into the *morung*, where they were prepared for their roles as adults, and where they stayed until marriage, see Julian Jacobs, *The Nagas: Hill Peoples of Northeast India* (Stuttgart 1990), p. 56.

27 Jacobs, *The Nagas: Hill Peoples of Northeast India*, p. 53.

28 Ibid., p. 56.

29 Ibid., p. 64.

30 J. H. Hutton, *The Angami Nagas: With Some Notes on Neighbouring Tribes* (Bombay 1969 [1921]), p. 142.

31 Jakobs, *The Nagas*, p. 72.

32 Ibid., p. 75.

33 Ibid., pp. 70–2.

34 *Proceedings of the Government of Eastern Bengal and Assam (PEBA)*, 1910, P/8340, Nov. 1910, From The Subdivisional Officer Mokokchung, To The Deputy

Commissioner, Naga Hills, No. 744G., dated Mokokchung, the 26th March 1910, p. 52 and *Proceedings of the Chief Commissioner of Assam (PCCA)*, 1913, P/9110, August 1913, Doc. No. 53, From J. E. Webster, Deputy Commissioner, Naga Hills, To The Commissioner, Surma Valley and Hill Districts, No. 250G., dated Kohima, the 25th April 1913.

35 Jacobs, *The Nagas*, p. 72.
36 The nowadays Chindwin in western Myanmar.
37 Captain Butler, 'Butler's account of the Naga tribes, 1873', in Alexander Mackenzie, *History of the Relations of the Government with the Hill Tribes of the North-East Frontier of Bengal* (Calcutta 1884), pp. 77–88, pp. 77–78.
38 Ibid., p. 82.
39 Ibid., p. 83.
40 Butler, 'Butler's account of the Naga tribes, 1873', p. 86.
41 Ibid., p. 85.
42 'Assam Census Record (Extracts from)', in Mackenzie, *History of the Relations of the Government with the Hill Tribes of the North-East Frontier of Bengal*, pp. 537–550, p. 549.
43 Ibid., p. 556.
44 Ibid.
45 R. G. Woodthorpe, 'Meetings of the Anthropological Institute', in Verrier Elwin (ed.), *The Nagas in the Nineteenth Century* (Bombay 1969 [1881]), pp. 46–82, p. 49.
46 J. H. Hutton, 'Introduction', in J. P. Mills, *The Lhota Nagas* (London 1922), pp. XI–XXXIX, p. XVI.
47 Ibid., p. XVI.
48 Ibid., p. XXI.
49 Butler, 'Butler's account of the Naga tribes, 1873', p. 86.
50 Woodthorpe, 'Meetings of the Anthropological Institute', p. 56.
51 Jacobs, *The Nagas*, p. 17.
52 Mackenzie, *History of the Relations of the Government with the Hill Tribes of the North-East Frontier of Bengal*, p. 122.
53 Woodthorpe, 'Meetings of the Anthropological Institute', p. 56.
54 Sir Robert Reid, *History of the Frontier Areas Bordering on Assam: From 1883–1941* (Guwahati 1997 [1942]), p. 159.
55 Henry Balfour, 'Foreword', in Hutton, J. H. *The Sema Nagas* (London 1921), pp. XV–XVIII, p. XV.
56 Ibid., which is unlikely, at least those who travelled to the plains must have been confronted with the external terms for them.
57 Hutton, *The Sema Nagas*, p. VII.
58 Hutton, *The Angami Nagas: With Some Notes on Neighbouring Tribes*, p. XXXV.
59 If Hutton and Mills had started out not as administrators but as professional anthropologists of the nascent discipline social anthropology, they surely would have smoothed the dissonance and presented monographs on neatly demarcated tribes.
60 Mills, *The Lhota Nagas*, pp. 1–3.
61 Ibid., p. 4.
62 Ibid., p. 5.
63 Ibid., p. 89.
64 Ibid., p. 90.
65 J. P. Mills, *The Rengma Nagas* (Gauhati 1980 (1937), p. 4.
66 J. P. Mills, *The Ao Nagas* (London 1926), p. 1.
67 Hutton, *The Sema Nagas*, p. 121.
68 *Proceedings of the Government of Eastern Bengal and Assam (PEBA)*, 1910, P/8340, Nov. 1910, From The Subdivisional Officer Mokokchung, To The Deputy Commissioner, Naga Hills, No. 744G., dated Mokokchung, the 26th March 1910, p. 52.
69 Mills, *The Lhota Nagas*, pp. 92–95.

70 The formation of tribes is a continuous process. Mills, *The Lhota Nagas,* counts 17 tribes; Verrier Elwin, *Nagaland* (Guwahati, 1997 [1961]), counts 14; Yonuo, *The Rising Nagas*, 35; Gangmumei Kamei, 'Origin of the Nagas', in R. Vashum, Aleube Ihleilung et al. (eds.), *Nagas at Work* (New Delhi, 1996), pp. 7–20, p. 41; and R. Vashum, *Nagas' Right To Self-Determination: An Anthropological-Historical Perspective* (New Delhi, 2000), even 49. Even though we acknowledge that these authors partially took different geographical units as frameworks of reference, there is an undeniable tendency towards multiplication. Tribes split, form alliances, change into tribes – all that makes one wonder if there was not just only a new name given to an old thing, even though collective identities during British colonial time became wider and more inclusive.

71 *India Foreign Proceedings – Political (IFP-P)*, Vol. P/1743, Aug. – Sept. 1881, Aug. 1881, Document 628, Major T. B. Michell, Political Agent, Naga Hills, to Secretary. CC Assam, dated Kohima, 14th January 1881, pp. 659–662, p. 659.

72 IFP-P, Vol. P/1916, Jan. 1882, Doc. 88, Brigadier General J. S. Nation, Commanding Eastern Frontier District to Quartermaster General in India, Headquarters, dated Shillong, 25th June 1880, pp. 91–92: 'the experience we have gained up to the present time clearly shows that, as long as the force in the Naga Hills is maintained at its present strength, it can only be fed by means of an independent transport. Reports from the political and military Officers now at Kohima all show that the Nagas are perfectly willing to submit to our rule in every way except one – and that is the excessive demand for forced labour. This they object to so strongly as to say openly that, if enforced, it will again cause them to rise against us. It is quite probable that, as they settle down, they will give labour voluntarily and in sufficient quantities as they are, as a rule, fond of money; but they are utterly averse to being seized for labour, and there is no doubt that such a practice, carried to the great extent which has hitherto been necessary, is a most fertile cause of discontent and ill-feeling which might at any time burst out into rebellion. (. . .) If we are to retain possession peaceably of the Naga Hills, it is imperative that we should as much as possible avoid the pernicious and dangerous system of forced labour . . .'.

73 *Proceedings of the Chief Commissioner of Assam (PCCA)*, Military Department, Shillong, September 1884, Doc. 3, DC NH to The Personal Assistant to the CC of Assam, dt. 19th March 1884, pp. 3–4.

74 Mills, *The Ao Nagas*, p. 404.

75 Asoso Yonuo, *The Rising Nagas: A Historical and Political Study* (Delhi, 1974), p. 109.

76 P. D. Stracey, *Nagaland Nightmare* (Bombay, 1968), pp. 12–13.

77 Ibid., p. 12.

78 Yonuo, *The Rising Nagas: A Historical and Political Study*, p. 110.

79 Mills, *The Ao Nagas*, p. 407.

80 Shibanikinakar Chaube, *Hill Politics in North-East India* (New Delhi, 1973), pp. 33–34.

81 Mills, *The Ao Nagas*, p. 409.

82 Ibid., p. 406.

83 Ibid., p. 409.

84 Ibid., p. 406.

85 Ibid. That the *dobashis* were also important in another respect was already stressed in the wake of conquest: 'I am to remind you that these interpreters are also delegates, who are accredited to the political officer on the part of the principal villages and tribes of the Naga hills, and that besides acting as interpreters, they serve as the medium for all communications between the political officer and those whom they represent. They reside at the headquarters, and convey the orders of the political officer to their villages, and in various ways render themselves useful to him.' C. J. Lyall, Officiating Secretary to the CC of Assam, to Sir A. C. Lyall, Secretary to the Government of India in the Foreign

Department, IFP-P, Vol. P/1743, Aug. – Sept. 1881, Aug. 1881, Document 283, dated 20th June 1881, pp. 239–240.

86 Mills, *The Ao Nagas*, p. 406.
87 Yonuo, *The Rising Nagas*, p. 110.
88 Mills, *The Ao Nagas*, p. 404.
89 Ibid., p. 405.
90 Reid, *History of the Frontier Areas Bordering on Assam: From 1883–1941*, p. 110.
91 Ibid., p. 152.
92 Yet Fürer-Haimendorf tells us that many Nagas volunteered, especially as porters for punitive expeditions, since these were the only occasions where they could locate the dead, and might even be able to lay a hand on a finger or an ear and thus, according to downgraded requirements due to the colonial ban on headhunting, could acquire the status of a head-hunter. Very often it was sufficient to touch a body with ones' own *dao*. Fürer-Haimendorf wrote in his report of participation in one such punitive expedition, that the Nagas, who participated in it as porters, lived in permanent fear that the differences could be settled peacefully and that therefore no one would be killed, see Christoph von Fürer-Haimendorf, *Die nackten Nagas: Dreizehn Monate unter Kopfjägern Indiens* (Wiesbaden, 1946 [Leipzig, 1939]).
93 According to Yonuo the Nagas had to pay fees. Until 1903–04 there were 22 primary schools in the NHD, one secondary school and two special schools. More than two-thirds of the 647 students were in primary schools, the literacy rate was *c.* one per cent, see Yonuo, *The Rising Nagas*, p. 110.
94 Mills, *The Ao Nagas*, p. 405.
95 Ibid.
96 Mills, *The Lhota Nagas*, p. 48.
97 Chaube, *Hill Politics in North-East India*, p. 41.
98 Ibid., p. 35.
99 Ibid.
100 Ibid., p. 41.
101 Lal Dena, *Christian Missions and Colonialism: A Study of Missionary Movement in Northeast India With Particular Reference to Manipur and Lushai hills 1894–1947* (Shillong, 1988), p. 117.
102 Yonuo, *The Rising Nagas*, p. 155.
103 Dena, *Christian Missions and Colonialism: A Study of Missionary Movement in Northeast India With Particular Reference to Manipur and Lushai hills 1894–1947*, p. 117.
104 See for example Rawle Knox, 'Nagaland To-day: Why Nehru Cannot "Free" Hill Tribesmen', New Delhi, Jan. 7, *The Observer*, Jan. 8, 1961; Gavin Young, 'Commonwealth's Unknown War – 2: Jungle Baptists Fight It Out With India' *The Observer*, May 7, 1961; Ursula Graham Bower, 'Sifting the Evidence on Naga Problem' *The Observer*, July 2, 1961 and George Patterson, 'Nagas: Indians killed one in ten', Karachi, June 9, *The Observer*, June 10, 1962.
105 Yonuo, *The Rising Nagas*, pp. 123–124.
106 Balfour, 'Foreword', pp. XVI–XVII.
107 Yonuo, *The Rising Nagas*, p. 126.
108 M. Horam, *Naga Insurgency: The last thirty years* (New Delhi, 1988), p. 35.
109 Ibid.
110 Ibid., p. 37.
111 *Proceedings of the Government of Assam*, 1923, P/11282, February 1923, Doc. 14, From A. W. Botham, Chief Secretary to the Government of Assam, To Major F. H. Humphrys, Deputy Secretary to the Government of India, Foreign Department, dated Shillong, the 3rd September 1921.
112 M. Alemchimba, *A Brief Historical Account of Nagaland* (Kohima, 1970), p. 162.
113 Yonuo, *The Rising Nagas*, pp. 126.

114 Nehemiah Panmei, 'Naga movement and its ramifications', in R. Vashum, Aleube Iheilung et al. (eds.), *Nagas at Work* (New Delhi, 1996), pp. 85–100, p. 86.

115 Alemchimba, *A Brief Historical Account of Nagaland*, p. 62.

116 Jacobs, *The Nagas*, p. 151.

117 Yonuo, *The Rising Nagas*, pp. 131.

118 Ibid.

119 Panmei, 'Naga movement and its ramifications', p. 86.

120 Horam, *Naga Insurgency: The last thirty years*, p. 37.

121 Yonuo, *The Rising Nagas*, pp. 160.

122 See Central Office of Information, *The Campaign in Burma* (London, 1946), p. 15; Vice-Admiral The Earl Mountbatten of Burma, *Report to the Combined Chiefs of Staff by the Supreme Allied Commander South-East Asia, 1943–1945* (New York, 1951 [London, 1951]), pp. 12–14 and Basil Collier, *The War in the Far East, 1941–1945: A Military History*, (London, 1969), pp. 314ff.

123 Mountbatten, *Report to the Combined Chiefs of Staff by the Supreme Allied Commander South-East Asia, 1943–1945*, p. 14.

124 Central Office of Information, *The Campaign in Burma*, p. 155.

125 Yonuo, *The Rising Nagas*, p. 142.

126 Collier, *The War in the Far East, 1941–1945: A Military History*, p. 316. Among the first refugees using the hitherto un-surveyed route from the Hukawng valley across the Paungsao pass to Ledo was the Life magazine photographer George Rodger who, in his personal account, wondered himself about the friendliness of the Nagas who were supposed to be fierce headhunters, and resolved 'Perhaps it was not the headhunting season.' See George Rodger, *Red Moon Rising* (London, 1943), p. 125. Later, however, this route was to be used on a regular basis to get troops (in the main American and Chinese) into Northern Burma, see Mountbatten, *Report to the Combined Chiefs of Staff*, Map on pp. 9–10.

127 Ursula Graham Bower, *Naga Path* (London, 1950), pp. 205–212.

128 W. J. Slim, *Defeat into Victory* (London, 1961 [1956]), p. 65.

129 Arthur Campbell, *The Siege: A Story from Kohima* (London, 1956), p. 34.

130 Central Office of Information, *The Campaign in Burma*, p. 91.

131 S. Woodburn Kirby, *The War Against Japan. Volume III: The Decisive Battles* (London, 1961), pp. 23 and 30.

132 Ibid., p. 319.

133 Collier, *The War in the Far East*, p. 415.

134 Kirby, *The War Against Japan. Volume III: The Decisive Battles*, pp. 329–341.

135 So wrote Mills, for example, when informing Archer in August 1946 on his posting in Kohima: 'Kohima was completely wrecked in the war & accommodation there is . . . very bad.' *Archer Papers* MSS Eur F 236/80, Oct. 25th 1946, Shillong.

136 Central Office of Information, *The Campaign in Burma*, p. 157.

137 Kirby, *The War Against Japan. Volume III: The Decisive Battles*, pp. 302–306.

138 Mountbatten, *Report to the Combined Chiefs of Staff*, p. 196.

139 Yonuo, *The Rising Nagas*, p. 146–147.

140 Central Office of Information, *The Campaign in Burma*, p. 161.

141 Kirby, *The War Against Japan. Volume III: The Decisive Battles*, pp. 336–337. Kirby reported that all men from Khonoma volunteered to serve the Allies '. . . as porters, on condition that troops were sent to protect the village during their absence.' Ibid., p. 337.

142 Slim, *Defeat into Victory*, pp. 291–292.

143 Kirby, *The War Against Japan. Volume III: The Decisive Battles*, p. 300.

144 *Archer Papers*, Tour Diary, 31.12.1946 – 11.2.1947, MSSEur F 236/74, dt. 8.1.1947, p. 8.

145 Central Office of Information, *The Campaign in Burma*, p. 166–167.

146 Yonuo, *The Rising Nagas*, p. 147.

147 So we find in an outline of a presentation Ian Bowman gave on the 28th April 1971

at the Stirling and Clakmannen Burma Club under points three and four: '1942 – Nagas + Lushais loyal. . . . Promise of backing by British after War (. . .) 1947 – 'Betrayal' of Tribes by . Political expediency and ignorance.' *Bowman Papers*, MSSEur F 229/26.

148 Bower, *Naga Path*, pp. 186–192.
149 S. Woodburn Kirby, *The War Against Japan. Volume IV: The Reconquest of Burma* (London, 1965), p. 32.
150 Two weeks of conversation with Mr. T. Muivah in Bangkok in March 2001.
151 Telephone conversation with Mr. Yong Kong, Heidelberg – London, 28th October 2004.
152 Kirby, *The War Against Japan. Volume IV: The Reconquest of Burma*, p. 21.
153 Ibid., p. 150.
154 Yonuo, *The Rising Nagas*, p. 150.
155 D. R. Mankekar, *On the Slippery Slope in Nagaland* (Bombay, 1967), p. 22.
156 Nirmal Nibedon, *Nagaland: The Night of the Guerrillas* (New Delhi, 1983), p. 23.
157 Nari Rustomji, *Imperilled Frontiers: India's North-Eastern Borderlands,* Delhi, 1983), p. 21.
158 Yonuo, *The Rising Nagas*, p. 149.
159 Ibid., p. 150.
160 Ibid.
161 Ibid.

5 India's nationbuilding and the Nagas, 1947–64

1 Benedict Anderson, *Imagined Communities: Reflections on the Origin and Spread of Nationalism* (London and New York, 1991 [1983]).
2 Walker Connor names that 'nation-killing' and argues that this was widely practised by post-colonial regimes, see his *Ethnonationalism: The quest for understanding* (Princeton, 1994), pp. 16, 20–24.
3 See Robert L. Hardgrave and Stanley A. Kochanek, *India: Government and Politics in a Developing Nation* (San Diego, 1986), p. 112; Ishtiaq Ahmed, *State, Nation and Ethnicity in Contemporary South Asia* (London, 1996), p. 102 and H. M. Rajashekara, 'The Nature of Indian Federalism: A Critique', *Asian Survey*, Vol. 37, No. 3, March 1997, pp. 245–253.
4 Gurharpal Singh, *Re-examining Centre-State Relations in India* (Unpublished inaugural lecture, 2000), p. 2. See also Ahmed, *State, Nation and Ethnicity in Contemporary South Asia*, p. 104.
5 Ahmed, *State, Nation and Ethnicity in Contemporary South Asia*, p. 103.
6 Singh, *Re-examining Centre-State Relations in India,* p. 3.
7 Stephen P. Cohen, *The Indian Army: Its contribution to the development of a nation* (Berkeley, Los Angeles, London, 1971), pp. 181ff.
8 Cohen, *The Indian Army: Its contribution to the development of a nation*, pp. 170 and 181ff.
9 Ibid., p. 171.
10 Even today, and even in Assam, the Indian Army has not only a free hand against local officials but in general behaves like an occupational army, see Kunja Medhi, 'Human Rights in North-East India: A Contemporary Perspective', in Aftab Alam (ed.), *Human Rights in India: Issues and Challenges* (Delhi, 2000), pp. 289–304.
11 Cohen, *The Indian Army*, p. 176. Cohen stressed that not only did the officer corps have no experience, but also the political leadership, especially Nehru and Menon, meddled with detailed military questions until the disaster of 1962.
12 That the Indian soldiers had worse gear than even the CIA's Tibetan guerrillas, see Kenneth Conboy and James Morrison, *The CIA's Secret War in Tibet* (Kansas, 2002), p. 172.

13 See John Kenneth Galbraith, *Ambassador's Journal: An American view of India* (Bombay, 1972 [1969]), pp. 169ff and passim, and especially illustrative his recollection of Nehru's reaction to the Chinese offer of ceasefire: 'The Prime Minister was inclined to think that the Chinese offer of ceasefire and withdrawal was real. He cited two factors as inducing the Chinese offer. One of these was the unexpected anger of the Indian people when aroused – an anger that was unfortunately unmatched by military effectiveness. And the second factor was the speed of the American response.' Ibid., p. 179. That the Indian Army's prestige had been created by its predecessor and shattered only after a few days of fighting the Chinese, was supported by its inability to come to terms with the Nagas, see Guy Wint, 'India faces the Shadows', *The Observer*, October 10, 1962.

14 Judith M. Brown has it that the Indian army was in every respect in a miserable state after their rout by the Chinese, leading to a massive build up, so that by 1966 the number of armed forces had been doubled as compared to a decade before and the expenditure more than trebled. *Idem, Nehru: A Political Life* (New Haven and London, 2003), pp. 325–330.

15 *Times* correspondent, Delhi, Jan. 15, *The Times*, 16.1.1961.

16 See Rajesh Rajagopalan, 'Innovations in counter-insurgency: the Indian Army's Rashtriya Rifles', *Contemporary South Asia* 13 (1), March 2004, pp. 25–37.

17 *The Times*, 20.11. and 23.12.1946; 2. and 27. 1., 24.3. and 12.4.1947; 30.12.1948; 8.3., Aug.–Sept. (major earthquake) and 30.10.1950; 16.4.1952.

18 *The Times*, 22.9. and 30.10.1950; 1.9.1951.

19 *Lok Sabha Debates*, Vol. 8, 1951, 26.5., Columns 4679–4681 and *Lok Sabha Debates*, Vol. 1, 1952, 19.5.

20 *Lok Sabha Debates*, Vol. 8, 1951, 26.5., Columns 4646–4647; Interview with Mr. Yong Kong, London, 7.8.2001 and with Mr. Kevilevor Phizo, London, 19.7.2001.

21 Through the provisional constitutional order of August 15th 1947 the previously excluded and tribal areas were no longer under the jurisdiction of the governor and his representatives, but now fell under the Assamese administration, see Shibanikinkar Chaube, *Hill Politics in North-East India* (New Delhi, 1973), p. 82.

22 Luingam Luithui and Nandita Haksar, *Nagaland File: A question of Human Rights* (New Delhi, 1984), p. 23; Nari Rustomji, *Imperilled Frontiers: India's North-Eastern Borderlands* (Delhi, 1983), p. 60.

23 Girin Phukon, *Assam Attitude to Federalism* (New Delhi, 1984), pp. 5, 20, 46, 55, 57, 68–73, 91 and passim. Phukon's book seems to me the best covering the time around the Transfer of Power.

24 Thus a typical explanation of the Naga's uprising is to blame collectively the CIA, British secret agents, Communist China and Christian missionaries, all threatening the unity of India, see for example Saroj Chakrabarty, *The Upheaval Years in North-East India: A documentary in-depth study of Assam holocausts 1960–1983* (Calcutta, 1984), p. 97.

25 Rustomji, *Imperilled Frontiers: India's North-Eastern Borderlands*, pp. 11, 27–28 and 36.

26 Nehru had earlier been approached several times by Naga delegations in general, and by Phizo (who had gradually crystallised as the Naga national leader) in particular. In the words of the head of the intelligence bureau, Mullik: 'Phizo saw Pandit Nehru . . . some time in 1949 in Delhi, but at that time the Prime Minister got the impression that Phizo was a crank and had not to be taken seriously. Phizo again met Pandit Nehru in Shillong or Dibrugarh in April 1950. The latter gave Phizo almost a blank cheque within the Constitution and told him that the provisions made in the 6th Schedule should be tried, and anything not found to be satisfactory by the Nagas could be amended and there would be no difficulty about it. But this assurance did not satisfy Phizo. He wanted a definite clause to be inserted on the terms of the nine-point agreement that the Nagas would have the right to secede, if they so desired, after ten years

from the date the Constitution came into force. This, however, the Prime Minister was naturally not willing to concede.' See B. N. Mullik, *My Years With Nehru: 1948–1964* (Bombay, 1972), p. 299.

27 Associated Press, Delhi, March 11, *The Times*, 12.3.1953.
28 Ibid.
29 Reuter, Kohima, March 30, *The Times,* 31.11.1953.
30 Gita Mehta, *Snakes and Ladders: A View of Modern India* (London, 1997), pp. 95–96.
31 Nehru, albeit informed by officer S. M. Dutt on the potentially dangerous situation in the Naga hills, trusted the judgement of the Assamese government and considered it as an internal affair of Assam, see Mullik, *My Years With Nehru,* p. 301.
32 Reuter, Shillong, Assam, Nov. 28, *The Times*, 29.11.1954.
33 Reuter, Shillong, Assam, April 21, *The Times*, 22.4.1955.
34 Reuter, Delhi, May 5, *The Times*, 6.5.1955.
35 *Lok Sabha Debates*, Vol. 4, 25th July 1955, Columns 2944–2946.
36 *Lok Sabha Debates*, Vol. 4, 28th July 1955, Columns 3111–3112.
37 *Lok Sabha Debates*, Vol. 4, 10th August 1955, Columns 3541–3542.
38 *Lok Sabha Debates*, Vol. 4, 16th August 1955, Columns 3683–3685.
39 *Times* correspondent, Delhi, Aug. 19, *The Times*, 20.8.1955.
40 Bertram Jones from Calcutta, in *Express*, Tuesday, 31.8.1955.
41 C. L. Proudfoot, *Flash of the Khukri: History of the 3rd Gorkha Rifles, 1947 to 1980* (New Delhi, 1984), pp. 53–61.
42 Delhi, Dec. 20, *The Times*, 21.12.1955.
43 Ibid.
44 *Manchester Guardian (MG)*, 28.4.1956.
45 Mainly *MG*, 28.4.1956, but minor info also from Times correspondent, Delhi, April 20, *The Times*, 21.4.1956.
46 BUP, New Delhi, May 3, in *MG*, 4.5.1956 and Reuter, Shillong, Assam, May 2, *The Times*, 3.5.1956.
47 BUP, New Delhi, May 4, in *MG*, 5.5.56.
48 *Times* correspondent, Delhi, May 4, *The Times*, 5.5.1956.
49 BUP, New Delhi, June 19, in *MG*, 20.6.56.
50 *MG*, 5.7.56.
51 *Lok Sabha Debates*, Vol. 5, 31st July 1956, Column 639.
52 *Times* correspondent, Delhi, July 31, *The Times*, 1.8.1956.
53 *Lok Sabha Debates*, Vol. 5, 3rd Aug. 1956, Columns 784–785. The questions of the MP Bibhuti Mishra betrayed a concern whether the chief of army staff had also had an opportunity to meet the village people.
54 *Lok Sabha Debates*, Vol. 5, 10th Aug. 1956, Column 1101.
55 Graham Greene, in To the Editor of *The Times*, 3.9.1956.
56 *Times* correspondent, Calcutta, Sept. 6, *The Times*, 7.9.1956.
57 *Times* special correspondent, Shillong, Assam, *The Times*, 12.10.1956.
58 *Times* correspondent, Calcutta, Oct. 19, *The Times*, 20.10.1956.
59 *Times* correspondent, Calcutta, Oct. 21, *The Times*, 22.10.1956.
60 Brown, *Nehru, A Political Life*, p. 141 and chapters 10 and 11, pp. 185–222.
61 *Times* correspondent, Delhi, Dec. 7, *The Times*, 8.12.1956.
62 *MG*, 18.12.56.
63 *Times* correspondent, Delhi, Jan. 10, *The Times*, 11.1.1957.
64 Anthony Mann from Calcutta, in *Daily Telegraph*, Tuesday, one week after the second general election (no exact date). The number of 30,000 for the troops fighting in the Naga hills was later confirmed to be the official number by Stephen Harper from New Delhi in *Weekly Dispatch*, Sunday, 31.3.57.
65 Taya Zinkin from Bombay, March 26, in *MG*, 27.3.57.
66 The NPC was a joint venture of dissident NNC leaders, members of the Naga church, and Mullik's intelligence bureau, see Aosenba, *The Naga Resistance Movement:*

Prospects of Peace and Armed Conflict, pp. 52 and 56. While the intention of the Nagas engaged in the NPC was to find a negotiated settlement, the intent on the Indian side was clearly to divide the Nagas. This policy was already criticised in the *Rajya Sabha* in 1958 as short-sighted, see *Rajya Sabha Debates*, Vol. 22, No. 1, 27. Aug. 1958, Column 1263. Bhola Nath Mullik's intelligence bureau as an organisation had '. . . deep colonial roots. Established in 1887 as the Central Special Branch, it had been organized by the British to keep tabs on the rising tide of Indian nationalism. Despite several redesignations before arriving at the title intelligence bureau, anticolonialists remained its primary target for the next sixty years.' See Conboy and Morrison, *The CIA's Secret War in Tibet*, p. 32. At least in the periphery, the intelligence bureau could continue its institutional tradition.

67 Rawle Knox, 'Nagaland To-day: Why Nehru Cannot "Free" Hill Tribesmen', New Delhi, Jan. 7, *The Observer*, Jan. 8, 1961.
68 Gavin Young, 'A meeting with Nagas' prisoners', *The Observer*, April 9, 1961.
69 Taya Zinkin from Bombay, Aug. 26, in *MG*, 27.8.57.
70 *Times* correspondent, Delhi, Sept. 26, *The Times*, 27.9.1957.
71 *Times* correspondent, Delhi, Oct. 3, *The Times*, 4.10.1957.
72 *Lok Sabha Debates*, Vol. 8, 11th Nov. 1957, Columns 9–12.
73 *Lok Sabha Debates*, Vol. 8, 20th Nov. 1957, Columns 1437–1438.
74 Reuter, Shillong, Assam, May 2, *The Times*, 3.5.1958.
75 *Rajya Sabha Debates*, Vol. XXII., No. 1, 25. August 1958, Columns 963–976; 27. August 1958, Columns 1253–1312 and 28. August 1958, Columns 1313–1474; Nehru's statement is, of course, at the end, i.e., 28. August 1958, Columns 1473–1474.
76 Reuter, Delhi, Sept. 2, *The Times*, 3.9.1958.
77 *Rajya Sabha Debates*, Vol. 22, 24th Sept. 1958, Columns 4431–4433.
78 Associated Press, Calcutta, Oct. 6, *The Times*, 7.10.1958.
79 *Times* special correspondent, *The Times*, 28.10.1958.
80 *Times* correspondent, Delhi, *The Times*, 20.3.1959.
81 Reuter, Imphal, N.E. India, Nov. 1, *The Times*, 2.11.1959.
82 Reuter, Delhi, June 16, *The Times*, 17.6.1960; Times correspondent, Delhi, June 17; *The Times*, 18. 6. 1960; *The Times*, 20., 27. and 29. 6. 1960.
83 *The Times*, 27.7.1960.
84 *Times* correspondent, Delhi, July 26, *The Times*, 27.7.1960.
85 *Lok Sabha Debates*, Vol. 44, 1st and 4th Aug. 1960, Columns 146–157 and 899–915.
86 *Times* correspondent, Delhi, July 31, *The Times*, 1.8.1960.
87 *Times* correspondent, Delhi, Aug. 4, *The Times*, 5.8.1960.
88 *Lok Sabha Debates*, Vol. 46, 5th Sept. 1960, Columns 6913–6918.
89 *Times* correspondent, Delhi, Oct. 10, *The Times*, 11.9.1960.
90 *Lok Sabha Debates*, Vol. 47, 22nd Nov. 1960, Columns 1516–1521.
91 *Times* correspondent, Delhi, Nov. 22, *The Times*, 23.11.1960.
92 *Times* special correspondent, Mokochung, Nagaland, Dec. 17 (delayed), *The Times*, 19.12.1960.
93 *Times* correspondent, Delhi, Jan. 11, *The Times*, 12.1.1961.
94 *Times* correspondent, Delhi, Jan. 1, *The Times*, 2.1.1961.
95 *Times* correspondent, Delhi, Jan. 11, *The Times*, 12.1.1961.
96 *Times* correspondent, Delhi, Jan. 1, *The Times*, 2.1.1961.
97 See for example his two articles in *The Observer*, 20. and 27.8.1950.
98 *Times* correspondent, Delhi, Jan. 15, *The Times*, 16.1.1961.
99 *Rajya Sabha Debates*, Vol. 32, 15th Sept. 1961, Columns 57–58.
100 *Times* correspondent, Delhi, Aug. 24, *The Times*, 25.8.1961 and Delhi, Sept. 22, *The Times*, 23.9.1961.
101 Bombay, Jan. 30, in *The Guardian*, 31.1.62; Times correspondent, Delhi, Feb. 1, *The Times*, 2.2.1962, Delhi, March 23, *The Times*, 24.3.1962, Delhi, May 4, *The Times*,

5.5.1962 and *Lok Sabha Debates*, Vol. 61, 23rd March 1962, Columns 1306–1307, Vol. 2, 4th May 1962, Columns 2593–2594 and Vol. 3, 14th May 1962, Columns 4419–4426. By August 21, 1962 Nehru motioned two bills in the *Lok Sabha* to provide for a union state of Nagaland disjoined from Assam, a move that from the start was intended to split the Nagas, see P. H. M. Jones, 'India and the Nagas', in *Far Eastern Economic Review*, Vol. 37, No. 9, 30 Aug 1962, p. 389 and Guy Wint, 'India's "Irish" Problem', *The Observer*, April 15, 1962.

102 *Times* correspondent, Delhi, May 17 and 18, *The Times*, 18, 19.5.1961 and June 20, 21.6.1961. While Nehru signalled willingness to grant certain autonomy in the Northeast, he opposed the Sikh demand for a Punjabi-speaking state.

103 Galbraith, *Ambassador's Journal: An American view of India*, p. 110.

104 *Times* commentary, *The Times*, 19.12.1961.

105 Staff Reporter, *The Observer*, 27.1.63.

106 Comment, *The Observer*, 27.1.63.

107 Staff Reporter, *The Observer*, 18.11.62; Staff Reporter, *The Observer*, 27.1.63; *The Guardian*, 9.3.63; Weekend Review, 'Guide to Little Wars', *The Observer*, 10.3.63.

108 Reuter, New Delhi, March 2, *The Observer*, 3.3.63.

109 James Mitchell, 'Still hope for Naga truce', New Delhi, April 13, *The Observer*, 14.4.63; *Idem.*, 'Nagaland offer by Nehru', New Delhi, April 20, *The Observer*, 21.4.63; Special Correspondent, 'Flare-up in Naga war feared', *The Observer*, 12.5.63.

110 Comment, *The Observer*, 12.5.63. Nehru had been politically decidedly weakened through the border war debacle, and those who thought he had a conciliatory influence on the jingoistic forces in his country and military now saw this restraint fast evaporating, see Michael Scott, 'A People in Danger' *The Observer*, 25.8.63. For Nehru's fall from grace, see Guy Wint, 'Nehru's declining grip' *The Observer*, 26.5.63.

111 Observer correspondent, New Delhi, June 1, *The Observer*, 2.6.63.

112 I took the terminology from the anthropologist Ursula Graham Bower who used it in, 'Nagas Fight On in Closed Land' *The Observer*, Nov. 13, 1960. The term 'concentration camp' is certainly used here to refer to the practice of colonial powers – British and German – in Africa, and not to German death camps during the SecondWorld War. Yet, the Indian terminology of 'regrouping' or 'self-sufficient centres' trivializes a ruthless practice.

113 *The Observer*, 28.7.63.

114 Bombay, July 24, *The Guardian*, 25.7.63.

115 James Mitchell, 'Naga rising spreads', Delhi, August 10, *The Observer*, 11.8.63.

116 *Observer* correspondent, New Delhi, September 28, *The Observer,* 29.9.63.

117 James Mitchell, 'Naga peace move dropped', *The Observer*, 1.12.63.

118 Special correspondent, 'More torture by India, say Nagas', *The Observer*, 23.2.64.

119 James Mitchell, 'Peace talks reopened quietly' New Delhi, April 25, *The Observer*, 26.4.64; *Observer* correspondent, 'Breakthrough in Naga peace talks', New Delhi, May 9, *The Observer*, 10.5.64; Editorial, 'The Man Behind The Saint', *The Observer*, 31.5.64.

120 Brown, *Nehru, A Political Life*, p. 187.

121 For this argument, see Heike Behrend, 'Frauen und Krieg. Zur Gewalt in postkolonialen Widerstandsbewegungen in Afrika', in Peter J. Bräunlein and Andrea Lauser (eds.), *Krieg und Frieden: Ethnologische Perspektiven.* (Bremen, 1995), pp. 161–172.

6 The Nagas' War

1 Walker Connor, *Ethnonationalism: The quest for understanding* (Princeton, 1994), pp. 7 and 22–24; Leo Kuper, 'The Genocidal State: An Overview', in Pierre L. Van den Berghe (ed.), *State Violence and Ethnicity* (Niwot, 1990), pp. 19–52, p. 20; Cultural Survival Report 22, *Southeast Asian Tribal Groups and Ethnic Minorities* (Cambridge,

1987) and James Mayall and Mark Simpson, 'Ethnicity is not enough: Reflections on Protracted Secessionism in the Third World', in Anthony D. Smith (ed.), *Ethnicity and Nationalism* (Leiden, 1992), pp. 5–25.

2 Richard Jenkins, *Rethinking ethnicity: arguments and explorations* (London, 1997), pp. 69, 107, 137 and 139; Carole Nagengast, 'Violence, Terror, and the Crisis of the State', *Annual Review of Anthropology*, 1994, 23, pp. 109–136, p. 122 and Donald L. Horowitz, *Ethnic Groups in Conflict* (Berkeley, 1985), pp. 230–231 and 262.

3 See chapter four.

4 Isaiah Berlin, *The Crooked Timber of Humanity: Chapters in the History of Ideas.* London, 1990 [1959], p. 261 and Charles Taylor, 'Nationalism and modernity', in John A. Hall (ed.), *The State of the Nation: Ernest Gellner and the Theory of Nationalism* (Cambridge, 1998), pp. 191–218, p. 212.

5 M. Horam, *Naga Insurgency: The Last Thirty Years* (New Delhi, 1988), p. 55.

6 Hand-written copy of article by the newspaper *The Statesman*, from 26.12.46 by Archer, in *Archer Papers*, MSS Eur 236/78, paper 2.

7 Ibid., paper 2b.

8 *Archer Papers*, MSS Eur 236/78, paper 2*c*. and 2d.

9 Further evidence about efforts to finding a common solution for all the hill people is that the Assam Hills Students Association, founded in Calcutta in 1945, proclaimed on 8th January 1947 an Indo-Burma Movement with the aim of unifying the tribal people and territories of Indo-Burma and of making them independent or autonomous via a plebiscite, see *Archer Papers*, MSS Eur 236/78, paper 3.

10 On 18th April 1946 Kevichusa and Mayangnokcha were chosen by the Kohima tribal council to represent the Nagas vis-à-vis the cabinet mission, if they were called upon. Kevichusa was E.A.C. (we get to know later that he was assistant to the DC) and Mayangnokcha headmaster of the government Middle English school Mokokchung, in ibid., paper 1, dated 2.5.46.

11 Ibid., paper 5 and 6. It is not clear whether Mayangnokcha's listing for the advisory committee was inconsequential or not known. To recapitulate, the basis for the Transfer of Power in India was created on May 16th 1946 through the cabinet mission's plan. The constituent assembly of India set up an advisory committee on the aboriginal tribes, which was divided into three subcommittees. One of them was meant to report on the north-eastern region, and should make suggestions on its future administrative form. The chairman of this subcommittee was Gopinath Bardoloi, the then chief minister of Assam, one of its members was to be Aliba Imti Ao, see Shibanikinkar Chaube, *Hill Politics in North-East India* (New Delhi, 1973), p. 76.

12 Lord Pethick-Lawrence to Rear-Admiral Viscount Mountbatten of Burma, India Office, 12 April 1947, in Nicholas Mansergh and Penderel Moon (eds.), *The Transfer of Power, 1942–7, Volume X, The Mountbatten Viceroyalty: Formulation of a Plan, 22 March – 30 May 1947* (London, 1974), No. 134, pp. 217–220.

13 Personal communication from Mills to Archer, dated Shillong, 23rd April 1947, in *Archer Papers*, MSS Eur 236/78, paper 28.

14 Mayangnokcha to Archer, dated Mokokchung, 26th April 1947, in ibid., paper 40.

15 Pawsey to Archer, dated Kohima, 29th April 1947. In ibid., paper 41. In the end, however, the subcommittee only came as far as Kohima, and did not even make it to Mokokchung.

16 J. P. Mills, Adviser to the Governor of Assam to G. E. D. Walker, Political Officer, Tirap Frontier Tract, Confidential, Memo. No. All/46, dated Shillong, 16th April, 1947 and Memo No. 63/G., by C. R. Pawsey, Deputy Commissioner, Naga Hills, dated 30th April, 1947. In ibid., paper 13.

17 Constituent Assembly of India, to The Hill peoples of the Naga Hills, Mikir Hills, Cachar Hills, Khasi and Jaintia Hills, and Garo Hills, signed R. K. Ramadhyani, Deputy Secretary Constituent Assembly of India, dt. 22nd April 1947, in ibid., paper 25. The members of subcommittee were the Assamese Gobinath Bardoloi, the Khasi J. J.

Nichols-Roy, Rup Nath Brahma, the Naga Aliba Imti, and A. V. Thakkar, in ibid., paper 109 and 115.

18 Memo No. 688–371/C., Governor's Secretariat, Shillong, the 25th April, 1947, sd/ P. R. Adams, Secretary to the Governor of Assam. In ibid., paper 26.

19 Telegram to SDO Mokokchung, dated Shillong, 7th May [1947], 11:55h. In ibid., paper 45.

20 Office of the Naga National Council. 7th May 47. No. 94–112/NNC, Joint Secretaries N.N.C. T. Sakhrie. In ibid., paper 46.

21 Office of the Naga National Council. Provisional Programme. T. Sakhrie, Joint Secretary Naga National Council, 8.5.1947. In ibid., paper 47.

22 Archer to Pawsey, Mokokchung, 8th May 1947, in Ibid., paper 90.

23 Archer to Pawsey, Mokokchung, 12th May 1947. In *Archer Papers*, MSS Eur 236/78, paper 94.

24 Undated notes by Archer. In *Archer Papers*, MSS Eur 236/78, paper 102.

25 Pawsey to Archer, Kohima Naga Hills, Assam, 27.6.47. In ibid., paper 57.

26 *Archer Papers*, MSS Eur 236/78, paper 58. See previous chapter for wording of Point Nine.

27 Minutes of the meeting of the Assam Tribal and Excluded Areas Sub-Committee at Shillong on the 4th, 5th and 7th July 1947, dated 8th July 1947 at Shillong, sd. R. K. Ramadhyani. In ibid., papers 60–70.

28 Pawsey to Archer, 18.7.47, Kohima, Naga Hills, in ibid., paper 72.

29 Confidential. Memo. No. 61/C., dated Kohima the 30th July, 1947. Copy of D.O. No. 973/*c*. dt. 18.7.47 from P. F. Adams, Adviser to the Governor of Assam, to C. R. Pawsy, Deputy Commissioner, Naga Hills. In *Archer Papers*, MSS Eur 236/78, paper 79.

30 Pawsey to Archer, Kohima, 3.8.47. In ibid., papers 82 and 83.

31 *Archer Papers*, MSS Eur 236/79, paper 7, dated Wokha, 7th August 1947.

32 Communication from NNC (president Aliba Imti, secretary Kumbho Angami) to governor of Assam, dated Kohima, 15th August 1947. Copy in *Archer Papers*, MSS Eur 236/78.

33 Extract from a letter dated 26th and 27th August, 1947 from His Excellency The Governor of Assam, copy as Memo. No. 6462–63/G., dated Kohima the 1st September 1947, Sd/ C. R. Pawsey, Deputy Commissioner, Naga Hills. In ibid.

34 *Archer Papers*, MSS Eur 236/79, papers 7 and 18, undated.

35 Ibid., paper 13, dated August 24 – September 2 [1947] and paper 14, undated.

36 Aliba Imti, president, NNC to His Excellency, The Governor of Assam, Shillong, dated Kohima, the 6th September 1947. In ibid., as copy to the ADC Mokokchung for information.

37 Aliba Imti, president, NNC to chairman, tribal council, dated Kohima the 9th Sept. '47. In ibid.

38 Aliba Imti, president, NNC to Pundit Jawaharlal Nehru, The Prime Minister of Indian Union, dated Kohima the 9th Sept. '47. In ibid., as copy to the SDO Mokokchung for information.

39 Ibid.

40 Ultimatum to the Government of India, To Jawaharlal Nehru, Prime Minister, Indian Union, from T. Aliba Imti, president & Kumbho Angami, secretary, on behalf of the NNC, dated Kohima, 4th November 1947. In L/PJ/7/10635.

41 Memo No. /83/NNC, Urgent, Subject: Precautionary Measures. Office of the Naga National Council, Kohima, Naga Hills, Assam, 9/11/1947, T. Aliba Imti, President, NNC. In *Archer Papers*, MSS Eur 236/78.

42 Copy of telegram from the Secretary, NNC to the Chairman, Mokokchung Central Council. Date of dispatch: 20.11.47 Date of receipt: 21.11.47. In ibid.

43 *Archer Papers*, MSS Eur 236/79, paper 4, dated Charali, 2nd and 3rd December 1947.

44 Office of the adviser to His Excellency the governor of Assam for tribal areas & states, Walker, to W. G. Archer, ADC, Mokokchung, Naga Hills, dated Camp Margherita, the 26th Dec. '47. In *Archer Papers*, MSS Eur 236/78.
45 Asoso Yonuo, *The Rising Nagas: A Historical and Political Study* (Delhi, 1974), p. 177.
46 Luingam Luithui and Nandita Haksar, *Nagaland File: A question of Human Rights* (New Delhi, 1984), p. 23.
47 Nehemia Panmei, 'Naga movement and its ramifications', in R. Vashum, Aleube Iheilung et al. (eds.), *Nagas at Work* (New Delhi, 1996), p. 89.
48 M. Alemchimba, *A Brief Historical Account of Nagaland* (Kohima, 1970), p. 174.
49 Special correspondent, *The Times*, 28.10.1958.
50 Rawle Knox, 'Nagaland To-day: Why Nehru Cannot "Free" Hill Tribesmen', New Delhi, Jan. 7, *The Observer*, Jan. 8, 1961. The best and most competent account is given by Nari Rustomji, *Imperilled Frontiers: India's North-Eastern Borderlands* (Delhi, 1983), passim. Rustomji, a Parsi and previously DC in Assam ,was part of this administration as adviser on tribal questions. He served under nine different governors.
51 Horam, *Naga Insurgency: The last thirty years*, p. 45.
52 Ibid. To underestimate Phizo's role, for Aosenba, is to fail to comprehend Naga reality, see Aosenba, *The Naga Resistance Movement: Prospects of Peace and Armed Conflict* (New Delhi, 2001), pp. III–IV.
53 Nirmal Nibedon, *Nagaland: The Night of the Guerrillas* (New Delhi, 1983), pp. 23–34.
54 Nibedon, *Nagaland: The Night of the Guerrillas*, p. 57. Nibedon saw Sakhrie as the strategic head of the NNC, and as the visionary of the Nagas. (ibid., pp. 57 and 60). Sakhrie later was murdered and Phizo was held responsible for ordering his murder. Sakhrie was against armed resistance.
55 See Pieter Steyn, *Zapuphizo: Voice of the Nagas* (London, 2002). Steyn, though mostly not giving his sources, must have moved through the Naga hills with Angami Nagas in the course of the Second World War operations, and part of his book is a recollection of oral history narrated on these occasions.
56 Horam, *Naga Insurgency*, p. 59.
57 Ibid.
58 Panmei, 'Naga movement and its ramifications', p. 89.
59 Yonuo, *The Rising Nagas*, p. 201.
60 Luithui and Haksar, *Nagaland File,* p. 24.
61 Z. A. Phizo, 'A Letter to the President of India', in Luithui and Haksar, pp. 57–60, p. 57.
62 Chaube, *Hill Politics in North-East India*, p. 108.
63 Yonuo, *The Rising Nagas*, p. 202.
64 Chaube, *Hill Politics in North-East India*, p. 108.
65 Yonuo, *The Rising Nagas*, p. 202.
66 Alemchimba, *A Brief Historical Account of Nagaland,* p. 174.
67 Chaube, *Hill Politics in North-East India*, p. 108.
68 Horam, *Naga Insurgency*, p. 50.
69 Yonuo, *The Rising Nagas*, p. 204. Nehru's statement on that occasion became infamous among the Nagas: 'Whether heaven falls or India goes to pieces and blood runs red in the country, I don't care. Whether I am here or for that matter any other body comes in, I don't care. Nagas will not be allowed to become independent.' Kaka D. Iralu, *Nagaland and India: The Blood and the Tears*, (no publishing place mentioned, 2000), p. 80.
70 Rustomji described Medhi as '. . . shrewd, narrow-minded and parochially Assamese.' Rustomji, *Imperilled Frontiers*, p. 36.
71 Nibedon, *Nagaland: The Night of the Guerrillas*, pp. 54–56.
72 Alemchimba, *A Brief Historical Account of Nagaland,* p. 175.
73 Panmei, 'Naga movement and its ramifications', p. 89.
74 Rustomji, *Imperilled Frontiers*, p. 31.

75 Alemchimba, *A Brief Historical Account of Nagaland*, p. 180.
76 Ibid.
77 Yonuo, *The Rising Nagas*, p. 204.
78 Nibedon, *Nagaland: The Night of the Guerrillas*, p. 48.
79 Yonuo, *The Rising Nagas*, p. 205.
80 Horam, *Naga Insurgency*, p. 51.
81 Yonuo, *The Rising Nagas*, p. 205.
82 Luithui and Haksar, *Nagaland File*, p. 26.
83 Yonuo, *The Rising Nagas*, p. 205.
84 Luithui and Haksar, *Nagaland File*, p. 25.
85 Alemchimba, *A Brief Historical Account of Nagaland*, p. 182.
86 Panmei, 'Naga movement and its ramifications', p. 90.
87 Luithui and Haksar, *Nagaland File*, p. 26.
88 Horam, *Naga Insurgency*, p. 55.
89 Ibid., p. 52.
90 'Report of the Naga Goodwill Mission to Assam (22th December 1953)', in Luithui and Haksar, pp, 74–94, pp. 91–92.
91 Panmei, 'Naga movement and its ramifications', p. 90.
92 Aosenba, *The Naga Resistance Movement: Prospects of Peace and Armed Conflict*, p. 50.
93 Yonuo, *The Rising Nagas*, p. 211.
94 Nibedon, *Nagaland: The Night of the Guerrillas*, p. 49. 'Hongking' means 'Get out' in Chang language, see Aosenba, *The Naga Resistance Movement*, p. 50. Phizo had already been to Tuensang from late 1952 onwards, and enjoyed a strong standing among the tribes there, see Steyn, *Zapuphizo: Voice of the Nagas*, pp. 86–87. Thus it is clear that if there was a president of this government, it was Phizo. See also ibid., p. 94.
95 Aosenba, *The Naga Resistance Movement*, pp. 50–51.
96 Luithui and Haksar, *Nagaland File*, pp. 26–27. See also Aosenba, *The Naga Resistance Movement*, p. 51.
97 Yonuo, *The Rising Nagas*, p. 213.
98 Ibid. and Aosenba, *The Naga Resistance Movement*, p. 52.
99 Luithui and Haksar, *Nagaland File*, p. 27.
100 Neville Maxwell, *India and the Nagas* (London, 1973), p. 11.
101 Yonuo, *The Rising Nagas*, p. 214.
102 See the beginning of the following sub-chapter and Kaka D. Iralu, *Nagaland and India: The Blood and the Tears*, pp. 86–89.
103 Luithui and Haksar, *Nagaland File*, p. 27.
104 Nibedon, *Nagaland: The Night of the Guerrillas*, p. 41.
105 Ibid., p. 57.
106 Ibid., p. 36.
107 Ibid., p. 63.
108 Ibid., p. 74.
109 Panmei, 'Naga movement and its ramifications', p. 91.
110 Nirmal Nibedon, *North East India: The Ethnic Explosion* (New Delhi, 1981), p. 28.
111 Luithui and Haksar, *Nagaland File*, p. 27.
112 'Village Diary – People of Mokokchung Village, Nagaland, dated 27 April 1964', in IWGIA Document 56, *The Naga Nation and its Struggle Against Genocide: A Report Compiled by IWGIA* (Copenhagen, 1986), pp. 136–140.
113 Imtiaz Ahmed, 'The Cry of Sakeena: A post-nationalist critique of violence in South Asia', *Mainstream*, Vol. 37, No. 11, March 6, 1999, pp. 14–21, p. 15.
114 C. L. Proudfoot, *Flash of the Khukri: History of the 3rd Gorkha Rifles, 1947 to 1980* (New Delhi, 1984), pp. 53–61.
115 Special Correspondent, *The Times*, 28.10.1958.

116 Ibid.
117 *Rajya Sabha Debates*, Vol. 22., No. 1, 25. August 1958, columns 963–976; 27. August 1958, columns 1253–1312 & 28. August 1958, columns 1313–1474; for Sapru's comment, see 27. August 1958, column 1287.
118 'Three case studies', in IWGIA Document 56, *The Naga nation and its struggle against genocide: A report compiled by IWGIA* (Copenhagen, 1986), pp. 73–82.
119 Gavin Young, 'Commonwealth's Unknown War – 2: Jungle Baptists Fight It Out With India', *The Observer*, May 7, 1961.
120 Gavin Young, 'Commonwealth's Unknown War – 3: Charges of Atrocities on Nehru's Doorstep', *The Observer*, May 14, 1961.
121 Easwar Sagar in *The Hindu*, undated, cf. Ursula Graham Bower, 'Nagas Fight on in Closed Land', *The Observer*, Nov. 13, 1960.
122 Ibid. That 30,000 Indian troops were fighting ca. 2,000 Naga army were the official Indian government numbers, Gavin Young, 'An Unknown War – 1', *The Observer*, April 30, 1961. Regarding the terminology employed here, see chapter five, note 112.
123 Special correspondent, Mokokchung, Nagaland, Dec. 17 (delayed), *The Times*, 19.12.1960.
124 Special correspondent, Jorhat, Assam, Dec. 22, *The Times*, 23.12.1960. On the officials shielding off of the correspondents from the population and its surreal results the journalist gave us the following notable anecdote: 'The feeling that they were being denied free access to all opinions reached its strongest pitch perhaps – and certainly the tour its most bizarrely comic moment – when, after a tribal dance, an imposingly barbaric chieftain came forward to make a long and passionately chanted declamation, emphasizing his points by driving his spear into the ground: according to the translator all this was about his people's satisfaction with the hospitals and dispensaries the Government had built, but according to the ubiquitous whisperers of the "overground" it was in fact a turbulent affirmation of the Nagas' desire for independence. The annoyance of the officials seemed to reinforce this claim.'
125 Rawle Knox, 'Nagas Slip Messages to Reporters', Kohima, Naga Hills, Dec. 17, *The Observer*, Dec. 18, 1960.
126 Rawle Knox, 'Nagaland To-day: Why Nehru Cannot "Free" Hill Tribesmen', New Delhi, Jan. 7, *The Observer*, Jan. 8, 1961.
127 Ibid.
128 Ibid.
129 Gavin Young, 'A meeting with Nagas' prisoners', *The Observer*, April 9, 1961.
130 Gavin Young, 'An Unknown War – 1', *The Observer*, April 30, 1961.
131 Gavin Young, 'Commonwealth's Unknown War – 3', *The Observer*, May 14, 1961.
132 Gavin Young, 'A meeting with Nagas' prisoners', *The Observer*, April 9, 1961.
133 Gavin Young, 'Commonwealth's Unknown War – 2', *The Observer*, May 7, 1961.
134 Ibid.
135 Gavin Young, 'Commonwealth's Unknown War – 3', *The Observer*, May 14, 1961.
136 See Chapter Five, Note 112.
137 Gavin Young, 'Commonwealth's Unknown War – 3', *The Observer*, May 14, 1961.
138 Ibid.
139 'Letters to the Editor: The War In Nagaland', *The Observer*, May 28, 1961.
140 Ibid.
141 T. N. Kaul, 'A Reply to Gavin Young: The Nagas of India', *The Observer*, June 25, 1961.
142 Ursula Graham Bower, 'Sifting the Evidence on Naga Problem', *The Observer*, July 2, 1961.
143 Ibid.
144 Ibid.
145 Guy Wint, 'India's "Irish" Problem', *The Observer*, April 15, 1962.
146 Wint quotes the Nagas on claiming 70,000 casualties to that point, but adds that he

thinks this number is excessive, Guy Wint, 'India's "Irish" Problem', *The Observer*, April 15, 1962.

147 In granting, for example, as much autonomy to the Nagas as had been granted to Bhutan. Editorial, 'The need of Asian unity', *The Observer*, November 4, 1962.

148 Among these we may list the direct and indirect casualties, devastation of infrastructure (villages, fields etc.) and environment, prevention of economic and cultural development, destruction of social fabric, creation of culture of violence, a gun culture with many opposed and irreconcilable actors, groups of war-winners, rampant drugs abuses and epidemic spread of HIV etc., in short the denial of a decent, dignified life to whole generations of people.

149 Special Correspondent, *The Observer*, May 20, 1962.

150 George Patterson, 'Naga General: I have Indian "atrocity" proof', *The Observer*, June 3, 1962.

151 Ibid.

152 George Patterson, 'Nagas: Indians killed one in ten', Karachi, June 9, *The Observer*, June 10, 1962.

153 Ibid.

154 Luithui and Haksar, *Nagaland File*, p. 29.

155 Rustomji, *Imperilled Frontiers*, p. 31.

156 Michael Scott, *The Search for Peace* (London, 1968), p. 14.

157 Ibid.

158 Ibid., p. 17.

159 Ibid., p. 31.

160 Maxwell, *India and the Nagas*, p. 11.

161 Ibid., p. 12.

162 Ibid., p. 11.

163 P. D. Stracey, *Nagaland Nightmare* (Bombay, 1968), p. 83.

164 Ibid., p. 84.

165 Ibid., p. 83.

166 Ibid., p. 141.

167 Ibid.

168 Rustomji, *Imperilled Frontiers*, pp. 49–50.

169 See, for example, the former chief minister of Nagaland S. C. Jamir, 'Nagaland and the Special Constitutional Provision', in Luithui and Haksar (eds.), *Nagaland File*, pp. 61–73, p. 63.

170 Horam, *Naga Insurgency: The Last Thirty Years*, p. 206.

171 Nibedon, *North East India: The Ethnic Explosion*, p. 46.

172 Ibid.

173 Horam, *Naga Insurgency*, p. 88.

174 Ibid., p. 52.

175 Rustomji, *Imperilled Frontiers*, p. 48.

176 Jenkins, *Rethinking ethnicity: arguments and explorations*, p. 137.

177 Ernest Gellner, *Nations and Nationalism* (Oxford, 1983), pp. 43–50.

178 Connor, 'Homelands in a World of States', p. 61.

179 Linda Colley, *Britons: Forging the Nation 1707–1837* (New Haven and London, 1992).

7 Divide-and-rule

1 Bimol Akoijam, 'How history repeats itself', *Economic and Political Weekly*, 28.07.2001, pp. 2807–2812.

2 The colonial legacy in structure, mindset and action, especially but not exclusively towards the periphery, is for example acknowledged in the following works: Sumit

Sarkar, *Modern India* (Delhi: Macmillan, 1983). Ayesha Jalal, *Democracy and Authoritarianism in South Asia: A Comparative and Historical Perspective* (Cambridge, 1995). Sugata Bose and Ayesha Jalal, *Modern South Asia: History, Culture, Political Economy* (Delhi, 1998) and Nivedita Menon and Aditya Nigam, *Power and Contestation: India since 1989* (London, New York, 2007).

3 Cobden, Richard, *How wars are got up in India: the origin of the Burmese war* (London: William & Frederick G. Cash, 1853). Cobden, a Whig, critical of British imperial policy described and decried in this book how the second Anglo-Burman War was facilitated under certain pretexts and carried out with the most ruthless superiority of fire power.

4 *Current Intelligence Weekly, Special Report: India's Rebellious Eastern Tribes* (Central Intelligence Agency, Directorate of Intelligence, 1 July 1966).

5 Dinesh Singh, deputy minister in the ministry of external affairs, in the *Lok Sabha* on an encounter in June 1963, *Lok Sabha Debates*, Vol. 21, 16th September 1963, Columns 6207–6208.

6 Cyril Dunn, 'Is Shastri just a stop-gap?', *The Observer,* 07.06.1964 and *The Observer*, 09.08.1964. Note the title of the article: 'Shastri: I want peace.'

7 *Times* correspondent, *The Times*, 15.08.1964.

8 *Times* correspondent, Kohima, *The Times*, 19.08.1964.

9 *Times* correspondent, Delhi, *The Times*, 19.08.1964.

10 *Times* correspondent, *The Times*, 07.09.1964.

11 *Times* correspondent, Kohima, *The Times*, 15.09.1964 and *The New York Times*, 15.09.1964 (Calcutta, 14.09.1964).

12 *The New York Times*, 25.09.1964 (Calcutta, 24.09.1964). Gundevia is described as foreign secretary leading the Indian delegation and Chedema as a village being five miles from Kohima.

13 *Times* correspondent, *The Times*, 30.09.1964.

14 *Rajya Sabha Debates*, Vol. XLIX, 29. Sept. 1964, Columns 3427–3430.

15 *The Times*, 15.10.1964.

16 *Times* correspondent, Kohima, *The Times*, 19.10.1964.

17 Thomas F. Brady 'India Sets Rationing for Kerala, But All Other States Reject Plan', *The New York Times*, 29.10.1964, p. 3.

18 *Lok Sabha Debates*, Vol. 35, 17. Nov. 1964, Columns 37–39; 18. Nov. 1964, Columns 457–470; 20. Nov. 1964, Columns 691–709 and 24. Nov. 1964, Columns 1456–1461.

19 *Times* correspondent, *The Times*, 18.11.1964 and *Rajya Sabha Debates*, Vol. 50, 15. Dec. 1964, Columns 3724–3727.

20 Cyril Dunn, 'Call to end Naga peace mission', *The Observer*, 27.12.1964 (New Delhi, 26.12.1964).

21 *Times* correspondent, *The Times*, 31.12.1964, 22.01.1965 (Kohima), 23.01.1965 and 09.02.1965; *The Observer*, 28.03.1965 and 18.04.1965 (New Delhi, 17.04.1965).

22 *The Observer*, 13.06.1965.

23 Ibid.

24 *The Observer*, 18.07.1965.

25 Ibid.

26 *The Observer*, 24.10.1965.

27 *Times* correspondent, *The Times*, 08.11.1965 (Gauhati, 07.11.1965).

28 'India: Tenuous Peace', *Far Eastern Economic Review*, Vol. 50, No. 7, 18.11.1965, p. 319.

29 Indira Gandhi in the Indian parliament informing on the meetings, *Lok Sabha Debates*, Vol. 50, 21. Feb. 1966, Column 1301.

30 *Times* correspondent, *The Times*, 21.02.1966 and *Lok Sabha Debates*, Vol. 50, 21. Feb. 1966, Columns 1300–1311.

31 *Lok Sabha Debates*, Vol. 51, 02. March 1966, Columns 3425–3440.

32 *Times* correspondent, *The Times*, 03.03.1966.

33 *Times* correspondent, *The Times*, 04.03.1966.
34 Commentary, *The Times*, 04.03.1966.
35 *The Observer*, 27.03.1966.
36 *Times* correspondent, *The Times*, 11.04.1966.
37 *Times* correspondent, *The Times*, 25.04.1966. When I, more than 30 years later, inquired about the reasons for that attacks, I was told that these trains brought IA reinforcements to the Naga hills.
38 *The Times*, 04., 06., 07. and 11.05.1966.
39 Cyril Dunn, 'India: Hard or soft line against rebels', *The Observer*, 22.05.1966.
40 *The Times*, 31.05.1966.
41 Ibid.
42 Jaime Malamud Goti, 'State terror and memory of what?', *University of Arkansas at Little Rock Law Review*, Vol. 21, Fall 1998, No. 1, pp. 107–118.
43 Ibid.
44 *The Guardian*, 20.07.1966.
45 *The Observer*, 06.08.1967 and Michael Scott, 'The Nagas', *The Observer*, Letters to the editor, 06.08.1968.
46 Cyril Dunn, 'India takes powers to crush secession', *The Observer*, 19.06.1966 (New Delhi, 18.06.1966).
47 Inder Malhotra, 'India to curb the "rebels"', *The Guardian*, 18.06.1966 (New Delhi, 17.06.1966).
48 *The Times*, 12.08.1966.
49 *The Times*, 28.10.1966.
50 Cyril Dunn, 'Nagas are weary but talk on', *The Observer*, 30.10.1966 (New Delhi, 29.10.1966).
51 *The Times*, 03.01.1967 and *The Guardian*, 04.01.1967 (New Delhi, 03.01.1967, Reuters).
52 *The Guardian*, 06.01.1967 (New Delhi, 05.01.1967, Reuters) and *The Observer*, 08.01.1967 (New Delhi, 07.01.1967).
53 *The Times*, 14.01.1967 and *The Guardian* 14.01.1967 (New Delhi, 13.01.1967).
54 *The Times*, 06.02.1967.
55 *The Times*, 08.04.1967.
56 *The Observer*, 16.04.1967.
57 *Lok Sabha Debates*, Vol. 6, 15. July 1967, Columns 12233–12238.
58 *Lok Sabha Debates*, Vol. 7, 17. July 1967, Columns 12352–12496 and 27. July 1967, Columns 15208–15213.
59 *Lok Sabha Debates*, Vol. 9, 13. November 1967, Columns 1000–1009 and 24. November 1967, Columns 2829–2836.
60 *The Times*, 22.09.1967, by Peter Hazelhurst.
61 Inder Malhotra, 'Statehood call from Assam hills', *The Guardian*, 25.09.1967 (Calcutta, 24.09.1967).
62 *The Observer*, 05.11.1967.
63 *The Times*, 19.01.1968.
64 *Lok Sabha Debates*, Vol. 14, 19.03.1968, Columns 1506–1516. See also *The Times*, 20.03.1968.
65 Ibid.
66 *The Observer*, 24.03.1968.
67 *The Times*, 25.03.1968.
68 *The Times*, 27.03.1968.
69 *Lok Sabha Debates*, Vol. 15, 01.04.1968, Column 1194.
70 *The Guardian*, 20.04.1968 (Reuters).
71 *The Times*, 25.04.1968.
72 *The Observer*, 05.05.1968.
73 *The Guardian* (Inder Malhotra), 20.05.1968; *The Times*, 27.05.1968 and 05.06.1968.

74 Inder Malhotra, 'Arms from China put Naga truce in danger', *The Guardian*, 25.05.1968 (Calcutta, 24.05.1968).

75 *The Times*, 27.05.1968 (Peter Hazelhurst from Delhi, 26.05.1968).

76 Inder Malhotra, 'Nagas fight with Chinese arms', *The Guardian*, 10.06.1968 (Calcutta, 09.06.1968), *The Times*, 15.06.1968 (Shillong, 14.06.1968) and Cyril Dunn, 'Nagas rout Indians', *The Observer*, 23.06.1968.

77 *The Observer*, 04.08.1968.

78 Colin Legum, 'New nations, old scores: Colin Legum answers Indian charges against The Observer.', *The Observer*, 11.08.1968.

79 Ibid.

80 *The Guardian*, 12.09.1968 (New Delhi, 11.09.1968) and *The Observer*, 15.09.1968 (New Delhi, 14.09.1968).

81 C. P. Ramachandran, '"Pro-China Naga leaders kidnapped,' say Indians"', *The Observer*, 03.11.1968 (New Delhi, 02.11.1968).

82 Cyril Dunn, 'India steps up forces in Nagaland', *The Observer*, 17.11.1968.

83 Cyril Dunn, 'Naga resistance leaders fall out – president seized', *The Observer*, 15.12.1968.

84 C. P. Ramachandran, 'Burma and India talk of Nagas', *The Observer*, 30.03.1969 (New Delhi, 29.03.1969).

85 *Lok Sabha Debates*, Vol. 27, 01.04.1969, Columns 212–213.

86 Inder Malhotra, 'India overcomes Naga rebels', *The Guardian*, 02.04.1969 (Calcutta, 01.04.1969).

87 *The Observer*, 13.04.1969.

88 Cyril Dunn, 'Mystery of missing Naga hero', *The Observer*, 20.04.1969.

89 *Lok Sabha Debates*, Vol. 31, 05.08.1969, Columns 204–210 and Inder Malhotra, 'Naga rebels kill troops', *The Guardian*, 06.08.1969 (Calcutta, 05.08.1969).

90 *The Observer*, 09.11.1969.

91 *The Guardian*, 02.04.1970 and Inder Malhotra, 'Indian State within State ushers in new era', *The Guardian*, 03.04.1970.

92 Inder Malhotra, 'New threat by Naga guerrillas', *The Guardian*, 15.04.1970 (Calcutta, 14.04.1970).

93 *The Observer*, 22.11.1970.

94 *Lok Sabha Debates*, Vol. 9, 08.12.1971, Columns 40–54 and Vol. 9 (no. 20), 09.12.1971, Columns 3–75.

95 David Loshak, 'Naga chiefs end rebel hopes', *The Telegraph*, 12.01.1972.

96 Cyril Dunn, 'India puts more troops in Nagaland', *The Observer*, 20.02.1972.

97 *The Observer*, 01.04.1972.

98 *Lok Sabha Debates*, 28.03.1972, Columns 161–200.

99 *Lok Sabha Debates* 1972, Volume 20, point 1331.

100 Cyril Dunn, ' Naga plea to UN to stop 'genocide'', *The Observer*, 03.09.1972.

101 Colin Legum, 'Indian troops start push into Nagaland', *The Observer*, 01.10.1972.

102 *The Observer*, 03.03.1974.

103 *The Observer*, 04.08.1974.

104 *The Observer*, 07.09.1975.

105 *Lok Sabha Debates,* Volume 58, 11.03.1976, Column 226.

106 Ibid., Columns 227–8.

107 Ibid., Column 234.

108 Ibid., Column 238.

109 Ibid., Columns 239–241.

110 Ibid., Column 241.

111 Ibid., Column 243.

112 Ibid., Columns 243–245.

113 Ibid., Column 250.

114 Ibid., Column 258.

115 *Lok Sabha Debates,* Volume 63, 20.08.1976, Columns 186–194.
116 Gavin Young, 'Naga battle will "flare up" ', *The Observer*, 19.06.1977.
117 Michael T. Kaufman, 'Legislators Welcome Mrs. Gandhi', *The New York Times*, 11.01.1980.
118 Michael T. Kaufman, 'Indira's Power Politics', *The New York Times*, 23.03.1980.
119 Salman Rushdie, *Imaginary Homelands: Essays and Criticism 1981 – 1991* (London, 1991), p. 50.
120 Gita Mehta, *Snakes and Ladders: A View of Modern India* (London, 1997), p. 13.
121 If the reading of Rohinton Mistry's *A Fine Balance* (London, 1997) is of any indication, or phrased differently, has any relevance for what it describes, then the latter is definitely the case.
122 Michael T. Kaufman, 'Indira's Power Politics', *The New York Times*, 23.03.1980.
123 Ibid.
124 Ibid.
125 Ibid.
126 Katherine Frank, *Indira: The Life of Indira Nehru Gandhi* (London, 2001), see esp. Chapters 13–15; P. N. Dhar, *Indira Gandhi, the 'Emergency', Indian Democracy* (New Delhi, 2001 [2000]), pp. 132–3.
127 *The New York Times*, 20.04.1980 (New Delhi, 19.04.1980).
128 Michael T. Kaufman, 'Assam balks at joining the Indian Melting Pot', *The New York Times*, 27.04.1980.
129 Michael T. Kaufman, 'Once-Timid Tribal Groups Vent Anger Violently in India', *The New York Times*, 04.07.1980 (New Delhi, 03.07.1980).
130 *The New York Times*, 21.02.1983 and Michael T. Kaufman, 'In Delhi, Shock but No Rush to Judgement', *The New York Times*, 25.02.1983 (New Delhi, 24.02.1983).
131 Ibid.
132 *The New York Times*, 04.03.1983 (New Delhi, 03.03.1983).
133 William K. Stevens, 'Gandhi tells cheering crowd bullets will not shake India', *The New York Times*, 20.11.1984 (New Delhi, 19.11.1984).
134 Sanjoy Hazarika, 'A rebel group in India turns from arms to talks', *The New York Times*, 07.04.1985 (New Delhi, 06.04.1985).
135 Steven R. Weisman, 'India's Northeast seems like a world of its own', *The New York Times*, 15.12.1985 (Gauhati, India).
136 *The New York Times*, 26.06.1986 (New Delhi, 25.06.1986) and Steven R. Weisman, 'A corner of India stirs hope for unity', *The New York Times*, 22.02.1987 (Aizawl, India, 17.02.1987).
137 Sanjoy Hazarika, 'New Delhi imposes direct rule in a turbulent state', *The New York Times*, 08.09.1988 (New Delhi, 07.09.1988).
138 Arindam Sarkar, 'Battle for Assam', *Sunday*, 2–8.08.1998, pp. 40–47.
139 Avirook Sen, 'Disarming Action', *India Today*, 10.08.1998, pp. 44–45.
140 Robert Bryniki, 'Premierminister Inder Kumar Gujral hat allen bewaffneten Gruppierungen im Nordosten Verhandlungen ohne Vorbedingungen angeboten – eine geschickte Geste, die Neu-Delhi eine Verbesserung des geopolitischen Umfelds einge-tragen hat', *Le Monde diplomatique*, No. 5275, 11.07.1997, p. 19.
141 Avirock Sen, 'On the Offensive', *India Today*, 01.09.1997, pp. 52–53.
142 'Long road to peace in Nagaland', *Economic and Political Weekly*, 02.08.1997.
143 *BBC News* http://www.news6.thdo.bbc.co.uk, 05.04.1998 (accessed on 12.02.2001).
144 *BBC News* http://www.news6.thdo.bbc.co.uk, 02.05.1998 (accessed on 12.02.2001).
145 *BBC News* http://www.news.bbc.co.uk, 26.06.1998 (accessed on 12.02.2001).
146 *BBC News* http://www.news.bbc.co.uk, 31.07.1998 (accessed on 12.02.2001).
147 Nitin A. Gokhale, 'Route to Suicide', *Outlook*, 01.02.1999, pp. 38–44.
148 'Naga Saga', *Economist*, 31.07.1999, Vol. 352, Issue 8130, p. 33.
149 Northeast Vigil, Editorial, http://www.northeastvigil.com, 01.08.1999, (accessed 02.03.2001).

150 Sukumar Muralidharan, 'A peace process unravels', *Frontline*, 14.04.2000, pp. 44–45.
151 *The Hindu*, 22.09.2000, online edition (accessed on 03.07.2007).
152 Barun Das Gupta, 'No solution for Nagas within Constitution', *The Hindu*, 05.07.2001 (Mokokchung, 04.07.2001), online edition (accessed on 17.04.2007).
153 *BBC News* http://www.news.bbc.co.uk, 19.01.2001 (accessed on 12.02.2001).
154 *The New York Times*, 22.06.2001.
155 *The Hindu*, 12.07.2001 (New Delhi), online edition (accessed on 17.04.2007).
156 *The New York Times*, 28.07.2001.
157 Radhabinod Koijam, 'Naga ceasefire and Manipur', *The Hindu*, 13.07.2001, online edition (accessed on 17.04.2007).
158 *Economist*, 16.01.2003.
159 K. T. Rajasingham, 'Nagas ready to resort to arms struggle for independence, if peace talks fail – Muivah', *Asian Tribune*, 02.10.2002.
160 Amy Waldman, 'India: peace gesture to rebels', *The New York Times*, 27.11.2002.
161 *Economist*, 16.01.2003.
162 Udayon Misra, 'Naga Peace Talks: High Hopes and Hard Realities', *Economic and Political Weekly*, 15.02.2003, pp. 593–597.
163 Subash Gatade, 'Why the Armed Forces Special Powers Act should be Dumped', *Mainstream*, Vol. XLII, No. 32, 31.07.2004., pp. 3–5.
164 B. K. Roy Burman, 'The Other Manipur', *Mainstream*, Vol. XLII, No. 36, 28.08.2004, pp. 2–6.
165 Bimol Akoijam, 'How history repeats itself', *Economic and Political Weekly*, 28.07.2001, pp. 2807–2812, p. 2808.
166 J. K. Dutt, 'Outlook for Peace in North-East', *Economic and Political Weekly*, 11.01.2003. pp. 109–110.
167 Monirul Hussain, 'Governance and Electoral Processes in India's North-East', *Economic and Political Weekly*, 08.03.2003.
168 Ibid., and see for one additional example also the *Economist*, 07.10.2004 for the fact that violence and terror continue to spread regionwide in the Northeast. For the argument that governance is absent in the border states and the Indian state solely present in the form of its security forces that are empowered by martial law and because of this has lost all legitimacy that it may have had, see Sushanta Talukdar, 'Cross-border challenges', *Frontline*, 16.07.2004, pp. 37–40.
169 Gautam Navlakha, 'Naga Peace Process: Larger Issues at Stake', *Economic and Political Weekly*, 22.02.2003. pp. 683–684.
170 Sanjib Baruah, *Durable Disorder: Understanding the politics of Northeast India* (Delhi, 2007 [2005]), pp. 211–236.
171 Christophe Jaffrelot, 'India's Look East Policy: An Asianist Strategy in Perspective', *India Review*, vol. 2, no. 2, April 2003, pp. 35–68.

8 From nation to civil society

1 See for example 'Third Degree' (Cover Story), *Sunday*, 3–9.08.1997, p. 32ff and note that by 2004 one third of India's districts were affected by Naxalism, *Economist*, 04.11.2004.
2 *Frontline*, August 27, 2004, pp. 37–9 and September 10, pp. 4–23 (several articles).
3 Lakshmi Menon, minister of state in the ministry of external affairs, in the *Lok Sabha*, *Lok Sabha Debates*, Vol. 22, 18th November 1963, Columns 45–46, see also *Times* correspondent, *The Times*, 18.11.1963.
4 *Times* correspondent, *The Times*, 03.01.1964.
5 *Times* correspondent, *The Times*, 08.01.1964.
6 *Times* correspondent, *The Times*, 16.01.1964, see also *The Observer*, 5. and 12.01.1964.

7 *The Observer*, 23.02.1964.
8 Cyril Dunn, 'Peace is nearer for Nagas', *The Observer*, 05.07.1964 (New Delhi, 04.07.1964).
9 *The Observer*, 10.05.1964 (Delhi, 09.05.1964).
10 *Times* correspondent, *The Times*, 20.05.1964.
11 *New York Times*, 12.11.1964 (Calcutta, 11.11.1964).
12 *Lok Sabha Debates*, Vol. 35, 17. Nov. 1964, Columns 37–39; 18. Nov. 1964, Columns 457–470; 20. Nov. 1964, Columns 691–709 and 24. Nov. 1964, Columns 1456–1461.
13 Cyril Dunn, 'Call to end Naga peace mission', *The Observer*, 27.12.1964 (New Delhi, 26.12.1964).
14 *Times* correspondent, *The Times*, 22.01.1965.
15 *Times* correspondent, Kohima, The Times, 22.01.1965.
16 *Times* correspondent, *The Times*, 23.01.1965.
17 *Times* correspondent, *The Times*, 09.02.1965.
18 *The Observer*, 13.06.1965.
19 *The Observer*, 18.07.1965.
20 *Times* correspondent, *The Times*, 08.02.1966 (Delhi, 07.02.1966) and 19.02.1966; *Lok Sabh Debates*, Vol. 50, 21. Feb. 1966, Column 1301.
21 *Times* correspondent, *The Times*, 11.04.1966.
22 See Temsula Ao, *These hills called home: stories from a war zone* (New Delhi, 2006), pp. 13–22; *The Observer*, 27.03.1966 and Cyrril Dunn, 'India: Hard or soft line against rebels', *The Observer*, 22.05.1966.
23 Letter to the editor, *The Times*, 01.04.1966.
24 Times correspondent, *The Times*, 18.04.1966 (New Delhi, 17.04.1966).
25 *The Times*, 12.08.1966.
26 *Lok Sabha Debates*, Vol. 7, 17. July 1967, Columns 12352–12496 and 27. July 1967, Columns 15208–15213.
27 *The Times*, 27.07.1967 (Bombay, 26.07.1967).
28 Inder Malhotra, 'Naga talks at critical stage', *The Guardian*, 22.01.1968 (Calcutta, 21.01.1968).
29 *The Guardian*, 23.03.1968 (Inder Malhotra, Calcutta, 22.03.1968).
30 Inder Malhotra, 'Nagas fight with Chinese arms', *The Guardian*, 10.06.1968 (Calcutta, 09.06.1968), *The Times*, 15.06.1968 (Shillong, 14.06.1968) and Cyril Dunn, 'Nagas rout Indians', *The Observer*, 23.06.1968.
31 Inder Malhotra, 'Division among the Nagas', *The Guardian*, 11.06.1968 (Calcutta, 10.06.1968).
32 *The Times*, 10.06.1968 (by Peter Hazelhurst, New Delhi, 09.06.1968).
33 *The Times*, 15.06.1968 (Shillong, 14.06.1968).
34 Michael Ross, 'Inside a forbidden Land on the brink of war', *The Observer*, 16.06.1968.
35 Ibid.
36 *The Times*, 17.06.1968 (by Peter Hazelhurst, Shillong, 16.06.1968).
37 *The Observer*, 04.08.1968.
38 C. P. Ramachandran, '"Pro-China Naga leaders kidnapped,' say Indians"', *The Observer*, 03.11.1968 (New Delhi, 02.11.1968).
39 Cyril Dunn, 'Naga resistance leaders fall out – president seized', *The Observer*, 15.12.1968.
40 C. P. Ramachandran, 'Burma to put curb on Nagas', *The Observer*, 23.03.1969 (New Delhi, 22.03.1969).
41 C. P. Ramachandran, 'Burma and India talk of Nagas', *The Observer*, 30.03.1969 (New Delhi, 29.03.1969).
42 Cyril Dunn, 'Mystery of missing Naga hero', *The Observer*, 20.04.1969.
43 C. P. Ramachandran, 'General "held in Red Fort"', *The Observer*, 27.04.1969 (New Delhi, 26.04.1969).

44   *The Observer*, 18.05.1969.
45   *The Observer*, 27.07.1969.
46   *Lok Sabha Debates*, Vol. 31, 05.08.1969, Columns 204–210 and Inder Malhotra, 'Naga rebels kill troops', *The Guardian*, 06.08.1969 (Calcutta, 05.08.1969).
47   *The Observer*, 10.08.69 (Kohima, 09.08.1969).
48   Major Melvin Kiesel, 'Nagaland: An Unending Guerrilla War', *Military Review* (US Army Comman & Gen. Staff Coll., Fort Leavenworth, Ka.), Vol. 51, No. 12, December 1971, pp. 80–87, p. 80.
49   Ibid., pp. 84–87.
50   David Loshak, 'Naga chiefs end rebel hopes', *The Telegraph*, 12.01.1972.
51   *The Observer*, 01.04.1972.
52   *Lok Sabha Debates*, Volume 17, 09.08.1972, point 1419 and 10.08.1972; Cyril Dunn, 'Nagaland search for Minister's attackers', *The Observer*, 13.08.1972.
53   Cyril Dunn, 'Nagas 'plot' may be freed', *The Observer*, 22.10.72.
54   Patrick Montgomery, 'Reading the writing on the wall in Nagaland', *The Times*, 14.11.1973.
55   Ibid.
56   Colin Legum, 'The war that India hides', *The Observer*, 18.11.1973.
57   *The Observer*, 03.03.1974.
58   *The Observer*, 04.08.1974.
59   *The Observer*, 07.09.1975.
60   Sanjoy Hazarika, Northeast, Nagas and future of Muivah', *Northeast Vigil*, July 2000, http://www.northeastvigil.com (accessed on 02.03.2001).
61   Sanjoy Hazarika, 'In India's Northeast: The Taming of the Guerrilla', *The New York Times*, 13.03.1984 (Imphal, no date).
62   Ibid.
63   Sanjoy Hazarika, 'Burmese army is said to fight India rebels', *The New York Times*, 11.04.1984 (New Delhi, 10.04.1984) and *idem.*, 'Naga insurgents said to kill 300 who refused to give aid', *The New York Times*, 12.04.1984 (New Delhi, 11.04.1984).
64   Steven R. Weisman, 'India's Northeast seems like a world of its own', *The New York Times*, 15.12.1985 (Gauhati, India).
65   *The New York Times*, 26.06.1986 (New Delhi, 25.06.1986) and Steven R. Weisman, 'A corner of India stirs hope for unity', *The New York Times*, 22.02.1987 (Aizawl, India, 17.02.1987).
66   Sanjoy Hazarika, 'New Delhi imposes direct rule in a turbulent state', *The New York Times*, 08.09.1988 (New Delhi, 07.09.1988).
67   Sanjoy Hazarika, Northeast, Nagas and future of Muivah', *Northeast Vigil*, July 2000, http://www.northeastvigil.com (accessed on 02.03.2001).
68   Sanjoy Hazarika, '3 Rebel organizations in India link activities', *The New York Times*, 19.08.1990 (New Delhi, 18.08.1990).
69   U A Schimray, 'Ethnicity and Socio-Political Assertion: The Manipur Experience', *Economic and Political Weekly*, 29.09.2001.
70   Sanjoy Hazarika, 'Insurgents in India's Northeast call for peace talks', *The New York Times*, 20.02.1991 (Gauhati).
71   Sanjoy Hazarika, 'Rebel group ends uprising in India', *The New York Times*, 18.12.1991 (New Delhi, 17.12.1991).
72   Sanjoy Hazarika, '100 Dead in India in religious strife', *The New York Times*, 05.05.1993 (New Delhi, 04.05.1993).
73   *The Guardian*, 16. and 24.09.1993.
74   Ibid.
75   'Nagaland: Continuing Violence', *Economic and Political Weekly*, 15.01.1994.
76   Sanjoy Hazarika, 'Bombs kill 25 soldiers in Northern India', *The New York Times*, 26.02.1995 (New Delhi, 25.02.1995).

77 Walter Fernandes, 'Limits of Law and Order Approach to the North-East', *Economic and Political Weekly*, 16.10.2004, pp. 4609–4611.

78 Sanjay Sangvai, 'Nagaland: Beyond Politics of Identity', *Economic and Political Weekly*, 30.11.1996, pp. 3103–4.

79 Ibid., p. 3103.

80 Ibid., p. 3104.

81 *The New York Times*, 01.01.1997 (Sesapani, India, 01.01.1997, AP).

82 Avrook Sen, 'Blood Brothers', *India Today*, 28.07.1997 (Churachandpur), pp. 42–3.

83 Samudra Gupta Kashyap, 'Cease-fire in Nagaland from today', *The Indian Express*, 01.08.1997.

84 'Long road to peace in Nagaland', *Economic and Political Weekly*, 02.08.1997.

85 Mike Wooldridge, 'The forgotten war in Nagaland', (Reporting from Nagaland), *BBC News* http://www.news6.thdo.bbc.co.uk, 21.11.1997 (accessed 12.02.2001).

86 *BBC News* http://www.news6.thdo.bbc.co.uk, 22.01.1998 (accessed 12.02.2001).

87 *BBC News* http://www.news6.thdo.bbc.co.uk, 28.01.1998 (accessed 12.02.2001).

88 *BBC News* http://www.news6.thdo.bbc.co.uk, 07.02.1998 (accessed on 12.02.2001).

89 *BBC News* http://www.news.bbc.co.uk, 26.06.1998 (accessed on 12.02.2001).

90 Kalyan Chaudhuri, 'A deadlocked peace process', *Frontline*, 14.08.1998, pp. 41–42.

91 *BBC News* http://www.news.bbc.co.uk, 13.11.1998 (accessed 12.02.2001).

92 *The New York Times*, 28.07.1999.

93 *Economist*, 29.07.1999.

94 *The New York Times*, 20.08.1999.

95 Northeast Vigil, Editorial, http://www.northeastvigil.com, 22.08.1999, (accessed 02.03.2001).

96 *BBC News* http://www.news.bbc.co.uk, 26.08.1999 (accessed on 12.02.2001).

97 *BBC News* http://www.news.bbc.co.uk, 27.01.and 02.02.2000 (accessed on 12.02.2001).

98 *Bangkok Post*, 27.05.2000.

99 *BBC News* http://www.news.bbc.co.uk, 29.01. and 06. and 09.02.2000 (accessed on 12.02.2001).

100 *BBC News* http://www.news.bbc.co.uk, 02.03.2000 (accessed on 12.02.2001).

101 This I can confirm from my own conversations with a wide range of Nagas.

102 Sanjoy Hazarika, Northeast, Nagas and future of Muivah', *Northeast Vigil*, July 2000, http://www.northeastvigil.com (accessed on 02.03.2001).

103 Sanjoy Hazarika, Hope of peace lives on in Naga hills', *Northeast Vigil*, 30.07.2000, http://www.northeastvigil.com (accessed on 02.03.2001).

104 Sanjoy Hazarika, 'Kashmir and Nagaland: Lessons from the latter', *Northeast Vigil*, 14.08.2000, http://www.northeastvigil.com (accessed on 02.03.2001).

105 Sanjoy Hazarika, 'India's Northeast: Ethnic Conflict, Peace and Civil Society', *the little magazine*, vol. III, issue 5 & 6, 2002, pp. 36–41.

106 Udayon Misra, 'Assam: Roll-Call of the Dead', *Economic and Political Weekly*, 14.09.2002, pp. 3781–3785.

107 Sanjoy Hazarika, 'India's Northeast: Ethnic Conflict, Peace and Civil Society', *the little magazine*, vol. III, issue 5 & 6, 2002, pp. 36–41.

108 J. K. Dutt, 'Outlook for Peace in North-East', *Economic and Political Weekly*, 11.01.2003. pp. 109–110.

109 Ibid.

110 *Economist*, 16.01.2003.

111 U A Shimray, 'Equality as tradition: women's role in Naga society', *Economic and Political Weekly*, 02.02.2002, pp. 375–377 and Udayon Misra, 'Naga Peace Talks: High Hopes and Hard Realities', *Economic and Political Weekly*, 15.02.2003, pp. 593–597.

112 *Economist*, 16.01.2003.

113 'Editorial', *Economic and Political Weekly*, 16.10.2004.

114 Sanjay Barbora, 'Rethinking India's Counter-insurgency Campaign in North-East', *Economic and Political Weekly*, 02.09.2006.

115 Hiren Gohain, 'The North-East: Post-Colonial Trauma?', *Economic and Political Weekly*, 04.11.2006. p. 4537.
116 Ibid.
117 *Economist*, 11.01.2007.
118 J. K. Dutt, 'Outlook for Peace in North-East', *Economic and Political Weekly*, 11.01.2003. pp. 109–110.
119 Rajesh Dev, 'More Space for Democratic Politics', *Economic and Political Weekly*, 26.04.2003, 1637–1640.
120 U A Shimray, 'Equality as tradition: women's role in Naga society', *Economic and Political Weekly*, 02.02.2002, pp. 375–377 and Udayon Misra, 'Naga Peace Talks: High Hopes and Hard Realities', *Economic and Political Weekly*, 15.02.2003, pp. 593–597, quote Misra, pp. 595–596. As well as U A Shimray, 'Women's Work in Naga Society: Household Work, Workforce Participation and Division of Labour' *Economic and Political Weekly*, 24.04.2004, pp. 1698–1711, especially p. 1711, Note 6.
121 Norbert Hoerster (Hrsg.), *Klassische Texte der Staatsphilosophie* (München, 2006 [1976]), pp. 176–188; Isaiah Berlin,'Montesquieu', in Idem., *Against the Current: Essays in the History of Ideas* (London, 1979 [1959]), pp. 130–161 and Immanuel Kant, 'Beantwortung der Frage: Was ist Aufklärung?', in *idem.*, *Schriften zur Anthropologie, Geschichtsphilosophie, Politik und Pädagogik 1*, Werkausgabe Band XI (Frankfurt a. M., 1968 [1784]), pp. 53–61.
122 *Economist.com*, 09.03.2007.

Conclusion

1 For the argument that centralisation leads to discrimination and this in turn to demands for secession and that the formal right to secede is the most effective check against centralisation and thus against secession, see Detmar Doering and Jürgen G. Backhaus, 'Introduction: Secession as a Right', in *Idem* (eds.), *The Political Economy of Secession: A Source Book* (Neue Zürcher Zeitung Publishing, 2004), pp. 7–17.

2 See Paula Banerjee's findings on the women's resolve to become independent in her 'Between Two Armed Patriarchies: Women in Assam and Nagaland', in Rita Manchanda (ed.), *Women, War and Peace in South Asia: Beyond Victimhood and Agency* (New Delhi, Thousand Oaks & London, 2001), pp. 131–176.

3 See O'Leary who, by engaging with Gellner's theory of nationalism, makes the observation that after the First World War and despite the Wilsonian doctrine the victorious powers redrew the boundaries not on the basis of self-determination but along geopolitical lines, and during the Cold War borders were preserved with the complete disrespect of the principle of self-determination, so he concludes that '... power politics, and power resources, provide an alternative (or at least a supplementary and over-determining) selection mechanism to that implicit in Gellner's theory.' Brendan O'Leary, 'Ernest Gellner's diagnosis of nationalism: a critical overview, or, what is living and what is dead in Ernest Gellner's philosophy of nationalism?', in John A. Hall (ed.), *The State of the Nation: Ernest Gellner and the Theory of Nationalism* (Cambridge, 1998), pp. 40–88, p. 61.

4 More than half a century before acquiring nominal control.

5 These are the reasons *in addition* to those leading to the empire in the first place.

6 As Neville Maxwell reminded me of in a letter, dated January 29, 2001.

7 See John McGarry and BrendanO'Leary, *The Politics of ethnic Conflict Regulation: Case Studies of Protracted Ethnic Conflict* (London, 1993), see chapter 1.

8 Chandler, for instance, has demonstrated with the example of the notorious Tuol Sleng prison under the Democratic Cambodia regime that to understand the unique form of state terror we have to abolish the tradition-modern divide, see David Chandler, *Voices from S-21: Terror and History in Pol Pot's Secret Prison* (Berkeley, 1999).

9 For the use of this term in the Indian case, see Iqbal A. Ansari, 'Human Rights Situation in India – An Overview', in *Idem* (ed.), *Human Rights in India* (New Delhi, 1998), pp. 1–23, p. 8.

10 Isaiah Berlin, *The Crooked Timber of Humanity: Chapters in the History of Ideas* (London, 1990 [1959], p. 261 and Charles Taylor, 'Nationalism and modernity', in John A. Hall (ed.), *The State of the Nation: Ernest Gellner and the Theory of Nationalism* (Cambridge, 1998), pp. 191–218, p. 212.

11 On torture and terror as deliberate policy, see Herbert C. Kelman, 'The Social Context of Torture: Policy Process and Authority Structure', in Ronald D. Crelinsten and Alex P. Schmid (eds.), *The Politics of Pain: Torturers and Their Masters* (Boulder: Westview Press, 1995), pp. 19–34; Ronald D. Crelinsten, 'In Their Own Words: The World of the Torturer', in Ibid., pp. 35–64 and Michael Taussig, 'Culture of Terror – Space of Death: Roger Casement's Putumayo Report and the Explanation of Torture', *Comparative Studies in Society and History*, 1984, 26, pp. 467–497.

12 The previous summary rests not only on our case study, but draws from a wide range of literature on state formation, nationalism, war and 'nationalities' war employed and quoted throughout this book.

13 Imtiaz Ahmed, 'State, military and modernity: the experience of South Asia', *Contemporary South Asia* (1994), 3 (1); pp. 53–66; Joyce Pettigrew, *The Sikhs of the Punjab: unheard voices of state and guerrilla violence* (London and New Jersey, 1995); Cynthia Keppley Mahmood, *Fighting for Faith and Nation: Dialogues with Sikh Militants* (Philadelphia, 1996); Sumantra Bose, *The Challenge in Kashmir: Democracy, Self-Determination and a Just Peace* (New Delhi, Thousand Oaks and London, 1997); E. Valentine Daniel, *Chapters in an Anthropology of Violence: Sri Lankans, Sinhalas and Tamils* (Delhi, 1997); Cynthia Keppley Mahmood, 'Trials by Fire: Dynamics of Terror in Punjab and Kashmir', in Jeffrey A. Sluka (ed.), *Death Squad: The Anthropology of State Terror* (Philadelphia, 2000), pp. 70–90.

14 Immanuel Kant, 'Beantwortung der Frage: Was ist Aufklärung', *Schriften zur Anthropologie, Geschichtsphilosophie, Politik und Pädagogik 1: Werkausgabe Band XI* (Frankfurt am Main, 1968), pp. 53–61.

Glossary and spelling

alhou	supreme being in Sema cosmology
ang	chief among the Konyak Nagas
dobashi	interpreter
gaonbura	village headman
genna	auspicious days during which certain activities were taboo
godown	warehouse (here for storing food provisions)
khel	territorial division of Naga villages
lungkizumba	supreme being in Ao cosmology
mandala	symbolic figure representing the universe
morung	young men/women dormitory with social and educational tasks
raj	British rule in South Asia
raja	king
ryat	settler-cultivator
satyagraha	non-violent non-cooperation
sepoy	soldier in British service
swaraj	self-rule
thana	police post
tsungrem	earth spirits
ukepenopfu	supreme being of Angami cosmology

It was endeavoured to standardise the spelling of names and places in the main body of the text. However, the spelling in the quotes and the sources in the footnotes that is often random, was left untouched. The important places and names will be recognisable, in the same way the spelling in the quotes was left in the original, despite often being mistaken or dated.

Select bibliography

1. Private and other Papers; Official Records, Oriental and India Office Library, London

Archer Papers MSS Eur F 236/74, 76 and 78–80.

Bowman Papers, MSS Eur F 229/26.

Curzon Collection, MSS Eur F 111/323, Minute by His Excellency the Viceroy on Territorial Redistribution in India,. 1 June 1903, pp. 9–10.

Curzon Collection, MSS Eur F 111/536. (Confidential) Summary of the Principal Events and Measures of the Viceroyalty of his Excellency Lord Curzon of Kedlestar, Viceroy and Governor-General of India, in the Foreign Department, for the time span of Jan. 1899–April 1904. Volume 5.

Hutton Papers, Tour Diaries, IOR Neg 11711 and 11712.

Extract from private and secret letter from Lord Wavell to Mr. Amery, dated 27 July, 1944, in L/PJ/7/6787.

Extract from private and secret letter from Mr. Amery to Lord Wavell, dated 9/10 August, 1944, in L/PJ/7/6787.

Notes exchanged between the Office of the High Commissioner for the United Kingdom, New Delhi, the Commonwealth Relations, and the Foreign Office, London, dated between April 1948 and May 1950 and *Confidential (FL 10114/11). L. A. C. Fry, Foreign Office to B. J. Greenhill, Commonwealth Relations Office*, dated 7 March 1950, both in L/PJ/7/10635.

Letter from Khetoi, Kukishe H. Q., Free Nagaland, P. O. Kohima, Naga Hills, to His Excellency, the Governor General of India, New Delhi, dated February, the 16, 1949, in L/PJ/7/10635.

Ultimatum to the Government of India, To Jawaharlal Nehru, Prime Minister, Indian Union, from T. Aliba Imti, president and Kumbho Angami, secretary, on behalf of the NNC, dated Kohima, 4 November 1947, in L/PJ/7/10635.

Bengal Secret and Political Consultations (BSPC) and Indexes, 1824–1833.

Bengal Political Consultations (BPC) and Indexes, 1832–1837.

India Political Consultations (IPC) and Indexes, 1838–1843.

India Political and Foreign Proceedings (IPFP) and Indexes, 1843–1851.

India Foreign and Political Proceedings (IFPP) and Indexes, 1854–1855.

India Foreign Proceedings (IFP) and Indexes, 1866, 1877–1882.

Proceedings of the Chief Commissioner of Assam (PCCA), 1884–1889, 1891, 1894–1899, 1913–1914.

Assam Secretariat Proceedings (ASP), 1900–1901, 1903–1904.
Proceedings of the Government of Eastern Bengal and Assam (PEBA), 1906–1910.
Proceedings of the Government of Assam (PGA), 1923, 1925, 1929 & 1931.

2. Official Publications

'Assam Census Report (Extracts from 1881)', in Alexander Mackenzie, *History of the Relations of the Government with the Hill Tribes of the North-East Frontier of Bengal* (Calcutta: Printed at the Home Department Press, 1884), pp. 537–550.

Balfour, Henry, 'Foreword', in J. H. Hutton, *The Sema Nagas* (London: MacMillan and Co., Limited, 1921), pp. XV–XVIII.

Butler, Major John, *Travels and Adventures in the Province of Assam, During a Residence of Fourteen Years* (London: Smith, Elder and Co., 1855).

Butler, Captain John, 'Butler's account of the Naga tribes, 1873', in Alexander Mackenzie, *History of the Relations of the Government with the Hill Tribes of the North-East Frontier of Bengal* (Calcutta: Home Department Press, 1884), pp. 77–88.

Central Office of Information, *The Campaign in Burma* (London: His Majesty's Stationery Office, 1946).

Coryton, J., 'Trade Routes between British Burmah and Western China', *Journal of the Royal Geographical Society*, Vol. 45, London, 1875, pp. 229–249.

Cotton, General Sir Arthur, 'On a Communication between India and China by the Line of the Burhampooter and Yang-tse', *Journal of the Royal Geographical Society*, Vol. 37, London, 1867, pp. 231–239.

Current Intelligence Weekly, 'Special Report: India's Rebellious Eastern Tribes' (Central Intelligence Agency, Directorate of Intelligence, 1 July 1966).

Government of India Proposals and Dispatch of the Secretary of State, 1907, Vol. I.

Hutton, John Henry, *The Angami Nagas: With Some Notes on Neighbouring Tribes* (Bombay: Oxford University Press, 1969 [1921]).

Hutton, John Henry, *The Sema Nagas* (London: MacMillan and Co., Limited, 1921).

Hutton, John Henry, 'Introduction', in J. P. Mills, *The Lhota Nagas* (London: MacMillan and Co., Limited, 1922), pp. XI–XXXIX.

Hutton, John Henry, 'Note, dt. Kohima 17 March 1928', iIn *Indian Statutory Commission*, Volume XIV, Appendix B, 1930, pp. 111–117.

Kirby, S. Woodburn, *The War Against Japan. Volume III: The Decisive Battles* (London: Her Majesty's Stationery Office, 1961).

Kirby, S. Woodburn, *The War Against Japan. Volume IV: The Reconquest of Burma* (London: Her Majesty's Stationery Office, 1965).

Lok Sabha Debates, Vol. 8, 1951, 26.5., Columns 4646–4647 and 4679–4681.

Lok Sabha Debates, Vol. 1, 1952, 19.5., Column 36

Lok Sabha Debates, Vol. 4, 25 July 1955, Columns 2944–2946; 28 July 1955, Columns 3111–3112; 10 August 1955, Columns 3541–3542 & 16 August 1955, Columns 3683–3685.

Lok Sabha Debates, Vol. 5, 31 July 1956, Column 639; 3 Aug. 1956, Columns 784–785 & 10 Aug. 1956, Column 1101.

Lok Sabha Debates, Vol. 8, 11 Nov. 1957, Columns 9–12 & 20 Nov. 1957, Columns 1437–1438.

Lok Sabha Debates, Vol. 44, 1 & 4 Aug. 1960, Columns 146–157 & 899–915.

Lok Sabha Debates, Vol. 46, 5 Sept. 1960, Columns 6913–6918.

Lok Sabha Debates, Vol. 47, 22 Nov. 1960, Columns 1516–1521.

Lok Sabha Debates, Vol. 61, 23 March 1962, Columns 1306–1307.

Lok Sabha Debates, Vol. 2, 4 May 1962, Columns 2593–2594.

Lok Sabha Debates, Vol. 3, 14 May 1962, Columns 4419–4426.

Lok Sabha Debates, Vol. 21, 16 September 1963, Columns 6207–6208.

Lok Sabha Debates, Vol. 22, 18 November 1963, Columns 45–46.

Lok Sabha Debates, Vol. 35, 17 Nov. 1964, Columns 37–39; 18. Nov. 1964, Columns 457–470; 20. Nov. 1964, Columns 691–709 and 24 Nov. 1964, Columns 1456–1461.

Lok Sabha Debates, Vol. 50, 21 Feb. 1966, Column 1300–1311.

Lok Sabha Debates, Vol. 51, 02 March 1966, Columns 3425–3440.

Lok Sabha Debates, Vol. 6, 15 July 1967, Columns 12233–12238.

Lok Sabha Debates, Vol. 7, 17 July 1967, Columns 12352–12496 and 27 July 1967, Columns 15208–15213.

Lok Sabha Debates, Vol. 9, 13 November 1967, Columns 1000–1009 and 24 November 1967, Columns 2829–2836.

Lok Sabha Debates, Vol. 14, 19 March 1968, Columns 1506–1516.

Lok Sabha Debates, Vol. 15, 01 April 1968, Column 1194.

Lok Sabha Debates, Vol. 27, 01 April 1969, Columns 212–213.

Lok Sabha Debates, Vol. 31, 05 August 1969, Columns 204–210.

Lok Sabha Debates, Vol. 9, 08 December 1971, Columns 40–54 and Vol. 9 (no. 20), 09 December 1971, Columns 3–75.

Lok Sabha Debates, 28 March 1972, Columns 161–200.

Lok Sabha Debates 1972, Volume 20, point 1331.

Lok Sabha Debates, Volume 58, 11 March 1976, Column 226–258.

Lok Sabha Debates, Volume 63, 20 August 1976, Columns 186–194.

Mackenzie, Alexander, *History of the Relations of the Government with the Hill Tribes of the North-East Frontier of Bengal* (Calcutta: Home Department Press, 1884).

Mansergh, Nicholas and Penderel Moon (eds.), *The Transfer of Power, 1942–7, Volume X, The Mountbatten Viceroyalty: Formulation of a Plan, 22 March – 30 May 1947* (London: Her Majesty's Stationery Office, 1974).

'Memorandum submitted by the government of Assam to the Indian statutory commission 1930', in *Indian Statutory Commission*, Volume XIV (London: His Majesty's Stationery Office, 1938), pp. 78–98.

Mills, J. P., *The Lhota Nagas* (London: MacMillan and Co., Limited, 1922).

Mills, J. P., *The Ao Nagas* (London: MacMillan and Co., Limited, 1926).

Mills, J. P., *The Rengma Nagas* (Gauhati: Spectrum Publications, 1980 [1937]).

Mountbatten of Burma, Vice-Admiral, The Earl, *Report to the Combined Chiefs of Staff by the Supreme Allied Commander South-East Asia, 1943–1945* (New York: Philosophical Library, 1951 [London, 1951]).

Parliamentary Debates, Fifth Series – Volume 301 H.C., (London, 1935), 10 May 1935, columns 1343–1449.

Rajya Sabha Debates, Vol. 22, No. 1, 25. August 1958, Columns 963–976; 27. August 1958, Columns 1253–1312; 28. August 1958, Columns 1313–1474 & 24th Sept. 1958, Columns 4431–4433.

Rajya Sabha Debates, Vol. 32, 15th Sept. 1961, Columns 57–58.

Rajya Sabha Debates, Vol. XLIX, 29. Sept. 1964, Columns 3427–3430.

Rajya Sabha Debates, Vol. 50, 15. Dec. 1964, Columns 3724–3727.

Reid, Sir Robert, *History of the Frontier Areas Bordering on Assam: From 1883–1941* (Guwahati, Delhi: Spectrum Publications, 1997 [1942]).

Report on the Administration of Assam for the year 1921–22 (Shillong: Government Press, Assam, 1923).

Report of the franchise committee, 1918–1919 (Calcutta: Superintendent Government Printing, India).

Shakespear, L. W., *History of Upper Assam, Upper Burmah and North-Eastern Frontier* (London: MacMillan, 1914).

US Department of State, *India Country Report on Human Rights Practices for 1998*, released by the Bureau of Democracy, Human Rights, and Labor, February 26, 1999, pp. 6–7, http://www.state.gov/www/global/human_rights/1998_hrp_report/india.html.

Welsh, Captain, 'Welsh's Report on Assam, 1794', in Alexander Mackenzie, *History of the Relations of the Government with the Hill Tribes of the The North-East Frontier of Bengal* (Calcutta: Home Department Press, 1884), Appendix A., 377–394.

Woodthorpe, R. G., 'Meetings of the Anthropological Institute', in Verrier Elwin (ed.), *The Nagas in the Nineteenth Century* (Bombay: Oxford University Press, 1969 [1881]), pp. 46–82.

Yule, Captain Henry, 'On the Geography of Burma and its Tributary States, in illustration of a New Map of those Regions', *Journal of the Royal Geographical Society*, Vol. 27, London, 1857, pp. 54–108.

3. Books

Ahmed, Ishtiaq, *State, Nation and Ethnicity in Contemporary South Asia* (London: Pinter, 1996).

Alemchimba, M., *A Brief Historical Account of Nagaland* (Kohima: Naga Institute of Culture, 1970).

Anderson, Benedict, *Imagined Communities: Reflections on the Origin and Spread of Nationalism* (London, New York: Verso, 1991 [1983]).

Andreski, Stanislaw, *Military Organisation and Society* (London: Routledge Kegan Paul, 1954).

Ao, Temsula, *These hills called home: stories from a war zone* (New Delhi: Penguin Books, 2006).

Aosenba, *The Naga Resistance Movement: Prospects of Peace and Armed Conflict* (New Delhi: Regency, 2001).

Ash, Timothy Garton, *History of the Present: Essays, Sketches and Dispatches from Europe in the 1990s* (London: Penguin Books, 2000).

Atkinson, Ronald R., *The Roots of Ethnicity: The Origins of the Acholi of Uganda Before 1800* (Philadelphia: University of Pennsylvania Press, 1994).

Banerjee, Anil Chandra, *The Eastern Frontier of British India 1784–1826* (Calcutta: A. Mukherjee and Co., 1946[1943]).

Barooah, Nirode K., *David Scott in North-east India 1802–1831: A Study in British Paternalism* (New Delhi: Munshiram Manoharlal, 1970).

Baruah, Sanjib, *Durable Disorder: Understanding the politics of Northeast India* (Delhi: OUP, 2007 [2005]).

Bayly, C. A., *Imperial Meridian: The British empire and the world 1780–1830* (London: Longman, 1989).

Bayly, C. A., *The Birth of the Modern World, 1780–1914* (Oxford: Blackwell, 2004).

Berlin, Isaiah, *The Crooked Timber of Humanity: Chapters in the History of Ideas* (London: John Murray, 1990 [1959]).

Boehm, Christopher, *Blood Revenge: The Enactment and Management of Conflict in Montenegro and Other Tribal Societies*. (Pennsylvannia: University of Pennsylvania Press, 1984).

Bose, Sumantra, *The Challenge in Kashmir: Democracy, Self-Determination and a Just Peace* (New Delhi, Thousand Oaks & London: Sage Publications, 1997).

Bose, Sugata and Ayesha Jalal, *Modern South Asia: History, Culture, Political Economy* (Delhi: OUP, 1998).

Bower, Ursula Graham, *Naga Path* (London: Butler & Tanner Ltd., 1950).

Brewer, John, *The Sinews of Power. War, Money and the English State, 1688–1783* (London: Unvin Hyman, 1989).

Brown, Judith M., *Nehru: A Political Life* (New Haven and London: Yale University Press, 2004).

Cain, P. J. and A. G. Hopkins, *British imperialism, Vol. 1: Innovation and Expansion 1688–1914* (London: Longman, 1993).

Cain, P. J. and A. G. Hopkins, *British Imperialism, Vol. 2: Crisis and Deconstruction, 1914–1990* (London: Longman, 1993).

Campbell, Arthur, *The Siege: A Story from Kohima* (London: George Allen & Unwin Ltd., 1956).

Chakrabarty, Saroj, *The Upheaval Years in North-East India: A documentary in-depth study of Assam holocausts 1960–1983* (Calcutta: Sree Saraswaty Press Limited, 1984).

Chandler, David, *Voices from S-21: Terror and History in Pol Pot's Secret Prison* (Berkeley: University of California Press, 1999).

Chaube, Shibanikinkar, *Hill Politics in North-East India* (New Delhi: Orient Longman, 1973).

Cobden, Richard, *How Wars are got up in India: The Origin of the Burmese War* (London: William & Frederick G. Cash, 1853).

Cohen, Stephen P., *The Indian Army: Its Contribution to the Development of a Nation* (Berkeley, Los Angeles, London: University of California Press, 1971).

Colley, Linda, *Britons: Forging the Nation, 1707–1837* (New Haven and London: Cape, 1992).

Colley, Linda, *Captives: Britain, Empire and the World, 1600–1850* (London: Yale University Press, 2002).

Collier, Basil, *The War in the Far East, 1941–1945: A Military History* (London: Heinemann, 1969).

Conboy, Kenneth and James Morrison, *The CIA's Secret War in Tibet* (Kansas: University Press of Kansas, 2002).

Connor, Walker, *Ethnonationalism: The Quest for Understanding* (Princeton: Princeton University Press, 1994).

Cultural Survival Report 22, *Southeast Asian Tribal Groups and Ethnic Minorities* (Cambridge: Cambridge University Press, 1987).

Dena, Lal, *Christian Missions and Colonialism: A Study of Missionary Movement in Northeast India With Particular Reference to Manipur and Lushai hills 1894–1947* (Shillong: Vendrame Institute, 1988).

Dhar, P. N., *Indira Gandhi, the 'Emergency', Indian Democracy* (New Delhi: Oxford University Press, 2001 [2000]).

Diamond, Jared, *Guns, Germs and Steel: The Fates of Human Societies* (London: Jonathan Cape, 1997).

Duara, Prasenjit, *Rescuing History from the Nation: Questioning Narratives of Modern China* (Chicago: The University of Chicago Press, 1995).

Elwin, Verrier, *Nagaland* (Guwahati: Spectrum, 1997 [1961]).

Fortes, M., and E. E. Evans-Pritchard (eds.), *African Political Systems* (London and New York: KPI, 1987 [1940]).

Frank, Katherine, *Indira: The Life of Indira Nehru Gandhi* (London: HarperCollins, 2001).

Fürer-Haimendorf, Christoph von, *Die nackten Nagas: Dreizehn Monate unter Kopfjägern Indiens* (Wiesbaden: Eberhard Brockhaus Verlag, 1946 [1939]).

Galbraith, John Kenneth, *Ambassador's Journal: An American View of India* (Bombay: Jaico Publishing House, 1972 [1969]).

Gellner, Ernest, *Nations and Nationalism* (Oxford: Basil Blackwell, 1983).

Gellner, Ernest, *Anthropology and Politics: Revolutions in the Sacred Grove* (Oxford: Blackwell, 1995).

Gopal, S., *British Policy in India, 1858–1905* (Cambridge: Cambridge University Press, 1965).

Grossman, Wassilij, *Life and Fate* (New York: NYRB Classics, 2006 [1959]).

Hardgrave, Robert L. and Stanley A. Kochanek *India: Government and Politics in a Developing Nation* (Fort Worth and London: Harcourt Brace Jovanovich College, 1993).

Hoerster, Norbert (Hrsg.), *Klassische Texte der Staatsphilosophie* (München: dtv, 2006 [1976]).

Horam, M., *Naga Insurgency: The last thirty years* (New Delhi: Cosmo Publications, 1988).

Horowitz, Donald L., *Ethnic Groups in Conflict* (Berkeley: University of California Press, 1985).

Iliffe, John, *A Modern History of Tanganyika* (Cambridge: Cambridge University Press, 1979).

Iralu, Kaka. D., *Nagaland and India, the Blood and the Tears: A Historical Account of the 52 Years Indo-Naga War and the Story of those who were never Allowed to tell it* (2000 [neither place nor publisher given]).

Jacobs, Julian, *The Nagas: Hill Peoples of Northeast India* (Stuttgart: edition hansjörg mayer, 1990).

Jalal, Ayesha, *Democracy and Authoritarianism in South Asia: A Comparative and Historical Perspective* (Cambridge: Cambridge University Press, 1995).

Jenkins, Richard, *Rethinking ethnicity: arguments and explorations* (London: Sage, 1997).

Kant, Immanuel, *Grundlegung zur Metaphysik der Sitten* (Frankfurt am Main: Suhrkamp, 2007 [1786]).

Kulke, Hermann and Dietmar Rothermund, *A History of India* (Calcutta: Rupa, 1991 [1986]).

Lamb, Alastair, *Asian Frontiers: Studies in a Continuing Problem* (London: Praeger, 1968).

Leach, E. R., *Political Systems of Highland Burma: A Study of Kachin Social Structures* (London: G. Bell and Sons, Ltd., 1964 [1954]).

Lieberman, Victor, *Burmese Administrative Cycles: Anarchy and Conquest, c.1580–1760* (Princeton, New Jersey: Princeton University Press, 1984).

Löwith, Karl, *Meaning in History* (Chicago: University of Chicago Press, 1949).

Luithui, Luingam and Nandita Haksar, *Nagaland File: A Question of Human Rights* (New Delhi: Lancer International, 1984).

Mahmood, Cynthia K., *Fighting for Faith and Nation: Dialogues with Sikh Militants* (Philadelphia: University of Pennsylvania Press, 1996).

Mankekar, D.R., *On the Slippery Slope in Nagaland* (Bombay: Manaktalas, 1967).

Mann, Michael, *Bengalen im Umbruch: Die Herausbildung des britischen Kolonialstaates 1754–1793* (Stuttgart: Steiner, 2000).

Maxwell, Neville, *India and the Nagas* (London: Minority Rights Group, 1973).

Maybury-Lewis, David, *Indigenous Peoples, Ethnic Groups, and the State* (Boston: Allyn and Bacon, 1997).

McGarry, John and BrendanO'Leary, *The Politics of Ethnic Conflict Regulation: Case Studies of Protracted Ethnic Conflict* (London: Routledge, 1993).

Mehta, Gita, *Snakes and Ladders: A View of Modern India* (London: Secker & Warburg, 1997).

Mehta, Uday Singh, *Liberalism and Empire: India in British Liberal Thought* (New Delhi: Oxford University Press, 1999).

Menon, Nivedita and Aditya Nigam, *Power and Contestation: India Since 1989* (London, New York: Zed Books, 2007).

Metcalf, Thomas R., 'Ideologies of the Raj', *The New Cambridge History of India*, Vol. III.4. (Cambridge: Cambridge University Press, 1994).

Mistry, Rohinton, *A Fine Balance* (London: Faber and Faber, 1997).

Montaigne, Michel de, *Essais* (Frankfurt am Main: Eichborn, 1998 [1595, 1802]).

Moore, R. J., *Liberalism and Indian Politics, 1872–1922* (London: Edward Arnold, 1966).

Mullik, B. N., *My Years With Nehru: 1948–1964* (Bombay: Allied, 1972).

Nibedon, Nirmal, *North East India: The Ethnic Explosion* (New Delhi: Lancers Publishers, 1981).

Nibedon, Nirmal, *Nagaland: The Night of the Guerrillas* (New Delhi: Lancers Publishers, 1983).

Orwell, George, *Burmese Days* (Harmondsworth: Penguin Books, 1967 [1934]).

Pagden, Anthony, *Lords of All the World: Ideologies of Empire in Spain, Britain and France c.1500–c.1800* (New Haven & London: Yale University Press, 1995).

Pagden, Anthony, *Peoples and empires* (London: Weidenfeld & Nicolson, 2001).

Peers, Douglas M., *Between Mars and Mammon: Colonial Armies and the Garrison State in Early Nineteenth-Century India* (London: Tauris Academic Studies, 1995).

Pettigrew, Joyce, *The Sikhs of the Punjab: Unheard Voices of State and Guerrilla Violence* (London: Zed, 1995).

Phukon, Girin, *Assam Attitude to Federalism* (New Delhi: Sterling Publishers Private Ltd., 1984).

Proudfoot, C. L., *Flash of the Khukri: History of the 3rd Gorkha Rifles, 1947 to 1980* (New Delhi: Vision Books, 1984).

Reid, Anthony, *Southeast Asia in the Age of Commerce, 1450–1680. Volume One: The Lands Below the Winds* (New Haven and London: Yale University Press, 1988).

Reid, Anthony, *Southeast Asia in the Age of Commerce, 1450–1680. Volume Two: Expansion and Crisis* (New Haven and London: Yale University Press, 1993).

Rodger, George, *Red Moon Rising* (London: The Cresset Press, 1943).

Rorty, Richard, *Contingency, Irony, and Solidarity* (Cambridge: Cambridge University Press, 1989).

Rosaldo, Renato, *Ilongot Headhunting 1883–1974: A Study in Society and History* (Stanford, California: Stanford University Press, 1980).

Rushdie, Salman, *Imaginary Homelands: Essays and Criticism 1981–1991* (London: Granta, 1991).

Rustomji, Nari, *Imperilled Frontiers: India's North-Eastern Borderlands* (Delhi: Oxford University Press, 1983).

Sanyu, Visier, *A History of Nagas and Nagaland: Dynamics of Oral Tradition in Village Formation* (New Delhi: Commonwealth Publishers, 1996).

Sarkar, Sumit, *Modern India, 1885–1947* (Delhi: Macmillan, 1983).

Schiller, Friedrich, *Wilhelm Tell* (Stuttgart: Reclam, 1979 [1804]).

Scott, Michael *The Search for Peace* (London: Zed, 1968).

Shimmi, Y.L. Roland, *Comparative History of the Nagas: From Ancient Period Till 1826* (New Delhi: Inter-India Publications, 1988).

Slim, W. J., *Defeat into Victory*. London: Cassell, 1961 [1956]).

Sluka, Jeffrey A. (ed.), *Death Squad: The Anthropology of State Terror* (Philadelphia: University of Pennsylvania Press, 2000).

Steyn, Pieter, *Zapuphizo: Voice of the Nagas* (London: Kegan Paul, 2002).

Stocking, G. W., *Victorian Anthropology* (New York: The Free Press, 1987).

Stracey, P. D., *Nagaland Nightmare* (Bombay: Allied Publishers Private Ltd., 1968).

Swartz, Marvin, *The Politics of British Foreign Policy in the Era of Disraeli and Gladstone* (New York: St. Martin's Press, 1985).

Tambiah, Stanley J., *World Conqueror and World Renouncer: A Study of Buddhism and Polity in Thailand Against a Historical Background* (Cambridge: Cambridge University Press, 1976).

Tarling, Nicholas, *Imperialism in Southeast Asia: 'A fleeting, passing phase'* (London and New York: 2001).

Taylor, Charles, *Sources of the Self: Making of the Modern Identity* (Cambridge: Cambridge University Press, 1989).

Tinker, Hugh, *Viceroy: Curzon to Mountbatten* (Karachi: Oxford University Press, 1997).

Todorov, Tzvetan, *Die Eroberung Amerikas: Das Problem des Anderen* (Frankfurt am Main: Suhrkamp, 1985 [*La conquête de l'Amerique. La question de l'autre*, 1982]).

Todorov, Tzvetan, *Facing the Extreme: Moral Life in the Concentration Camps* (London: Weidenfeld & Nicolson, 1996 [1991]).

Van den Berghe, Pierre L., (ed.), *State Violence and Ethnicity* (Niwot: University Press of Colorado, 1990).

Vashum, R., et al. (eds.), *Nagas at Work* (New Delhi: NSUD Publication, 1996).

Vashum, R., *Nagas' Right To Self-Determination: An Anthropological-Historical Perspective* (New Delhi: Mittal, 2000).

Weber, Max, *Gesammelte Aufsätze zur Wissenschaftslehre* (Tübingen: Mohr, 1973).

Webster, Anthony, *Gentlemen Capitalists: British Imperialism in South East Asia 1770–1890* (London: Tauris Academic Studies, 1998).

Yonuo, Asoso, The Rising Nagas: A Historical and Political Study (Delhi: Vivek Publishers, 1974).

4. Articles

Ahmed, Imtiaz Ahmed, 'State, military and modernity: the experience of South Asia', *Contemporary South Asia* (1994), 3 (1); pp. 53–66.

Ahmed, Imtiaz Ahmed, 'The Cry of Sakeena: A post-nationalist critique of violence in South Asia', *Mainstream*, Vol. 37, No. 11, March 6, 1999, pp. 14–21.

Ansari, Iqbal A., 'Human Rights Situation in India – An Overview', in *idem* (ed.), *Human Rights in India* (New Delhi: Institute of Objective Studies, 1998), pp. 1–23.

Banerjee, A. C., 'The East-India Company and Assam', in H. K. Barpujari (ed.), *The Comprehensive History of Assam. Vol. II: Medieval Period: Political. From Thirteen Century AD to the Treaty of Yandabo, 1826* (Guwahati: Publication Board, Assam, 1992), pp. 300–331.

Banerjee, A. C., 'Internal Dissensions and Foreign Invasions', in H. K. Barpujari (ed.), *The Comprehensive History of Assam*, Vol. II: *Medieval Period: Political. From Thirteen Century AD to the Treaty of Yandabo, 1826*, (Guwahti: Publication Board, Assam, 1992), pp. 332–352.Banerjee, Paula, 'Between Two Armed Patriarchies: Women in Assam and Nagaland', in Rita Manchanda (ed.), *Women, War and Peace in South Asia: Beyond Victimhood and Agency* (New Delhi, Thousand Oaks & London: Sage Publications, 2001), pp. 131–176. Barpujari, H. K., 'Preface', in *idem* (ed.), *The Comprehensive History of Assam, Vol. I: From Pre-historic Times to the Twelfth Century AD* (Guwahati: Publication Board, Assam, 1990) pp. IX–XII. Barpujari, H. K., 'Introduction', in *idem* (ed.), *The Comprehensive History of Assam, Vol. I: From Pre-historic Times to the Twelfth Century AD* (Guwahati: Publication Board, Assam, 1990), pp. 1–24.

Barpujari, S.K., 'Paramountcy in the Hills, 1874–1914', in H. K. Barpujari, *The Comprehensive History of Assam. Volume III: Modern Period: Yandabo to Diarchy, 1826–1919 AD* (Guwahati: Publication Board, Assam, 1992), pp. 220–257.

Barua, Pradeep, 'Strategies and Doctrines of Imperial Defence: Britain and India, 1919–45', *The Journal of Imperial and Commonwealth History*, Vol. XXV, May 1997, No. 2, pp. 240–266.

Bayly, C. A., 'The First Age of Global Imperialism, c.1760–1830', *The Journal of Imperial and Commonwealth History*, Vol. XXVI, May 1998, No. 2, pp. 28–47.

Bayly, C. A., 'The British and indigenous peoples, 1760–1860: power, perception and identity', in Martin Daunton and Rick Halpern (eds.), *Empire and Others: British Encounters with Indigenous Peoples, 1600–1850* (Philadelphia, 1999), pp. 19–41.

Behrend, Heike, 'Frauen und Krieg. Zur Gewalt in postkolonialen Widerstandsbewegungen in Afrika', in Peter J. Bräunlein & Andrea Lauser (eds.), *Krieg und Frieden: Ethnologische Perspektiven* (Bremen: kea-edition, 1995), pp. 161–172.

Bell, Morag, Robin Butler and Michael Heffernan, 'Introduction: Geography and Imperialism, 1820–1940', in *idem* (eds.), *Geography and Imperialism 1820–1940* (Manchester: Manchester University Press, 1995), pp. 1–12.

Benyon, John, 'Overlords of Empire? British 'Proconsular Imperialism' in Comparative Perspective', *The Journal of Imperial and Commonwealth History*, Vol. XIX, 1991, No. 2, pp. 164–202.

Berlin, Isaiah, 'Nationalism: Past Neglect and Present Power', in *idem, Against the Current: Essays in the History of Ideas* (London: Pimlico, 1979, edited by Henry Hardy [1959]), pp. 333–355.

Berlin, Isaiah,'Montesquieu', in *idem., Against the Current: Essays in the History of Ideas* (London: Pimlico, 1979 [1959]), pp. 130–161.

Berlin, Isaiah, 'Does Political Theory Still Exist?', in *idem., Concepts and Categories: Philosophical Essays* (London: The Hogarth Press, 1978), pp. 143–172.

Bhattacharyya, 'Publishers Note', in H. K. Barpujari (ed.), *The Comprehensive History of Assam, Vol. I: From Pre-historic Times to the Twelfth Century AD* (Guwahati: Publication Board, Assam, 1990), pp. V–VI.

Brands, H. W., 'India and Pakistan in American Strategic Planning, 1947–54: The Commonwealth as Collaborator', *The Journal of Imperial and Commonwealth History*, Vol. XV, October 1986, No. 1, pp. 41–54.

Brown, Judith M., 'India', in *idem* (ed.), *The Oxford History of the British Empire, Vol. IV, The Twentieth Century* (Oxford: Oxford University Press, 1999), pp. 421–446.

Bryant, G. J., 'Pacification in the Early British Raj, 1755–85', *The Journal of Imperial and Commonwealth History*, Vol. XIV, Oct. 1985, No 1, pp. 3–19.

Cannadine, David, 'Empire', in *idem, History In Our Time* (New Haven and London: Yale University Press, 1998), pp. 143–154.

Cannadine, David, 'The Context, Performance and Meaning of Ritual: The British Monarchy and the "Invention of Tradition", c.1820–1977', in Eric Hobsbawm and

Terence Ranger (eds.), *The Invention of Tradition* (Cambridge: Cambridge University Press, 1983), pp. 101–164.

Canny, Nicholas, 'The Origins of Empire: An Introduction', in *idem* (ed.), *The Oxford history of the British Empire. Vol. 1: The Origins of Empire: British Overseas Enterprise to the Close of the Seventeenth Century* (Oxford: Oxford University Press, 1998), pp. 1–34.

Chakrabarty, Dipesh, 'Subaltern Histories and Post-Enlightenment Rationalism', in *idem.*, *Habitations of Modernity: Essays in the Wake of Subaltern Studies* (Chicago and London: University of Chicago Press, 2002), pp. 20–37.

Chattopadhyaya, S., 'Economic condition', in H. K. Barpujari (ed.), *The Comprehensive History of Assam, Vol. I: From Pre-historic Times to the Twelfth Century AD* (Guwahati: Publication Board, Assam, 1990), pp. 233–264.

Comaroff, John and Comaroff, Jean, 'On Totemism and Ethnicity', in *idem*, *Ethnography and the Historical Imagination* (Boulder: Westview, 1992) pp. 49–68.

Connor, Walker, 'Homelands in a World of States', in Montserrat Guibernau and John Hutchinson (eds.), *Understanding Nationalism* (Cambridge: Polity Press, 2001), pp. 53–73.

Connor, Walker, 'The timelessness of nations', *Nations and Nationalism* 10 (1/2), 2004, pp. 35–47.

Crelinsten, Ronald D., 'In Their Own Words: The World of the Torturer', in Ronald D. Crelinsten and Alex P. Schmid (eds.), *The Politics of Pain: Torturers and Their Masters* (Boulder: Westview Press), pp. 35–64.

Darwin, John, 'Imperialism and the Victorians: The Dynamics of Territorial Expansion', *English Historical Review*, CXII (1997), pp. 614–642.

Doering, Detmar and Jürgen G. Backhaus, 'Introduction: Secession as a Right', in *idem* (eds.), *The Political Economy of Secession: A Source Book* (Neue Zürcher Zeitung, 2004), pp. 7–17.

Drake, Richard Allen, 'Construction Sacrifice and Kidnapping Rumor Panics in Borneo', *Oceania* 59, 1989, pp. 269–279.

Dunn, John, 'The History of Political Theory', in *idem*, *The History of Political Theory and other essays* (Cambridge: Cambridge University Press, 1996), pp. 11–38.

Edney, Matthew H., 'The Ideologies and Praxis of Mapping and Imperialism', in *idem*, *Mapping an Empire: The Geographical Construction of British India, 1765–1843* (Chicago: University of Chicago Press, 1997).

Fieldhouse, D. K., 'Gentlemen, Capitalists, and the British Empire', *The Journal of Imperial and Commonwealth History*, Vol. XXII, 1994, No. 3, pp. 531–541.

Fortes, M. and E. E. Evans-Pritchard, 'Introduction', in *idem.* (eds.), *African Political Systems* (London and New York: KPI, 1987 [1940]), pp. 1–23.

Foucault, Michel, 'Nietzsche, Genealogie, die Historie', in *idem.*, *Von der Subversion des Wissens* (Frankfurt am Main: Fischer Wissenschaft, 1987), pp. 69–90.

Galbraith, John S., 'British War Aims in World War I: A Commentary on "Statesmanship"', *The Journal of Imperial and Commonwealth History*, Vol. XIII, October 1984, No. 1, pp. 25–45.

Gibson, Thomas, 'Raiding, trading, and tribal autonomy in insular Southeast Asia', in Jonathan Haas (ed.), *The Anthropology of War* (Cambridge: Cambridge University Press, 1990), pp. 125–145.

Goti, Jaime Malamud, 'State terror and memory of what?', *University of Arkansas at Little Rock Law Review*, Vol. 21, Fall 1998, No. 1, pp. 107–118.

Guha, Sumit, 'The Politics of Identity and Enumeration in India *c*.1600–1990', *Comparative Studies in Society and History*, 2003, Vol. 45, pp. 148–167.

Hoskins, Janet, 'Introduction: Headhunting as Practice and as Trope', in *idem* (ed.) *Headhunting and the Social Imagination in Southeast Asia* (Stanford, California: Stanford California Press, 1996), pp. 1–49.

Hyam, Ronald, 'The Primacy of Geopolitics: The Dynamics of British Imperial Policy, 1763–1963', *The Journal of Imperial and Commonwealth History*, Vol. XXVII, May 1999, No. 2, pp. 27–52.

Jaffrelot, Christophe, 'India's Look East Policy: An Asianist Strategy in Perspective', *India Review*, vol. 2, no. 2, April 2003, pp. 35–68.

Jamir, S. C. 'Nagaland and the Special Constitutional Provision', in Luingam Luithui and Nandita Haksar (eds.), *Nagaland File: A Question of Human Rights* (New Delhi: Lancer International, 1984), pp. 61–72.

Kamei, Gangmumei, 'Origin of the Nagas', in R. Vashum, Aleube Ihleilung et al. (eds.), *Nagas at Work* (New Dehli: NSUD Publication, 1996), pp. 7–20.

Kant, Immanuel, 'Beantwortung der Frage: Was ist Aufklärung?', in *idem., Schriften zur Anthropologie, Geschichtsphilosophie, Politik und Pädagogik 1*, Werkausgabe Band XI (Frankfurt a. M.: Suhrkamp, 1968 [1784]), pp. 53–61.

Kelman, Herbert C., 'The Social Context of Torture: Policy Process and Authority Structure', in Ronald D. Crelinsten and Alex P. Schmid (eds.), *The Politics of Pain: Torturers and Their Masters* (Boulder: Westview Press, 1995), pp. 19–34.

Kende, Istvàn, 'Terrorism, wars, nuclear holocaust', *International Social Science Journal* 110, 1986, pp. 529–538.

Keyes, Charles F., 'Presidential Address: "The Peoples of Asia" – Science and Politics in the Classification of Ethnic Groups in Thailand, China, and Vietnam', *The Journal of Asian Studies* 61, no. 4 November 2002): pp. 1163–1203.

Kiesel, Major Melvin, 'Nagaland: An Unending Guerrilla War', *Military Review* (US Army Comman & Gen. Staff Coll., Fort Leavenworth, Ka.), Vol. 51, No. 12, December 1971, pp. 80–87.

Leach, E. R., 'The Frontiers of "Burma"', *Comparative Studies in Society and History*, Vol. 3, No. 1, Oct. 1960, pp. 49–68.

Leach, E. R., 'Tribal Ethnography: past, present, future', in Elizabeth Tonkin et al. (eds.), *History and Ethnicity* (London: Routledge, 1989), pp. 34–47.

Lieberman, Victor, 'Local Integration and Euroasian Analogies: Structuring Southeast Asian History, *c.*1350-*c.*1830', *Modern Asian Studies* 27, 3 (1993), pp. 475–572.

Lieberman, Victor, 'Transcending East-West Dichotomies: State and Culture Formation in Six Ostensibly Disparate Areas', *Modern Asian Studies* 31, 0 (1997), pp. 463–546.

Long, Ngo Vinh, 'Vietnam: The Real Enemy', *Bulletin of Concerned Asian Scholars*, Vol. 21, Nos. 2–4/April-Dec. 1989, pp. 6–34.

Louis, Wm. Roger, and Ronald Robinson, 'The imperialism of decolonization', *The Journal of Imperial and Commonwealth History*, Vol. XXII, 1994, No. 3, pp. 462–511.

Mahmood, Cynthia K., 'Trials by Fire: Dynamics of Terror in Punjab and Kashmir', in Jeffrey A. Sluka (ed.), *Death Squad: The Anthropology of State Terror* (Philadelphia: University of Pennsylvania Press, 2000), pp. 70–90.

Marshall, P. J., 'The Transfer of Power in India: Lord Wavell and his Political Masters', (Review Article) *The Journal of Imperial and Commonwealth History*, Vol. V, October 1976, No. 1, pp. 331–334.

Mayall, James and Mark Simpson, 'Ethnicity is not enough: Reflections on Protracted Secessionism in the Third World', in Anthony D. Smith (ed.), *Ethnicity and Nationalism* (Leiden: E. J. Brill, 1992), pp. 5–25.

Medhi, Kunja, 'Human Rights in North-East India: A Contemporary Perspective', in Aftab Alam (ed.), *Human Rights in India: Issues and Challenges* (Delhi: Raj Publ., 2000), pp. 289–304.

Moore, Robin J., 'Imperial India, 1858–1914', in Andrew Porter (ed.), *The Oxford History of the British Empire, Vol. III, The Nineteenth Century* (Oxford: Oxford University Press, 1999), pp. 422–446.

Morgan, Kenneth O., 'Imperialists at Bay: British Labour and Decolonization', *The Journal of Imperial and Commonwealth History*, Vol. XXVII, May 1999, No. 2, pp. 233–244.

'Naga Memorandum to Simon Commission 1996 (10. January 1929)', in R. Vashum, Aleube Iheilung et al. (eds.), *Nagas at Work* (New Delhi: NSUD Publication, 1996), pp. 151–152.

Nagengast, Carole, 'Violence, Terror, and the Crisis of the State', *Annual Review of Anthropology*, 1994, 23, pp. 109–136.

O'Leary, Brendan, 'Ernest Gellner's diagnosis of nationalism: a critical overview, or, what is living and what is dead in Ernest Gellner's philosophy of nationalism?', in John A. Hall (ed.), *The State of the Nation: Ernest Gellner and the Theory of Nationalism* (Cambridge: Cambridge University Press, 1998), pp. 40–88.

Otterbein, Keith F., 'Feuding – Dispute Resolution or Dispute Continuation?', in *idem* (ed.), *Feuding and Warfare: Selected Works of Keith F. Otterbein* (Amsterdam: Gordon and Breach, 1994), pp. 133–146.

Panmei, Nehemiah, 'Naga movement and ist ramifications', in R. Vashum, Aleube Iheilung et al. (eds.), *Nagas at Work* (New Delhi: NSUD Publication, 1996), pp. 85–100.

Pannel, Sandra, 'Travelling to Other Worlds: Narratives of Headhunting, Appropriation and the Other in the Eastern Archipelago', *Oceania*, 62, 1992, pp. 162–178.

Peers, Douglas M., 'Introduction', in *idem* (ed.), *Warfare and Empires: Contact and conflict between European and non-European military and maritime forces and cultures.* (An Expanding World: The European Impact on World History, 1450–1800: Vol. 24, Aldershot: Ashgate, Variorum, 1997), pp. XV–XXXIV.

Porter, Andrew, '"Cultural Imperialism" and Protestant Missionary Enterprise, 1780–1914', *The Journal of Imperial and Commonwealth History*, Vol. 25, No. 3, September 1997, pp. 367–391.

Porter, Andrew, 'Introduction: Britain and the Empire in the Nineteenth Century', in *idem* (ed.), *The Oxford History of the British Empire, Vol. III, The Nineteenth Century* (Oxford: Oxford University Press, 1999), pp. 1–28.

Proschan, Frank, 'Peoples of the Gourd: Imagined Ethnicities in Highland Southeast Asia', *The Journal of Asian Studies*, 60, no. 4 (November 2001), p. 999–1032.

Radcliffe-Brown, A. R., 'Preface', in M. Fortes and E. E. Evans-Pritchard (eds.), *African Political Systems* (London and New York, 1987 [1940]), pp. XI–XXIII.

Rajagopalan, Rajesh, 'Innovations in counterinsurgency: the Indian Army's Rashtriya Rifles', *Contemporary South Asia* 13 (1), March 2004, pp. 25–37.

Rajashekara, H. M., 'The Nature of Indian Federalism: A Critique', *Asian Survey*, Vol. 37, No. 3, March 1997, pp. 245–253.

Ranger, Terence, 'Kolonialismus in Ost- und Zentralafrika: von der traditionellen zur raditionalen Gesellschaft – Einsprüche und Widersprüche', in Jan-Heeren Grevenmeyer (ed.), *Traditionale Gesellschaften und europäischer Kolonialismus* (Frankfurt am Main: Syndikat, 1981), pp. 16–46.

Reid, Anthony, 'Introduction: A Time and a Place', in *idem* (ed.), *Southeast Asia in the Early Modern Era: Trade, Power, and Belief* (Ithaca and London: Cornell University Press, 1993), pp. 1–23.

'Report of the Naga Goodwill Mission to Assam (22nd December 1953)', in Luingam Luithui and Nandita Haksar (eds.), *Nagaland File: A Question of Human Rights* (New Delhi: Lancer International, 1984), pp. 74–94.

Robinson, Ronald, 'Wm. Roger Louis and the Official Mind of Decolonization', *The Journal of Imperial and Commonwealth History*, Vol. XXVII, May 1999, No. 2, pp. 1–12.

Sahlins, Marshall, 'Goodbye to *Tristes Tropes:* Ethnography in the Context of Modern World History', *Journal of Modern History* 65 (March 1993), pp. 1–25.

Sankalia, H. D. & T.C. Sharma, 'The Prehistoric Age', in H. K. Barpujari (ed.), *The Comprehensive History of Assam, Vol. I: From Pre-historic Times to the Twelfth Century AD* (Guwahati: Publication Board, Assam, 1990), pp. 25–43.

Sarkar, Sumit, 'Postmodernism and the Writing of History', in *idem., Beyond Nationalist Frames: Relocating Postmodernism, Hindutva, History* (Delhi: Permanent Black, 2002), pp. 154–194.

Singh, Gurharpal, *Re-examining Centre-State Relations in India* (Unpublished inaugural lecture, 2000).

Sircar, D. C., 'Epico-Puraanic Myths and Allied Legends', in H. K. Barpujari (ed.), *The Comprehensive History of Assam, Vol. I: From the Pre-historic Times to the Twelfth Century AD* (Guwahati: Publication Board, Assam, 1990).

Stokes, E. T., 'Bureaucracy and Ideology: Britain and India in the Nineteenth Century', *Transactions of the Royal Historical Society*, Fifth Series, Vol. 30, London 1980, pp. 131–156.

Taussig, Michael, 'Culture of Terror – Space of Death: Roger Casement's Putumayo Report and the Explanation of Torture', *Comparative Studies in Society and History*, 1984, 26, pp. 467–497.

Taylor, Charles, 'Interpretation and the sciences of man', in *idem., Philosophy and the Human Sciences: Philosophical Papers 2* (Cambridge: Cambridge University Press, 1985), pp. 15–57.

Taylor, Charles, 'Nationalism and modernity', in John A. Hall (ed.), *The State of the Nation: Ernest Gellner and the Theory of Nationalism* (Cambridge: Cambridge University Press, 1998), pp. 191–218.

Thornton, A. P., 'With Wavell on to Simla and Beyond', *The Journal of Imperial and Commonwealth History*, Vol. VIII, October 1979, No. 2, pp. 175–185.

'Three case studies', in IWGIA Document 56, *The Naga nation and its struggle against genocide: A report compiled by IWGIA* (Copenhagen, 1986), pp. 73–82.

Tonkin, Elizabeth, 'Borderline questions: people and space in West Africa', in Hastings Donnan and Thomas M. Wilson (eds.), *Border Approaches: Anthropological Approaches on Frontiers* (Lanham: University Press of America, 1994), pp. 15–30.

'Village Diary – People of Mokokchung Village, Nagaland, dated 27 April 1964', in IWGIA Document 56, *The Naga nation and its struggle against genocide: A report compiled by IWGIA* (Copenhagen, 1986), pp. 136–140.

Washbrook, D. A., 'India, 1818–1860: The Two Faces Of Colonialism', in Andrew Porter (ed.), *The Oxford History of the British Empire, Vol. III, The Nineteenth Century* (Oxford: Oxford University Press, 1999), pp. 395–420.

Wesseling, H. L., 'Colonial Wars: An Introduction', in J. A. de Moor and H. L. Wesseling (eds.), *Imperialism and War: Essays on Colonial Wars in Asia and Africa* (Leiden: E. J. Brill/Universitaire Pers Leiden, 1989), pp. 1–11.

White, Hayden, 'The Forms of Wildness: Archaeology of an Idea', in Edward Dudley and Maximillian E. Novak (eds.), *The Wild Man Within: An Image in Western Thought from the Renaissance to Romanticism* (Pittsburgh: University of Pittsburgh Press, 1972), pp. 3–38.

Young, Crawford, 'Ethnicity and the Colonial and Postcolonial State in Africa', in Paul Brass (ed.), *Ethnic Groups and the State* (London: Croom Helm, 1985), pp. 57–93.

5. Newspapers, Journals and Web News Sites

Assam Tribune
Bangkok Post
BBC News
Daily Telegraph
Economic and Political Weekly
Economist
Economist.com
Far Eastern Economic Review
Frontline
India Today
Le Monde diplomatique
Mainstream
Manchester Guardian
North-East Sun
Northeast Vigil
Outlook
Sunday
The Express
The Guardian
The Hindu
The Indian Express
The Little Magazine
The New York Times
The Observer
The Telegraph
The Times
Weekly Dispatch

Index

For Product Safety Concerns and Information please contact our EU
representative GPSR@taylorandfrancis.com
Taylor & Francis Verlag GmbH, Kaufingerstraße 24, 80331 München, Germany

www.ingramcontent.com/pod-product-compliance
Lightning Source LLC
Chambersburg PA
CBHW050427280326
41932CB00013BA/2015